DECOLONISATION AND THE
BRITISH EMPIRE, 1775–1997

D. GEORGE BOYCE

First published in Great Britain 1999 by
MACMILLAN PRESS LTD
Houndmills, Basingstoke, Hampshire RG21 6XS and London
Companies and representatives throughout the world

A catalogue record for this book is available from the British Library.

ISBN 0–333–62103–4 hardcover
ISBN 0–333–62104–2 paperback

 First published in the United States of America 1999 by
ST. MARTIN'S PRESS, INC.,
Scholarly and Reference Division,
175 Fifth Avenue, New York, N.Y. 10010

ISBN 0–312–22325–0

Library of Congress Cataloging-in-Publication Data
Boyce, David George, 1942–
Decolonization and the British Empire, 1775–1997 / D. George
Boyce.
p. cm.
Includes bibliographical references (p.   ) and index.
ISBN 0–312–22325–0 (cloth)
1. Great Britain—Colonies—History. 2. Decolonization—Great
Britain—Colonies—History. 3. Imperialism—History. I. Title.
DA16.B64 1999
941—dc21   99–12192
                                                                                    CIP

This book is printed on paper suitable for recycling and made from fully managed and sustained forest sources.

10   9   8   7   6   5   4   3   2   1
08   07   06   05   04   03   02   01   00   99

Printed in Hong Kong

Nevertheless, as a rule, when Divine Providence has put a part of the world under English rule, it has usually stayed, often quite willingly, in the state unto which it pleased God to call it. And contemplating this fact we are inclined to agree with Mark Twain; the English are mentioned in the Bible.

D. W. Brogan, *The English People: Impressions and Observations* (1947)

CONTENTS

ACKNOWLEDGEMENTS

I should like to thank Val and Roy Anthony for rising to the challenge of my typescript.

Crown copyright material in the Public Record Office is reproduced by permission of the Controller of Her Majesty's Stationery Office.

A NOTE ON THE TEXT

Although this book is mainly concerned with English political traditions, I have, like most people, used the terms 'English' and 'British' interchangeably, except where I want to identify specifically English characteristics. This, I hope, avoids any awkward linguistic and therefore political infelicities.

INTRODUCTION:
EXPERIENCE AND EMPIRE

It is a truth, universally acknowledged, that all empires fall; but they fall after their own fashion, though there are common themes in their demise. For this reason the 'how' of decolonisation is as important to an understanding of the British imperial experience and its special character, as is the 'why'. There are many fine books devoted to the latter; this book concentrates on the former, while acknowledging, of course, that the two experiences are inseparable. As the English expanded and consolidated their empire, they used and adapted their own institutions and ways of thinking about politics to their new possessions; as that empire contracted they also drew upon these traditions, showing (with the exception of Ireland in 1921) no rigid theoretical position, but rather an ability to adapt what they were familiar with to their new experiences. But because they had a way of seeing contingency as a kind of destiny,[1] they got the best of both worlds. When Winston Churchill claimed in September 1941 that British policy goals for the empire had already been stated in declarations which were 'complete in themselves', and 'free from ambiguity', an embarrassed Colonial Office, when pressed by Members of Parliament to make public the declarations, found that they had no complete list of pledges and commitments.[2] But this was a strength rather than a weakness, especially when mixed with a kind of Whiggish discourse that could be used to justify and explain decisions often taken under the most acute political and economic pressure.

This belief in contingency as a form of destiny – in short, providence – reaches far back into English history, perhaps even as far as the Venerable Bede's eighth-century history of the English.[3] It developed a particular significance from the Middle Ages to the eighteenth century, as the English expanded their power over the British Isles, incorporating different peoples into their political system or at least bringing them under their jurisdiction. They invited these peoples, the Welsh, the

1

Scots, the Protestant and even the Catholic Irish, to join them in their enterprise of making themselves masters of much, eventually most, of the world. The Celtic nations accepted the invitation and there is a corner of most foreign fields that is forever Celtic. But the politics of empire were essentially English in origin and practice, and when pressures from within or without obliged the English political élite to respond to the exigencies of imperial change, it did so in the light of its own ideas and institutions, modified and adapted to the particular predicaments that the imperial power faced, but still always recognisably English. Above all, at the heart of this lay a belief that what had been done before could be repeated (even in less favourable circumstances); and an assumption too that the English could get things right – so that their self-belief facilitated the management of most dangerous challenges; and, even if they did not always manage them well (and there are sufficient examples of failure to support this reservation), they still believed that, by and large, they had.

Imperialism, colonisation and decolonisation were essential to the United Kingdom's role in the world. Empire, as Alfred Cobban remarked, 'at bottom . . . means no more than the extension of power over a large area including a variety of nations'.

> It may represent the domination of one element, as it usually has, or it may recognise the equality of its national or racial components. Consequently, under the common heading of imperialism diametrically opposed political systems may be included.

Imperialism, he noted, 'seeks its own interest; as a political institution it cannot do anything else. Its scope is a function of its power and this is basically military.'[4] But there were also in the English tradition concepts of consent, liberty and latitude in government. And as for power, Cobban explained, 'moderation in its use is a condition of the survival of power'. Military conquest and annexation were not as successful as the basis of empire as they formally were. 'Political consciousness had, by 1945, become a factor of world wide significance.'[5]

The empire that England built was meant to survive this new political consciousness and both express and uphold military and economic power. But, although efforts were made in the nineteenth century to turn this empire into a centrally managed political institution, the English contrived to construct their empire without any grand organising theory, and this helped them lose it without the destabilising consequences that usually accompanied the loss of great empires, ancient or modern. This was because of the practical thinking characteristic of English political behaviour and expressed in key episodes in English history, from the Glorious Revolution of 1688 to the Great Reform Act of 1832, and beyond. Historical and conceptual thinking were applied to concrete problems. This gave England a peculiar approach to the governing of an empire; and, equally important, of transforming and relinquishing its government in a way that appeared then (however it may appear now) as compatible with, and conformable to, the English way of thinking about what they regarded, rightly or wrongly, as their particular, even singular, place in the world.[6] For, while England is always portrayed as a nation dealing with other people's nationalisms, she was imbued with a powerful nationalism of her own, which is ineluctably present in her imperial story. This book is intended as a contribution to what Elizabeth Mancke calls the need 'to put political considerations of empire-building . . . into our interpretations of the British Empire';[7] or, in this case, empire-ending, as the English political vocabulary combined empire with *libertas*, devolution of power with *imperium*, a language of liberty with a lexicon of authority. For political language is not merely an adjunct of, or secondary to, political activity but forms and guides it; it lies at the heart of the world of politics, and is integral to the imperial experience of modern England.

1

THE EXPANSION OF ENGLAND

England is amongst the oldest of the European imperial powers. Her imperial expansion is often assumed to have begun with the voyages of discovery in the sixteenth century; but her experience of dominion over other lands and people, with its catalogue of war, conquest, treaty, settlement, administrative and legal innovation, and governance began not overseas, but in the British Isles. The temptation to intervene in, dominate, and if need be to conquer, the Celtic lands of Wales, Ireland and Scotland proved too strong to resist, though not always easy to accomplish. This long process of conquest and settlement lasted from the twelfth century to the eighteenth, and England drew upon her even earlier history of consolidation and domination of the Anglo-Saxon lands, with King Alfred promoted as the ancestor of an English and English–British imperial ancestry (and with reference even to 'an ancestry at once British and Roman Imperial').[1] England was a state and nation answerable only to God. From such confidence, from this early experience of dominion or aspiration to dominion, sprang the early modern British Empire, with its complex English–British identity, and with the prime mover, England, bent on pursuing its destiny in lands outside the 'British island of England'.[2]

The British Empire was not the most powerful of the early modern European empires, but it was distinguished by its capacity to endure hard knocks, to reinvent as well as reconstruct itself, and to outlast the rest of its rivals. Some European states enjoyed an equally early beginning in their imperial experience: the Spanish and the Dutch, the French and the Portuguese. Some, like Germany, Italy and Belgium, were late arrivals, or managed to establish colonies only to lose them. Even the French could not claim the same continuity as the British. The French began early, in India and North America; but their defeat by the

5

British in both those continents left them virtually bereft of empire until their renewed interest in Africa in the early nineteenth century. Spain lost virtually all her South American possessions in the early nineteenth century. The British Empire, 'on which the sun never set', lasted, on the face of it, from the early modern age to the present day, and (if the Falkland Islands remain under British sovereignty) will continue into the twenty-first century.

But the use of the word 'continue' must not blind us to the fact that the British Empire is a history of several empires, though there are connecting themes. The loss of most of the North American colonies in 1783 is often taken as changing the character of the empire: from colonies of white settlement to colonies of European rule over non-European peoples; from a centre of gravity in America to one in the Indian Ocean. Yet there were new colonies of white settlement, new areas of the British diaspora, and these provide a certain continuity, not least in the arena of political theories about empire and its ordering.

In his celebrated lectures delivered at Cambridge University in 1883,[3] J. R. Seeley categorised empires into the Roman kind and the Greek kind. He delivered his homilies at a time when the British Empire's fulcrum lay between its colonies of 'white' settlement (Australia, Canada, New Zealand), and its Indian empire, and when it was on the eve of its great expansion into Africa, and just establishing its presence in Egypt. His ideas can only be reviewed in the context of the state of the empire in 1883: but his views throw light on the character of the empire as it was, and as he hoped it to be – and, even, as it subsequently developed. Seeley believed that the empire could be a source of power only in so far as it was an extension of the state. This was because it was an empire of migration. The empire comprised the United Kingdom and 'four great groups of territories, inhabited either chiefly or to a large extent by Englishmen, and subject to the Crown'. India was different; there was no significant English population there, but in the great four territories there were populations 'of our own blood'. Ten million Englishmen abroad gave the British Empire a stable footing.[4] There was a community of race, of religion and of interest. The United Kingdom of Great Britain and Ireland was likewise 'for all purposes one nation', despite the presence of what Seeley called the Celtic blood and (rather unkindly) the 'utterly unintelligible' languages of Wales, Scotland and Ireland.[5] This common bond made the expansion of England not unlike that of ancient Greece, which populated the Mediterranean with people of their own blood and religion.

But expansion of people was not enough to create a powerful empire. The migration of peoples made England powerful because it was an extension of the state. The migration of Germans to America created no greater Germany.[6] And in this respect the Greek empire was different from the British, because it was not an expansion of the state, but only of the population. The British Empire was an empire of power. It had, in Seeley's view, been gained by warfare. Seeley claimed that in the eighteenth century Britain had waged seven great wars (1688–97, 1702–13, 1739–48, the Seven Years War, the American War of 1775–83, and the Revolutionary and Napoleonic wars of 1793–1802 and 1803–15), and that all these were motivated by imperial needs. Even the wars of the Revolutionary and Napoleonic period were imperial; the possession of the new world was 'among the grounds of quarrel'. Napoleon saw England as a 'world empire', and in 1798 he sought to seize its weaker parts in Egypt, and to stir up trouble in India. The mainsprings of British national development were military strength and the expansion of her industrial and commercial growth. The expansion of England was therefore not merely one of 'race', but had the authority of the English state behind it.[7]

Yet Seeley denied that this was merely an empire of conquest: for the people who spread out into the British Empire were the same as those who stayed at home. Other empires were different; they contained only a few Europeans and a large number of native races.[8] India was the exception in the British Empire because, although there the state was indeed strong, English people were few in number. The danger was that in India the subject or rival nationalities could only be imperfectly assimilated; there they remained a cause of danger.[9] But – this aside – Seeley alleged that the British Empire was not like the other great empire of the ancient world, that of Rome. It was not an empire of conquest, not an empire of 'violent military character'. If it were, he concluded, then like most empires it would indeed be short-lived and subject to a 'speedy decay'.[10]

It might be said, therefore, that the British Empire in Seeley's view was poised between the Grecian and Roman models. An empire in which war played a key role in the making, but which was not merely an empire of conquest; an empire of common population and culture, which was yet not merely an empire of the expansion of peoples, but one of expansion of the British state. It had absorbed 'alien races' but its real strength lay in its common nationality, held together by British institutions. If the empire lost that homogeneous character, it therefore followed, it might indeed be at risk; its 'Grecian' dimension would be fatally diluted. But if it did not build on its institutional strength, then it might suffer the fate of the Roman and Grecian empires, in that it must fall between two contradictory models: it could not survive merely on the Grecian example of its peoples living abroad; but neither could it act in the Roman capacity of a violent military edifice. And if the empire expanded beyond the limits of British nationality – if it gathered more Indias – then its power would become precarious and artificial. 'This is the condition of most empires; it is the condition, for example, of our own empire in India.'[11]

Seeley traced the most salient fact of modern English history – the long succession of wars with France – not to any European cause, but to the colonial competition that was first seen in North America in the eighteenth century, and which found another field of competition in Asia. His explanation of British expansion was simple: fear of France.[12] But Seeley misunderstood the complex and mixed motives for the expansion of the English state, first over the British Isles, or much of them, and then abroad. The English Elizabethan state was a powerful neighbour of the other nations and peoples of the British Isles; it had already absorbed Wales and, in order to secure its internal frontiers, was driven to conquer Ireland. Scotland remained England's most vexatious neighbour, and the Scottish question was not resolved until the Union of 1707.

The Elizabethan state drew upon the idea of a civilising mission, one that conveniently ignored the contribution of Christian Ireland to the making of European civilisation; but an internal *imperium* necessitated a moral as well as political imperative, and this sense of the moral and the political – a neat combination of principle and expediency – was significant for the development of the empire in the future. At the time, however, England ruled less territory than she did in the Middle Ages, before the loss of her French possessions. Following the war against Spain and the conquest of Ireland, England enjoyed some 40 years of peace, during which she began her search for trading posts in North America, the West Indies and India. These early colonies, gained before 1641, were established by the authority of the Crown, and not of Parliament. The usual form was to make grants in fief, or corporate charters; thus in the Letters Patent from James VI and I to Sir George Calvert on 7 April 1623, the King, noting that Calvert intended to 'transport thither [to Newfoundland] a very great and ample Colony of the English nation', granted 'all the said Region with certain privileges and jurisdictions requisite for the good Government and State of the said Colony and

Territory to him, his Heirs and Assigns for ever'.[13] Early colonies were established in North America, at Virginia and New York, with some small West Indian islands and a foothold in India. They were a mixture of trading posts, settlement colonies and plantation colonies. But, while they were essentially an economic venture, they immediately raised the question of how best they could be governed, how they could be governed cheapest and how their newly settled peoples would govern themselves. In this sense the small, initial colonial expansion confronted the essential problems of the major colonial expansions of the modern age. Settlement colonies were engaged in the business of establishing working institutions that could cooperate harmoniously with the Crown. Trading colonies were different: here the emphasis was on seeking and exploiting markets, and this involved only a small number of officials and soldiers in the early days of their establishment. The East India Company founded bases in Surat, India in 1611 and Madras in 1642. In the West Indies the first effective post was established in 1624 at St Christopher Island; the Barbados in 1622 and Nevis in 1628. The enterprise was based on tobacco and then, from the 1640s, on sugar. The economy was based on black slavery.[14]

These posts differed greatly from the colonies of religious settlement, where God-fearing people had emigrated to create and live by the best rules and laws by which men could live: religiously based, with power and votes restricted to the Godly. In these colonies of settlement (Massachusetts, New Haven, Connecticut, Rhode Island, Maryland) there were no royal charters, and the colonists devised their own constitutions. Nevertheless, the Crown was anxious to assert its authority. In Maryland in 1637 the Crown was obliged to declare that an already existing assembly had no legal status, that the laws passed by it were 'voyd' (*sic*) and that the Crown authorised Governor Calvert to call an assembly 'of the freemen within our said province, and to propound and prepare other wholesome laws and ordinances, for the general and well ordering of the said province, and people within the same, to be by us assented to and confirmed, if upon new and mature consideration had of the same, we shall in our judgement approve thereof'.[15] This concept of empire, that of a royal *imperium*, did not alone hold the field. There was in the seventeenth century also another theory, that of the Republican tradition, which claimed that the English empire was a protectorate of several interests rather than an *imperium*.[16] The debate on the character of the empire was not, therefore, one confined to the nineteenth and twentieth centuries, but was already opened up, and was focused on the alternatives of colonies enjoying a devolved arrangement serving the interests of the English abroad, or under a tight central control, and subjected to government by authority; in this case, royal authority.

The beginnings of the empire, both in motivation and in governance, were as varied as the expansion of the later British Empire; nevertheless, trade was the most powerful driving motive. But trade was also a weapon of war. In the new world it was an extension of the rivalry between England and Spain; war and trade went hand in hand, and since this was an extension of European rivalries, control – political control – was an essential, but not the only, part of the development of empire. But in the east there was, especially in the East India Company's activities, a desire to trade, not govern, to seek commercial outlets, not territorial acquisition, and to use force to secure the needs of trade, but not to establish government.[17]

But the expansion of the English commercial and imperial state brought with it difficulties – difficulties in sustaining the new colonial possessions and in keeping the enterprise going. Small, remote colonies, with harsh living conditions and great distances between home and colony, were vulnerable: to military disaster, attacks from the indigenous populations, or simple hardship. The frequent references to establishing appropriate links between the Crown and its possessions, the need to govern the colonies, sat beside the grave difficulties in sustaining them against natural and man-made disasters. But by the middle of the seventeenth century England was perceived as a coming great imperial power. The possessions gained in the seventeenth and eighteenth centuries – in America, the Caribbean, India and the West Indies – were to form the basis of British Imperial identity before the dissolution of most of the North American empire by 1783. A seaborne empire had been built; and from the beginning of the eighteenth century it began to take on an air of permanence.[18]

It was helped towards this by the fact that, however diverse this empire was, the British treated it as an integrated unit, for economic purposes; and this was to prove in time a fatal weakness. It was important to secure the best arrangements conducive to the wealth of Britain; again, precedent was called in to assist practice. The medieval concept of control and restriction was extended in the Navigation Act of 1651, and then expanded between 1660 and 1696. All trade must be carried in British vessels; all goods going to the colonies had to proceed through English ports; colonial exports must be exported direct to an English port, even if their final destination was elsewhere.[19] The dynamic combination of trade, settlement and war was vital to the creation of the empire, and the empire had to justify its existence, through its potential to strengthen and enrich the mother country. But it would be a mistake to see the empire merely in terms of trading links. The establishment of Englishmen overseas did involve the English, later the British Crown, in working out some durable constitutional relationship between Crown and Colony. Government could not be ignored, and questions of authority must be settled in the North American colonies, if the empire was to work as an integrated unity – and, above all, if the Crown was to demonstrate its essential role as the binding symbol and effective authority of the empire.

The expression 'British Empire' was first popularised, if not invented, in 1578;[20] this again revealed the importance of projecting the empire in the political sphere, in endowing it with some kind of inclusive character, in emphasising its unity. The empire, in its eighteenth-century expansion, offered opportunities to the Scots who, relieved of the burden of their persistent fear of their large neighbour, England, both promoted, and took advantage of, the North American enterprise. Seeley exaggerated when he claimed that virtually all eighteenth-century wars were imperial wars; but some of them, and especially the Seven Years War of 1756–63, developed a vital imperial dimension. The consciousness of empire as a source and a symbol of British wealth and power was given new urgency by the war with France. Informal clashes took place, in America and India, before the formal outbreak of hostilities in 1756. The European origins of the war, and its centrality in Europe, cannot be disputed; but the struggle became a worldwide affair, and the British victory added territory and populations to the empire: including the French Canadians and inhabitants of the Indian subcontinent. Trade expanded, and exports to the new American colonies increased. The shipment of slaves from Africa rose from 3 million in 1760–70, to more than 4 million in 1790–1800.[21] Outside the formal empire, private enterprise established a whole network of seaborne trade from British India to the Philippines. But, as always, it was hard for British Governments to establish a uniform system of governing this empire with its 'informal' trading posts in any consistent way. Its diversity, its lack of a uniform machinery for administering and governing the colonies, meant that problems were dealt with as the need arose. Worse, it was becoming evident that the empire was expensive to defend, and yet it must be defended, against, in the case of North America, external threat and internal attacks from the American Indians.

The expansion of England, then, was a two-edged weapon. The empire enriched the mother country; but its defence was expensive, and armies could either be raised locally (American colonial militias, Indian sepoys) or the British army could, and indeed must, add a strengthening element to the colonial forces. It seemed not unreasonable for the British state to assert that those people who were the subjects of the Crown, but abroad, should pay their way, just as subjects of the Crown did at home. Obligation, however, had to be enforced and there was a wider issue at stake: the Crown's authority, its central role as the symbol as well as the reality of British Dominion overseas, must be weakened fatally, and the whole empire weakened fatally, if it were defied in any of its colonies. The long, costly and in the end unsuccessful war with the American colonies, waged between 1775 and 1783, was a war of principle. The Atlantic, Caribbean and North American colonies were subject to the Crown in Parliament, whose laws protected the subject at home or abroad. Parliament in the eighteenth century represented 'interests' – the church, the universities, the merchants in the ports – yet the American colonies were 'corporations' (as their charters described them) and were not represented in parliament. But from the start these colonies, founded by charters as they were, also spoke the language of their legal and political rights as Englishmen. They were not conquered but, on the contrary, brought with them the liberties that they enjoyed in England. Thus they could not be taxed without the consent of their representatives – and they had their representatives in their own legislative institutions. The problem was exacerbated by that fact that, except in trading matters, the Crown in Parliament rarely troubled the North American colonies before the 1760s; it was all the harder for them to accept the assertion of the British legislature, of the Crown in Parliament, which had shown so much laxity before.

The American colonists were Englishmen abroad; they claimed all the rights and privileges of their fellow-countrymen at home, and were imbued with a powerful sense of the rightness too of their religious beliefs and their strongly Protestant character. North America was, arguably, the first British experience of decolonisation, and this will be considered in the next chapter. It had remarkably little impact on the British state itself, though at the time it seemed to many to be indicative of the failure of the British constitution to work properly – if it had done so there would have been no war, or the war would have been won. Ireland, in its turn, took the opportunity afforded by the American war to assert some limited degree of legislative initiative in her parliament; but she clung to the theory of the 'sister kingdom', and there was, as yet, no separatist element on the political horizon. But the American Revolution did not usher in a speedy demise to the early British Empire. The empire may have in a sense diminished in theory – the Crown was defied, and America, or most of it except Canada, was lost – but there were sound and immediate reasons why the British should continue collecting colonies, bases, territories, as the need arose. As always, war was the great persuader. The Revolutionary and Napoleonic wars between 1793 and 1815 were an incentive to expand. The wars were fought in Europe, which was the only place, and which provided the only allies, to defeat the French. But the struggle had its worldwide aspect, and the old British Empire, with its diversity and flexibility, could usefully influence the new. There was in any case continuity: there was no alteration in the relationships between the Crown in Parliament and the legislative assemblies in Jamaica and Barbados. Assemblies were created in Upper and Lower Canada in 1791, thus emphasising the governmental traditions of the empire since the seventeenth century.

With continuity came innovation. Yet, again, the innovation reflected only British needs, and these were hardly new. Colonial possessions were gained: from the Netherlands came Grenada, the Cape and Ceylon. There was further expansion into India. There was the migration of British people, as there had been to America; to Australia as a penal colony; and a strengthening of British immigration to Canada, and then to Australia which doubled their numbers between 1820 and 1840. New Zealand and South Africa saw an expansion of population, and by 1820 5000 settlers, encouraged by Britain, went to the Cape. As before, Britain picked and chose in her imperial expansion. She could have taken more from the list available between 1793 and 1815, but she kept little of the French and Dutch possessions; the Cape was retained as part of the control of the sea route to the east, which might in the hands of the Dutch be controlled by an enemy power. She kept certain islands, such as Trinidad, Guiana, Tobago and St Lucia, all for naval strategic reasons.[22] But she gave Indonesia back to the Dutch, and later acquisitions from Holland – Singapore and Malacca – were negotiated by treaty, and again for strategic reasons. Malta and the Ionian islands were likewise part of the British naval presence in the Mediterranean. Value – both trading and naval – was calculated, and decisions made to keep, relinquish or leave alone were made on the basis of protecting and maintaining existing British interests. No significant European settlement was made in such colonies.

These motives were hardly different from those of the early phase of imperial expansion. Before 1783 there was always a calculation of gain or loss. Trade was a key factor in this 'new' phase of expansion. Trade did not necessarily require direct British rule, but in India the perception of its economic value to Britain drew her ever deeper into military expansion and political control. Trade did not necessarily require direct control, though it might require ports to be kept open, recalcitrant peoples to be subdued, foreign powers sent packing, and informal control to be asserted. Power and wealth were what the British state pursued. But there was also the continuing acceptance that certain parts of the empire were different, and required a constitutional response. Canada, for example, must have legislative institutions. The American disaster must not be repeated. Though here, the purpose of the British was less well conceived, less deliberate than posterity came to believe. The Royal Navy saw to it that the diverse empire was policed and retained. During the French revolutionary and Napoleonic wars a new expedient – crown colony government – was introduced in the various acquisitions made between 1793 and 1815.

When British interests were threatened, as they were by the Sepoy mutiny and peasant rebellion in India in 1857, the British responded with the necessary military force and, indeed, ruthlessness. British control of India was originally driven by trade; trade required military support; military support required finance; and finance required some central supervision of the East India Company, which was secured in Pitt's India Act of 1784. Now British power was asserted by the gun, and India was subjected to the authority of a Viceroy and his advisers. This quick and stern response, however, left India controlled by a few officials, a British and British Indian army, a police force, and the acquiescence of the population, or most of it. Despite this, peasant uprisings and protests were endemic in British India in the late nineteenth century. Contemporaries as well as historians regarded India as a special case, and this further emphasised how the means by which bits of empire were acquired deeply influenced their subsequent government and place in the empire. Heterogeneous acquisitions meant heterogeneous control.

The motives that sustained this empire – an empire of settlement, conquest, of the survival of the old colonial system (in the Caribbean, Nova Scotia and New Brunswick), of the system reformed (Canada), of the autocratic government of captured colonies and of the empire of India – were mixed. Trade, power, the denial of power to potential rivals, sheer force of habit, and an assumption that the empire, however unpopular it might be, however politicians might grumble about it being a 'millstone' around the neck of Britain, was part of the British experience – so that, if there was no great incentive to expand, then there was no great desire to contract either. And the empire *would* expand. The discovery of diamonds in South Africa in 1867 encouraged the British to support expansion there and then annex and defend new territory. The island of Fiji was added because British settlers moved there and obliged the British Government in 1874 to take it over. Also in 1874 Cyprus was acquired as a useful means of checking the Russians. A war was fought with the Afghans in 1878–80 and then with the Boers of the Transvaal in 1881, the former to check Russian expansion into India, the latter because the Boers were determined to resist the British desire to control them and stabilise South Africa, a desire which arose partly out of the necessity to defeat the Zulus in 1879, and protect Natal. In 1882 Egypt was occupied to serve British interests, and then Britain was obliged to secure the Sudan in order to stabilise her control of Egypt.

These wars were hard-fought and occasionally unsuccessful, or accompanied with only a limited degree of success. Armies were roughly handled; prestige forfeited. Yet the mood of anxiety that gripped the British political élite in the 1880s was only deepened by the prospect of Britain losing the race for control, direct or indirect, of areas that she though vital to her interests. She was moving deeper into the assumption that her position as a great world power, and especially as a great trading power, was at risk. Internal politics, international politics and imperialism could not be separated any more – if ever they could be separated. A rich, satiated power, with no ambitions but to maintain the peace, might take only piecemeal and even reluctant steps forward; but, after 1884, when the fear of other European states and their ambitions grew, it was becoming axiomatic in British official thinking that Britain must not be left behind. Also, the advance of democracy in the United Kingdom, and the small but growing concern with what was called the 'social question', meant that Britain had to ensure that her empire was a source of, and a means of, alleviating, social distress at home. Great empires and little Englanders seldom went together, and little Englanders might, through their narrow vision, cut Britain off from the very sources not only of her foreign power, but of her ability to respond to domestic political demands.

Thus, between 1884 and 1904, the British Empire changed radically: not only were vast new territories gained, as a result of the 'scramble for

Africa'. Not only did the British assert their power in the Middle East, where the Sudan was now designated a vital British interest. But the whole question of the government of the empire took on a new urgency. In truth, since the seventeenth century the British had to concern themselves with affairs of government; and the idea of subordinate, but representative, colonial legislatures, subject to the Crown in Parliament, but enjoying English liberties, was as old as the empire itself. The question now was whether this tradition of subordination, representation, and the British need for a more directed and coherent form of imperial government could be reconciled. The Roman military empire of conquest sat beside the Grecian empire of colonies of settlement – and now Seeley's point about the empire of settlement as an expansion of the English *state* was to be put to the test.

From the late 1880s there was a new self-consciousness about the empire. It must of course serve British interests, as it had always done. But the question arose – could there be created with the colonies of white settlement a great imperial federation, which would design a tighter structure of the empire, a federal system, with Britain as the sovereign power, but with the colonies sending representatives to London to debate and decide matters common to all? In a world of great powers, could the empire itself constitute a great, or indeed, super, power? And another theory was articulated: the old colonial empire had been an empire of trade, with the navigation acts acting as the sinews of imperial and British prosperity. This had long disappeared, and had been replaced by an empire of free trade. But, again, in the new competitive world of states it might be that this empire of free trade was now obsolete: that it must be replaced, not of course by reviving the old colonial system, but by a modern version of that system; modern in the sense that it combined the establishment of firm rules for trade between colonies and the mother country, with the exclusion of other trade rivals. This idea, of offering preference to imperial goods, and encouraging the empire to export at favourable rates their raw materials in return for British products, would, moreover, answer the social question, in that it would provide the wealth necessary for social reform, without the danger of socialism. And the tropical empire, especially that of Africa, could be developed – the imperial garden could be cultivated, not neglected as hitherto, and territories taken to deny other powers' ambitions could again be put to good and profitable use. The empire would then indeed conform to Seeley's somewhat ambitious claim that it was an extension of the English state – more, it would be an extension of the English economy as well, and anyway state power and economic power were inseparable.

Thus the Greek character of empire (its peoples abroad, organised in a loose political arrangement) and the Roman character (powerful military force) could be combined in the making of the British state as a director and leader of the white settlement colonies. The rest of the empire would not form part of this extension of the state – could not, because of the non-European nature of their populations. But Joseph Chamberlain, Colonial Secretary between 1895 and 1903, believed that the tropical empire too could be developed. The vision of the great imperial federation was launched in the 1880s; the campaign for tariff reform and the end of free trade in the empire and abroad was launched in 1904.

The idea of a new, revived, organised empire that would be more closely wedded than before to the British state itself raised as many questions as answers. It presupposed that the colonies of settlement would be prepared to accept a kind of permanent economic tutelage to the mother country. The idea of imperial federation presupposed a parallel political subordination, and the difficulty of getting the colonies to think in a truly imperial way was illustrated by the near impossibility of securing from them a reasonable contribution to their defence by the Royal Navy. There were easier ways of extending British economic influence, using or adapting some of the old *laissez-faire* methods: chartered companies, for example, like the British East Africa Company, might suffice.

By 1914, in any event, Britain seemed to have reached the limits of her imperial ambitions; she seemed to be a satiated power. In 1914 British investment overseas was worth about £4 billion: of this, £¾ billion went to the United States of America; £½ billion to Canada; £¾ billion to the rest of the Americas (with half to the Argentine alone), £400 million to Australia and New Zealand; just over £400 million to India; just over £200 million to various European countries, and £200 million to other foreign countries with most going to Japan.[23] The empire was an important, but not an exclusive, adjunct of British financial investment.

Yet the empire reflected, even if it did not exclusively encompass, the wealth and power of England. It stood for her economic might, on which rested her military strength as a great power. It was simply assumed that the empire must be held. And yet another great European war, like that of 1793 inspired by British fears of the domination of Europe by one great power, and not at all inspired by colonial rivalries, in the event, like its predecessor, ended up with Britain stripping other belligerents of their colonies. The war was a world war, and the British fought on several imperial fronts: against the Germans in Africa, against the Turks in the Middle East. These were side-shows; yet, as before, they ended up adding major new territories to the British Empire. The British war effort was greatly helped by the white colonies and India. It saw the creation in 1917 of an Imperial War Cabinet, in which sat, for one, General Smuts, who had fought the British between 1899 and 1902, and seemed the very epitome of the way in which the empire, ever adaptable, could absorb its former enemies. The war brought into the Cabinet what before 1914 would have seemed unfamiliar figures to the British electorate: Lord Curzon, former Viceroy of India; Lord Milner, former Governor-General of South Africa. The white colonies were loyal; they acted in concert with Britain at the Versailles Peace Conference. In territorial terms the British Empire now added Jordan (known then as Transjordan), Iraq and Palestine as mandated territories, with British rule endorsed by the newly established League of Nations. German colonies in Africa were swept into the empire and the sign of the new imperial partnership seemed to be given real form in the entrusting of South Africa with the former German South West Africa, also as a mandated territory.

But war was also a modernising and unsettling influence on the empire. It provoked the British into offering to Indian nationalists the promise (no date given) of a move towards the ultimate goal of self-government. It heightened nationalist sentiment in the white settlement colonies, now invariably called Dominions. It even caused a partial break-up of the United Kingdom, with Ireland, after an armed struggle, becoming a Dominion. The new acquisitions in the volatile Middle East were to prove difficult to manage.

Still, the whole direction of British foreign and defence policy was predicated on the assumption that the empire had to come first, and that it was itself a source of military strength. Yet it was not easy to control the vast territorial range of empire. The 1914–18 War expanded the empire; but it also stretched its resources. After 1919 British political parties, and the electorate, were more concerned with domestic problems – unemployment, strikes, depression – than with a grand vision of a Curzon or a Milner. They assumed that Britain was an imperial power, and would remain so. But if they were asked in what sense was there a British Empire, and what kind of character did it possess, they would have found it hard to give a coherent answer. The Dominions were keen to conduct their own foreign policy; India was, as always, a special case, and Britain was seeking ways to maintain her control there, while offering what she regarded as reasonable concessions to the nationalist Congress Party. There was more turbulent, dangerous nationalism in Egypt and the Middle East; the Jewish–Arab conflict proved increasingly hard to handle. The long string of small bases, islands and territories still existed; they were still, too, essential bases for a world naval power. But four pillars of empire could be discerned: Ireland; India; Egypt and the Middle East; and Africa. Of the non-white empire, three stood out for their sheer size, or strategic importance or, in India, both. No responsible British statesman had the remotest idea of decolonising these, or any part of the empire; yet an empire held together by the symbol of the Crown, and with no institutions uniting its parts, could hardly any longer be considered an extension of the British state. It was a bit Roman, in its military control; a bit Grecian in its populations of the Dominions (except Ireland, which liked to lay claim to a European heritage) and their relaxed political connection; and above all vulnerable to shifts in the balance of world politics and economics, as was the British state itself, now less competitive economically, and very stretched militarily. In 1920, when the empire seemed at its strongest, the Chief of the Imperial General Staff, Sir Henry Wilson, feared that the army simply could not cope with the military and policing duties that confronted it; as he put it, 'in no single theatre are we strong enough'; Lloyd George had 'lost Ireland and the Empire'.[24]

Yet the British Empire was not lost so easily. It was still a priority in the making of British foreign policy in the 1930s; it remained a definition of British world status and power after 1945. But its long acquisition and varied character are important, for they emphasise the point that the empire was always in various stages of development: self-governing colonies sat side by side with dependencies; sometimes self-governing Dominions were evolving; another, Newfoundland in 1934, was collapsing.[25] It was necessary for the British to be flexible in their handling of imperial issues; yet they could draw upon a notion that there was some over-riding plan or purpose in all this; that, in retrospect, it could be seen as fitting into a pattern.[26] In a book written for school students in 1963 W. D. Hussey referred to the British Commonwealth as a 'living proof that the British Empire evolved from within itself sound principles of political development and progress based on the idea that freedom rather than coercion was the stronger political force'.[27] This was a peculiarly English way of looking at constitutional political and economic change. It emphasised the need to reconcile change and continuity in a way that was satisfying to English perceptions of their own, and other

people's, history. It gave the English the certainty that they had a manifest, but malleable, destiny. And while it is true that the colonised peoples
had their own history before they were taken over by the imperial
power,[28] it is equally the case that the imperial power had its own history
as well; and this history, or sense of history, which shaped the English
way of looking at the world played a significant, and at times decisive,
role in the making and then the unmaking of their imperial possessions.

2

NORTH AMERICA, 1775–1850: LESSONS FROM HISTORY?

The early British empire was heterogeneous in its composition, and this was revealed in the colonies' relationship with the mother country. There were colonies directly authorised by Royal Charter, and colonies of religious settlement, where the colonists had from the beginning very definite ideas about how, and for what purpose, they should regulate their own affairs. This could result in political turbulence on a considerable scale, as the power of religion and politics drove colonists to rebel against their lawful Governors: in Maryland in 1676, North Carolina in 1677–8 and New Hampshire in 1683.[1]

Religion and liberty were inseparable in the seventeenth century; yet the British empire was complicated by the heterogeneous nature, not only of the empire, but of the domestic British state itself. The Sister Kingdoms of Ireland, Scotland and England with Wales, admitted, as much as they disguised, the varied character of a domestic state constructed over several centuries, and with no purpose other than the security and religious stability of England. For example, England accepted Presbyterianism as the established religion in Scotland; this was the price of a Union in 1707 that would, it was hoped, end the mutually disastrous intervention of Scotland in English politics. Nevertheless, with this exception, the Anglican establishment was considered to be essential for the stability of the state and the authority of the Crown. This was hard to sustain, even in Ireland, where there was in Ulster a powerful local Presbyterian population with the ability to negotiate a financial concession from the Crown for its support (the *regium donum*). It would therefore be much more difficult for the English state to demand and secure religious conformity, as essential to governmental control, in the North American colonies; not least because of the large Presbyterian immigration from Ulster in the eighteenth century. Moreover, the Glorious Revolution of 1688 had based its legitimacy on the notion that an ancient constitution had been subverted; that English liberty was under threat from a Catholic and would-be tyrannical king. How much more difficult, then, would it be for any king, whether absolutist, or constitutional, as the 'King in Parliament' was after the Glorious Revolution, to impose royal authority in the empire. Navigation acts and commercial control, those economic sinews of the British Empire, might well become caught up in, and inseparable from, the colonists' ideas of how God insisted that they conduct their affairs of government. The assumption in the internal British *imperium*, that the state had the right to command its citizens' obedience, and levy taxes upon them, was all very well: but what was the 'state'? It was based on the relationship between King, Parliament and People, as represented in the House of Commons. How strong was the King's authority in this system? That would be tested domestically, and with some political instability in the 1760s; how strong the King's authority was in the Colonial Empire, an empire of God-fearing, liberty-loving ex-Englishmen and Irish Presbyterians remained to be seen.

This set the scene for a conflict between Britain and her North American empire that has become central to the idea, and the myth, of the British Empire, summed up in Edmund Burke's resounding phrase, 'A Great empire and little minds go ill together'.[2] When Alistair Cooke interviewed Charles, Prince of Wales, on the centenary of the American Revolution's Declaration of Independence, the Prince argued that 'I have a feeling that the American colonies at the time leading up to the Declaration of Independence would have been quite happy to have King George III as King of America; but what they did not want was the British Parliament as the Parliament of America'. He added:

> I think we've learnt from this now. For instance, the present Queen is Queen of Australia, is actually Queen of Canada, is Queen of New Zealand, is Queen of Fiji.... They are quite happy to have the monarch – but not an alien Parliament.
>
>   George III saw things in black and white, which in some ways was unfortunate.[3]

This way of seeing the North American experience as central, not
to the loss of empire, but to its evolution, is difficult to resist, though
modern historians find it harder to sustain. This series of events, the
American Revolution, and then the concession of Responsible Government to the remnant of the North American Empire in Canada (and
subsequently to other colonies of settlement, and colonies that were not
colonies of settlement), were the product of widely differing circumstances. Yet they were seen in retrospect as in some sense the natural
outcome of the loss of the American colonies, and the making of responsible government in Canada in the 1830s. When W. D. Hussey prepared
to educate British schoolchildren into understanding the empire/Com-
monwealth, he claimed that 'these changes have taken place gradually
and in an orderly way; they are in accordance with the ideas expressed a
century or more ago by such men as Lord Durham, Earl Grey and Earl
Elgin that the colonies would develop as free communities towards
nationhood and independence'.[4] And whatever the qualifications that
historians place on this idea – and they are considerable – the idea itself
proved of great significance in the British imperial experience. All political systems require sustaining myths; the remarkable thing about the
British imperial system is that it managed – and as part of the same process – to acquire a sustaining myth and a myth that deeply influenced the
eclipse of empire. Few empires have been as fortunate; and the origins
of both the sustaining and the declining myths lie in the events that
spanned the history of the North American continent between the late
eighteenth and the first half of the nineteenth century.

The conflict between Britain and her North American colonies
followed quickly upon the British triumph in the Seven Years War
(1756–63) which placed North America at the heart of British calculation
of her interests – economic and strategic – that compelled her to annex
Canada, and to regard the North Atlantic as vital to her protection of
her sugar colonies in the West Indies. British trade now ran into 'one
great channel', as Adam Smith put it in his *Wealth of Nations*.[5] Empire was
both a symbol and a basis of British power; British victories had sealed a
colonial system that presupposed that the colonies existed for Britain's
self-interest; but of course Britain offered in return the protection of her
navy and her army – a not inconsiderable factor in North America where
native Indian uprisings were a serious threat to the colonists' lives. But
this mutual dependence might be jeopardised if the colonists wished,
not to break away from the empire – that was not their first intention as
they moved into their dispute with the mother country after 1763 – but

to negotiate an arrangement that enabled them to influence British policy towards the colonies in respect of financial matters and the general supervision of matters such as the expansion of the colonies westwards. This seemed in itself a dangerous path to take; for while the Glorious Revolution had created the great English political solution to absolutism – the concept of the King in Parliament, and of the mutual checks and balances that made the system work – there was even in England the acceptance of the idea that at the heart of English Government, as of all governments, there was, and must be, a great engine of power – that the King in Parliament was at once mutually checking, and thus a constraint on arbitrary power, and yet working together to provide that legal source of power that was to be found in all states and which was essential to their proper and efficient working.[6] It might reasonably be assumed that this great engine of power would make itself felt equally in all parts of the British Isles. Ireland felt its weight in 1720 when, following a legal dispute and an appeal to the Irish House of Lords, the British Parliament passed an act 'for the better securing of the dependency of the kingdom of Ireland on the Crown of Great Britain', declaring that it had full authority to make laws of 'sufficient force and validity to bind the kingdom and people of Ireland', and denying that the Irish Lords had any appellate jurisdiction.[7]

There could be no doubt that the North American colonies would feel its weight as well. In the 1760s, indeed, the British domestic political scene was excited by accusations that King George III was seeking to emulate King Charles I, and subvert the checking mechanism of Parliament through the use of corruption. But the test of any system is found when it is opposed by those who, while not denying its fundamental right to claim the allegiance and compliance of its subjects, nevertheless resolve to test the application of that right – both in theory and in practice. Americans countered the claim of the British Parliament's Declaratory Act of 1766 to unitary sovereignty over America with an appeal to natural law – subjects could withdraw from societies with which they were dissatisfied and in so doing they recovered their 'natural freedom and independence'.[8] When King George III asserted his government's right to tax the American colonists he did so on the grounds that the empire, like his own kingdom, was subject to the unitary sovereignty of the Crown. Thus two systems of law were in conflict with each other. George III defended the British constitution, arguing that the Americans were represented in the way that every Briton was represented, through the system of virtual representation, whereby a subject without a vote was represented by like subjects with a vote. But the question for the King, and for the British Empire, was whether or not the sovereignty of the King in Parliament could in practice be applied across the Atlantic.[9]

The British attempt to raise money from the colonies which were most expensive to defend raised wider constitutional questions. British decisions and colonial responses were not merely decisions and responses; the question asked in Britain was, could the King in Parliament oblige his subjects in America to meet the reasonable demands that the British Empire needed for its security and defence; the question asked in America was, if the British state were indeed a unitary one, with American subjects regarded as ordinary British subjects at several removes of distance only, then the whole British system of church and state, king and parliament, laws and ordinances, would shape and mould their political, religious and economic futures in ways that could not yet be foreseen, but must raise anxieties on the head of fundamental liberties. Moreover, these anxieties were felt at a time when the British political system itself was the subject of debate and when the liberties of English men in England were represented as being in jeopardy. Even if it were possible to incorporate some representatives from America in the British Parliament (and these must be few enough in number, exercising no decisive or perhaps significant voice), these representatives would be entering into a closer relationship with an already suspect political system.

·The solution to this problem, Edmund Burke claimed, was to acknowledge the value of a more informal imperial system; to rule through practical moral prudence rather than doctrine.[10] Burke's appeal in 1775 was seen by one British subject, Dean Josiah Tucker of Gloucester, as a 'heaven-born pacific scheme' that granted the colonies 'all that they shall require, and stipulate for nothing in return; then they will be at peace with us'.[11] This was to misinterpret Burke, who was certain that the very specific power of levying money in the colonies must be retained by Great Britain as a 'sacred trust': 'it is obvious that the presiding authority of Great Britain as the head, the arbiter, and director of the whole empire would vanish into an empty name, without operation or energy.... If Great Britain were stripped of this right, every principle of unity and subordination in the empire were gone for ever.' But the only way to resolve the controversy was not reasoning but wisdom; 'It is reconciled in policy.'[12] Burke's advice was unacceptable to those who saw the American challenge for what it was – a test of the will, and the resolve to apply that will, of the British Crown in Parliament.

In resolving to go to war with the colonists if need be, King George III and his ministers were certain that they were acting in defence of the Crown's prerogative to demand allegiance and obedience from its subjects, and in such a way that would preserve the British Empire. A weak crown would be the sign and admission of a fundamentally flawed British imperial constitution. Those who would impose Britain's will on the colonies were not political backwoodsmen, nor rampant imperialists, but men basing their decision to go to war if need be on the real and careful calculation of the future of the empire. They were drawing upon a theory of empire that would enable the American colonists to be dealt with in a way that would maintain the sovereignty of the unitary British state and its imperial possessions. Thus two theories of empire developed: the Crown's, that the British constitutional system must be applied to the Americans, by force if need be; that without this there would be no empire to apply it to. And the theory that the colonies were, in the last resort, entitled to rest their case for the assertion of their right to govern themselves on natural law; and since the dispute did come to war, then it would be hard to find a resting ground somewhere between these competing claims. Indeed, rebellion made it impossible for the colonies to do other than aim to win, and then find that winning ended the prospect of any kind of compromise arrangement with the British state.[13]

The colonies were convinced that they had the right to withhold consent from laws passed by the British King in Parliament; that their regional legislatures had the right to give or withhold consent.[14] The colonists were British subjects, or they were not. Their victory in arms ensured that they were not. But the alternative, which Burke offered, was to see the Americans as a distinctive people with a distinctive right to be governed in ways that were appropriate to their particular situation and their peculiar character. Burke would later apply this notion to India, where he argued in 1785 against the deposition of the Rajah of Tanjore by the British East India Company. An empire thus governed would be an empire of peace; but would it be an empire of power? And what would the consequences be for the Crown in Parliament's authority over the rest of the empire? Burke's idea of 'salutary neglect' was based on the idea of a loosely regulated empire, not its demise. Burke hoped to reconcile subordination and freedom; the colonists in 1774 spoke of a 'federalistic empire' made up of equal and independent legislatures.[15]

This idea of empire had been explored in 1768 by the anonymous author of *The Present State of the British Empire in Europe, America, Africa and Asia*, a geographical survey explaining the power of the empire, which was, the author claimed, even greater than that of Rome. But this empire was distinguished by its freedom from the blemish of 'ambition', for it was based on liberty. Major Cartwright, a leading radical pamphleteer, urged in 1774 that the empire should be a free association of states endowed with British liberties.[16] But the British were guided by their King's determined statement in his speech from the throne in November 1774 that 'you may depend upon my firm and steadfast resolution to withstand any attempt to weaken or impair the supreme authority of this legislature over all the Dominions of my crown; the maintenance of which I consider as essential to the dignity, the safety and the welfare of the British Empire'. There could be no choice but one of war, in the last resort.[17]

Had Britain won the war of American independence, then she would still have been faced with the problem of what to do with her subjugated colonies. This would have involved her in awkward and complex questions of exercising sovereignty across vast distances, and over a country divided by the civil war fought in the colonies between loyalists and rebels. Any attempt at incorporating the colonies into the British political system would have proved very difficult and, if at all practicable, would have involved the British constitution itself in considerable upheaval. When imperial questions threatened to change the system enjoyed by the mother country (as imperial federation proposals were to do in the late nineteenth century) it was best to leave that alternative alone. But the American experience showed that the determination to enforce the authority of the Crown upon a set of people of European origin would not work: victory could achieve little; defeat demonstrated its inadequacy. The American defeat was not the first 'decolonisation', a model for the British Empire in future crises or difficulties, an example of intransigence that must be avoided in the future, a vindication of Burke's idea that 'a nation is not to be governed which is perpetually to be conquered'.[18] Britain was soon to expand her imperial role and possessions in other directions, as she became locked into the long wars with revolutionary and Napoleonic France. The American war was an eighteenth-century war, which took place against the background of contemporary ideas of freedom, religion and laws. But it revealed how difficult it would be to establish proper and working relationships between colony and mother country. This was of no consequence in most of the colonies which Britain retained, or was soon to acquire. Authoritarian rule, military conquest raised no problems (as yet) in India. Small colonies could be acquired with no need to think about their future constitutions, or their general role in British Government. At home, the sovereignty of Parliament enabled the British state to pursue policies of reform and centralisation without much reflection on the consequences of this trend for the British subject. Historians have frequently commented on the apathy that seized Britain when it came to colonial affairs in the early nineteenth century; certainly Britain had no need (and certainly no desire) to address the fundamental issues raised by the American Revolution; and since the colonies had broken away, this closed down any further need to work out the relationship between the British subject at home and the British subject abroad, or the application of sovereignty with no easy or adequate means of representing the subject abroad in the British Parliament.

II

But the residue of the first British Empire, in North America, was to have some significance for the British idea of empire: 'it meant a spon-taneous revival of that interpretation of the British Empire which had been offered to the mother country by many a patriot in the old Amer-ican colonies during the conflicts which Britain finally failed in solv-ing'.[19] The British victory over the French in the Seven Years War was the culmination of frictions between the two powers that had occasioned hostilities before the formal declaration of war in 1756. This victory proved in many ways more troublesome than the defeat of 1775–83. It incorporated into the empire a European people, the French Cana-dians, a people of different (and dangerous) religion, potentially recal-citrant, resentful and troublesome. It incorporated too the British loyalist majority, reinforced by those loyalists who fled to Canada after the American Revolution. Both were now encompassed in the British Empire and in a place where Britain had considerable strategic interests, a trad-ing interest, and a political interest.

In these circumstances it is hardly to be wondered at that the British Government should approach the question of governing Canada with some caution. In 1763 the governor-general was authorised to call a general assembly, but no assembly was instituted. This was abandoned in 1774 for a system which created a nominated legislative council for Quebec (i.e. British Canada). This was a direct response to the need to provide a strong, but tolerant, government as the American colonies and the British Government moved into conflict, but it drew criticism not least from the British Parliament itself, where it was denounced as a threat to domestic as well as colonial freedoms. The balance shifted against the act, especially following the influx of loyalists from the American colonies after 1775, but the British Government faced a real dilemma: to concede a generous grant of self-government to Quebec might only lead to the kind of separatist feeling that had undermined the British link with the American colonies, which had enjoyed too much, rather than too little, liberty. But the only way to reconcile French Canadians to British rule would be to ensure a peaceful and stable Quebec which would enjoy the benefits of the imperial connection. The inability of Quebec to pay its way forced the issue: Upper and Lower Canada were separated and ruled by a governor with the assistance of legislative and executive councils; bodies, however, that represented property and were meant to provide stability. There was also a 50-strong representative assembly. The 1791 Act which implemented these policies was compromised from the start because it was applied to a country where there was no natural aristocracy to provide political ballast, and where loyalists resented the French Canadians' enjoyment of the same privileges as themselves.[20] There remained serious constitutional problems in the relations within the two provinces of Upper and Lower Canada. These colonies had legislatures; they had nominated executive and legislative councils; and there were tensions between the legislatures on the one hand, and the executive and legislative councils on the other. There were also tensions between the French Canadian majority in Lower Canada – a majority which was a local one and which was accused of not knowing its proper place as merely a local majority – and the British population. The French local majority, after all, existed in a place where its mother country's power had been overthrown in battle.

The French Canadian problem was one of a distinct people, separated by religion and language, and also social structure, from the British colonists. The French, over 300,000 in number, were Roman Catholic in religion, French-speaking and rural; the British were Protestant and middle-class merchants, professionals and businessmen. They could claim a monopoly of loyalty to the Crown and empire; the Crown and empire could hardly set this claim aside, yet its fulfilment might provoke continued unrest amongst the French Canadians. A progressive and loyal class must be preferred to a potentially disloyal and backward Catholic people. The tension between the two could lead to conflict, rebellion and distraction for the British. If Britain lost control of yet

another part of North America (however indifferent she might in general feel about colonies) and if the United States were to fish in these
troubled waters, then there must be at least a weakening of the British
state, and this at a time when it had demonstrated its superiority in the
long wars with France. British prestige, recovering after the American
débacle in 1783, would suffer yet another reverse.

In Upper Canada the British population, strongly reinforced by the
infusion of Loyalists after the American Revolution, claimed that they
should have a monopoly of control over the administration: by the 1820s
their leaders formed a clique, called the 'Family Compact', which sought
to manage all patronage and persuade the governors that they alone
must constitute the executive council. They dismissed more recent settlers as interlopers, to be excluded from power and privilege. There was
also a dispute over the system of allocating the reserve lands of the province, which the British Crown controlled. Land reserved for ecclesiast-
ical purposes was restricted to the use of the Anglican Church; yet
dissenters, including Methodists and Scots Presbyterians, pointed out
that they were more numerous than Anglicans, and that the lands allo-
cated to the Church of England were not put to use, and were a barrier
to communications. Large tracts of land were secured by the Family
Compact and left vacant for speculative purposes. But the opponents
of the Family Compact were divided amongst themselves, with the
Methodists splitting into reformers and anti-reformers, which some critics alleged was because Methodists were benefiting from government
grants.[21]

American power could grow only at the expense of British power. To
let go of Canada was impossible; but to maintain the essentials of Britain's interest would not be easy. French Canadian discontent was complex and, in a sense, it obscured the difficulties involved in reconciling
the different interests and perspectives of any colonial legislature and
the British Government. But the conflict of cultures in Canada posed
especially difficult dilemmas for a British Government anxious not to
experiment with colonial relationships, or think too deeply about her
imperial system and its justification. It raised issues of principle: could
power be placed in the hands of Catholic French Canadians? What
would happen to the loyalist Protestant people if it were placed in the
hands of the French Canadians? If any concession were to be made in
Lower Canada, it would open up the danger that, as Edward Ellice
wrote in 1838, 'we shall abandon our own people established in the
Country by our encouragement'. Moreover, this would create the dan-

gerous possibility that the British would be 'cut off from all intercourse with this Country, by leaving the key of the Navigation in the hands of the French'.[22]

British interests, and the interest of a particular set of people in the British colony, were in this view inseparable. If Lower Canada were lost to the empire, then the British in Upper Canada would be cut off from the sea, and might therefore throw their lot in with the United States of America. As in the case of the Americans in the 1760s, to reward a recalcitrant people with concessions might arouse the resentment of already contented loyal people, and might further jeopardise the whole country by provoking the loyalists to demand concessions for themselves. Yet some measure of political stability must be attained; for if the British were to continue to emigrate to Canada and thus strengthen the British link, then they must be certain that they were going to a country which held out the possibility of prosperity and stability.

Therefore, while the British Government had no desire to depress French Canadians into the status of second-class subjects, they had to consider the consequences of permitting too much freedom and power in their assemblies. In Lower Canada in the 1820s there were almost 400,000 French Canadians and 80,000 English. This balance of population remained fairly steady over the next two decades.[23] In Nova Scotia and New Brunswick the English predominance was assured. As always in the nineteenth century, religious affiliation was politically significant and the British state supported the Anglican Church in all the colonies, much to the disgust of the numerous and vigorous Protestant sects – Methodists, Presbyterians, Calvinists and (of course) Roman Catholics. The religious practice of the people had powerful political implications. Dissenters resented Anglicans and all their privileges; but the French Canadians took the matter further, and saw their religion as a mark of identity: religious customs and beliefs must be defended against Anglican enslavement. The land system, with its French landlords granting land to *habitants* in return for the payment of dues and the performance of services, was regarded by the British as old-fashioned and almost feudal. Yet the French, backward and feudal as they might be, claimed the rights and privileges of a free people. They spoke the language of liberty because it suited their purpose to do so; so did the English Canadians. The British Government was therefore confronted with demands which, should they withhold them from one or other of these groups, would provoke instability, and the charge of behaving in a way contrary to the history and traditions of the British constitution. Yet to grant them to one or other of the contending parties would be to provoke the charge of favouritism and arbitrary government.

But Britain was not concerned only with the clash of religions and nationalities in Canada; after 1815 Canada assumed a significance for British economic development because of the rise of the lumber industry in New Brunswick and the St Lawrence regions. This increased the importance of the North American colonies for British naval power; and naval power was British power in the nineteenth century. In 1815 New Brunswick exported 92,553 loads of timber to Britain, Nova Scotia sent 19,382 loads and Lower Canada sent 11,676.[24] Then there was the development of the wheat industry, as the expansion of wheat growing in the west became of increasing significance by the 1820s. This in turn attracted British investment and engineering skills. The Atlantic provinces were less valuable (with the exception of New Brunswick and its timber) but even here Newfoundland had her fisheries industry and was regarded as a great trading area for British seamen.

With Canada now becoming a land of some economic potential it was easy to see this potential handicapped by the feudal, anti-modern society of Lower Canada. It was inevitable, therefore, that the British would want to secure their interests. The constitutional link between Britain and her colony was the system whereby the governor, representing the Crown, was given advice by the Council, with an assembly to allow a proper representation of public opinion. The Governor could veto, or reserve to London, acts of the legislature of which he disapproved. The Councillors were usually appointees of the King in Council, giving advice, and acting in a judicial capacity. The Assembly was elected on a franchise of the 40-shilling freeholder in the counties and the £5 householder in the towns.

Representative government had been introduced to help reconcile French Canadians to imperial rule and, once reconciled, the stability which ensued would attract British settlement there and make Lower Canada a British-dominated colony as well. A clash between the oligarchic Legislative Council and the elected Assembly was likely to occur in an increasingly self-assertive age. But the French had a particular grievance against the English-speaking members of the Council. Relations between Canada and the United States of America were bound to cause problems and more anxiety for the imperial power. The legislatures were prone to follow the same arguments as the eighteenth-century American colonial legislatures, and claim rights based on British precedents. There was potential for another clash similar in some respects at least to that which cost Britain her American colonies in the 1770s. The loss of the American colonies was still fresh in the memory; another North American crisis could only prove a distraction at least, and at worst a serious blow to British power and prestige. A second secession of her North American colonies, or of part of them, was hardly to be borne. There was even an ominous financial aspect to the uneasy relationship between colony and the British Government, as the British sought to make governors more financially independent, by appointing certain revenues to them and by making, at the same time, the colonists pay their way for their own establishment.

These were problems that might provoke any self-respecting colonist. But the French in Lower Canada were more assertive than the British, and resented the British determination to exact more funds from the colonists to defray the cost of administration. The 1820s saw deteriorating relations between the governor and the French representatives in the Assembly who, in 1827, refused to vote monies and as a result the Assembly was dissolved. When Louis Joseph Papineau, the leader of the more radical French Canadians, was elected Speaker in the New Assembly, the Governor, Lord Dalhousie, refused consent.[25] This was a serious dispute with implications for the relations between colony and imperial power: an assembly which claimed to control expenditure and an elected Upper Chamber (instead of a nominated one) in the assembly was likely to collide with the mother country and perhaps, at worst, provoke another North American crisis for the British Empire.

The British Government sought some means of accommodating local and imperial interests. In 1831 the Howick Act, called after the Under-Secretary of State for the Colonies, conceded the Assembly's claim for financial control, in return for a Civil List of £19,500, designed to secure the continuation of government in all circumstances.[26] Papineau used control of supply to confront the Governor by cutting off all revenue to the civil government. Further concessions seemed impossible, without endangering British control overall. The tendency to postpone a solution was abruptly interrupted by a rebellion sparked off by an attempt to arrest Papineau in November 1837. In Upper Canada also there was a small French Canadian rebellion. No grand theories, no appeal to the rights and liberties of man, inspired those rebellions; yet there was a degree of borrowing from the American colonial precedent. This was adopted by the English as well as the French Canadians. In December 1835 the Deputy Post-Master General, T. H. Stayner, a large landholder and no irresponsible agitator, wrote from Quebec to the Hon. John

Macaulay, who was about to become a member of the Legislative Council of Upper Canada, that the English were becoming convinced that 'the crisis is at hand *when blows must be come to* and the question be decided whether they are to be slaves or freemen'. The French must be pandered to no longer and the English were now 'desirous of any change that may relieve them of the odious tyranny which now rules the country'. In the same month the *Montreal Gazette* warned that:

> The Americans prior to their Revolution for grievances of a lighter character addressed themselves patiently and calmly to the Imperial Parliament, and when it turned a deaf ear to their complaints, they appealed to arms, and the result to them was success. They acted in the spirit of their fathers, and the Constitutionalists of Lower Canada are animated by feelings equally powerful and honourable. They are fully resolved, let the consequences be what they may, to uphold and preserve the inheritance bequeathed to them by their ancestors.

Papineau adopted this American-style language, widening what the dissidents regarded as a struggle between a local oligarchy and their aspirations into a general attack upon the role of the British Government, and drawing parallels with the American colonial predicament preceding the revolution. The cry of taxation and its inseparability from representation was raised, even though the parallel was somewhat forced; British goods were boycotted, and even the terms used to describe the American patriots, such as 'sons of Liberty', were adopted.[27]

The crisis was a constitutional one, and the drift towards a more serious outcome seemed likely. In July 1837 the governor of Lower Canada issued a warning against illegal assemblies; three months later he dismissed 18 magistrates and 35 militia officers for disobedience, and predicted the suspension of *habeas corpus*. In August the Governor, Gosford, prorogued the legislative assembly because of its refusal to pay arrears and its condemnation of resolutions made by the British Government in Parliament in May 1837, which were designed to tame the legislative assembly, and deny any possibility of allowing for an executive responsible to the assembly. In September Gosford reported that the Papineau party was now aiming at separation and a republic, and that it might be necessary to suspend the constitution.[28] The British reinforced their military strength, and while this was merely precautionary, it had no other policy in view. The result was insurrection and the British were obliged to confront what they had hoped to avoid: a colonial rebellion in

North America, with the need, once order was restored, to rethink the principles on which settlement colonies were to be governed. But there was an alternative tradition for Britain to draw upon. The early modern empire had always included representative assemblies governing themselves under the supervision of governors representing the Crown. The American Revolution had not ended this system, which survived in the British colonies in the Caribbean, in Nova Scotia and New Brunswick (from 1783) and in Quebec from 1791. Authoritarianism did not establish itself in these older colonies, and the British found themselves living with irritating frictions between executives and legislatures, though with no major upheaval on the American colonial scale. Governors needed money from assemblies which in turn endeavoured to influence policy.[29] The Canadian model adopted in 1791 sought to ease the position of governors in Upper and Lower Canada by making them more financially independent, and by creating an upper house nominated by the Crown, to check the more popular lower house. Now that this had failed, it was necessary to think about some modification of a system that was not in itself bad, but had failed to achieve the desired results, of reconciling colonial liberties with imperial control. This need not be a new, radical departure, a break with traditions; and it could arise from the English domestic habit of using contingencies and even contradictions in such a way as to create harmony out of discord. It was easy, in the first instance, to adopt a strong line, and suspend the assembly of Lower Canada, replacing it with a special council, nominated by the governor. But Lord Howick and Sir George Grey opposed this, suggesting instead that the governor should be given a discretionary power to call a purely advisory convention of delegates from both Canadas to gauge the state of public opinion and discuss the possibility of a union between the two provinces. In January 1838 the Whig Prime Minister, Lord John Russell, announced that the government would dispatch the Earl of Durham as high commissioner and governor-general to deal with the emergency.[30]

It is tempting to see Durham as having put into constitutional form the solution that evaded the British Government in the dispute with the American colonies; to draw a direct line between the two crises, and thus regard Lord Durham's visit to Canada, and his report, published in February 1839, as in direct lineal descent from the 'mistakes' of 1775. It was this that inspired the twentieth-century imperialist Reginald Coupland to describe Durham's mission and report as the 'Magna Carta' of the British Empire. But, in fact, the British attempt to learn from the American Revolution – to be careful about applying taxation to their British people abroad – only led them to commit errors of perception: the friction in Canada resulted from a number of factors (some of them indeed present in the American crisis). Now the British Government was faced by the resentment of colonial legislatures on restrictions placed upon their legislation, the refusal to vote supplies, and London's anxiety not to allow too much freedom of manoeuvre for their governors in Canada.[31] Nor could Durham have anticipated the idea of Cabinet Government in a democratic legislature (or at least partly democratic legislature) which did not exist in Britain in the 1830s.

As a man of his time, searching for a resolution of metropolitan–colonial disputes, Durham sought to strengthen the British connection with Canada, but did so in a way that profoundly influenced British theories of empire; and that influence was only enhanced by the way in which his report was invested with the same kind of awe that surrounded Magna Carta and, in his own time, the Great Reform Bill of 1832.

Durham was from one of the great radical Whig families of England, but he had a deep suspicion of French Canadians. His stay in Canada was short (from May to 1 November 1838) and he spent a mere 10 days investigating the affairs of Upper Canada. He suffered a rebuttal from his own Government over his attempt to banish the leaders of the French Canadian rebellion to Bermuda on pain of death; Durham, on learning this, issued an angry statement, which provoked his recall, but he had already left before news of his recall arrived.[32] Nevertheless, in December 1838 Lord John Russell suggested that Durham be contacted to see if he had any useful information to impart to the Government. Durham agreed to write up his report 'to enable you to form a correct opinion as to the state of the North American provinces'.[33]

Durham's report revealed the flaws arising from his hurried visit. He set aside the constitutional questions, and underestimated the internal tensions within the English people in Canada, whose religious divisions he hardly understood. Instead he concentrated on the clash of nationalities, declaring that the question was one of institutions, 'laws and customs as are of French origin, which the British have sought to outlaw, and the Canadians have sought to preserve'.[34] This ignored the possibility that, had the inhabitants of Lower Canada been exclusively English, then they might have tried their strength against the British Government as did the Americans in the 1760s and 1770s.[35] Durham hardly mentioned Upper Canada, where there were serious difficulties between the Legislature and the local oligarchy which controlled the executive and legislative Councils, and some reformers in the Assembly even

advocated the American principle of an elective Upper House.[36] There
was even the American religious parallel, for most of the oligarchy in
Upper Canada was Anglican in religion. Governors sought to support
an Anglican establishment and secure for the church all the privileges of
an establishment, but the majority of the province's inhabitants were
Dissenters, with an eye to clipping the wings of the Anglican Church.[37]

Durham, obsessed with the conflict of nationality, directed his gaze
towards the resolution of this, as he perceived it, vital issue. He believed
that the British were bound, inevitably, to predominate in Lower Canada as well as Upper Canada, and he thought it unwise to devise a future
form of government that placed the English minority under the control
of a French Assembly. Lord Melbourne doubted whether what he called
'swamping them' (the French) would do 'in these days'.[38] But swamping
them was Durham's preferred option. He explained why:

> Without a change in the system of government the discontent which
> now prevails will spread and advance. As the cost of retaining the Col-
> onies increases their value will rapidly diminish. But if by such means
> the British nation shall be content to retain a barren and injurious
> sovereignty, it will but tempt the chances of a foreign aggression by
> keeping continually exposed to a powerful and ambitious neighbour a
> distant dependency, in which the invader would find no resistance,
> but might rather reckon on active co-operation from a portion of the
> resident population.[39]

Therefore, British power and a settlement of the French Canadian
problem were inseparable. But Durham acknowledged that two possibilities were excluded: Canada could not be governed from Downing
Street, nor could absolute constitutional freedom be given to Lower
Canada. Therefore the joining of Upper and Lower Canada in a legislative Union would, he urged, fuse the two 'races'. But this would not and
indeed must not be a fusion of equals. It was vital to subject Quebec to
the 'vigorous rule of a clear English majority' and thus oblige the minority to 'abandon their vain hopes of nationality'.[40]

Durham looked to the precedent of the British Isles; here again British imperial thinking was dominated by what was believed to be the
domestic precedent. Durham maintained that Union in the British Isles
revealed how 'effectively the strong arm of a popular legislator will compel the obedience of a refractory population'. Durham called on the
state to encourage emigration to populate North America: 'one year's

emigration' could 'redress the balance', in the united legislature. The problem must be resolved because of the 'extensive' interests 'involving the welfare and security of the British Empire, which are perilled by every hour's delay', and the 'state of feeling' in North America and especially in the two Canadas.[41]

To resolve this problem Durham advocated that the two Canadas be joined; and the means by which they were then to be governed was based on his premise that the weakness of the present system lay in the perpetual clash of executive and assembly. This was caused by the combination of representative institutions with irresponsible government. A small group of governor's advisers had exercised political power without regard to the wishes of the people or their responsibilities, and had done so through their control of the councils and the support or acquiescence of governors. The assembly opposed this but could not create its own programme or remove the governor's advisers. This in turn opened the way to demagogues who acted without restraint. Therefore, the solution was to extend the British style of Cabinet Government, or what became known as 'responsible government' to the colonies. Governors should entrust the administration of local affairs to people who could command the confidence of a majority in the assembly. British control should be restricted to matters of essential imperial interest alone: the form of colonial government, the regulation of commercial and foreign relations, the disposal of public lands. Thus would the desire for internal self-government be reconciled with imperial supremacy, and separatist aspirations discouraged.[42] When Durham referred to 'Cabinet Government' he spoke at a time when Cabinet Government was in itself in the process of formation in England; and it was still a process in which the Crown enjoyed considerable influence in the appointment of ministers. But, here again, Durham was governed by his English experience; he refused, for example, to accept that the Great Reform Act of 1832 would be or could be a final measure, recognising that the world of politics was a changing one.[43]

The reception of the Durham Report was complicated by the fact that it coincided with a ministerial crisis in Britain, long discussion in the Cabinet, and the resignation of the ministry when its majority in the Commons over a bill to suspend the constitution of Jamaica resulted in a Government defeat. But in the 1830s the British Constitution was itself undergoing modification and adaptation; and in 1841 the question of whether or not an administration could sustain itself if it enjoyed the confidence of the sovereign, but not of the House of Commons, was

resolved in favour of the latter; and government by Ministers command-
ing a majority in the House would be government by party – though the
party lacked the organisation and rigidity of the modern British party
system and was soon, after 1847, to dissolve into the loose, shifting
groups described by Walter Bagehot in his *English Constitution* (1866):
one which made the Commons into an institution where, while the
'atoms' were hot the 'body' itself was cool. But if party was supreme in
the English constitution, then it might prove a more efficacious, as well
as constitutionally appropriate, means by which the colonies of settlement could be governed.[44]

The idea of responsible government was still one that required careful
handling in the colonies. As Lord Howick put it in May 1840, it would, if
it meant an executive government directly responsible to a Colonial
Assembly, prove 'incompatible with the maintenance of Colonial Government'.[45] The Durham Report was once thought to have played the
most significant role in moving the British Government towards a Canadian settlement based on the principle of responsible government. But
while this is too simplistic an explanation,[46] it was part of the growing
certainty that Canada, peopled largely with a community of British origin, could be modelled in some respects at least on the mother country's
stable political system, now based on party government.[47]

The appointment of Poulett Thomson as governor-general moved
forward the Union of Canada; and he managed to gain the support of
the two Canadian legislatures for Union, which was enacted in 1841,
with the full support in the British Parliament from Sir Robert Peel. This
Union did not follow the lines laid down by Durham. The constitution
assumed a more federal shape, which secured the French Canadians
in their interest, rather than swamping them, even after the number
of British colonists increased. British ministers did not immediately
endorse the principle of what was now commonly referred to as 'responsible government' (though Durham's use of the term was 'loose, general
and varied'),[48] but they at least required the governor-general and the
colonial executive to govern in harmony with the assembly. Moreover,
the French Canadians benefited from the tendency of the British (which
Durham seemed to regard as a homogeneous 'nation') to divide rather
than form one party representing the English interest. And there would
be no 'assimilation'.

Durham's report was firmly fixed in its time, though leaving open the
door to natural constitution evolution. He was sure that, just as Queen
Victoria played a role in selecting her ministers, so too would the

governor-general. The governor-general was expected to gather support in the assembly. The question of the governor-general's primary responsibility – whether to the Government in London, or the ministers in Canada – was unclear. It would not be easy to separate 'internal' from 'imperial' affairs. Colonial politicians would, naturally, seek to expand the scope of their powers.[49] Lord John Russell would not concede any general principle of separating local from imperial affairs, though there were clearly matters so central to imperial interests that they could not be delegated to a colonial assembly. But it was anticipated that no governor-general should attempt to defy Canadian wishes as expressed in the Assembly. In the 1840s governors found themselves making concessions in order to conduct harmonious relations with their assemblies. A sign of the times came in 1849 when Lord Elgin accepted the Rebellion Losses Act compensating the residents of Lower Canada for damage to property and other losses suffered during the 1837 disturbances: an Act which the English Canadians disliked intensely, but which they had to accept, since the majority in the assembly supported it, and since it was a 'local' matter.[50]

Durham's report was based not only on what he believed was the best British practice of government, but on the constitutional experience that underlay it; one based on the assumption that the British political élite could manage change, and that it could do so by structuring and re-structuring the machinery of government and administration. Ideas were not things imposed from some political theory textbook; but they existed, and were secreted in the practice of statecraft itself. Contradictions – such as the role of the governor-general, who might at one and the same time represent the Crown in Canada, acting on the advice of his Canadian Ministers, and also the Government in London, and holding himself responsible to that Government for his Canadian administration – were not necessarily important, because the idea of British government since at least the Glorious Revolution was that a constitutional system could be based on contingencies and even contradictions. The whole North American experience since the American Revolution, now reinforced by resolution of the Canadian crisis, was that the British Empire of settlement could be reconciled to imperial rule simply because, unlike America (now fortunately lost), British concepts of liberty 'remained stubbornly specific, resisting incorporation into the generalised natural rights rhetoric of 1789'.[51]

The American and Canadian experiences are significant for the British Empire, even though the mistakes made in the former, and the remedies sought in the latter, were located in their own time, and not easily translated into what earlier historians of North America liked to call 'a new departure, sagacious and enlightened in itself, and memorable and far-reaching in its issues, not only in Canada, but wherever the task of Empire-building has called forth the splendid energy of the English race'.[52] It is necessary to take a narrower view, and see the Canadian experiment as the product of the same perception that informed the Great Reform Act of 1832: as a cure for what had gone wrong in the Canadian constitutional crisis, and not a concession to the modern world of colonial nationalism. But, like 1832, a specific, pragmatic, concrete measure (electoral reform) could and perhaps must prepare the way for the application of political experience, and the knowledge derived from experience. This was seen in the movement of Nova Scotia, New Brunswick and even the small Prince Edward Territory towards what was now defined as 'responsible government' between 1847 and 1854 – even though Nova Scotia, for its part, was hardly the model of a responsible political society because of its religious animosities and divisions. But the 'solution' attributed by later enthusiasts to the Durham Report left many questions unanswered. There was as yet of course no suggestion that it could be applied to colonies other than those of settlement. But, even here, might it not cause difficulties in welding the empire into a coherent strategic and economic bloc? The French Canadian question had been side-stepped rather than resolved; if distinct nationalities could not be, to use Melbourne's phrase, 'swamped', then could they be reconciled for good to the imperial connection and rule? But the British seemed to have discovered a half-way house, or perhaps more accurately a corridor, between the disaster of the American precedent and the alternative voiced by some statesmen in the 1830s and 1840s of letting the empire go its own way in a form of voluntary decolonisation (and after all, Melbourne, in his letter inviting Durham to investigate the affairs of Canada of 22 July 1837, referred pointedly to the fact that the loss of the colonies 'might possibly not be of material detriment to the interest of the mother country', though he did place the 'honour' of Britain and the survival of his Government on the same plane).[53]

The British had developed an approach to empire that, in the future, they might find it expedient to apply to other, hardly analogous situations, but to situations which they preferred to think of as analogous. Of course, colonial rule was more complex than this Anglo-centric view allowed. Durham's misunderstanding of the varied tensions in English as well as French Canadian society was to be repeated in other colonial predicaments, from India to South Africa. But whereas this failure of understanding helped produce disaster in the case of the American colonies, it was at least concealed by Durham's invitation to colonial subjects to drink at the wells of the British domestic constitution. Durham reinforced the belief that lessons could be drawn from history, especially English history. In 1831 Lord Macaulay prophesied that the governing forces in history were generated by the constant tendency of intelligence and property to increase and diffuse themselves in an ever-widening circle; India could not be isolated from this tendency.[54] 'We can no more prevent property and intelligence from aspiring to political power than we can change the courses of the seasons and of the tides', he remarked when urging that Parliament pass the Great Reform Bill of 1832. 'We tried a stamp duty – a duty so light as to be scarcely perceptible – on the fierce breed of the old Puritans, and we lost an empire.'[55]

The North American experience seemed to vindicate the avoidance of the kind of doctrinaire approach that had alienated the Americans (the 'old Puritans'). The Durham Report appeared to endorse the kind of mixture of principle and pragmatism that Edmund Burke, apparently, advocated, securing British sovereignty while offering scope for colonial rights to be admitted. It provided what later generations identified as a fund of wisdom which could be drawn upon to provide the justification, perhaps also the means, of resolving later, and very particular, imperial problems. This was especially so in the twentieth century, when the empire was faced with complex problems of colonial relationships. In 1905 the Earl of Selborne, as governor-general of the Transvaal and High Commissioner for South Africa, considered, though he ultimately rejected as not quite analogous, the Durham Report as a guide to his task of saving South Africa for the British, while reconciling as far as possible the Dutch.[56] The Canadian representatives at the Imperial Conference in 1937 claimed that on Empire Day it was 'fitting to recall the words of Burke: "The ties of Empire are as light as air but strong as links of iron"'. 'Let them strive that at the conclusion of this conference these links were not broken by placing too much strain on them, but that, as the result of their deliberations here and a real earnest spirit of co-operation they should be stronger than they had ever been before.'[57] Clement Attlee suggested in 1942 that 'Lord Durham saved Canada to the British Empire' and concluded that 'we need a man to do in India what Durham did in Canada'.[58] But the most bizarre analogy was the statement by Sir Arthur Dawe in 1942 that the white settlers in the Kenyan Highlands were ripe for self-government: 'Such a solution would be indicated by the whole history of British settlement overseas from the time of Lord Durham's Report.' The 'physical effects of an equatorial climate add a note of feeling and excess to their Anglo-Saxon independence'.[59]

The belief that the North American experience facilitated the escape from the disaster of the too-rigid application of sovereignty which had lost the American colonies took hold. 'It was an experiment in the consolidation of power that failed,' wrote the English-domiciled historian D. W. Brogan, in 1947; 'And the real claim to political wisdom of the rulers of England is that when they failed they noticed the fact and retraced their steps.'[60] That the two examples were not wholly analogous – that the Americans wanted to restore what they saw as the diminishing rights that they had once possessed in full, whereas the Canadian Loyalists and British generally wanted to gain new responsibilities so that they could better dominate Canada – seemed not to matter. An imperial version of the Whig writing of history was born: the English ability to re-write history in the interests of practical politics that facilitated not only ways of governing a large part of the empire but, equally important, of modifying its governance and, in the very distant future, of transforming it altogether.

3

RATIONALISM AND
EMPIRE, 1850–1914

In 1853 Earl Grey, who was most closely associated with the successful introduction of responsible government to Canada, surmised that the British Colonial Empire ought to be maintained, not only because it was a responsibility that could not lightly be set aside, but also because of the fact that 'much of the power and influence of this Country depends upon its having large Colonial possessions in different parts of the world'. These gave Britain 'a number of steady and faithful allies in various quarters of the globe' and also the strength of 'opinion and moral influence' which, if lost would diminish British power 'to a degree which it would be difficult to estimate'.[1]

This quotation is not only important for its argument for empire; it reveals that, by the mid-nineteenth century, the British assumption that she was, and must remain, a great world power was axiomatic. And to be a successful world power would mean that economic strength, military force, and prestige, which drew their inspiration and origin from the empire, were integral to Britain's world supremacy. This was not so in the eighteenth century, where the loss of the American colonies did not prevent the British state, within a decade, waging war and waging it successfully until 1815. A well-organised, industrialising, hierarchical society, believing strongly in its own destiny and confident in its own resources, might be in search of imperial possessions, and might take them from other powers, but did not see them as essential to its survival: there were no colonial forces deployed in the vital theatres of war, the Peninsula and Belgium, nor even in Egypt. Other parts of the conflict were side-shows: and Britain's best allies were her Hanoverian regiments whose participation in the French wars took their origin in the

Hanoverian homeland of the English Kings. This was a Europe-centred conflict, and the navy, which certainly needed ports of call as it swept the seas for the enemy fleets, did its best work blockading French-dominated Europe.

But by the mid-nineteenth century the picture had altered. It is doubtful if British economic strength depended on colonial control; a colony, after all, indicated a 'territory occupied and ruled by a foreign power'[2] and the British belief in free trade, world-wide, meant trading with every nation and state equally. This required peace, order, but not necessarily occupation of territories; unless another power should threaten this world-wide trading system. It required railways, steamships, cheap communications, all of which were available in abundance after 1870; but the question remained open of whether or not this premier trading position required formal control, won by invasion, war, and then held by a military garrison and locally recruited police or military forces.

At the same time, it was by the 1850s inconceivable that an empire, once acquired, could not be the subject of political debate. The British expansion in India in the 1840s and the hard-fought campaigns against the Sikh Empire in 1845 and 1849–50 were not repudiated by the British Government, even though the serious losses in the pitched battles fought against a well-trained and armed Sikh army provoked consternation in Britain. Territories once acquired were not, with only a few exceptions, let go. British prosperity and pride rested upon the assumption that these were connected directly with colonial expansion. But if the empire were to be expanded, and retained, then its strengths and weaknesses must sooner or later become a matter for concern. And there were weaknesses, even in the 'responsible' colonies which, led by Canada, might be considered to have had their relationship with the mother country settled for good. Lord Grey warned in 1853 that there was a proper role for Britain in the internal affairs of her self-governing colonies: oppression and corruption might require to be checked; British economic interests, he warned, must not be jeopardised by colonial government's policies.[3] In 1873 he warned again that, for the empire to be an empire 'in the true sense of the word', then there must be 'one paramount authority invested with sufficient power over all the separate communities that form the empire to insure that on matters which concern them all they shall not follow different and conflicting lines of conduct, but shall cooperate with each other'. Unless the colonies could be persuaded or required to act in concert and in subordination to the imperial authority 'in everything that concerns the general interest, they cannot be said to constitute a real Empire'.[4]

When Lord Durham wrote his report he did not spend much time on these questions; but the fact that he spent any time on them at all in an era when colonies were (allegedly) unfashionable, was itself of significance. Durham wished to make a clear demarcation between imperial and local matters, which governments were reluctant to implement; and in truth this was difficult to make. But there was no doubt that the imperial authority must be retained. He also drew upon new thinking about the empire in his concern to secure a 'wise system of colonisation'. This was a reflection of Edward Gibbon Wakefield's theory of colonisation, which maintained that the Government should sell land, and then use the revenue to bring out immigrants who would work for wages. The British Government set up a Board of Colonial Land and Emigration Commissioners which between 1840 and 1873 helped 6.5 million people to go overseas. But two-thirds of them went to the United States of America.[5] In any case, Wakefield's prognosis involved keeping land prices high; and this could lead to friction between colony and mother country.[6]

Canada again raised further questions of the nature of imperial power and responsibility. Canada was a close and at times very uneasy neighbour of the United States of America. When colonies needed protection then they must realise and acknowledge their dependence on the mother country. This was a sound poposition, but, as Lord Elgin pointed out, it all depended on the enemy that the colony was being defended against. Would not Canada have greater, rather than less, security if she tied herself to the United States? Would she not have as much security against aggression as the state of Maine?[7] If the United States were serious about invading Canada, could the British protect her? And were Britain's enemies the same as Canada's enemies?

These were questions that were very far ahead of their time; the reckoning up of where Britain's 'true' interests lay, and how far they coincided with the colonies' interest was to wait until after the mid-twentieth century for its resolution. But in the 1850s and 1860s it was assumed, despite Earl Grey's warnings, that colonial self-government on the Canadian model was gathering momentum in the colonies of settlement, with British sympathy and assistance. As the preamble to the British North America Act of 1867 stated, 'such a Union [of the Canadian provinces] would conduce to the welfare of the Provinces and Promote the interests of the British Empire'. Significantly, however, one of the key advantages for Britain was that the strengthening of the bonds between the provinces would enable them to defend themselves more effectively. The political advance of the colonies from local to national and state identity was, then, not only compatible with, but an essential adjunct to, the interests of Britain in defending her empire and holding it against enemies, but at no overwhelming cost.[8] The idea of federation in South Africa from the 1850s to 1870s was part of this desire to ensure that, when necessary, federation of colonial states would be a means of reconciling colonial and British interests.[9]

There was also the 'informal' empire; what historians have defined as Britain's ability to dominate foreign economies, such as Argentina or China. The former was achieved peacefully, the latter after wars in 1839, 1842 and 1856–60. The paradox of informal empire was that it did offer Britain economic opportunity, but that trade itself was not sufficient for the demonstration and application of British power. Trade, in fact, needed the visible deployment of British military and naval force if need be. Trade needed imperial power as much as imperial power needed trade. The modern penetration by Japan of world markets made her a great economic actor, but did not raise her to the status of a great, or even medium, world power. British thinking about empire was slow to arrive at the conclusions uttered by Earl Grey in 1873, but in the end it was forced upon those who pondered on the nature and extent of British power – of the British need to be an empire 'in the true sense of the word'. But the problem was that any attempt to assert tighter control from the centre might provoke resentment from the periphery. This point was made by one of Grey's critics, Charles Adderley, later Lord Norton, in 1879: colonial affairs would be in danger of being treated as 'the materials of party struggles in England, with which they have no concern'.[10]

The questions that the Durham Report posed, though indirectly and by implication, were now coming to the fore: was the process of responsible government in the colonies of settlement one that constituted a formula for consolidating the empire, for reconstructing it, or deconstructing it? Was Britain actually decolonising, even as she reflected on her rise to imperial and world power status, and would this paradox of granting responsible government, to Canada, and then to other colonies of settlement, even in 1910 to South Africa after a prolonged and bitter war, end in the fatal weakening of imperial bonds? This was a question which exercised a debate amongst some luminaries in England from the 1870s to the 1890s, and beyond.

It is hard to assess the depth or even the importance of the debate. It had little popular interest, though there was after 1870 a quickening popular if sporadic public awareness in imperial affairs, especially in times of crisis: the defeat of an army in South Africa by the Zulus in 1879, the death of General Gordon in 1885, the defence of a fortress by brave Sikhs in 1895, the threat to Britain from the French in Fashoda on the Nile in 1898 – all provoked a popular response that politicians could not, except at peril of their political lives, ignore. These famous episodes, and others like them, became the subject of music-hall songs, slogans and fervid emotion; for a while. But seeing to the heart of what it meant to have an empire in an age of great power rivalry, when Germany, Russia and France were all accepting that to be a great power in Europe it was essential to be a great power in the world, was a different matter. This required sustained thinking about how best to harness and use the power, economic, diplomatic, military, that an imperial nation was supposed to possess. It called for clear, unemotional assessment about where the empire was going in an age of contested power. Was Russia a threat to the Indian empire, and if so what was to be done about it? Were the French a danger in the Middle East? How could British interests be secured and maintained? There seemed no alternative but to find means of bolting together an empire systematically: but the empire, heterogeneous, comprising colonies of settlement, crown colonies, India and areas of influence only, would not lend itself easily to the kind of logical and clear-sighted plan that the times and seasons seemed, to some at least, to demand.

The necessity to attack the problems and assess the potential of empire was increased by the growing concern about the future of British economic paramountcy in the world. Peace and free trade went together; and this belief would continue to underpin British thinking about how best to order the affairs of the world to suit her position as both a major trading nation, and as an importer of food; the empire, or at least the colonies of settlement (including South Africa) were major destinations for British investment. There might, in the future, be possibilities of investment and trade in the territories acquired in the rest of Africa in the 1880s; at any rate the empire seemed to be essential for the production of wealth: the wealth was necessary for the provision of the military resources which would defend the empire, and Britain, against any possible enemy, either near to home, or further abroad. This could answer the question posed to British statesmen in the 1840s, when they were concerned about the threat to Canada from the United States of America: the question of how best to strike a balance between defending the colonies and paying too much for the cost of their defence. It was again raised by expansion and settlement in South Africa and New Zealand, when imperial troops were required to subdue the inhabitants of territories now becoming attractive to European settlement. If troops were needed to subdue the Maories in New Zealand, for example, then it would be preferable if the colonists could themselves defray the cost. To 'withdraw the legions', however costly it might be to retain them throughout the empire, was alarmingly like the Roman experience, not in that it was a prelude to the decline of empire, but that it revealed the weaknesses of military and financial resources. Unless, of course, the colonists could not only raise money or local forces to defend themselves, but, better still, if they might even prove a source of manpower to the Empire, a reservoir of armies that could be used to spread the burden of war. And empire and war, however much Britain's position as a trading nation needed peace, were inseparable.

The answer to the problem of what constituted a 'real' empire is an essential aspect of decolonisation, because the attempts to construct such an empire, and their failure or success, must throw light on the strengths and weaknesses of the empire, which would be exposed in the future. The devolution of power to those colonies which could support the transplanting of British institutions was a means of separating local from imperial affairs, and thus stabilising the imperial edifice; but whereas the emphasis in the 1840s was placed on the need to loosen the ties of empire only in order to strengthen them through the Canadian model; the emphasis in the last quarter of the nineteenth century was on the best means of reconciling this necessary division of powers with the need for a central directing control. That part at least of the English politicians and public opinion were in a centralising mood was seen in the crisis over home rule for Ireland in the 1880s, when the Conservative party, identifying itself as the Unionist party, refused to contemplate even a mild measure of local devolution in the United Kingdom itself.

Yet devolution had been granted, or was being granted, to the colonies of settlement; there could be no refusal, nor a withdrawal of these devolved powers. The case of Ireland was different, for it was a domestic affair, concerned with the integrity of the British state itself, though the empire did not necessarily see it this way. In May 1882 the Parliament of Canada transmitted an address to the throne, urging the British Government to find 'some means . . . of meeting the expressed desire of so many of your Irish subjects' for self-government, possibly on the lines of

Canadian federation, 'so that Ireland may become a source of strength to your Majesty's Empire'. They were told, however, that this matter was the exclusive concern of the imperial parliament and ministers.[11] But the empire was 'Anglo-Saxon', and here British practice of devolution of power could be seen to work in the right spirit. Seeley in his lectures certainly thought that this was so, though he worried about the presence, indeed the centrality, of India in the empire. But, setting India aside, the other colonies of settlement were now living in a world where, as J. A. Froude put it, these were 'not the days of small states'.[12]

The United Kingdom was a small state, when considered within the borders of the British Isles. But it might be possible, indeed it was imperative, to look to the white colonies to make her into a large state. The white colonies themselves seemed to be willing to promulgate the idea that there was a 'race', a 'broader British loyalty' and a 'recognition of wider citizenship'. These ideas took root even in colonies with a large Irish Roman Catholic immigrant population. Australia declared her intention of creating a 'British Australia', of developing a white colony for the British race. One Irish–Australian even coined the phrase 'Anglo-Celtic' to incorporate this vision.[13] Australian immigrants from Ireland kept their home identities, though their children lost contact with the motherland.[14] But the fact that the colonies of settlement were peopled by the diverse nations of the United Kingdom kept alive the idea that there was an empire that belonged to all the 'British'.

By themselves, however, these British nations abroad constituted only very small populations. Separately they could be gobbled up by an enemy; and, after all, the first half of the nineteenth century was one when the United States at times seemed inclined to help herself to Canada, or bits of it. There were just under five million Canadians in 1891; just under four million Australians in 1901.[15] These were very small nations when compared to the European powers: France had a population of 39 million in 1901, and the German Empire had nearly 56.5 million.[16] Broadly based, but well-organised imperial defence institutions were more likely to deter an aggressor than were local forces locally controlled. An imperial navy, for example, with appropriate financial, manpower or material contributions, would demonstrate to foreigners that there was strength as well as prestige to be gained from the reorganisation of the imperial system.

Sir Charles Wentworth Dilke was one of the foremost advocates of turning imperialism into the way of power politics. In his *Greater Britain*, published in 1886, he anticipated the arguments that were to dominate the imperial debate until the First World War. Nearly 20 years before, in 1868, he expressed his pessimism about the possibility of Australian and Canadian separation. He drew attention to the 'one sided nature of the partnership which exists between the mother and the daughter lands'. The Briton, surveying his relationship with the colonies, could not but help being struck by one singular fact:

> No reason presents itself to him why our artisans and merchants should be taxed in aid of populations far more wealthy than our own, who have not, as we have, millions of paupers to support. We at present tax our humblest classes, we weaken our defences, we scatter our troops and fleets, and lay ourselves open to panics such as those of 1855 and 1859, in order to protect against imaginary dangers the Australian gold-digger and the Canadian farmer. There is something ludicrous in the idea of taxing St. Giles's for the support of Melbourne, and making Dorsetshire agricultural labourers pay the cost of defending New Zealand Colonists in Maori wars.[17]

Dilke's argument seemed to imply that the colonies might be relinquished to Britain's advantage. But Dilke had no desire to push his argument towards such a conclusion, though it is significant that he answered his own question only very obliquely. In answering his question, Dilke drew a distinction between what he called 'true colonies' and what he termed 'new dependencies'. True colonies had one great advantage for Britain, in that they raised 'us above the provincialism of citizenship of little England' through 'our citizenship of the greater Saxondom which includes all that is best and wisest in the world'.[18] But this was, he admitted, only half an answer, for it was no substitute for trade and defence. Indeed, trade and defence were hindered, not assisted, by the possession of colonies. England had more trade with the United States of America than with Canada: 'For the purposes of commerce and civilisation, America is a truer colony of Britain's than is Canada.' England's real empire was small in 1650, but her prestige stood higher then than now.[19]

By 1890 Dilke had altered his view; and this alteration corresponded to the changes in the international scene over the previous decades. Now, in his *Problems of Greater Britain*, Dilke dedicated his work to Lord Roberts, Commander in Chief of the Indian military forces, to whom the 'peaceful progress of Greater Britain' was 'made securer by his sword'. Appropriately, Dilke devoted the last section of his book, following a general survey of the various colonies that constituted the empire, to imperial defence. He urged a more systematic, rational defence arrangement, listed a detailed programme for imperial defence, and threw doubt upon the idea of foreign alliances – the navy, not doubtful allies, was the backbone of defence. Food supplies must be maintained in time of war; home supplies developed; the command of the seas retained. A General Staff must be created; and such a staff would 'constitute a form of Imperial Military Federation'. Our 'children across the seas' were now (he alleged) ready to make 'clear and distinct proposals', and the mother country 'with her concentrated population and her provision of skilled military talent, ought to set an example to her children by working out a practical system, in which many of them would gladly take their part'.[20]

The tone, as well as the substance, had greatly changed since 1868. Whereas Dilke then spoke of the colonies in a dismissive tone, he now insisted that it was Britain herself who had failed to make the best use of the relationship. 'At present it would seem as if our attitude towards the great colonies should be rather one of gratitude for the good nature with which they accept our shortcomings than of doubt whether they will consent to bear their legitimate part in Imperial Defence.'[21] There must be an appreciation of the colonies' point of view. If imperial defensive federation in any form were to be brought to a successful issue,

> the colonists will wish to know whether the fleet, which is to be our main contribution to the safety of their trade, and of their shores, can be spared for its world-wide work, or must be kept selfishly in the Channel, because we have not organised for England that land defence which we ask them on their part to have ready for themselves.[22]

The colonists must make their contribution, in raising and paying armies. Dilke did not speculate on whether or not the British worker, or the London businessman, might ask why he should be expected to contribute to the defence of far-away places such as Darwin or Durban. The empire stood or fell together when it came to defence preparation. Thus, if France were to threaten Australia, then this would necessitate the destruction of France's New Caledonian port, and that would be done by Australian troops carried in Royal Navy vessels. The creation of an Imperial General Staff brought to mind 'a clearer image of the stupendous potential strength of the British Empire, and of our equally stupendous carelessness in organising its force'. The German Chancellor, Bismarck, spoke of the potential for offensive war that the British Empire possessed, but our concern was for a defensive stance, and it was in pursuing this goal that Britain needed 'consistent plans for supporting the whole edifice of British rule by the assistance of all the component parts of the Empire'.[23]

The empire, then, must be seen as a power bloc, not simply as an asset to British trade and investment (though these were, of course, part of its inner strength). When in 1877 Gladstone argued that England's greatness as a nation lay within 'these islands' and not in the empire (least of all in India),[24] Edward Dicey answered him with the claim that 'England, like Rome, is the corner-stone of an Imperial fabric such as it has fallen to the lot of no other country to erect, or uphold when erected'; Great Britain must not be pulled down. He admitted that some said that England gained, rather than lost, by the secession of the American colonies; some would not even regret the loss of Canada. But, even if these views were accepted, the maintenance of the empire, of British authority over outlying territories, was England's chief object. England won her empire because she was strong, and would keep it only if she were believed to be strong still. India must be retained because 'to us has been given a mission like to that of ancient Rome'. It was conducive to England's reputation and interest alike.[25]

But money alone did not make power, though it was the means of buttressing power. What would make the empire a powerful organisation, able to counter a threat from any quarter of the globe? In 1877 Earl Blatchford argued that there must be a common purpose to the empire, otherwise it could be of no value in international relations. He agreed that it was wise to give self-government 'unreservedly'; but this left the empire vulnerable. In what European questions had the colonies any interest? What interest was there in England for matters relating to the cod fisheries of the Atlantic? A common purpose was needed as a basis for unity, for 'every increase of colonial wealth, or numbers, or intelligence, or organisation, is in one sense a step towards disintegration'.[26] But how could a common purpose be given expression? How could it be forged and made effective? The answer lay in a more systematic organisation of the empire; that which had been gained over time and in varying circumstances must be shaped in a new mould. The image of British invincibility must be given institutional reality; and the way forward, some argued, was the making of imperial federation – the application to the empire as a whole (or, rather, to its white colonies) of the federal idea that had proved a means of uniting individual parts of the empire, especially Canada.

The idea of imperial federation pre-dated the foundation of the Imperial Federation League in 1884, but the League gave strength and focus to what had until then been only a general suggestion. An inaugural conference was held in the Westminster Palace Hotel in London in July 1884, and the new organisation took as its objective the need to 'secure by federation the permanent unity of the Empire'. Important public figures attended, from both the Conservative and Liberal parties, and from the colonies themselves. This campaign needed leadership, and control from the top. The League would offer these essentials. It propagandised the idea with a confidence born of the certainty that this was a scheme whose time had come. Branches of the League were established in Britain and the colonies. The Liberal politician W. F. Forster set the tone for the debate when he argued that, having given self-government to the colonies, Britain had introduced a principle 'which must eventually shake off from Great Britain, Greater Britain, and divide it into separate states', if federation were not achieved. A 'colonial Board of Advice' would start the process off.[27]

The two key issues were identified as the creation of a kind of imperial *zollvereien*, or economic unit, which would mean radical change in British trade and economic policy; and the making of an imperial political organisation, a kind of imperial *kriegsverein* to ensure the military security of the empire. The latter did not necessarily require the former – free trade could exist side by side with imperial federation. But the question of defence necessarily raised considerations of a financial kind; in particular, the necessity for some kind of colonial financial support. This would of course have to be acceptable to the colonies. The whole idea of imperial federation necessitated England's taking the lead, and the colonies falling in behind. The League's idea of a 'Council for the Empire', was deeply enmeshed in defensive strategy, in evaluating and creating foreign policy goals. This raised the question of how far the colonies were prepared to commit themselves to British leadership and, more important, British definition of what her defensive and foreign policy goals were. The Imperial Federalists believed that the colonies would indeed be persuaded to share these aims, and work towards unity, because they would be invited to participate in a common nationality and a common danger 'which united defence alone can avert'.[28]

This plan, and the League itself, faltered when Gladstone rejected it on behalf of the Liberal Government in April 1893. But it had from its beginning received serious and sustained criticism from those who believed that, as Henry Thring put it, the 'true character of the British Colonial Empire is described by Burke'. The Parliament of the United Kingdom was a local legislature and an imperial legislature, superintending several legislatures. The colonies could not be represented in Parliament; and Burke was right in claiming that 'close affection' growing from kindred blood, similar privileges, and equal protection were 'ties which, though light as air, are strong as iron'.[29] Some colonial politicians added their doubts. Robert Stout of New Zealand warned that imperial federation meant a written constitution and a supreme court; and English statesmen must meet this 'face to face'.[30] John Merriman of the Cape legislative assembly was more hostile. The American Revolution had arisen from British efforts to tax the American colonies. Democracies would not abandon their own interest, not even for a cause as lofty as the unity of the British Empire. A common fleet for defence of the empire would be difficult to organise. The history of Greece showed how such an arrangement carried in it the seeds of decay, and 'England would occupy with regard to her colonies the same position as Athens did to hers before the outbreak of the Peloponnesian War'. 'Allowing for the differences between ancient and modern civilisation, there will be the same causes of disintegration of the Empire at work.'[31]

Imperial federation did not disappear, for the times were ripe for a debate on the relationship between England, her empire, and indeed her own United Kingdom, for the question of whether or not Ireland should have home rule within the United Kingdom was increasingly perceived as having imperial resonances. Gladstone's adoption of the policy of home rule for Ireland in 1886, and his presentation of his idea of 'justice for Ireland' in two home rule bills in 1886 and 1893 was originally seen as a purely domestic matter, though one which, if it broke up (or united more firmly) the United Kingdom, must have important implications for British power. The empire was watching from the sidelines, but the onlooker often saw more of the game, and the Irish issue was bound to have imperial repercussions, if only because of the large number of Irish immigrants who lived in Australia and Canada, and because there were nationalist stirrings in the oriental jewel of the empire, India, where the Congress Party was founded in 1885 and looked to the Irish nationalist party in the British House of Commons both as a model and as an ally. The last decade of the nineteenth century, and the first of the twentieth, provided timely reminders that Britain had to look to herself, and to her role in the world, in an age when

European states were consolidating their newfound political unity (Germany, Italy) and when the United States of America was in the wings at least of the world stage. Germany and France were pursuing their colonial ambitions, in the Pacific, in Africa; and the Russians, as always, were perceived not only as standing dangerously near the borders of Britain's Indian empire, but as now pushing for concessions, economic and diplomatic, in China. On the continent the great European powers, Germany, France and Russia, were setting their minds towards creating and maintaining armies that could be mobilised quickly in the event of a day of reckoning. Britain had, then, to look to her manpower and also to her technological expertise, for modern armies required modern weapons. But she also needed re-education in the importance of her empire to her place in the modern world. Sidney Low, historian and prophet of empire, devoted himself to the creation of educational institutions which would help make the British think imperially. He drew attention to the way in which federation could help Britain rival the larger populations of her rivals in the world, Germany, the United States of America, and Russia. Again, the history of dead empires was brought out: the Greeks were unable to reconcile democracy with imperialism, state self-government with a larger unity, and because there was no real union, there could be no 'common centre of political energy'.[32] In the autumn of 1912 he addressed a meeting of members of the British Academy in London on 'The organisation of imperial studies in London'. Oxford and Cambridge placed imperial studies behind every other subject, and London University ignored them altogether. An imperial school or faculty must be located in London which was 'the centre of imperial government, imperial administration, imperial finance, and imperial commerce'. The graduate of such an academy would go on to hold high places in the India Office and the Colonial Office, and in the great banks and business corporations of the City of London 'which are in the closest touch with the overseas communities'. Young men aspiring to good careers and honours in public life, would be able to attend lectures in the Institute. Low canvassed leading public figures, Lord Haldane, Lord Esher, Earl Grey and others, and in February 1914 he gave an 'Empire Study Dinner' at which Lord Milner and various professors from the University of London were present. A month later the first formal meeting of the Imperial Studies Committee was held at London University. The war interrupted this development, and a chair in imperial history in the University was delayed until July 1919, when the Rhodes Trust endowed one. This was a symptom of the political and educational élite's awareness of the need to think imperially and use history as a preparation for the imperial life.[33]

Britain also became more aware of the economic vulnerability that now underlay her free trade position. She invested much capital overseas, though not all or even the greater part of it in the colonies (some 40 per cent). But this 40 per cent was not unimportant, and in any case British investment was directed largely towards the colonies of settlement, making it all the more imperative to think about their potential for British economic development. Britain depended on foreign foodstuffs for home consumption and on foreign industrial raw materials; this again must make her rethink her position in the world. She was aware too of the increasingly fierce competition in distant markets for manufactured goods; if it were accepted that not only must a nation acquire wealth, but that it must also deny it to others, then these economic factors had also political implications. British imperial consolidation therefore had a very significant economic aspect, and this was not separable from the political and military spheres.[34]

Imperial manpower, imperial economic cooperation, the establishment of a common defence policy, the whole untapped potential of empire were central to the thinking of Joseph Chamberlain when he became Colonial Secretary in 1895. Chamberlain thought imperially; he looked at populations, claiming in 1897 that the colonies of settlement would double their populations 'in the lifetime of our descendants'. They would themselves become great nations, and through their willingness to give military assistance to Britain, help maintain her status and power as a great nation.[35] It was with some justification that Henry Birchenough wrote a panegyric in *Nineteenth Century* in March 1902, hailing Chamberlain as an 'empire builder' who had taken up the tradition created by Seeley in his *Expansion of England*, by Forster and the Imperial Federation League, and Lord Rosbery and the Liberal Imperialists. But Chamberlain had, Birchenough claimed, quickened and vitalised this great principle, educating people at home, and demonstrating in the South African war of 1899–1902 that the empire was willing to rally to the mother country 'with unswerving firmness' as the Northern States had rallied to the cause of Union in the American Civil War. But the corollary of this help was that the colonies must be consulted, and the result was that 'imperial public opinion' had formed. 'It is difficult to believe that henceforth any man can be Prime Minister of Britain-within-seas who has not gained in equal measure the confidence and support of Britain-beyond-seas.'[36]

Chamberlain embraced the arguments for imperial consolidation in the 1890s, advanced them, and promoted the idea of economic and political union. Britain must negotiate a new arrangement with the colonies of settlement through the creation of a kind of *zollverein*. The colonies could be inducted into a special trading area. They would contribute raw materials to Britain, and she would export her manufactured goods to them. But she would also erect tariff barriers against her foreign competitors, while offering preferential rates to her colonies, and waiving these rates for her colonies, who could export, say, their grain to Britain and undercut competition from the United States of America. The colonies would respond by reducing tariff rates on the import of British manufactured goods. This would have the added advantage that the wealth needed by government to meet the demands for social reform at home would be raised not from the British taxpayer, but at the expense of the foreigner, and this, in turn, would bind the working classes to the idea of empire, for it would have direct implications for their own livelihood and welfare.

Chamberlain also entertained more ambitious plans of an imperial system based on regular conferences, that would be turned into political and even executive institutions; the empire might have a parliament representing all its white subjects. When Sir Robert Giffen raised doubts about the project, warning that an Imperial *zollverein*, through preferential tariffs, would encounter problems of the physical separation of the different parts of the empire, the variety of race and business, and the deleterious impact on the various economies involved,[37] Henry Birchenough replied that a practical arrangement of tariffs could be achieved, and indeed was already working in some cases, such as Canada. But more vital was the grouping of the world into great states, politically and economically. 'A natural instinct is driving us into closer union.' Preferential treatment within the empire, the development of the material as well as the moral resources of the empire, was a patriotic duty. It was difficult to create political union without creating a desire for some sort of commercial union. 'People do not keep the various interests and activities of life in a series of watertight compartments.' 'It was now for the first time possible for all the States of the Empire to adopt in principle the policy of preferential treatment. ... At first the practical application of this principle would no doubt be more favourable to the Mother Country than to the Colonies, but ... the Colonies would probably be willing to show some confidence in the future, and in the gradual modifications which ever growing financial necessities are sure to effect in the fiscal system of the Mother Country.'[38]

This was to go too fast for the empire, and indeed for the Conservative Party. But the idea of imperial preference seemed to meet many needs, including the needs of British domestic politics, and this was the goal that Chamberlain set himself to achieve, through capturing the Conservative Party and the British electorate for his proposals. He launched his Tariff Reform Campaign in 1903, but it failed to capture the party or the country, and only split the Conservatives and sent them into the political wilderness for a decade. But this failure cannot hide the importance of the problems that Chamberlain identified for Britain in the new century. 'Old ideas of trade and free competition have changed', he declared on 16 May 1902:

> We are face to face with great combinations, with enormous trusts, having behind them gigantic wealth. . . . At the present moment the Empire is being attacked on all sides, and in our isolation we must look to ourselves. We must draw closer our internal relations, the ties of sentiment, the ties of sympathy – yes, and the ties of interest. If by adherence to economic pedantry, to old shibboleths, we are to lose opportunites of closer union which are offered us by our Colonies, if we are to put aside occasions now within our grasp, if we do not take every chance in our power to keep British trade in British hands, I am certain that we should deserve the disasters which will infallibly come upon us.[39]

Chamberlain's warnings were not readily taken up even by his Cabinet colleagues. At an Imperial Conference in 1903 Canada suggested an extension of her 33 per cent preference to the United Kingdom, if the United Kingdom responded by the preferential remission of the shilling duty on colonial corn. Within a short time the Cabinet abolished the corn duty altogether, thus shutting the door on the prefential principle. Chamberlain protested to the Duke of Devonshire on 21 September 1903 that a decision to give Canada preference had been taken, only to be thrown over as if it were of no importance. Devonshire replied that he had failed 'to understand that . . . a decision was even provisionally taken of such importance as that to which you refer, and it must have been taken after very little discussion'.[40] This was hardly the mood on which Chamberlain's party could build a new imperial spirit. But the intrusion of imperial matters into British domestic affairs, and the question of the empire's role in keeping Britain a great world power, invaded British politics before 1914 in an uneven, but at times highly pertinent way. The chief dangers to the empire and Britain's future lay in the forces of nationalism and separatism; the remedy lay in convincing both the empire and the home country that the time had come to turn wealth into power – power that, when tested, would not crumble away. These two issues were closely related. Indeed, the defeat of separatism might well require the mobilisation of imperial manpower and its movement into the battle line. A far-flung empire was vulnerable; the fall of the Roman Empire demonstrated that a widespread empire could hold its own, just, provided that the onslaught from without, or trouble within, was confined to one area or at most a few trouble spots.

In the 1890s the British Empire began to resemble a bush fire that broke out now in one place, now in another. There were disputes with the United States of America over Venezuela, Portugal over South Africa, France over Siam. Then, after 1898, came the most alarming confrontation of all. Relations between Afrikaaner and Briton in the South African Transvaal came to a head with Dr L. S. Jameson's raid into the colony to try to raise a British uitlander rising in protest against the Afrikaaner denial of their political rights.

All these caused Lord Selborne, Chamberlain's Under-Secretary of State at the Colonial Office, to regard the moment of crisis as having come. When he ruminated on the confrontation with America in 1895, Selborne wrote of the American President, Cleveland, as having been 'smitten' by the 'mad thought for war'.[41] Chamberlain, returning to a fear that had dogged Britain between 1812 and 1870, spoke of the danger that the United States would take the step of invading Canada as a retaliatory measure. The sense of isolation and danger which these disputes aroused seemed to be realised when Britain manoeuvered the Afrikaaner republics, the Transvaal and the Orange Free State, into war in 1899.

The South African War was the most significant conflict in British imperial history before the Suez crisis of 1956. It was not simply that the republics proved harder to defeat than anyone, including Chamberlain and Selborne, could have imagined. At least there was the compensation of the support given by the white colonies for the British cause. What was really troublesome about the whole business was that the dispute with the Boer republics was not only about the uitlanders, nor about the discovery of gold in the Transvaal after 1886, but the certainty that this crisis was the turning point for the empire as well as South Africa. The dispute was one between two civilisations, the British – progressive, modernising, efficient – and the Afrikaaner – medieval, backward and indelibly set in its ways. This reflected the larger dispute which was that if Britain failed in this war, then the hub of her empire in South Africa would break, and the empire as a whole would suffer from the disaster. Lord Milner, the strongest advocate of what he called a 'forrarder' policy in South Africa, believed firmly in imperial union and did not see why the self-governing colonies should drop away from the mother country.[42] Lord Selborne, quoting Rudyard Kipling's 1897 poem, 'Recessional', wrote to Lord Curzon on 23 December 1899: 'lest we forget',

> I think we had largely forgotten and that we relied too much on ourselves and too little on God, the giver of our greatness. We are of course in no sense necessary to Him, but I believe from the bottom of my soul that He still means to use us in working out His immutable purposes, and that we shall emerge from this ordeal, chastened indeed, but stronger and more united.[43]

The British did win the war, though not without deep divisions in public opinion at home, and the irritating sight of Irish nationalists support for the Boer cause, a fight for freedom that they declared they only wished they had the military means to emulate. But what was perhaps even more daunting than the war was the peace; for this raised the question of how an embittered, recalcitrant Boer population could be incorporated into the British Empire for good. There were two ways of securing this: one was that the Boer states should remain with the most minimalist of representative institutions, and that Britain should concentrate on building up the prosperity of the Transvaal gold mines, thus encouraging economic revival generally. This would in turn invite more British immigrants to South Africa and achieve what Britain hoped to set in train in Canada in 1839, to 'swamp' the recaclitrant peoples. This necessitated the continuation of crown colony government in the republics, which Lord Selborne, when he went as governor-general to replace Lord Milner in 1905, fully intended to maintain – if his new masters, from 1905, the Liberal Government, would let him.[44] But Selborne was also aware of the legacy of the British liberal tradition. He feared that the Liberals would instead embrace the principle of maintaining the empire through granting responsible government to its component nations, which would mean, Selborne declared, 'a Boer Ministry ... Boer Police, Boer Railways, Boer everything, except the British flag, and how long that would stay would be merely a question of opportunity and historical accident'.[45] Selborne saw another parallel with Canada in the 1840s, in that whereas the British population tended to split politically and so reveal political weakness, the foreign element – then French, now the Afrikaaner – did not thus divide into parties.[46]

But the Liberal Government also was aware of the history of the British Empire that seemed, at least to them, to be exemplified in the earlier history of British response to armed revolt in her colonies. The view was expressed by J. A. Hobson while the South African war was still being waged: that to base British control of the Boer Republics on military force would fail, and that 'if historical precedents have any weight', would 'sap the loyalty of even the most loyal British colonists, and at no distant date sever South Africa from the British Empire'.[47] The Liberals were in no sense prepared to give South Africa away; they were as convinced of the need to maintain a strong imperial system as were Milner or Selborne. But they believed that the Boer republics could best be secured by the grant of responsible government which, Asquith reassured Selborne in March 1906, must 'by all legitimate means . . . stand upon the lines of British predominance'.[48] Selborne, dismayed nonetheless at the grant of responsible government to the republics, now worked for the federation of the whole of South Africa which, he believed, could have several beneficial results:

> federalism . . . or better still unification, will bring stability, that stability will bring prosperity and capital, that prosperity and capital will develop mining and industrial enterprise and commerce, and that development of these enterprises and commerce will *surely* bring with it the essential growth of the British population.[49]

In the event, and after hard bargaining, the Union of South Africa was created in 1910. But its eventual fate was not secured, despite British hopes for a British South Africa. Even while Selborne and the group of young imperialists, led by Lionel Curtis, were congratulating themselves on their part in preparing the 'egg' that, they believed, led to Union, Louis Botha, Boer General and now first head of the new state, confided to Francis Malan in April 1910 that he was 'anxious to see the politics of Union crowned with success. The day must go to the Afrikaaners.'[50] In the end it did, as Afrikaaner domination was ushered in, not stopped, by the Union; but the question of whether or not Afrikaanerdom was compatible with the integrity of the British Empire was to be tested in 1914 and, it appeared, answered positively, as Botha not only supported the British war effort, but suppressed a dissident Afrikaaner revolt against it. The precedent on which the Liberals rested their decision to grant responsible government seemed vindicated. Selborne, for his part, reflected years later on the 'gamble' taken by the Liberals, concluding that 'the luck of the British Empire did not desert it and we found Botha'; but in the Orange River Colony, 'where there is no Botha', there the outcome was just as Selborne predicted: 'it has been racial, obscurantist and reactionary to the last degree'.[51]

The South African crisis, which Chamberlain assumed could, if need be, be settled by a quick, cheap war, gave rise to a whole debate on the question of the foundation on which the empire rested. The Liberal theory won the day; but this debate now became related to another, hitherto domestic debate, on the place of Ireland in the United Kingdom, and of both South Africa and Ireland in the empire. When Selborne was dealing with the Boers (whom he personally liked very much) he warned that the Boer was 'like the Irishmen, very pleasant to meet as friends, but when you do business with them, particularly political business, you must use a very long spoon'.[52] Yet they must be done business with. Asquith's third home-rule bill, introduced in April 1912, and intended to grant a modest measure of devolution to an Irish executive and parliament, met with resistance from both the Conservative Party and the Irish, especially the Ulster, Unionists. By 1900 the Irish question had begun to assume a more imperial aspect. There was an increasing awareness that what affected Ireland and Britain must have imperial repercussions; and what the empire thought could not be ignored when the British came to deal with Ireland. As the Liberals and Conservatives became more deeply engaged in bitter political dispute over Ireland between 1912 and 1914, there were those in the Party, and in Conservative circles generally, who thought that the imperial, and especially the South African, precedent, might indicate a way forward. J. R. Seeley had spoken of the idea of federal union of the empire as a means of keeping England on the same footing as the other great powers. England could lead the way to a United States of Empire. In 1897 Chamberlain had urged the need for a systematic method of consultation, perhaps 'a great Council of the Empire to which the colonies would send representative plenipotentiaries', thus leading towards that 'federal council to which we must always look forward as our ultimate ideal'.[53] In December 1902 a Committee of Imperial defence was created, and its administrative staff encouraged Dominion participation in high-level defence discussions, but the Committee was purely advisory, and Dominion attendance was at the discretion of the British Prime Minister. This suited Canada and South Africa, both of whom were satisfied at what Louis Botha called the destruction 'root and branch' of the 'proposal for an Imperial Council'.[54] In 1910 the journal *Round Table* was founded to advocate imperial cooperation, and preached the gospel of the great naval historian, Captain Mahan, that 'the balance of forces influence continually and decisively the solution of diplomacy'; the lesson to be drawn from this was that it was anomalous 'that there should be no means of marshalling the whole strength and resources of the Empire effectively behind its [the empire's] will, when its mind is made up'.[55]

Ireland seemed at first glance an odd place to begin this grand design. But the *Round Table* group had played their part in the unification of South Africa when they provided Lord Selborne with ideas and material to help his plan for 'closer union'. Ireland was another inviting prospect. And Ireland could be the beginning of something much larger. For a possible solution to the conflict of nationality in modern Ireland might lie in the reform of the United Kingdom on Federal principles, with Parliaments for Ireland, Wales and Scotland, perhaps also the English regions, which would keep nationalist Ireland in the empire, and deprive Unionist Ulster of its claim that the Irish nationalists were being treated as a special case through the unilateral grant of home rule. The *Round Table* group believed in what they called 'organic union' of the empire; by starting with Ireland and the United Kingdom they could then work outwards, and the result would be a grand parliament representing the United Kingdom and the Dominions 'on some basis of population or wealth'.[56] It seemed that, yet again, the British had discovered a theory of empire that fulfilled two tasks at once: the loosening of central control, through granting responsible government, to federal units (or to a single unit as in the case of South African Union); and the tightening of imperial control by the very same process. That it failed to work in Ireland and the United Kingdom before, during and just after the Great War, was perhaps troublesome; but then, the exceptionalism of Ireland could be regarded as no true guide to its validity. At any rate, it was an ambitious grand theory, and if it were set aside for the moment, then it could yet be taken out again to consolidate the empire in a great federal union.

All this was in the future; the empire had more pressing concerns besides Irish and imperial federation. These were the more mundane, but none the less important, considerations of money and military innovation, of the question of paying for power. Lord Salisbury put the point succinctly when he declared in 1900 that 'you must divide victories by taxation if you wish to know in solid figures the real worth of Empire';[57] taxation and victories were indeed inseparable, as Britain had demonstrated in her last great world conflict with France between 1793 and 1815. And taxation was usually spent on the navy, the one instrument that guaranteed British victories. The key question was now the level at which the navy could be maintained. Britain had adopted the 'two power standard' in 1889, which called for the construction and maintenance of a battleships fleet of first-class cruisers that were not merely equal to the combined fleets of the next two greatest naval rivals, but equal to beating them. This equality, moreover, was regarded as an absolute minimum: and 'equal to beating the next two powers' required expenditure on expensive, modern powerful vessels. This was an ever-increasing burden, and one that First Lords of the Admiralty hoped might be shared with the colonies which the navy helped defend. Sir Michael Hicks Beach, Chancellor of the Exchequer, suggested that Selborne, the First Lord, should obtain from Canada and Australia 'some *real* contribution to the naval defence of the Empire'.[58]

This always proved difficult; the colonies wanted naval protection, but were reluctant to pay for it: they had, after all, domestic electorates to consider also. But equally important was the role that the navy should play in British global strategy. That it was dangerously dispersed was becoming evident, as Germany's great naval programme began to attract official notice. But this was not recognised as the chief danger right away. Selborne saw Russia as the main threat. In April 1901 he warned that 'compared to our empire, hers is invulnerable' because 'her communications are secure'.[59] And, again, in a memorandum, 'The Balance of Power in the Far East', Selborne remarked that 'for us victory in such a war [with France or Russia] is a condition of continued existence as an Empire. To them defeat would bring no corresponding consequences.'[60] Where was the most vulnerable place in this empire? Selborne acknowledged that the answer was complex: to be defeated in the Chinese seas would matter little as long as Britain proved superior in the Channel or the Mediterranean; though a *serious* disaster in the Far East would certainly have dangerous repercussions: 'we could not afford to see our Chinese trade disappear, or to see Hong Kong and Singapore fall'.[61]

The Admiralty, at first, found two solutions to this problem. Britain concluded a naval treaty with Japan, on 30 January 1902, which stated that if either party found itself at war with a third power, the other party would remain neutral; but if this third power were joined by an ally, the other party to the agreement would intervene. This, Selborne noted, made 'a satisfactory disposition of our fleet easier'.[62] But the disposition of the fleet was radically altered when the Admiralty became aware of what Selborne called 'the intensity of the hatred of the German nation to this country'.[63] The question was whether or not the navy should follow the enemy wherever it went – as Admiral Sir Cyprian Bridge pointed out in April 1902, this strategy had sent Nelson to the West Indies. But this exposed Britain to the danger of a sudden invasion, with her fleet absent. From the beginning of 1904, then, the Admiralty's experts worked out the best strategic disposition for the fleet, and resolved to concentrate it in the North Sea, given that 'the great new German navy is being carefully built up from the point of view of war with us'.[64] In December 1904 Selborne's memorandum, 'Distribution and Mobilisation of the Fleet', was based on the belief that 'a new and definite stage has been reached in that evolution of the modern steam navy'. The fleets of the United States, Japan, Germany, Russia and France were powerful; they had been developing over the past 30 years. But British naval strategy was based on an era before the electric telegraph, when wind was the 'motive power'. Now new conditions dictated new methods. Care would be taken to maintain Britain's domination of the high seas, and to provide for 'peace duties of Imperial Police'.[65] But the protection of Britain's home shores was vital. Yet, barely a year earlier, Selborne had noted that, in the years to come, the United Kingdom by itself would not be strong enough to hold its own against the United States of America, or Russia, or possibly Germany. Britain would be swept aside by sheer weight. But 'the British Empire could hold its own on terms of more than equality'.[66]

Here was a paradox: the empire was vital to British world power; yet the navy – the very basis and mainstay of that power – must primarily defend Britain against a European state, an enemy close to home. British frontiers were wherever the flag flew; yet if the flag were hauled down at home, then the other frontiers would be rendered meaningless. Imperial rivalry, Selborne assured the German Admiral Eisendecker in February 1905, was not the point at issue between the two nations: 'I do not think that the existence of a German Colonial Empire or the marvellous expansion and prosperity of German commerce are in any way responsible for the Englishman's suspicion of Germany. He regards the former as quite natural and the latter with admiration although he feels the competition.' But Germany's building a fleet must be seen as a threat to Britain: 'says my fellow countryman to himself', he wrote, 'the Germans say their navy can be no menace to ours because it is so much smaller than ours'. But what would the German War Office say if there were suddenly created on the German land frontier a new army, first class in quality, which bore the same proportionate strength to the German Army as the German Navy does to the British Navy?'[67]

British foreign policy, however, was still, up to the outbreak of war in August 1914, based on her imperial prerequisites; European rivalries were considered only so far as they impinged upon her imperial interests. England's frontiers still lay on the Himalayas, and she now looked to Russia, not herself, to provide a balance of power in Europe. Yet, as the Liberal Foreign Secretary Lord Grey admitted in March 1914, 'all along the line we want something, and we have nothing to give'.[68] This raised the question of what kind of strength the empire provided to Britain, if indeed it was proving more difficult to defend, with 'apprehension and strain' in India the result of Britain's imperial role.[69] Lord Curzon, former Viceroy of India, had no doubt that the British mission must be an imperial one. In an address in Birmingham in December 1907 he drew attention to the 'loyalty and enthusiasm' of the empire. Rome had recalled her scattered legions when she was threatened by barbarians; but there never rallied to her aid the offspring of her own loins, as Australia and Canada provided when they poured their volunteer manhood into South Africa. This loyalty was found too in India's princes and Africa's chiefs.

Curzon believed that the Crown was the essential link between the imperial possessions. A British Empire that had no visible head but a prime minister or even a president of a republic would not last 25 years. This, he went on, was an age of empires – American, Italian, French, German, even Japanese. There was an inevitable compulsion of imperialism: 'if the dawn of small nations has not yet sounded, at least the day of great nations seems to have dawned'. The British Empire was not a military empire, as Rome had been. Around Britain swung her satellites: the self-governing colonies, the crown colonies, the Indian empire. 'If that empire fell, so would England, and your ports, coaling stations, dockyards would disappear, and England would become the inglorious playground of the world, with her antiquities, castles, parks and the like remaining to attract tourists, a crowd of meandering pilgrims.' People would come to visit England as they went to see the Acropolis at Athens. So England must keep her empire; and empire needed imperialism as its creed. The English, like the Romans, began as conquerors, but then brought law and order to their conquered lands. The Medieval Roman Empire had encapsulated the same idea. Socialism and empire went together also, and Curzon stressed this conjunction, although he was not a socialist. Curzon acknowledged the problems of creating imperialism: distance was one, though this was being removed by improved communications. Race was another, for the empire comprised many millions of people different from the imperial people. Government and administration was a third, and it was necessary to create some form of 'Imperial Council' as 'advisory, if no more'. The problem of imperial defence must be solved. Tariff reform was vital, for it would make the empire more self-sufficient. Curzon looked to the day when the King would hold his Court in Quebec or Calcutta.[70]

By 1914, therefore, even as the United Kingdom engaged in a major European war, she did so without any idea of involving herself permanently in Europe, or playing a key role in the balance of power. She hoped, after the war, that such a balance could be found by means other than close involvement in the affairs of the continent; it was the pursuit of this goal that would lead her into the policy of appeasement in the 1930s. But it was clear, or at least becoming clear, that some overall, fundamental rationalisation of the empire on political or economic grounds had failed to materialise; that imperial federation or imperial preference were unrealistic goals, or at least that a federal Parliament in Britain, or a kind of *zollverein*, was not what the colonies wanted. It was, as rationalist doctrines often are, an abridgement of a complex political and historical development. As one South African journalist and member of the Union Parliament put it – and he was an English South African – 'the mechanical difficulties in the way of an Empire Parliament and Government began to seem more insuperable the more logically they were exposed as rather imaginary than real'. The people of the colonies, he asserted, suspected that 'system and centralization . . . were so alien that they would do more harm than good', and they 'sniffed suspiciously for the motive of an attitude so un-British. Imperial federation, as a preventative against the risk of empire dissolution from inside, thus never became more than a plan of theorists.'[71]

But the federalists were not yet willing to abandon hope, and the Great War was to focus their attention yet again on the idea of a United Kingdom and an empire reorganised on basic constitutional principles that would secure England's place in the world. In the event their activities revealed that some at least of the pillars of empire must be based on a completely different foundation, but one that was not unknown in the British experience: that of devolving power to local élites, as the best means of preserving what could be preserved of British interests and influence, possibly even British power. This was done in South Africa in 1910, and as Dr Iain Smith has noted, it was a precedent to be followed 'elsewhere during the twentieth-century exercise in decolonisation'.[72]

4

PILLARS OF EMPIRE:
IRELAND AND INDIA, 1914–49

The British Empire by 1914 was extensive; by 1918 it was even larger. But this collection of territories, governed in various and contrasting ways, ranging from white colonies of settlement, now looking more like nations, to small islands with no perceptible sense of identity, and wholly dependent on Britain for their administration, was supported by three main pillars, or, if Ireland in the United Kingdom be considered, four – for, as Unionists saw it, the Irish home crises of 1886, 1893 and 1912–14 all challenged the integrity of the kingdom, which was, in the eyes of some, to jeopardise the whole empire. Even those who defended home rule did so on the grounds that, in strengthening the loyalty of Ireland to the kingdom, it would thereby strengthen the empire. The other pillars were the great subcontinent of India; the recently acquired British possessions in the continent of Africa; and the increasingly vital territories in the Middle East. These pillars were the main edifices on which the empire rested; if they were lost, then all the smaller bits and pieces would shrink to unimportance, for the empire would lose all coherence and meaning. They were unalike in the timing, method and reasons for their acquisition; but although the pillars of Ireland, India, Africa and the Middle East had little in common with the white colonies of settlement, three of them were eventually to be grouped into a special category named 'Commonwealth'. The white colonies of settlement had a history different in many respects from that of Ireland, which could (and did) claim to be a mother country in her own right, sending immigrants to the empire, and spreading the Roman Catholic religion, via the empire, throughout most of the world. This Commonwealth club provided a means of enabling England to continue her tradition of regarding the imperial connection as something to be re-negotiated, not abandoned. In the end all these different pillars were to weaken or, in some cases, reject the imperial link, but two of them, India and Africa, at least were to find themselves grouped in the Commonwealth club that was, originally, designed for white nations only.

The outbreak of war in August 1914 answered any questions about whether or not Britain could muster her imperial strength; the white colonies of settlement put their armies and manpower behind the war effort; India was enlisted in the war by the British Government, which was at last able to draw on numerous and loyal soldiers of the Indian Army to fight a European war. The recently acquired African territories, though of course on a lesser scale, did their bit. The chief enemy for Britain was necessarily Germany; and it was on the continent of Europe that the generals wanted to deliver the knock-out blow. But the war had vital imperial dimensions as well. The British carried the war, as they had done the wars against France over a hundred years earlier, into the imperial possessions of their German and Turkish enemies. Military campaigns in these spheres – South West Africa (mainly the concern of the South African armed forces), East Africa and Palestine were conducted, though it could not be said that they always showed British military endeavour at its best. In Mesopotamia a British and Indian Army was initially successful in pushing the Turks back to Kut, only to be besieged there and forced to surrender. In East Africa a handful of Germany's colonial subjects used guerrilla tactics to hold off a larger British force for several years. There was controversy, too, over the role of Dominion soldiers in Gallipoli, where the Australians complained that they had been sacrificed in the interests of British troops. The question of the military performance of the Dominions' soldiers lasted beyond the end of the war. There was friction between the British and the Canadians over the performance of the Canadians in the second battle of Ypres, on 24 and 25 April 1915, and even more dispute when the British Official History of the War provoked the Canadians to claim that it had an 'anti-colonial bias'. The Canadian Official History took a very different point of view, defending the Canadians and their officers.[1]

At home, in the hub of the empire, the United Kingdom began to experience the stresses of war, and find itself the object of criticism from the white Dominions for the Government's failure to resolve the problem of Nationalist and Unionist Ireland. John Redmond hoped to use the war to place Ireland firmly in the ranks of the Dominions, in terms of loyalty and resolve, if not yet in terms of constitutional status. Redmond saw the war as a chance to prove Irish loyalty and thus win for certain Irish home rule. But the heart of the empire was shocked by a dangerous, if unsuccessful, rebellion by Irish separatists in Dublin at Easter 1916; and the British Government failed to resolve the question by a series of expedients, including an Irish Convention in 1917 in which the representatives of Irish political opinion would, it was hoped, settle the matter by themselves. The Dominions were alarmed at this failure by the British to secure the full allegiance of their own subjects, and General Smuts of South Africa, in particular, showed an active interest in promoting a settlement.[2] But the British attempt to impose conscription on a recalcitrant Ireland in March 1918 helped move Irish Nationalist opinion away from the Home Rule party's imperial nationalism towards the rising star of Sinn Fein, a party which had never anything good to say about the British or their Empire. In South Africa the outbreak of war had occasioned an Afrikaaner conspiracy and rebellion in 1914, though one that was put down by the South African Government itself, which seemed to demonstrate the positive nature of Dominion Nationalism. In Canada there was serious French Canadian opposition to conscription; riots against conscription in the spring of 1918 provoked bad feeling between English and French Canadians.[3]

But these troubles were the exception; and they were as nothing set beside the spirit of loyalty and cooperation that swept the empire. An Imperial War Cabinet was established in London in 1917 to promote imperial cooperation, even though it was only the British Cabinet with the visiting Dominion Prime Ministers added on, and did not form a kind of supreme command of the imperial war effort. Lionel Curtis surfaced again, stressing in his book *The Problem of the Commonwealth*, published in 1916, that the organic union he sought could not be forged by ties of blood and sentiment only: some illogical British concept or compromise was insufficient. British politics, the constitutional crisis over the House of Lords in 1909–11, had shown that unwritten constitutional conventions were too weak; there must be practical plans to ensure that the electors of the empire could choose their imperial future. A Convention of the Commonwealth must be called to discuss how to promote democratic control of foreign policy. Other similar books were published at the same time. But they met with a mixed response, the *Times Literary Supplement* doubting whether the 'tangled facts of our Commonwealth are amenable to logic', and the constitutional expert on the empire, A. B. Keith, dismissing the idea of organic union as 'fantastic'. Local autonomy was the 'life-blood of the British Empire' and federation would remove the defects of Dominion status at the cost of that autonomy.[4]

But the idea of turning again to imperial preference in trade as a means of binding the empire together was resurrected; this was not surprising as Britain depended more upon imports from the empire, though she also relied considerably on the United States of America.[5] L. S. Amery, Assistant Secretary to the Imperial War Cabinet, spoke in grand terms of the great, indeed limitless, possibilities of economic development in 'India and in the Dominions of the Southern Hemisphere', and warned the Cabinet in February 1919 that 'we are in fact no longer the sort of country that can compete industrially in the open market except in certain industries. . . . It really comes to this, that we both carry out our social reform and develop an immense trade, but mainly if not entirely within the Empire.'[6]

The British Empire, then, passed the test of war, though war was more of a volatile, modernising force than her statesmen realised. The Imperial General Staff noted in July 1920 that 'as in India' there were 'few coloured races in the Empire who had not to some extent fought for us in a white man's war, have been trained to arms and imbued with fresh ideas on the subject of race equality', a state of affairs for which 'no parallel can be found in pre-war conditions'.[7] The Dominions, for their part, in 1918, opposed any attempt to establish an imperial navy under the control of an imperial naval authority.[8] In terms of territory, the empire gained German colonies and Turkish provinces. Palestine, Transjordan and Iraq became British 'mandates', a form of trusteeship under the aegis of the newly formed League of Nations, but with British control secured, and the defence of India made more secure than at any time since the British recognition of the importance of her Indian empire. India, the Middle East and the Far East absorbed British military garrisons; the continental commitment was reduced to diminishing point, and British foreign policy was as before conducted on the basis of imperial frontiers. But the war, which had revealed some disquieting signs about imperial solidarity, was followed by a crisis at home that had imperial implications. The assumption that empire – white empire – was based on consent, on the belief that the mother of parliaments, Britain, did not coerce her children, was now to receive a rude setback. Between 1919 and 1922 the British Government found itself obliged to coerce her children, when in Ireland she fought a bitter if low-intensity war, to prevent Irish republicans from seceding from the United Kingdom.

The war of the Irish Republican Army and the Crown forces was one
that could not help attracting the attention, and perhaps criticism, of the
Dominions. They saw the British using force against a small nation, and
using force of a particularly disreputable kind: the 'Black and Tans'
were not the barbarians of Sinn Fein propaganda, but they were hardly
models of good police work. The British Cabinet's policy of permitting
'unofficial' reprisals against people suspected of republican sympathies,
and then introducing official reprisals (the destruction of houses where
IRA members or their sympathisers were suspected to live), the declaration of martial law in some areas, all attracted the concern of the Dominions, who saw the conflict as one fundamentally at odds with the British
concept of civil order. The war revealed both the strengths and weaknesses, the lack of resolution, and yet the determination, of the British
Government when it came to holding on to her territory. Britain could
not win the war without a serious effort at making peace; only thus could
she put herself right in the eyes of the world.[9] But, in the negotiations for
an Anglo-Irish Treaty, Lloyd George and his colleagues made it clear
that they would not tolerate, not even if it meant a renewal of war
('immediate and terrible war'), the secession of Ireland from the empire.[10]
The United Kingdom might be reduced in territorial sovereignty, but
the empire would be augmented, for Ireland must become a Dominion
with the same power as Canada, though with some military restrictions
because of her proximity to the mainland of Britain. The Irish were not
a colonial people seceding from the empire; they were a part of the United
Kingdom which must be denied secession. The British were determined
to hold Ireland to certain important responsibilities (for example, to
accept a share in the British national debt and war pensions) which
would not apply in the case of a colony. But at least they abandoned her
original determination to make free trade with Ireland compulsory.[11]

But the Irish case forced the British to try to define what it was that
held the Dominions together; and the answer seemed to be that the
Crown was the means whereby the British Empire ensured that it was
a cohesive unit, and not merely an aggregate of scattered territories.
Moreover, this took a definite constitutional shape, for the governor-
general, the Crown's representative, was regarded by the British as
central to their determination to continue to direct the political destinies
of Ireland. The first governor, T. M. Healey, a former mainstay of the
Irish home-rule party, was given definite instructions about how best he
could defend British interests, which he did in 1923 when he fulfilled his
promise to give London warning of any controversial Irish legislation, and

even tried to persuade the head of the Irish Executive, W. T. Cosgrave, not to erect customs barriers on the Northern Ireland border.[12] Nevertheless Sir Edward Carson, in a bitter speech in the House of Lords on the Anglo-Irish treaty, warned the British that they had suffered a reverse that would exert serious and damaging repercussions on the empire as a whole:

> If you tell your Empire in India, in Egypt and all over the world that you have not got the men, the money, the pluck, the inclination and the backing to restore order in a country within twenty miles of your own shore, you may as well begin to abandon the attempt to make British rule prevail throughout the Empire at all.[13]

Carson's speech was a bitter attack on those in the British Conservative and Unionist Party whom he believed had betrayed the most loyal of people, the Protestants of the South and West of Ireland; and the personal nature of his attack, with Lord Birkenhead singled out for the full force of Carson's invective (a 'loathsome' politician who had used Ireland and Ulster to advance his own career), deprived it of some of its authority. But Carson's was not the only voice prophesying that Ireland had set a dangerous precedent. Writing in the *Nineteenth Century* Cyril Falls, Chichele Professor of the History of War and himself a Protestant Ulsterman, warned that 'the Treaty stands today a monument to the success of naked force', and would set the scene for more concessions. Egypt had a 'theoretical right to complete independence far more convincing than any that has been pleaded on behalf of Ireland'. Then there was India. The Government had given 'direct encouragement' to those in India who wanted independence. Falls concluded with the admonition that:

> Whatever this old Empire may be called upon to yield within the next few years, let us hope that it will either yield it swiftly with good grace or deny it decisively with bad. Above all, let us hope that it will not again permit the world to believe that it will surrender to violence what it refuses to reason.[14]

Lloyd George, for his part, was always aware of the importance of Ireland to the British concept of empire in the postwar period. In September 1921, while discussing with his Cabinet the possibility of moving into direct negotiations with Sinn Fein, he mused on the consequences if 'we gave in to them. It would lower the prestige and dignity of this country and reduce British authority to a low point in Ireland itself.' Such a policy would 'give the impression that we have lost grip, that the Empire has no further force and will have an effect in India and throughout Europe.'[15] During the treaty negotiations Lloyd George and his colleagues fought relentlessly against the Irish idea of association with, rather than full membership of, the empire. This was novel to the British, as Austen Chamberlain remarked when, on 24 October 1921, the British plenipotentiaries withdrew to consider the 'external association' option. 'They [the Irish] dwelt upon an elected head as representative of the Crown', he remarked. 'They seemed to think of a republic within the Empire.'[16] While the politicians tried to close with the elusive concept of Dominion status, Lionel Curtis, for his part, tried to square the circle of what he called 'the two conflicting principles of autonomy of the parts and unity of the whole'. He dwelt upon what Dominion status would become, rather than what it was, and was obliged by the British delegation to produce a revised version, which stressed that 'each Government is free to take any action it chooses, but each is expected to consult the others before taking action which affects the unity of the Commonwealth as a whole. And if the imperial conference is of opinion that the action proposed would affect that unity, the Government proposing it is expected to abstain.' He was certain that the Crown was essential to the Commonwealth unity; without this there must be a 'desperate struggle between the two islands, in which either Ireland would be crushed or the British Commonwealth destroyed. The concession of this demand will lead at once to agitation in India', and it must therefore be 'resisted up to and past the breaking point now'.[17] Curtis was adamant on this issue: whether a man was a subject of the King or an alien 'no more admits of an equivocal answer than whether he is alive or dead'.[18] The most the British would allow was that Ireland should be a 'free state of the British Empire with a Parliament'.[19] Nevertheless, the British conceded an oath of allegiance which tried to meet some of the Irish objections to placing themselves under direct allegiance to the Crown: the form of words used was:

> I . . . do solemnly swear true faith and allegiance to the Constitution of the Irish Free State as by law established and that I will be faithful to H. M. King George V, his Heirs and successors by law in virtue of the common citizenship of Ireland with Great Britain and her adherence to and membership of the group of nations forming the British Commonwealth of Nations.[20]

This was little more than legal verbiage, but it revealed a certain, if limited, flexibility in imperial thinking about Crown and citizenship.

When Lloyd George defended the Treaty in the House of Commons on 14 December 1921, he put up a spirited performance. The freedom of Ireland, he said, 'increases the strength of the empire by ending the conflict which has been carried on for centuries with varying success, but with unvarying discredit'. He rehearsed again the great advances made within the empire during the world war, where the British Government set up for the first time 'a great imperial war Cabinet. There were present representatives of Canada, Australia, South Africa, New Zealand and India, but there was one vacant chair, and we were all conscious of it. It was the chair that ought to have been filled by Ireland.' Ireland was angry because 'the people who were a nation when the oldest Dominion had not even been discovered had its nationhood ignored'. But now that empty chair would be filled by Ireland, a 'willing' Ireland, which could take part in the 'partnership of Empire, not merely without loss of self-respect, but with an accession of honour to herself and of glory to her own nationhood'. The 'previous loyalty' which Ireland once gave to kings she was now giving to the 'partnership and common citizenship of Empire'. But then Lloyd George looked beyond Ireland. Other dangers might arise to trouble the British Empire. 'Whence will they come?', he asked. 'From what quarter? Who knows?' What the British did know was that when they came, Ireland would be with her. 'Our peril will be her danger, our fears will be her anxieties, our victories will be her joy.'[21]

Lloyd George's view was shared by Lionel Curtis, whose influence on the making of the Anglo-Irish treaty was significant; but there was a possible problem here. Both Curtis and Lloyd George were, in effect, staking some at least of the future development of the Commonwealth on the resolution of the Irish question. This was something of a leap in the dark, as was demonstrated within a few months, when the British Government was to become disillusioned with the new Free State Government's efforts to maintain Nationalist unity in the face of the anti-treaty onslaught led by Eamon de Valera in the Dáil, and then by the anti-treaty or 'irregular' IRA. Voices were raised in questioning the way in which the British had glossed over Ireland's strange road to Dominion status, and the character of her politics which, some argued, would not sit easily with the concept of a Dominion. Professor A. B. Keith, constitutional expert, pointed out that Ireland's measure of freedom was greater than Canada's because the official description of the Articles of Agreement as a 'treaty' implied the recognition of Ireland as a sovereign power; and even where Ireland's constitutional position was coincident with that of Canada, it contained nothing to ensure the permanence of Irish allegiance to the Crown. On the Government's own admission, he concluded, the right of secession was inherent in Dominion status; and the Irish leaders were 'perfectly entitled to argue that next year they can declare Irish independence, as they accepted Dominion Status as defined by the Government with which the treaty was negotiated'. Sir Robert Horne, Chancellor of the Exchequer, took a less pessimistic view. In a meeting of Coalition Liberals and Conservatives he denied that Ireland would use her Dominion powers to secede from the empire. Many people had made the same melancholy predictions with regard to Canada, Australia and New Zealand, but this was true only as far as it went. Ireland was a reluctant Dominion which, as *The Times* admitted, had 'come to pass not by a slow process of evolution, but, as it were, in a night'.[22] It had also come to pass only after a threat by Lloyd George of 'immediate and terrible war' if the Irish delegates did not sign the treaty.

Ireland was a reluctant Dominion; and this was soon revealed in her attempts to republicanise the draft Free State constitution. In June 1921 the British prepared a response to the Irish draft constitution, in which Lionel Curtis (who was instrumental in helping the process towards South African self-government) pointed out that in the treaty 'the British Commonwealth of Nations is conceived as a single and undivided whole, owing allegiance to the Crown'; but the Irish conception of it was that 'there should be two quite separate and independent wholes, on the one hand the British Commonwealth of Nations and on the other hand an independent Irish State associated for certain limited and specified purposes with the British Commonwealth of Nations, and for those purposes and those alone recognising the Crown as the Head of that Association'. The British Government would remain 'unalterably opposed' to this latter concept of the empire, and Lloyd George put forward six questions to the Irish, setting out again the essential point of common citizenship and the necessity for Ireland to accept and work her status in the mode of Canada and the other Dominions. The oath of allegiance must be incorporated in the Constitution.[23] On 26 June 1922 Winston Churchill repeated the British ultimatum, this time in the House of Commons: either the provisional Government of the Irish Free State would loyally implement the treaty, or the Government would regard the Articles of Agreement as 'having been formally violated', and would 'resume full liberty of action in any direction that may seem proper and to any extent that may be necessary to safeguard the interests and the rights that are entrusted to our care.'[24]

The Irish case deserves consideration because it obliged the British to examine the basis on which their empire rested. They claimed it did not rest on force; but Kevin O'Higgins (later Minister for Justice in the Free State Government), argued, with justification, that 'the most objectionable aspect of the Treaty is that the threat of force has been used to influence Ireland to a decision to enter this miniature league of nations'.[25] Of course, it could be argued that coercion had been used to oblige the Boer republics to enter the empire, or at least to enter the Union of South Africa; and the Boers in the Great War had, it seemed, demonstrated their loyalty to the Crown and empire. But there was a disquieting note in the Irish case. Louis Botha had regarded the union as a means of securing eventual Afrikaaner domination of the new state; if this could be achieved within the empire, then so be it; there would be no objection in principle on his part and those of his fellow Afrikaaners to staying within and supporting the empire. But Ireland was different: Michael Collins defended the Anglo-Irish treaty, not because he considered Dominion Status a worthy end in itself, but because 'it gives us freedom, not the ultimate freedom that all nations desire and develop to, but the freedom to achieve it'; and Arthur Griffith, who had no objection to the monarchical principle, nonetheless urged that the treaty had 'no more finality than [that] we are the final generation on the face of the earth: we can move in comfort and peace to the ultimate goal'.[26]

There was another dimension to the Irish problem that was to have repercussions on the empire. In 1920–1 the British Government, anxious to appear to be acting fairly in response to Irish Nationalist demands for self-government, and Ulster Unionist resistance to those demands, partitioned Ireland into two states, 'Southern Ireland', consisting of 26 counties, and Northern Ireland, consisting of the remaining six. These two states were to have home rule or devolutionary forms of government, and whereas 'Southern Ireland' was a state that never materialised, Northern Ireland was founded in 1921, and by the end of 1922 was stabilising itself as a state for the protection of its two-thirds Protestant and Unionist population. When, in November 1921, Lloyd George's Government put pressure on the first prime minister of Northern Ireland, Sir James Craig, to place his Home Rule Parliament under Dublin rather than London sovereignty, Craig replied by referring to the Dominion examples: if Ulster were to be thrust out of the United Kingdom, then she would demand to go as a Dominion of the empire, rather than a subordinate state under Dublin's sovereignty. Lloyd George refused this request, arguing that Dominion status was a means of creating the 'gradual amalgamation of large territories and scattered colonies in natural units of self-government. We could not reasonably claim place for two Irelands in the Assembly of the League of Nations or in the Imperial Conference.' Boundaries would harden; the hoped-for ultimate reunification of Ireland would be compromised.[27]

In the end Craig resisted British pressure and his Northern Ireland state remained as a devolved region within the United Kingdom. This revealed what Nationalists always denied: that it was beyond the power of the British to deliver the Loyal minority in Ulster into Nationalist hands. The expedient of partition, as a means of separating peoples who could not live together, was born in the heat and burden of the Anglo-Irish quarrel, and the Unionist–Nationalist contest. It was not as clear-cut a solution as it looked, for, as Lloyd George himself pointed out to Craig when declining his request to have Northern Ireland made into a Dominion, partition and Dominion status would have serious effects on the minorities left behind in both Northern and Southern Ireland, 'cut off' as they would be 'from the majority of those to whom they are bound by faith, tradition, and natural affinity'.[28] But partition, however unsatisfactory as a means of mediating between contending peoples, between 'loyal Irishmen' and 'true Irishmen', was now a precedent that could be drawn upon in the future. Indeed, within a short time the unexpected (relative) tranquillity of Ireland and Irish politics seemed to indicate that it was a successful example, and one that would be applied again in the case of the Indian subcontinent as its crisis of nationality reached a climax in 1947.

The efforts made by Southern Ireland to move forward to the 'ultimate goal' of freedom absorbed an inordinate amount of time in British imperial circles between the world wars. Moving forward in comfort and peace was indeed more easily facilitated by the fact that Ireland was a member of the British Commonwealth of Nations, at a time when the Dominions reassessed their relationship to Britain. Australia and New Zealand were least restless, but South Africa pressed for some clearer definition of the Dominion relationship, and Canada, as the senior member of the club, and one with considerable power or at least the potential for power in her own right, was the most influential Dominion. The British were in 1926 persuaded to issue the declaration that the Dominions were indeed 'autonomous Communities within the British Empire, equal in status, in no way subordinate to one to another in respect of their domestic or external affairs, though united by a common allegiance to the Crown, and freely associated as members of the British Commonwealth of Nations'. Two years later Basil Williams asked the pertinent question, that if the empire was based on free association, then what kept it together as an empire? He answered with the tautology that it was the free association that kept it together; the 'real sanction for the permanence of this Commonwealth of Nations is the profit that ensues therefrom: not, indeed, material profit, for that is the least part of it'. The diversity of the empire was its strength, its free scope granted to each member to develop its individuality was its key, 'There can be no compelling force short of civil war, which we tried once and are never likely to try again.'[29]

A conference of constitutional experts was called in 1929 to consider the problem that the Dominions were subject to legislation passed by the 'imperial' Parliament at Westminster. Their recommendations were embodied in the Statute of Westminster of 1931, which declared that the Dominions would no longer be bound by any past or future British acts unless they so requested and consented. This further emphasised the importance of the Crown as the link which held the Commonwealth together.

But there was another, contrasting view, put forward by the historian Sir Sidney Low, who drew a distinction between a free alliance – an empire of will – and one that constituted an empire–realm, a kind of state unit which devolved power on the constituent parts, but acted indivisibly in a crisis.[30] Moreover, the Balfour Report provided ammunition for internal battles in South Africa, between the imperialist and pro-British General Smuts, and the Afrikaaner Nationalist Hertzog, and was not without impact even in Canada.[31] The British view was that there was but one King, and he was the same in every part of the empire. This was not merely a theoretical point, for the doctrine was that when the King declared war, which he did formally, then he declared war on behalf of the whole empire, as indeed he had done in 1914 (but was not to do in 1939). The Statute of Westminster further declared to the world that the Dominions were states in their own right.

Basil Williams was rather idealistic in his downgrading of 'material' ties as significant in keeping the empire together. The serious economic climate between the world wars, and the worsening international scene in the 1930s, gave every incentive for any loosening of the ties of empire to go no further. The empire was of material value to Britain, and Britain to the empire. Britain had investments and trade in the wider world, but the empire's share of trade grew larger, from 27 per cent of British imports and 37 per cent of her exports in 1920–4, to 39.5 per cent of her imports and 49 per cent of her exports in 1935–9.[32] And whereas investment in the empire stood at 46 per cent in 1911–13, in 1927–9 it stood at 59 per cent. The empire seemed to be paying its way and even offering good dividends to the British. At the Imperial Conference of 1932 the policy of imperial preference was extended; and at Ottawa 15 bilateral trade agreements were made to extend trade reciprocity between the Dominions. Britain agreed to continue the preferences already established and extend them to other commodities, notably minerals, wheat and meat products, in return for an enlargement of Dominion preferences: some by lowering tariffs on British goods, others by raising them on foreign goods.[33]

It was at this time that the concept of empire, and its significance for Britain's great power status, was closely examined, at least in élite circles. The work of the great geographer H. J. Mackinder was debated. Mackinder argued that Britain's naval power, which everyone emphasised was vital to her world status, rested on the solid base of British productivity, on her rich agricultural and mineral resources. He pointed out the strength of the great European heartland, the vast European plain from the Elbe to Vladivostock, which, if it were developed agriculturally and industrially, and knit together by railways, would provide a means of outflanking sea power and overwhelming it. Germany in the war of 1914–18 had come close to controlling this heartland, and it must be protected now from the control of communist Russia.[34]

Therefore, if Britain did not control this kind of heartland, she must then use her imperial resources as a counter-measure. This, however, brought forth a harder, more calculating edge to the British concept of Commonwealth, one which J. H. Thomas, Dominions Secretary in the National Government, outlined when he told the Cabinet in November 1931 that the United Kingdom must stop allowing itself to be put on the defensive, as if paying some 'overdue ... debt of economic gratitude owed by us to the rest of the Empire'. British policy at Ottawa must emphasise that any British concession to the empire producer must have reciprocal concessions.[35] Thomas's negotiating style at Ottawa came near at times to attacking Dominion representatives for their 'blackmail'.[36]

The British lack of a 'heartland' required the United Kingdom to spread her defensive resources more widely than any other European state, and it particularly necessitated the maintenance of British sea power in all its might and majesty. And all at a cost: by 1938 the naval base at Singapore was completed at the cost of £60 million. H. V. Hodson, editor of the *Round Table*, struck a pessimistic note when he warned in 1937 that the Dominions must share the 'common burden' of defence, and noted that:

> on her part the United Kingdom may continue to say: 'I will maintain naval and air forces which are designed for the defence of the Empire as a whole and its ocean routes of supply. With that object I identify my own interests'. . . . But I must warn the Dominions that with the rearmament of Europe, with the abandonment of old-fashioned reinsurances like the Anglo-Japanese alliance, with the danger that the Empire may be menaced at three danger-spots at once–in north-western Europe, in the Mediterranean, on the Singapore–Australia front – I cannot afford them that measure of security on which they have relied in earlier decades.[37]

These warnings were made only 15 years after Lloyd George had insisted that the 1921 Imperial Conference was proof that the bonds forged between Britain and her possessions were strong and would remain so. In December 1921, the very month that the Anglo-Irish Treaty was signed, he told the House of Commons that the foreign policy of Great Britain would be the foreign policy of the British Empire. The Foreign Office must direct; but the Dominions could contribute, combining with Britain to produce the advantage of joint control and

> joint control means joint responsibility, and when the burden of Empire has become so vast it is well that we should have the shoulders of these young giants to help us along. It introduces a broader and calmer view into foreign policy . . . it widens the prospect.[38]

But the Chanak Crisis of September 1922, when Lloyd George cabled the Dominions to support Britain against Turkey by armed force, produced a mixed response, which one contemporary historian described as: 'New Zealand had answered "yes" with enthusiasm, Australia had answered "yes" with resentment and misgiving, Canada had answered "this is a matter to be considered".' So the young giants had minds of their own.[39] But so, it seemed by 1937, had the old giant as well.

Nevertheless, the special 'league of nations' that was the Commonwealth seemed to have survived the Irish difficulty and, moreover, seemed capable of a flexibility that augured well for the future. India was in some sense an inferior member of the Commonwealth, perhaps more of an imperial possession than a Commonwealth member in terms of self-government. Yet her presence at the Imperial War Cabinet, and at the Imperial Conference of 1921 (and her membership of the League of Nations) all acknowledged India's status as 'the juniormost traveller on the highroad to self-government', as a British Command paper put it. Ireland drew attention to the anomaly of India's presence at the conference, but the very anomaly of the Indian presence suggested that the British system would never collapse, and contemporaries claimed that its flexibility and its anomalies enabled it to manage the irregularities of politics – irregularities which a too-long concentration on mere constitutional matters obscured.[40]

Therefore, despite the constitutional rigidity displayed by the British Government in the 1921 Anglo-Irish Treaty, it was possible in 1921 for an imperialist of the modern school to take stock, survey the old Dominions, the newest (Ireland) and the Dominion that was to be (at some unspecified time), India, and feel that the British Empire would survive all challenges, and emerge stronger than before. Certainly, when contemplating the Irish settlement, Lionel Curtis wrote of the Anglo-Irish treaty almost in wonderment as 'one of the greatest achievements in the history of the Empire. But the steps by which effect was given to its provisions was an even greater achievement, so great that one is almost tempted to believe in the intervention of a special providence. One gets the feeling that the curse which bedevilled Anglo-Irish relations for 700 years was deliberately lifted.'[41] Curtis's panegyric, written in a letter to Winston Churchill in 1928, contrasts sharply with the gloomy ruminations of the Earl of Birkenhead (another signatory of the Anglo-Irish Treaty) in 1924, when he spoke of the 'general malaise which succeeded the war in India, Ireland and Egypt'.[42] Egypt, at least, was apparently put to rights, with an Anglo-Egyptian Treaty of 1936 which preserved Britain's military presence in the Suez Canal, and her colonial rule in the Sudan. But in the 1930s Ireland manipulated the Commonwealth connection to her advantage, and India too was to test British resolve and, in the end, to find it wanting in the emergency conditions of the Second World War.

The Irish Free State's constitution described it as a 'co-equal member of the Community of Nations forming the British Commonwealth of Nations'. This co-equality was enhanced by the Statute of Westminster of 1931 which made Dominion Parliaments competent to legislate with regard to those matters of Dominion concern which had hitherto been regulated by legislation of the imperial legislature on the same matters, and the power to make laws having extra-territorial operation. They were also given the assurance that legislation of the Parliament of the United Kingdom would apply to them only at their request and with their assent.[43] This appeared as the ultimate act of wise statesmanship and generosity, and so it was; but there were stresses in the imperial family that were revealed even in the circumstances of its passing. In South Africa, General Hertzog insisted, against the wishes of Jan Smuts, that South Africa had the right of neutrality in war and secession from the Commonwealth; and a compromise was reached whereby Afrikaaner republicanism, never wholly reconciled to the Crown, was given the privilege that 'none will be denied the right to express his individual opinion about, or advocate his honest convictions in connection with, any change of our form of Government' – a proviso which became known as the 'republican propaganda clause' in that it met the conscientious objections of those who still clung to the republican ideal.[44]

This still left objectors such as Dr Malan who wished to defend Afrikaaner culture: 'the struggle against Imperialism would be as fierce as ever, but the spirit of young South Africa would win'.[45] South Africa was not then a simple success story for the empire; it might yet weaken it, and its three-dimensional political problem – Afrikaaner, English and the question of race equality – was far from resolved. But in Ireland too the republican ideal was about to be resurrected; and this time it would not be left as a matter of individual conscience, as the Smuts–Hertzog clause had decreed in South Africa. The pro-treaty government, led since 1922 by W. T. Cosgrave, affirmed that they remain loyal to the British Empire, though Cosgrave insisted that Irish relations with Britain were to be based on international law, and not, as the British insisted, on the special law and procedures of the empire and Commonwealth.[46] The Statute of Westminster again revealed the anxieties of both the British and Irish concerning their mutual understanding – or misunderstanding – of the nature of the Dominion relationship. Cosgrave was quick to promise the British, as he had reiterated 'time and again', that the Anglo-Irish treaty was not affected by the Statute of Westminster, in that 'the Treaty is an agreement which can only be altered by consent'.[47] In the British Parliament some Conservative peers and MPs attempted to exclude the Irish Free State from the operation of the Statute because they claimed the Irish would use it to amend the Treaty.[48]

The problem was – and it was not unique in the history of the British Empire – that the British perspective on her relations with her fellow members of the Commonwealth differed from that in the association at large. It was too easy, in the light of British imperial history, to assume that a gesture of magnanimity – in South Africa, in Ireland – was the answer to nationalist grudges or ambitions. In Ireland the return of Eamon de Valera, first to politics, then in 1932, with the support of Labour, to power, revealed that the alternatives which might be deployed to maintain the empire – force, or magnanimity – were equally shaky. Force had been used in South Africa and Ireland, and would be used again elsewhere; but it seemed at variance with the way in which the making of the empire was historically conceived. Magnanimity, especially in the troubled decade of the 1930s, was a more acceptable alternative, indeed a necessary one. When the Dominions' officials spoke of the virtues of moral obligation, they felt secure in their tradition; but this was a tradition which de Valera regarded as a barrier to the march of the Irish nation. Moral obligations were not binding on a nation deprived of its birthright or sovereignty. De Valera moved carefully and cautiously towards the republican goal, abolishing the oath of allegiance to the Crown and retaining land annuities (payments due to the British Government under the terms of the Land Purchase Acts of the late nineteenth and early twentieth centuries). The powers of the governor-general were reduced, the right of appeal from Ireland to the British Privy Council ended. The British Government showed that it took these threats to the Anglo-Irish treaty seriously, setting up a powerful Irish Situation Committee in March 1932. De Valera soon became the demon figure, a 'crank' and 'visionary', a 'fanatic' (to name but a few epithets).[49] The British Government hoped to bring de Valera to his senses, or perhaps even contrive his fall.[50]

The result of de Valera's republican manoeuvres was an 'economic war' between Britain and Ireland which took the form of the imposition of duties on Irish imports to Britain, and the Irish riposte of reciprocal duties on certain British imports to Ireland, which made up about one-third of the Irish import trade with Britain.[51] The British sought to rally support from the other Dominions for this policy, with some success, but again South Africa struck a troublesome note with its telegram to de Valera emphasising 'sovereign independence', rather than co-operation between members of the Commonwealth.[52] The British feared that the Irish problem would have unfortunate repercussions on the Statute of Westminster, resulting in its extension.[53] But, faced with Ireland unappeased, the British found themselves confronting a central question about the future of the empire (was secession allowed or was it not?) and proposed to ignore it, and treat it as an 'academic question'.[54]

It was not an academic question to de Valera, and between 1935, when the economic war was concluded, and 1939 de Valera pursued his policy of dismantling the Anglo-Irish Treaty of 1921. In 1937 a new Irish constitution was adopted, declaring that Ireland was a 'sovereign independent state'. This, again, caused problems for the British concept of the Commonwealth; they were sure that common allegiance to the Crown was an essential basis of the whole Commonwealth system; but they were not sure what this really meant, and even less certain about how it could be enforced. Even if 'enforcement' was part of the British Commonwealth tradition, it was hardly possible to send the Black and Tans back to Ireland to keep her a loyal member of the Commonwealth. The British Government responded to the Irish ratification of the 1937 Constitution in a plebiscite on 1 July by declaring that it was prepared to treat the new constitution 'as not affecting the fundamental alteration in the position of the Irish Free State, in future to be described under the new Constitution as "Eire" or "Ireland", as a member of the British Commonwealth of Nations'.[55] This prepared the way for negotiations to realign Anglo-Irish relations. In 1938 the British and Irish Governments met and agreed on a settlement of all outstanding issues. Most importantly Britain ceded the 'treaty ports' whose use they had retained under the terms of the Treaty of 1921, which effectively gave de Valera the option of Ireland remaining neutral in any future war involving Britain and her empire – an option which she exercised when war broke out in September 1939. Ominously, the South African, Eric Louw, a member of the Nationalist Party and later Minister of Foreign Affairs, told an audience of Afrikaaner students at Stellenbosch University in 1939 that 'the path which Ireland has followed now lies open for South Africa too. Ireland shows the way.'[56] The Anglo-Irish Agreement of 1938 was regarded by the British Chiefs of Staff, and by experienced negotiators such as Anthony Eden, as a 'complete surrender'.[57] This was countered by the argument, powerfully made by the Prime Minister, Neville Chamberlain, that it was safer for Britain to have an appeased Ireland on her western flank, than deal with an unappeased and hostile Ireland; and indeed de Valera always assured the British, quite honestly as it turned out, that 'a free Ireland in times of common risk could be for Great Britain only a friendly Ireland'.[58] In the Second World War Ireland proved herself to be a neutral state with a disposition to lean on the side of the British, especially in the repatriation of British members of the Royal Air Force who were forced to land on Irish soil.

In 1921 Lloyd George had referred to the 'young giants' whose influence on British foreign policy could only be supportive; but in 1939 'the young pygmy', Ireland, had demonstrated that the Dominion relationship could be used to advance the unappeased nationalism fuelled by history, myth and sense of grievance. Of course, it could be objected that Ireland was not a typical Dominion; and this opinion was well founded. It was, after all, the British who in 1921 decided, under pressure, to turn a dissident part of the United Kingdom into a Dominion of the British Empire, an expedient which might have worked in the days of John Redmond, and worked, up to a point, even in the era of W. T. Cosgrave. But the fact that Ireland was not a typical Dominion helped expose the incoherence of the British Government in December 1921 when they tried to define what it was that made the Empire and especially the Commonwealth, a powerful force in the world, supporting Britain's role as a great power – perhaps even, in the terms of extent of territory and material resources and manpower, a super-power.

India was another pillar of empire that was shaken in the 1930s, and finally crumbled at the end of the Second World War. Ireland and India were linked in the imperial context, though it is hard, at first and even last sight, to understand why – the geographical difference, the cultural contrasts, the political experience of the two countries, seem utterly at variance.[59] Yet the Irish home rulers in the 1880s acted as defenders and advocates of the Indian National Congress Party, which demanded reform of Indian Government and then home rule; and the Indian nationalists, for their part, always looked to Ireland as an example, both of parliamentary action, and, as M. K. Gandhi saw it, of the kind of civil disobedience and non-violent nationalism tactics which Arthur Griffith advocated. Violent nationalists also paid attention, this time to Irish terrorism. And the British response, the Amritsar massacre of 1919, when General Dyer ordered his troops to open fire on a crowd of demonstrators at the Jallianwallahbagh gardens, killing and injuring hundreds of people, was taken note of in the Black and Tan war. Some regarded the British disavowal of Dyer's tactics as a threat to the morale of the Crown forces in Ireland, whose hands would now be tied when they came to combat disorder; others read the opposite lesson, with the *Round Table*, which had exhorted Lloyd George to follow the example of Abraham Lincoln and oppose by force the secession of Ireland, declaring a few months later that 'the Government which dismissed General

Dyer least of all Governments can afford to leave subordinates in Ireland to take unauthorised measures'.[60]

The British response to the demand for more self-government in India was influenced by the need to keep India contented and supportive in the First World War. It was a growing recognition of these conditions that inspired the announcement by the Secretary of State for India on 20 August 1917, that:

> The policy of His Majesty's Government . . . is that of the increasing association of Indians in every branch of the administration and the gradual development of self-governing institutions with a view to the progressive realisation of responsible government in India as an integral part of the British Empire.[61]

This must be done with caution; there must be successive stages; the British Government and the Government of India must judge the time and measure of each advance. But, once again, the Durham Report could be cited as a precedent, even for a country as different from Canada as was India. Writing in 1944 about the Montagu–Chelmsford Report of 1917 on the Government of India, Reginald Coupland noted:

> Just as Durham accompanied his plan for responsible Government in the Canadian Provinces with a vision of the future nation of Canada, so Montagu and Chelmsford pointed to the goal of Indian nationhood, not only as an end in itself, but as a means of overcoming the dissensions which obstructed the path of political advance.

It was for this reason that they 'boldly recommended the concession of a wide measure of representative government'.[62]

In 1919 the Government of India Act was passed, the preamble of which declared that the British Parliament's purpose was 'the progressive realisation, of responsible Government in India',[63] with the word 'responsible' chosen accidentally, but one that Lionel Curtis and his colleagues regarded as implying Dominion status.[64] The Act introduced a new constitution in the form of Dyarchy, which set the pattern for reform of Indian Government in the inter-war years: a division of Government functions between locality and centre, with the offer to Indians of controlling policy at the local level, while denying them access to what were regarded by the British as the central areas of policy: foreign affairs, and economic and military decisions. In the provinces, power

was divided between 'transferred' subjects (education, health and agri-
culture) and 'reserved' subjects (law and order, finance). The electorate
was enlarged to 5.5 million in the provinces and 1.5 million for the
central or imperial Legislature, and representation was modified on
communal grounds, to give safeguards to special communities – Muslims,
Sikhs in the Punjab, Indian Christians, and Anglo-Indians. This was a
significant reform. It may have been intended to shore up the Raj; but if
so, it did this in an unprecedented way, for it was based on the principle
that parliamentary government was appropriate for India, a concept
that was unthinkable before 1914. As Montagu himself put it, 'we are not
dealing with a cattle-yard. We are dealing with men, and thinking men,
and business men, men who desire opportunities for their aspirations.'
He referred to a 'passion for self-government'. 'Nobody questions that it
must come gradually, but I say at this stage the transference of power
must be real and substantial.' We 'must make a beginning and go on
doing it. That is what I mean by the progressive realisation of responsible government'.[65]

The Congress Party at first ignored Montagu's words; but they soon
came to value the reform, and from 1923 they used it to build important
local power structures. This measure was preceded by the hated Rowlatt
Acts (called after Mr Justice Rowlatt, and passed by the Imperial Legislative Council in February–March 1918), which introduced trial without
jury and internment without trial. And the Dyer massacre was the
epitome of the other tradition of governing India, and one that was
supported strongly in the British House of Lords, which deplored the
treatment of Dyer as 'unjust to that officer, and as establishing a precedent dangerous to the preservation of order in face of rebellion'.[66] The
Dyer incident restored law and order in the short term; but it convinced
Gandhi, in particular, that the British had forfeited all moral authority
to govern India. He tested British resolve for the first time in 1919, by
his Rowlatt Satyagraha, which encouraged volunteers to adopt non-
cooperation rather than physical force. The deterioration of the Satyagraha into disorder, the severe British response at Amritsar, persuaded
Gandhi to call off the protest, and at a Congress meeting in Amritsar in
May 1919 he urged that the Montagu–Chelmsford reforms be given a
trial period. A year later he again moved to confrontation, convinced
now that the British professions of partnership were false, and sought to
build links with the Muslim community. A further outbreak of violence
drove him once again into despair that the 'movement had unconsciously
drifted from the right path'.[67]

Between 1923 and the 1930s Congress built up its base in the provinces; perhaps too successfully, because the taste of local power and patronage, the emergence of local Congress and mainly Hindu élites, all worked to blunt Indian political ambitions. In April 1927 Motilal Nehru wrote to his son Jawaharlal that there was not a Congressman who 'won't go into a fainting fit on hearing the words complete independence for India'.[68] The working of Dyarchy also had its impact on Muslim politics; in 1924 the Muslim League met separately from Congress for the first time since 1920 and it now looked to a federal India with mainly self-governing provinces, with only the slightest measure of control from the centre. Dyarchy provided a system that deeply influenced the making of Indian Nationalism and Muslim reaction alike. Above all, it gave the incentive for politically motivated élites to seek to inherit, rather than destroy, the developing political and administrative structures, especially since the British were also increasing the number of civil servants from India: by the end of the 1930s half its members would be Indian.[69]

In 1928 Congress itself established a committee to draft a constitution for India as a future Dominion. The Nehru Report sought to reconcile those who wanted complete independence and those who sought Dominion status, by claiming that the acceptance of the latter 'does not mean than any individual Congressman, much less the Congress itself, has given up or toned down the goal of complete independence'.[70] A constitution was drafted basing its first article on that of the Anglo-Irish Treaty of 1921:

> India shall have the same constitutional status in the comity of nations known as the British Empire, as the Dominion of Canada, the Commonwealth of Australia, the Dominion of New Zealand, the Union of South Africa and the Irish Free State, with a Parliament having powers to make laws for the peace, order and good government of India and an executive responsible to that Parliament, and shall be styled and known as the Commonwealth of India.

This went beyond previous Dominion convention, in that now responsible government was upheld by written law. But it was a nice example of the centrality of the Dominion concept and that of responsible government in the thinking, not only of the rulers, but of the ruled as well.[71]

But it still posed the question for the ruling power, the question posed by Seeley in 1883: could English institutions be safely transplanted in alien soil, amongst an Asian people? In May 1930 a Commission headed by Dr John Simon reported on the future of India in an atmosphere rendered more fragile by disturbances and demonstrations that seemed to darken the confident claims now being made that India could follow the British way. The report threw doubt upon the belief that parliamentary government could work in India: 'The British Parliamentary system has developed in accordance with the day-to-day needs of the people, and has been fitted like a well-worn garment to the figure of the wearer, but it does not follow that it will suit everybody.' British Parliamentarianism in India was 'a translation, and in even the best translation the essential meaning is apt to be lost'. The Provincial Councils established in 1919 had not worked. No true party system had emerged; communalism had battened on the system. And it would be 'some time before it is possible to judge how far it is likely that the party system obtaining in Britain will reproduce itself in the Provincial legislatures'.[72]

In 1930 Congress revived its agitation, calling for complete independence, denying the right of the British to rule, accusing them of 'exploiting the masses, and of ruining India, politically, culturally and spiritually'. This followed a two-year period of civil disobedience which ended with the 'Gandhi–Irwin' pact of 1931, when Irwin (later Lord Halifax) persuaded the British Government to make a declaration that Dominion status was the goal, and that a round table conference should be called to decide the next step. Gandhi refused these terms but then, perhaps worried that his leadership of the nationalist movement was slipping to young radicals, agreed to accept them, and attend the next session of the conference. The Government in return released all political prisoners except those convicted of violence. The round table conferences failed to make progress, but in 1935 the British Government drafted the Government of India Act which built upon the British belief that India could best be governed under a federal system; one that would not only appease nationalism and give the British a firmer base for their rule, but one that would secure also the future of the Indian Princely states.

The Act created autonomous provinces exercising jurisdiction over certain stated functions, free from central supervision, and enlarged the Indian electorate to 30 million. Provincial governors still had reserved powers intended for emergency use (law and order and the like). Ministers could give advice, but their views could be rejected on matters such as minority rights, the privileges of civil servants; and defence and foreign policy remained the exclusive concern of the Viceroy. Princely India was included in this system, and it was hoped also that Muslims would be satisfied through the federal plan. Congress, which at first boycotted the elections for the provincial assemblies, decided to contest them in 1937, and won six of the provincial governments outright, making itself the largest party in two more. The Muslim League failed spectacularly, achieving respectable results only in Bengal and Punjab and Sind. [73]

It is easy to dismiss the 1935 Act as a piece of fancy footwork; as a means of prolonging the British hold on India, rather than as a serious step towards Indian self-government; and certainly it was intended to refresh, not to end, British rule. But the Act did run counter to the pessimism of the Simon Report of 1930. It was modelled on the constitutions of the Dominions; it was parliamentary; it reaffirmed the declaration of 1917. It envisaged an Indian political system in which communalism would remain central, and retained separate electoral rolls for Hindu and Muslim, but it rejected the idea that there should be a representation of minorities in the various Cabinets, mainly because it conflicted with the doctrine of collective Cabinet responsibility on the British model. It was federal, unlike the British constitution; but it was federal on the Canadian precedent, with a strong unitary bias. It differed from Dominion status in several important respects, notably the persistence of Dyarchy at the centre, with foreign affairs and defence retained by the governor-general, responsible to the Secretary of State for India. There were 'safeguards' by which Indian Ministers were subject to the governor's control, for example in the protection of minorities; and legislation of the federal governments was subject to the refusal or assent of the governor-general, acting under the control of the Secretary of State, and to disallowance by the Crown under his advice. But these reservations, Sir Thomas Inskip noted on behalf of the Government, were 'not inconsistent with the ultimate attainment of the position of a Dominion within the Empire'.[74] They also reflected, as Sir Samuel Hoare put it in 1930, the British concern to maintain 'stability at the centre ... the ultimate bulwark against chaos in India'.[75] These developments took place against another, significant, though not yet decisive aspect of the British connection with India. Holding India for the empire was, by the 1930s, a declining economic prospect. The army and the bureaucracy had to be paid for. This required more revenue which, to collect, might require more bureaucrats. To impose new taxes might alienate those Indians, especially merchants, on whose goodwill the Government of India depended. Between 1914 and 1939 British exports to India halved in value; British investment in India declined. The Indian cotton industry suffered from Japanese competition. The British Government left to the

Government of India the option of imposing tariffs against foreign goods; but this was only a temporary measure. The British had to buy raw cotton in bulk to keep Indian trade healthy. Britain was not by any means envisaging leaving India in the immediate future; and the economic argument was not paramount. There was no expectation that decolonisation was imminent, and indeed the liberal-minded imperialist, Basil Williams, wrote in 1927 that it was 'safe to say that the home Government will for long preserve a more direct influence in India and provide more immediate protection than she does in the other Dominions. If for no other reason, the existence of the native states not directly under British rule, but dependent for their security and even their existence on British protection, will ensure this.'[76] But the point was that the economic reasons for holding India might be set in the balance against the economic reason for letting her go if there were compelling reasons why the holding of India was no longer a practical possibility.

The main problem for Congress – and the key to the British response to Congress – was that the nationalists had always to strike a balance between agitation and participation; between snubbing British offers, and recognising that these offers might well contain the means of strengthening Congress and establishing it as the successor to the Raj. Congress's power base rested on strong or 'dominant' peasants, the intelligentsia, and the commercial classes. But by the late 1930s it was clear that, while Congress still had some Muslim support, it had, partly at least through its triumphalism, alienated large sections of the Muslim community; and tensions were particularly high in the provinces, where local Congress politicians were apt to see themselves not as the arbitrators between the British and India, but as dominators of the Muslims who, in the United Provinces, were required by Nehru to take an oath of loyalty to Congress, which the Muslim League leader described as 'Congress Fascism'.[77]

When the Second World War broke out, Congress was the main representative of the Indian Hindus; it preferred to see itself as the sole legitimate representative of the Indian nation. It was always in the British interest to stress the internal divisions in India; it would have been foolish, in political terms, for the British to admit the full Congress claim. But the divisions were real, and the proposal of a federal India might have helped accommodate them. But while a loose federation or confederation might have preserved Indian unity in one way, in another sense it might have damaged it, and Congress for its part feared that such an arrangement would lead to the disintegration of any state that they might inherit. The Viceroy declared war on India's behalf, and failed to respond to Congress requests that he at least promise something like responsible government at the centre. The only morsel of temptation that the Viceroy would offer was the promise of Dominion status at some unspecified future time, and the modification of the 1935 Government of India Act. Britain was concerned about the wider strategic role of India in the world war, and so India must remain secured to the empire. The Viceroy's Executive Council was given an Indian majority (though without control of defence and finance), but the Muslims were promised that no system of government would be introduced which would transfer power to any government 'whose authority is directly denied by large and powerful elements in India's national life'.[78] This gave the Muslim League a veto on constitutional change, and in 1940 the League began to call for territorial readjustment with 'independent states' for Muslim majority areas. Muhammad Ali Jinnah harked back to the Irish question when he put his case.

> The Irish Nationalist Leader, Redman (sic), met Carson, Ulster Leader, and told him, 'Look here, can't we come to some settlement? Why do you want to separate from Ireland? Mind you, there is not one-millionth part of the differences between the people of Ulster and Ireland' What was Carson's reply? 'I do not want to be ruled by you'. My reply to Mr. Gandhi is, 'I do not want to be ruled by you'.[79]

The climactic events of the world war pushed matters on much faster than anyone, British, Hindu or Muslim, could have anticipated. In 1942 Singapore fell to the Japanese armies. Churchill warned against raising the Indian constitutional issue when the enemy 'is upon the frontier. . . . Bringing hostile political element (i.e. Congress) into the defence machine will paralyse action'.[80] This view was shared by the Viceroy, Lord Linlithgow, and by the Secretary of State for India, L. S. Amery, with Amery insisting that while the ultimate aim was to grant Dominion status to India, no further interim constitutional advance could be made for the present.[81] Clement Attlee disagreed. On 2 February he warned that India was deeply affected by the 'changed relationship between Europeans and Asiatics which began with the defeat of Russia by Japan at the beginning of the century'. Now the Japanese were continuing the process. If there were a successful outcome to the war, then what he called the 'Asiatic powers' in the 'Big Four' – the United States of America, the USSR, China and Britain – would claim a powerful voice in the settlement. The United States supported Indian freedom, and India was helping the war effort by her 'blood and tears and sweat'. A settlement therefore was urgent, not least because Britain had educated Indians to accept British principles of democracy and liberty.[82] By November 1942 Amery was admitting to Linlithgow that 'it may be that we are all wrong in hoping that a self-governing India, established with our goodwill and on a sound basis, may continue to stay in the Commonwealth of its own accord. But what is the alternative? Britain could not stand against Indian nationalism even if there were a united public opinion here to support it.'[83]

In March 1942 Sir Stafford Cripps led a mission to India to make a new offer to Congress: more participation in government at once, all the portfolios in the executive council (except defence) to be entrusted to Indians chosen in consultation with the political parties, and the promise of an elected assembly at the end of the war whose recommendations for the future of India would be implemented by the British Government. Cripps indicated to Congress that this arrangement was, in effect, full Dominion status. But the Viceroy, Lord Linlithgow, expressed his reservations to L. S. Amery about India's status as a Dominion; she was, like Burma, 'alien by race, history and religion . . . and both are in the Empire because they are conquered countries which had been brought there by force'. Churchill assured Linlithgow that there would be no settlement that would diminish his powers.[84] And there was another disincentive for Congress; any settlement was subject to guarantees for racial and religious minorities, and each province would be free to choose whether or not it would join the Indian Union. Congress naturally feared that the Muslim League would carry Bengal and the Punjab out of the Union, despite the presence there of considerable Hindu minorities.[85]

There were in Cripps' mission to India echoes of the Irish controversies of 1921. In 1921 Lloyd George regarded the (undefined) offer of Dominion status as essential to an Anglo-Irish *rapprochement*; in 1942 Cripps proposed it, and in 1947 it was used as the interim arrangement for the transfer of power to India. Cripps offered Dominion status, in which he echoed the words of the 1926 declaration, that members of the Commonwealth were equal in status and in no way subordinate in any aspect of their domestic or external affairs. When he was asked at a press conference if the Indian Union would be entitled to disown its allegiance to the Crown, he replied unequivocally:

Yes. In order that there should be no possibility of doubt, we have inserted in the last sentence of paragraph (c) (ii) the statement: 'but will not impose any restriction on the power of the Indian Union to decide in the future its relation to other Member States of the British Commonwealth'. The Dominion will be completely free either to remain within or to go without the Commonwealth of Nations.[86]

This offer stood for the rest of the war. But Congress, emboldened by British military reverses, launched, on 8 August 1942, its 'Quit India' campaign, demanding an immediate end to British rule and the summoning of an Assembly to decide on a constitution. Gandhi acknowledged that such an abrupt end to British rule might lead to anarchy; but out of anarchy a new India would be born. Nehru was anxious for a settlement, but the British Government itself was divided, and some feared that to grant India full control of defence was too dangerous. The 'Quit India' campaign was described by Lord Linlithgow as 'by far the most serious rebellion since that of 1857', but the British stood firm, imprisoning Congress leaders and using the army as well as the police to restore order.[87] But this victory was a temporary respite only.[88] Congress continued to advance as the coming power over most of India, but the Muslim League too made good its claim to represent most of the Muslims of India, making advances in Assam, Sind, Bengal, and the North West frontier provinces between 1942 and 1943. The idea of a state for Muslims – 'Pakistan' – grew more attractive, but might not have been pressed to the limit had Congress been prepared to accept a loose federal structure.

Lord Wavell, who replaced Linlithgow as Viceroy of India in June 1943, pressed the case for moving forward to Indian self-government. There could be no 'half-way house' between an official government and a government of political leadership, the one incapable and the other capable of initiative in the political and constitutional field.[89] And, while Churchill was still alarmed at the prospect of radical change in wartime, he admitted that the goal of the British Government was Dominion status for India, but as an integral member of the 'British Empire and Commonwealth of Nations'.[90] When Wavell met his provincial governors in conference in July 1945 he reported that the men on the spot felt they were still 'sitting pretty', but that, when the war ended, 'H.M.G.s cheque would be presented and would have to be honoured'.[91]

The victory of the Labour Party in the British General Election of 1945 did not change Wavell's assessment of the situation in India, but made its consummation more certain. There was, as always, hope that India would follow the pattern of earlier nations in the empire. On

11 January 1946 Sir Stafford Cripps wrote to Lord Pethwick-Lawrence, enclosing a letter from Major Short of the Ministry of Information, recalling that 'Milner's kindergarten had an earlier and very pertinent precedent. Durham worked his Canadian miracle with a team of three – Charles Buller, Gibbon Wakefield, and Turton. All three were, by ordinary standards, an odd choice – i.e. somewhat "uncivil" servants, shall we say! But the interesting point is that Durham went over to Canada for five months himself, plus these three, to do the job – and did it. So might you, on this precedent, I suggest.'[92] Cripps, Pethwick-Lawrence and the First Lord of the Admiralty did go to India in March 1946, but Wavell warned in June that a crisis in India was coming 'at perhaps quite an early stage' and that the Government must have what he called a 'breakdown policy'.[93]

British withdrawal from India caused anxiety amongst the Chiefs of Staff, who warned in August 1946 that 'from the military point of view it was as nearly vital as anything to ensure that India remained within the Commonwealth'.[94] British pragmatism came to the rescue. In February 1947 Sir D. Monteith, permanent Under-Secretary to the Secretary of State for India, wrote to an official at the Foreign Office setting out his thoughts on the 'Future Relations of India and the British Commonwealth'. India, he reckoned, was unlikely to remain in the Commonwealth under the existing form of Commonwealth allegiance 'which is primarily enshrined in the common allegiance to the Crown'. He asked whether or not a Republic could be reconciled with the Commonwealth, and if there was 'any possibility that India might be *induced* to remain in the Commonwealth if she were offered a new form of Commonwealth relationship which will enable her to remain a sovereign Republic within the Commonwealth and, if so, whether from the point of view of the Commonwealth as a whole this would have sufficient advantages over the relationship which we might secure with India as a foreign power to make it desirable for us to make a deliberate effort to obtain such a relationship.' The important point was that Monteith listed purely practical reasons why this might be an advantage (strategic requirements could be secured, Britain would suffer no loss in international prestige), and only one abstract reason why this might be a disadvantage (the absence of the common ties that bound the other Dominions to Britain, such as Crown, Christian and particularly Protestant civilisation), the rest of the arguments being of a purely practical kind also. He came down on balance in favour of flexibility. 'In essence this matter is one of estimating the degree of real cooperation that is likely to be forthcoming from India in the more distant as well as in the immediate future.' Ireland in 1938 adopted a constitution which was in effect Republican; but Britain let Ireland stay in the Commonwealth, and did not regard her as excluded, even though Ireland recognised the Crown for only limited purposes in the international field, and regarded obligations to other Commonwealth members as virtually non-existent.[95]

British withdrawal from India might not necessarily have led to the partition of the subcontinent; but the chances of a unitary state were diminishing. In 1946 the options still seemed open. Jinnah asked for the six Muslim majority provinces (Punjab, the North West frontier provinces, Baluchistan, Sind, Bengal and Assam) to be grouped as part of a loosely constituted federation. This plan of federal government with a weak centre was proposed in the spring of 1946 but rejected by Nehru and the Congress Party; Jinnah then withdrew it and turned to what he saw as the last alternative for the Muslim people – the creation of the state of Pakistan. Wavell sought to construct a coalition government which would include Jinnah, but Jinnah became obstructive. Nehru now began to think in terms of partition. On 20 February 1947 Prime Minister Attlee fixed June 1948 as the deadline for the transfer of power.[96]

This date was brought forward, under the last Viceroy, Lord Mountbatten's, advice. Mountbatten proceeded with speed, holding 133 interviews with political leaders between 24 March and 6 May 1947, and suggesting the transfer of power to separate provinces. Congress rejected this as Balkanisation, and partition was the last dangerous alternative. The Indian Princely states were incorporated into the new India through a mixture of persuasion and threat; all except three agreed to join the Union. This was a political arrangement brokered under pressure, and accompanied by violence and social disruption on a massive scale. But the British Government felt keenly the need to demonstrate that 'withdrawal from India need not appear to be forced upon us by our weakness nor to be the first stage in the dissolution of the Empire'. There was 'no occasion to excuse our withdrawal; we should rather claim credit for taking this initiative in terminating British rule in India'. The withdrawal must be presented as the 'final phase in this process of evolution' begun at the end of the Great War. Indian independence, Attlee claimed, was 'not the abdication, but the fulfilment of Britain's mission in India'. Fortunately for the British, the Indian National Congress Party in June 1947 accepted partition and Dominion status as the price of early independence.[97] Ceremonies appropriate to the grand occasion were planned, for it was important, for Congress no less than the British Government, that the day of independence should go well. A 'violent retreat' was given the aura of a job well done, and of a departure marked by 'the grace with which [the British] had relinquished India'.[98] At one minute past midnight on 15 August 1947 India became independent, preceded on 14 August by Pakistan.

The final stages of the making of modern India were influenced by the Irish example – both what was done and what was not done – some 25 years before. India found it expedient to adopt the essentials of what de Valera had wanted for Ireland in the treaty negotiations of 1921: de Valera sought external association of Ireland with the Commonwealth; Nehru opted for a republican state but still within the Commonwealth. The Secretary of State for Commonwealth Relations, Patrick Gordon Walker, led the way, arguing in a 'most important meeting' of the Commonwealth Affairs Committee of the Cabinet on 7 January 1949, that 'the Crown link is out. Let's fit in India as a Republic, based on the reality of a common act of will.'[99]

On 27 April 1949 the Cabinet recognised that India would be a 'sovereign independent republic', but was told that the Government of India had 'affirmed India's desire to continue her full membership of the Commonwealth of Nations and her acceptance of the King as the symbol of the free assocation of its independent member nations and as such the head of the Commonwealth'. The other Commonwealth members accepted this compromise, with only South Africa expressing concern that the description of the King as 'Head of the Commonwealth' might imply 'the existence of some sort of super-state'.[100] The Irish Constitution of 1937 was closely copied by India: Eire was described as a 'sovereign, independent, democratic state'; the Indian Union's constitution of 1948 described the new state as 'sovereign, democratic'.[101]

The idea, fondly held by the Attlee Cabinet in 1947, that the British Government in India was following some great tradition, illustrated the importance of interpreting and expressing British policy in the language of gradual and inevitable progress towards Dominion status and Commonwealth membership. Winston Churchill welcomed the Indian Republic; he was sure that it was 'wise' to avoid any chance of the Crown, hitherto the 'circle of unity', becoming an 'exclusive instrument in respect of India in its new guise'.[102] This was not self, or other, deception, though it bore a close resemblance to it: rather it was a neat and deliberate convergence of necessity and tradition. The role of necessity can be explained by the British handling of another piece of decolonisation after 1945, that of Burma. Burma seemed to be moving in the same direction as India in the 1930s; indeed her political élite was anxious not to fall behind India in any moves towards responsible government. The 1935 Government of Burma Act set up an elected House of Representatives with ministers responsible to it, on a more broadly based franchise than that of India. The governor of Burma still retained control of certain functions such as foreign policy, defence and currency.

When war with Japan broke out, Burma was quickly overrun and in 1943 was declared independent and given a government of Burmese nationalists. As the Japanese armies began to retreat in 1944 the question of the political future of Burma resurfaced, but the Government was in no mood to hurry: L. S. Amery complained about a leader in *The Times* 'practically suggesting that Burma be given Dominion Status immediately on re-occupation', and in the War Cabinet on 14 March 1945 Attlee warned against 'constitutional advances regulated by fixed dates. The inevitable result was pressure to accelerate those dates.'[103] But the memory of the British collapse, the political instability left by the military conquest, the presence of local military forces, of which the most significant was the Burmese 'National Army' led by a nationalist, Aung San, pressed the British Government forward. The governor, Sir Hubert Rance, told the Secretary of State for Burma, Lord Pethwick-Lawrence, in December 1946 that Burma wanted 'nothing less in any way than India'. 'The price has hardened.'[104] The Government was well aware that it could not, even if it wanted, hold Burma by force; and despite Winston Churchill's complaint that 'the British Empire seems to be running off almost as fast as the American loan',[105] the Government resolved to deal with Aung San, not least because he could be a bulwark against Communism.

But the question arose of Burma's future status as an independent state. The Government was determined to make it clear that a republican constitution was incompatible with Commonwealth membership, but speculated on the possibility that Burma was considering 'some adaptation of the Eire Constitution' (of 1937).[106] The Burma Office instructed Rance to stress the difficulties, financial, economic and international, should Burma insist on a republican constitution. This raised the question, which Rance posed to Lord Listowel, Secretary of State for India and Burma: was the time ripe for 'a new conception of association within the Commonwealth not necessarily using allegiance to the Crown especially for those countries which have no ties of blood, culture or religion'?[107] This was rejected by the Government, which held to the view (the Eire example notwithstanding) that the Crown was the essential symbol of Commonwealth unity. This decision seemed to fly in the face of the pragmatic management of change in the empire, and Malcolm MacDonald, governor-general of the Malayan Union, Singapore and Sarawak, wrote to the Secretary of State for the Colonies, Arthur Creech Jones, in June 1947, to urge flexibility. Burma should be kept in the Commonwealth if possible, not least because 'Asiatic people' would 'tend to be persuaded that Britain is the true friend and guide to Asiatic peoples desiring to be free and self-governing'. If Burma could be retained within the Commonwealth it would 'make possible the creation of a British Commonwealth of Nations including nations and peoples of many races, colours and civilizations', and vastly increase the moral influence of Britain as well as its material security. MacDonald appealed to 'our genius for political government' which had enabled 'our predecessors' in the last generation to transform a large part of the colonial empire into a Commonwealth of free and equal nations. This could now be applied to those not of British stock. He referred to the 1937 Irish precedent when he was Secretary of State for Dominion Affairs, and had advised the Cabinet to keep Eire in the Commonwealth, because when India, Burma and the rest came to attain Dominion status, some of them at least would adopt the same attitude as Eire to the Crown. MacDonald called for a settlement on something like the 'Irish model', perhaps offering Burma a means of distinguishing between giving full allegiance to the Crown, and recognising the Crown for certain purposes only. There could be 'two degrees of membership'.[108]

But MacDonald approached this question from the wrong angle. He was asking for some broad change in principle, some fundamental rethinking of the Commonwealth constitution. But this was against the grain of the English way of thinking about constitutional development; perhaps MacDonald was reflecting the more theoretical tradition of his native Scots ancestry. In a short time the Government did accept the concept of a Republic within the Commonwealth when, in 1949, India adopted this arrangement; but that was on purely pragmatic grounds. In November 1948 the Cabinet insisted that, having repudiated its allegiance to the Crown, Ireland, 'as before her Burma', must go, otherwise the 'essential feature of the Commonwealth relationship would become meaningless'. But the Cabinet was anxious that Burma would be 'the last to leave' and there were important strategic and other British interests at stake in the Indian case which persuaded the Government that now the occasion had come for the kind of rethinking of the Commonwealth relationship that MacDonald requested, but requested in the wrong spirit and language. The Government and the Commonwealth Prime Ministers agreed at a meeting held in London, in April 1947, that it would be a 'disservice to the Crown if Commonwealth Ministers allowed a position to develop in which the Crown was made to appear a stumbling block to the continued cohesion of the Commonwealth', a decision which the Government's legal experts dismissed as 'pragmatic nonsense', but one which was adhered to nonetheless.[109] India's decision to accept the British position likewise reflected her calculation of advantage, especially since she did not want Pakistan to exploit Commonwealth membership to India's detriment.

The Indian and Irish cases developed at almost the same time; their association surfaced yet again after the Second World War as a result of Eire's decision, made in the summer of 1948, and announced in September by the Irish Prime Minister J. A. Costello when he was in Canada, that she would repeal the External Relations Act and thus break the last link with the Commonwealth.[110] Attlee's Government responded, once more, by placing the issue on a practical rather than theoretical basis, in his own words, to bring it down to 'practical rather than theoretical questions'.[111] From the beginning his Government pointed out to Eire the practical problems involved if Eire left the Commonwealth, in trade and the position of Irish citizens in Great Britain; but it also acknowledged that to treat Ireland as foreign for all purposes would involve even more practical problems for Britain.[112] It was important, the Cabinet agreed on 28 October, that relations with Eire should be handled in 'a spirit which would not create bitterness between the two countries as might diminish the chances of Eire's returning to the Commonwealth'.[113] But, apart from this longer view, it was acknowledged that ties of blood, history and the intermingling of peoples made Ireland's 'foreign-ness' different from that of an 'Asiatic' country.[114] In any event the other Commonwealth countries, notably Canada, Australia and New Zealand, were anxious that, as the Canadian premier Mackenzie King put it, the 'larger vision' be 'kept to the fore'; the cohesion of the Commonwealth did not depend on the symbol of the Crown.[115] But he did not say what it did depend on.

In these circumstances the British Government, already instinctively adopting a practical approach to this development, and convinced of the expediency of tackling the problem in a conciliatory way, made special arrangements for Irish citizens living in Great Britain after Ireland departed from the Commonwealth. There was no talk of retaliation, but

the British Government acknowledged that it would be necessary to protect Northern Ireland's interests once Eire seceded. The Cabinet noted
that it would be 'embarrassing' for the United Kingdom to be put in the
position of having to support the continuation of partition, should Eire
raise this at the United Nations, which, as a sovereign state, she would
now be entitled to join.[116] But it was convinced that Britain must assure
the people of Northern Ireland about their status in the United Kingdom, otherwise the British would see a 'revival of the Ulster Volunteers
and of other bodies intending to meet any threat of force by force'. And
Northern Ireland was vital for the United Kingdom's defence needs.[117]
But the Cabinet agreed that, while it would protect Northern Ireland's
status by the Ireland Act, guaranteeing that the border would not
change without the consent of the parliament of Northern Ireland, it
would not vigorously react against the Irish Government's propaganda
campaign against partition; the Ireland Act should be sufficient to reassure the people of Northern Ireland.[118] The Irish Republic was proclaimed on Easter Monday 1949, the anniversary of the 1916 Rising.
The Ireland Act was published on 3 May and both, taken together,
showed that the ghosts of the Government of Ireland Act of 1920, and
the Anglo-Irish Treaty of 1921, still walked. But not in British politics:
for, as Herbert Morrison asserted in defending the Labour Government's Irish policy, 'The more we march together on Commonwealth
matters the better it will be.'[119]

A Canadian correspondent in the *Round Table* in December 1949, noted
that Irishmen 'respectfully pointed out' that the present penchant for a
lack of formalisation and for 'spontaneous cooperation' 'had not been
relied upon in the Anglo-Irish negotiations of the 'twenties'.[120] This
informality, what the Canadian correspondent in the *Round Table* called
a 'family atmosphere', while it provoked less drama than Lloyd George's
determination to hold Ireland to the spirit and letter of the 1921 Treaty,
could be taken as a sign of strength; or, more realistically, as a dilution of
the Commonwealth symbol to the point where British leadership of the
institution was at best ambiguous, at worst severely weakened. And there
is much to be said for the more sombre analysis: that the transfer of
power in India, and Ireland's decision to remain neutral in the Second
World War, and then to sever the last links with the Commonwealth,
marked the destruction of two pillars of the British Empire. They were
hardly equal in size or stature, nor very alike in their social and political
history. The British Government still intended to use its influence to
manipulate the foreign policy of the two successor states in the Indian

subcontinent. And of course Ireland, an irritant to the empire, might be regarded as no considerable loss.

Moreover, the British Empire and Commonwealth was of such a heterogeneous character, was composed of so many building blocks, that to lose one as small as Ireland, or to mislay one as large as India, seemed not to alter the remainder – and there was still a considerable remainder to keep. But, in another sense, these were great losses, not so much in themselves as in what they revealed about the British Empire. Its heterogeneous character, in one way its strength, was in another sense its weakness.

Putting it to work, mobilising it to keep British great power status, was hard to do; there was, as the geographer Mackinder remarked, no central heartland of empire but a widespread Dominion held together by the Royal Navy. And when the empire met, not only the challenge of other great powers, but internal difficulties and complications arising from the impact of nationalism and modernisation in a world that was rapidly and deeply altered by the two world wars, then the British were, quite simply, floundering: applying reckless coercion in Ireland; insisting at the point of a gun that Ireland become a Dominion while declaring that the Commonwealth rested on free association; seeking to retain control of India, yet providing the very institutional means that enabled the Congress Party to gradually wrest control from her; applying force again, especially in the 'Quit India' campaign of 1942, yet acknowledging that force was not the basis of her rule; then suddenly relinquishing control, as the burden of the Indian empire became too great, and other demands on British time and resources became more insistent.

Yet that long-standing British imperial tradition of stressing – sometimes against the facts – that the empire was one of free association, that devolution of power was in its very bones, that the medicine of the body politic was liberty and cooperation – enabled England to avoid confronting the deeper implications of the loss of these two pillars of empire. In 1932 Reginald Coupland, Beit Professor of the History of the British Empire at Oxford, drew up a memorandum on the lessons to be drawn from the Irish experience. He had visited Dublin, and encountered the usual Nationalist ideas of 'British tyranny' and a 'fight for freedom'. To lessen their impact it was, he believed, necessary to eliminate the imperial factor in Ireland. The task of the imperial statesman was to conserve the empire by consent, not force. Rigidity on points that were not 'demonstrably vital' would only weaken the empire '*at the present phase of its history*'. Coupland believed that the Irish 'drift' towards a republic would continue. No Catholic Irishman 'felt quite free'; Ireland saw herself not as a 'young "colonial" half-baked nation, but an ancient mother-country'. Britain should not resist such a decision by force, but respond by making a declaration that would include a recognition of the right, not of secession, but of freedom to disassociate (a neat use of language). She should pre-empt the declaration of a republic, thus depriving Nationalists of their prize of having defeated the mighty British Empire. The freedom to 'disassociate' would, he argued, have a beneficent impact on India, when the time came for it to move more closely to Dominion status: 'I believe it would greatly strengthen our position and make it more likely that the Indian leaders will ultimately acquiesce in India remaining within the empire.'[121] By 1936 the Dominions Office was expounding the view that the Commonwealth was 'an association of free and equal nations between whom war is ruled out as a method of settling differences. . . . Can Mr de Valera's idea be said to offend against this? On the other hand would not acceptance of the idea, by indicating the flexibility of the British Commonwealth, be a demonstration of wise statesmanship and of the value attached to membership of the Commonwealth, which would add enormously to its international influence?.' In vain did the *Round Table*, in disillusioned mood, retort in March 1949 that 'three-quarters of Ireland has now definitely seceded from the Commonwealth, and nothing can be gained by ignoring this unpleasant fact'.[122] And the Attorney-General's opinion, delivered on 27 April 1949, that 'from the legal point of view there was little content in the conception of the Crown as a symbol of the association of the Commonwealth people, once the element of common allegiance has been removed',[123] remained, in the Cabinet's eyes, a legal point of view only. The idea of an Empire–Commonwealth, stable not static, evolving yet coherent, firmly grounded yet tolerant of movement, seemed not to be shaken, but rather to be reinforced by what were, in another perspective, great reversals.

And there was always the consolation of Ceylon. Here the transfer of power, which was made in February 1948, seemed to confirm that the empire could get these things right. There was no history of political opposition as in India, and no unhappy defeat as in Burma; and minority–majority problems were carefully set aside for a future date, as ones best solved by the people concerned for themselves (as the senior Colonial Office official, Sir Charles Jeffries, put it).[124] Ceylon's Singhalese majority was anxious to take power before a serious threat from communists or the Tamil minority asserted itself, and it made sense to cooperate with the imperial power in negotiating Dominion status, though the Foreign Secretary urged the Colonial Office to delete the word 'independence' from the final draft agreement, because 'Eastern people' attached a different meaning to it than the British did.[125] At last it was possible, both then and later, for officials to resort to the language they liked best to use: Lord Soulbury, who chaired the Ceylon Commission on Constitutional Reform between 1944 and 1945, urged that giving too much too soon was better than giving too little too late;[126] Sir Charles Jeffries, writing in 1962, asked whether Ceylon had been 'ready' for independence in 1948, and answered that this was 'really one of those theoretical questions to which no answer is possible'.[127] Thus, consoled with positivist language, emphasising matters of fact and experience, did England take leave of most of her Asian empire.

5

THE CHANGING WORLD OF EMPIRE, 1939–59

The First World War had been a test of empire and empire had responded to it. Britain had emerged from the world struggle with her empire materially as well as emotionally stronger. And, while the war quickened the process of Dominion nationalism, which must at least present problems for any ideas of a centralised future for the empire, and had witnessed the defection of most of Ireland, it had not raised doubts about the whole relationship of Britain to her empire. The outbreak of the Second World War saw the Dominions rally round again, but without the deep sense of kith and kin that characterised August 1914, and with some 20 years of Dominion statehood, political calculation by Dominion political élites, and hard economic bargaining with the United Kingdom behind them. The Dominion partners had their own objectives, albeit they could see these as reconcilable with the wider war effort waged on Britain's behalf. The Second World war also obliged Britain to take note of the gap between the dependent empire and the rest. At a conference held in London, in October 1939, Reginald Coupland warned that nowhere was there 'any acceptance of the sincerity of our expressed intentions in the dependent Empire'. In India the British had delayed too long, and had alienated the educated part of the community. He urged that now was the time to 'get educated Africans on our side by starting constitutional advances in Africa'.[1] In October 1939 Malcolm MacDonald warned Sir John Simon that the war would exercise a profound impact on the colonial empire; it would have a 'somewhat unsettling effect on colonial minds' since the 'mere fact that white men are again fighting, with every manifestation of brutality, among themselves tends to lessen the respect for their rule and for the benefit it brings'. There was also the belief that the white man's war was the black man's opportunity, and political discussion and agitation was developing, with strikes and rioting. One of Britain's greatest strengths in the war was that she fought for a moral cause, the interests of 'small peoples'; it was important, therefore, to anticipate criticism of the British as a selfish imperialist power, and begin to think of finding additional money to provide for the welfare of the many millions of people in the colonial empire 'for whom we are the trustees'.

It was intended that this conference be followed by what Malcolm MacDonald, Secretary of State for the Colonies, called a 'seething of thought'.[2] But the centre of attention quickly shifted to the Far East. The rapid Japanese advance through Burma; the fall of Singapore in February, 1942; the Japanese threat to India, even Australia: all were the cause of much concern and introspection about where Britain had gone wrong in her government of her Far Eastern Empire. This introspection is not hard to understand: that the British Army performed at less than its best in Malaya and Singapore was bad enough; but that British naval power should be wiped out in a few minutes, with the sinking of the *Repulse* and *Prince of Wales* on 10 December 1941, was scarcely credible. To these disasters was added the unhappy acknowledgement that, as the High Commissioner for the Malay States put it, 'For the most part the Asiatic population up country has thrown up the sponge on the first sign of enemy activity. They just go away and do nothing.'[3] One civil servant in Malaya blamed this on the failure of Government to promote a 'strong spirit of patriotism and loyalty to the rulers of the country'.[4]

About a month after the fall of Singapore, investigations began in the Colonial Office to discover the origins of the collapse. Remedies were suggested. A better-informed public opinion at home was needed. Blame was placed on those who failed to regard colonial peoples as in any way equals to themselves, with the consequent deleterious effect on a working partnership between Britain and her colonial subjects.[5] And a joint Foreign and Colonial Office memorandum in August 1942 declared that public speculation in the United States that the 'age of imperialism' was 'dead' must be met 'effectively'.[6] The Far Eastern Empire was essential for British economic prosperity, for raw materials and markets for British manufacturers.[7] Accordingly, it must be Britain's intention to present to public opinion in the United Kingdom and elsewhere that, as indicated in the third article of the Atlantic Charter (which referred to the 'rights of all peoples to choose their form of government under which they will live'), Britain would foster self-government in 'accordance with the spirit' of this article, but this must be governed by considerations of the 'degrees of responsibility' which some peoples had not yet attained. Britain would 'promote and accelerate' these processes, and stand by her treaty obligations towards the inhabitants of these territories. She would fulfil article 6 (referring to the need to protect all peoples from fear and want) by discharging her obligations in all those territories at risk. The memorandum preferred to talk about restoring British 'administrative responsibility' rather than 'sovereignty'.[8]

The Cabinet discussed the memorandum on 11 September 1942. There were diverse reactions, with L. S. Amery urging that Britain should give up nothing, and Lord Cranborne rejecting any suggestion that British rule in her colonies was 'poor', but Attlee spoke in terms of the difficulty of bearing financial burdens for the sake of empire.[9] A few days later Cranborne explained to the Chinese Ambassador that Dominion status was unlikely to be given to backward territories in the near future; it required an 'adult' nation responsible for its foreign policy and defence.[10] But the need to make some concession to the new mood engendered by, in particular, American participation in the war, caused Lord Hailey, Chairman of the Colonial Research Committee, to warn that 'Adverse expressions of American opinion might not necessarily impair our cooperation in military operations, but they would strengthen the hands of our own domestic critics if they thought that our policy was not sufficiently "forward looking".' Critics would ask why the inhabitants of these areas did not support the British in their campaign against the Japanese or actively give assistance to British forces when they began to oust the Japanese. 'False impressions' must be corrected.[11] In May 1943 another memorandum, this time by G. E. J. Gent, as Assistant Under-Secretary of State supervising the Eastern Department, reinforced the point that 'a full restoration of the pre-war constitutional and administrative system will be undesirable in the interests of efficiency and security and of our declared purpose of promoting self-government in Colonial territories',[12] a sentiment echoed almost word for word by the Colonial Secretary, Oliver Stanley, in January 1944.[13] In February 1944 the Supreme Commander of the South East Asia Command warned that, to convince the troops that the war with Japan was worth continuing to fight after the European war ended, it would be necessary to assure them that Britain had a 'constructive plan' which their victory would enable her to put into effect, and stated that America and the 'democracies in general' were sharply critical of 'our handling of this part of the world'. Foreign occupation meant a 'clean break with the past'; Britain must not fulfil her critics' assumption that she had neither the will nor the vision to 'prevent a return to the bad old days'.[14] In September 1944 he again urged the Government to act quickly and devise 'suitable Political Warfare' and, above all, not to miss 'the bus'.[15] The war then had a modernising effect on significant parts of the empire, for example in Egypt. Britain relaxed her hold on Egypt in the treaty of 1936, but tightened it once more because of its vital importance in the war. The British war in the Middle East aroused resentment at the use of Egyptian, Persian and Arab territory for the conflict, and a new awareness of the inequalities of society and the British support for the rich and ruling classes.[16] Burma had fallen to the Japanese, and while no-one could maintain that Japanese rule was other than exploitative, it was nevertheless a blow to British control of Burma from which it never recovered. The problem of defending the Dominions, always contentious, was exposed by the war. Australia was a problem. In the 1930s Menzies, the Australian Premier, had declared that the navy's defence of Australia merited a reciprocal Australian response: 'The British countries of the world must stand or fall together.'[17] But in December 1941 the then Prime Minister, John Curtain, took a different view:

> Without inhibitions of any kind. . . . I make it quite clear that Australia looks to America, free of any pangs as to our traditional links with the United Kingdom. We know the problems that the United Kingdom faces. We know the continental threat of invasion. We know the dangers of dispersal of strength. But we know too that Australia can go and Britain can still hold on. We are, therefore, determined that Australia shall not go, and we shall exert all our energies towards the shaping of a plan, with the United States as its keystone, which will give to our country some confidence of being able to hold out until the tide of battle swings against the enemy.[18]

The fall of Singapore, and the imminent danger of a Japanese invasion of Australia, rendered these fears all the more vivid.

The phrase 'Australia can go and Britain can still hold on' deserves consideration. Britain was indeed central to the struggle against Nazi Germany, and Japan. Defence of the empire was a vital part of her wartime strategy, but the defeat of Japan was in the end left primarily to the United States, and Britain saw her European role as of greater and more immediate significance – not least when the Americans arrived in large numbers and used the United Kingdom as their base for the liberation of Europe. Even when fighting the Japanese in Burma, Field Marshal Slim found it necessary to explain to the men of his Fourteenth ('forgotten') army that they were not risking their lives in an imperialist war, but were fighting to defeat a cruel enemy, and liberate conquered peoples from that enemy – and then go home. [19] These were hardly the sentiments of a conquering imperial army. Australian troops made a vital contribution to the Middle East theatre of war; but their presence there only reinforced the point that the British perception of what was central to the war effort, and what was peripheral, again suggested that 'imperial defence' was not all of a piece, but was subject to a very British-centred order of priorities. Britain promised that, in the event of New Zealand and Australia being invaded by Japan, 'we shall then cut our losses in the Mediterranean, sacrifice every interest, except only the defence and feeding of this island'.[20] But this was greeted with scepticism in Australia.

The entry of the United States of America into the position that she has held ever since – that of the most powerful nation in the world – was another consequence of the war, and one that must help create a climate less congenial to the imperial idea. Roosevelt harboured deep suspicions that the British would use the opportunity of emerging as a victorious power to strengthen or recover her imperial possessions. The Atlantic Charter, which Churchill and Roosevelt signed in August 1941, was perhaps open to a conservative as well as a radical interpretation. Churchill sought to close the door on any radical view: article 3 applied only to European countries under German occupation.[21] But he was obliged to declare that Britain had already stated her policy goals for the empire. And L. S. Amery, who in February 1943, described the Charter as 'essentially an exposition of nineteenth century and not of twentieth century ideals, whether in economics or in politics', had to admit that 'on the other hand, that doesn't alter the fact of the growing intensity of nationalism in the Oriental world'.[22]

But if nationalism presented a danger to the British Empire, the other great ideology of the twentieth century, communism, offered as much an opportunity as it did a threat. The Soviet system was always regarded by America as the direct opposite of her liberal, free-enterprise culture; but now the advance of the Soviet Union to the heartland of central and eastern Europe seemed to give her the kind of powerful geopolitical status that Mackinder had identified in his diagnosis of imperial power. It was essential, then, that the British and their empire be placed at the disposal of the free world; and America acknowledged that the British

Empire was, in many vulnerable parts of the world, a defence against communism. Eventually the United States would find itself moving into the role that it had assigned to the British, either because the British could not or would not fulfil it, or because America believed she could fill it more effectively, in Turkey, Saudi Arabia, Persia and perhaps even in Palestine.[23] The 'special relationship' between Britain and America was, therefore, a complex and even contradictory one: the Americans were certain that they had not entered the war to keep the world safe for the British Empire; yet keeping the world safe for democracy involved mobilising Britain and her empire. The climate was not as yet settled; but the American presence was, to say the least, a troublesome one for the imperial powers.

There were those who believed that the English way of pragmatism and adaptability could enable them to ride out this period of change. L. S. Amery (as always with his eyes on the geopolitical facts of history) noted that:

> In spite of Atlantic Charters and all that sort of stuff, it looks as if the world were moving steadily towards more intensive national organisation and if so, our Empire may hope to follow suit or fall into the hands of others.[24]

America saw Britain as at least a reformable power: she conceded the case for the continuing British control over Libya, which at one stage Britain feared America would include in her vision of the 'inevitable independence of North African colonies, including Algeria, Morocco and Tunisia'.[25] The possibility of war between America and her western allies, and the Soviet Union, made it imperative that the British should retain their place in the Middle East. America had come to see the point of the British acting in defence of American interests, and those of the West. The American Head of Office of the Near Eastern and African Affairs of the State Department, Loy Henderson, appreciated that Britain wanted to remain a world power and therefore necessarily an imperial power; and he acknowledged also that Britain was an essential partner in combating Soviet influence.[26] But it was a world ever increasingly critical of the imperial idea; for example, the Government of Tanganyika, which Britain had gained in the wake of the German defeat in the First World War, was the subject of critical appraisal in the United Nations; appraisal that alarmed the British Government. The United Nations conducted five Visiting Missions to Tanganyika between 1948 and 1960, some of which were regarded as helpful by the Administration in Kenya, but the first of which, in 1948, provoked Lord Listowel to describe the United Nations as 58 back-seat drivers.[27] Such activities alerted political groups in Tanganyika to the possibility of gaining advantage and publicity by sending representatives to the United Nations to plead their case. And by 1954 the Trusteeship Council of the United Nations was urging acceptance of a timetable for political advance in Tanganyika. The United Kingdom Government showed itself sensitive to such commentary on its colonial policies, and the decision made in 1955 to take the first steps towards elections in Tanganyika was announced in New York before it was announced in Tanganyika itself.[28]

It suited America to help keep the world safe for British democracy – and therefore imperialism; at least until 1956 and to some extent after that as well. So the British Empire was given a place even in the developing anti-colonial mood of the post-war world. The two world wars convinced Britain that her land army should never again fight on the mainland of Europe. Her real interest lay in securing her sea communications and the Middle East: that vital area to strike against the USSR. The Cold War was indeed of central importance in the redefining and repositioning of the empire. In December 1954 a memorandum by the Minister of Defence, 'Internal Security in the Colonies', surveyed the scene, noting that the chances of a major war were declining, but that the Cold War would go on. And, during the next four years:

> our Colonial Empire in its varying stages of development is likely to be a vital 'cold war' battlefield. If we are defeated here much of our effort in Western Europe will be wasted. Trouble in the Colonial Empire may be directly inspired by the Communists. Alternatively, they may exploit troubles basically of a nationalist character.[29]

But the Cold War could work in the opposite direction. When trying to deal with the problem of Greek Cypriot demands for independence, backed by terrorism, Britain found herself referring not only to her own assessment of her interests, but to the anxiety of the North Atlantic Treaty Organisation, of which the United Kingdom was a key member, that she do her utmost to reach a settlement.[30]

But great power status and the possession of an empire depended not only on foreign perceptions of Britain's role in the world; it also depended considerably on her economic condition at home. Britain after 1945 was a country in an insecure and even alarming economic predicament.

Britain was owed accumulated debts of some £3.5 billion in sterling as a result of the Second World War; she was willing to allow these debts to continue because they helped her maintain her financial role as a banker in the non-communist world outside the western hemisphere.[31] But her dependence on the American loan of 3.75 billion US dollars made in July 1946, and her deployment of some two-thirds of this on military expenditure, and her inability to achieve the policy of convertibility with the American dollar by 1949, created problems of foreign debts, and in the end a devaluation of 30 per cent, a decision taken by Britain without consulting the Commonwealth nations. Sterling was still the currency for half the world's trade, and by 1952–3, despite the rearmament necessitated by the outbreak of the Korean War, United Kingdom trade with the dollar area was in balance.[32] Britain continued to develop the sterling area, and this meant that she wanted to ensure that her colonies remained within this area, as indeed they did. Britain also set out to impose controls on colonial trade and investment. There was no sign here of a post-war world inimical to the maintenance of empire; on the contrary, Britain showed a determination, amounting to ruthlessness, to protect her economic interests by using her imperial possessions and subordinating their economic interests to her own needs.[33]

But this soon changed. Britain's retreat from the idea of open competition in world trade had begun in the 1930s, when she first developed a protectionist policy. But the British response to the world economic crisis of 1929 was also to resurrect the Chamberlainite idea of preferential tariffs for Commonwealth countries. In 1932 a series of agreements were reached in Ottawa to foster a self-contained trading unit, protected against foreign competition by tariffs, thus responding to the economic crisis, but also bringing 'the Empire together again'. But the Commonwealth members were determined not to subordinate their own potential or actual industrial development to imperial needs, and the United Kingdom was unwilling to grant the Commonwealth countries the effective monopoly in the metropolitan market that they wanted. [34]

Once the western nations began to recover economically after the Second World War, inspired by American financial aid, they soon challenged Britain's otherwise promising post-war condition. While these European economies were weak, Britain was well-placed for economic leadership, despite the period of austerity introduced just after the war ended. But as the leading nations of Europe began to make economic progress, they began to take advantage of British economic backwardness. In 1954 Germany passed Britain in shipbuilding; in 1953 Japan did the same. Britain's share of the total value of world manufacturing exports declined from 25.5 per cent in 1950 to 16.5 per cent in 1960.[35] British assumptions that the Commonwealth and sterling area would enable her to maintain her world position in trade were misplaced. The Commonwealth nations wanted to make sterling convertible, and the United Kingdom effectively acquiesced in this by 1958. The European Economic Community was a rising economic bloc, and the United Kingdom chose to remain outside it. Sterling lost its pre-eminence and became a currency that its potential purchaser had to be persuaded to buy. This meant that Britain would have to retain high interest rates, and yet this would have an adverse effect on her domestic industry. Or Britain had to offer military and economic aid to countries such as Malaya, which she no longer controlled. Balance-of-payments crises became part of the British economic experience, and while devaluation was always a last option, it was feared that such an expedient might mean that sterling would cease to be an international currency.

The post-war economic world worsened, and must have an effect on British imperial ambitions, even if this was not felt right away. There was no immediate necessity to abandon great power status, and indeed Britain played a central role in the defence of Europe against possible Soviet aggression. But this meant that her chief military commitment was to Europe; there would not be much to spare for imperial commitments, though there would be a need to meet these in small wars. In these wars, like that in Malaya in the 1950s, imperial troops would play a role; but there would be no reciprocity: it was unthinkable as well as impossible that Australian or Canadian soldiers should be based in Europe and continue the military role that they had been prepared to play, at considerable sacrifice, in the liberation of Europe in 1944–5. The old question of just where British priorities lay, in terms of the geographical fact that Britain was only a thin strip of sea away from the continent of Europe (and a short time away from Soviet missiles) would be raised again. But not yet, and the British determination to hold her worldwide commitments and possessions was not diminished.

But the world in which these possessions sat was also undergoing significant changes. The war had helped unleash the force of nationalism outside Europe, a force which Britain had already encountered in Ireland, India and Egypt, but which was now to unsettle her in many of her colonies. Dominion nationalism had proved to be less disruptive than might have been expected; the Dominions all rallied to Britain in 1939, as they had done in 1914. And there was still a sense of belonging to some common stock of ideas and values, however weak this might be in political or military terms, and after all, a Commonwealth Brigade had served with the British army in the Korean War. It is easy either to exaggerate, or to underestimate, the influence of post-war nationalism on the British Empire. Some historians, notably Ronald Robinson and John Gallagher, have dismissed the idea that the empire was undermined from below. In a paper on the 'Decline, Rise and Fall of the British Empire' Gallagher wrote that 'colonial resistance movements, a romantic term, are not going to help us through our problems'.[36] Certainly the expression 'resistance movements' conveys a coherence and élan that opposition to British imperial rule hardly deserves.

Local officials, like the Governor of Kenya, in a reply to a Colonial Office circular, dismissed the concept of an 'African Nation' as non-existent: 'there is no place in Africa for the synthetic nationalisms which are being manufactured today, largely under the influence of Hindu politics'.[37] Nevertheless, the empire between 1918 and 1959 encountered enough nationalists, and reacted to them in a sufficiently rebarbative way, as to suggest that the names of Zaghlul (Egypt), de Valera (Ireland), Nasser (Egypt) and Makarios (Cyprus) would be engraved on the imperial mind as demonised enemies.

The post-war years saw an important political, propagandist and at times violent challenge to the notion that British rule was as secure as ever it had been. In 1945 Kwame Nkrumah, the Gold Coast African political leader, wrote and issued a 'Declaration to the Colonial Peoples of the World', which was approved by a pan-African Congress held in Manchester, on 15–21 October. The Declaration set out the 'rights of all people to govern themselves' and affirmed 'the right of colonial peoples to control their own destiny':

All colonies must be free from foreign imperialist control, whether political or economic . . . we say to the peoples of the colonies that they must strive for these ends by all means at their disposal.

The statement declared that the 'object of imperialist powers is to exploit' and that 'by granting the right of Colonial peoples to govern themselves, they are defeating that objective'. The Declaration made a specific reference to the need for 'workers and farmers of the Colonies to organise effectively. Colonial Workers must be in the front lines of the battle against imperialism.' Professional people and intellectuals must 'awaken to their responsibilities'; 'today there is only one road to effective action – the organisation of the masses'. The Declaration finished with the clarion call: 'Colonial and Subject Peoples of the World-Unite!'[38]

This was of course more rhetorical than substantive. Yet the language of the communication deserves serious study. The Declaration adopted a specifically socialist, even Marxist tone; and one of the difficulties confronting a colonial power was its vulnerability to the accusation that its rule was only another form of capitalist exploitation. This was not a new argument; J. A. Hobson had made it forcefully in 1902 in his book *Imperialism*.[39] Whether this theory was soundly based on economic fact is debatable: colonial powers were often out of pocket in their dealings with their possessions, as the British in India were by the 1930s (which is not to deny that they certainly had the desire to exploit their colonies economically). But the argument was one likely to hit the British in particular where they were most vulnerable; for the British liked to feel that they had a moral case for empire. The British Idealist philosophers spoke for a wide section of political and perhaps even public opinion when they wrote in the nineteenth century that the only justification for British rule was to rule on behalf of the native peoples, for all peoples had the 'capacity for a good life'.[40]

The question arose, after the Second World War, of where the British mission was going if it were branded as a mere tool of capitalist exploitation – an accusation which by now had gathered force from the general collectivist mood of post-war Europe, and the (apparently) successful Marxist experiment in the Soviet Union. Britain did not yet feel that her imperial rule needed an apologia, let alone an apology; but she was soon to confront a series of challenges to her position as the ruler of heterogeneous peoples, and the campaign of the Indian nationalists in the 1920s to the 1940s proved to be, not an end, but a presage of what was yet to come.

The British Government was alive to the danger posed by nationalist movements in the post-war world. In 1952 the Foreign Office prepared a memorandum on the 'Problem of Nationalism' which was circulated to Winston Churchill's Conservative Cabinet. The paper stated that its aim was to 'suggest means by which we can safeguard our position as a world power, particularly in the economic and strategic fields, against the dangers inherent in the present upsurge of nationalism'. The memorandum made it clear that it believed nationalism was a deliberate threat to Britain's world interests and power 'by less developed nations'. There were three options. 'Domination by occupation'; 'threat of intervention'; and 'creating a class with a vested interest in cooperation'.[41] The first two options certainly sounded like military ones; even the mere 'threat of intervention' necessitated the preparation of troops for any action that might be necessary. Britain showed herself ready to deploy military force in Malaya between 1948 and 1953 in an operation against communist guerrillas that has been taken as a model of counter-insurgency.[42] But it was one taken to support a nationalist government already installed in power, not to coerce or overthrow one; and this made Britain's determination to defend its economic interests in Malaya, and keep the country in the sterling area, feasible. Still, Britain had shown that she was not prepared to be what Lord Salisbury called 'hustled'.[43] But it was hard not to be 'hustled'. A Colonial Office paper, prepared in January 1955, warned that:

> For many years successive Governments in the United Kingdom have pursued, with a broad measure of public support, a Colonial policy of assisting dependent peoples to reach a stage of development at which they can assume responsibility for managing their own affairs. As a result, constitutional development is proceeding steadily in many parts of the Colonial Empire. This process cannot now be halted or reversed, and it is only to a limited extent that its pace can be controlled by the United Kingdom Government. . . . In the main, the pace of constitutional change will be determined by the strength of nationalist feeling and the development of political consciousness within the territory concerned. Political leaders who have obtained assurances of independence for their people normally expect that the promised independence will be attained within their own political lifetime; and if they cannot satisfy their followers that satisfactory progress is being maintained towards that goal, their influence may be usurped by less responsible elements.[44]

The Gold Coast experience helped to make this point. Here the colonial government had for a long time depended on the participation of traditional rulers who were directed from above, and the small, western-educated middle classes which, like the educated Indian middle classes in between the wars, were permitted to have access to a narrow range of professional and business opportunities and to the junior levels of public offices. This class would see itself, and was seen, as future inheritors of a more responsible government system, and thus would play their part in the economic development that was the main concern of the British

Government, far surpassing any notion of political change. The emphasis would be on administrative experience to which this élite would be exposed.

The Gold Coast was governed from October 1941 by Sir Alan Burns, who inherited this idea of preparation of an élite for a proper, if highly circumscribed, role in the colony's future development. He came to believe that there should be an unofficial majority in the Legislative Council, because it was the best means of defusing African opposition to any unpopular policies. He still regarded the colony as unfit for self-government; and, in any case, the Colonial Office was opposed to the idea of an unofficial majority on the Legislative Council.

The Colonial Office was thinking in terms of economic, not political or constitutional, development. But it did realise that the war made it necessary to train Africans in administrative skills. Educational reform was implemented. A university was suggested to train future élites. Tentative suggestions were made for modest constitutional change and development, and the unofficial majority principle in the Legislative Council was implemented as early as 1944. But, after 1947, unrest in the Gold Coast increased. There were economic problems, inflation and industrial discontent, and protests were organised. The United Coast Convention, led by its General Secretary, Kwame Nkrumah, began to foster political opposition. There were disturbances which the authorities put down: but they also responded with a Committee of Inquiry which investigated the unrest, and concluded that, in political terms, it was the consequence of the large number of African soldiers returning from service with the forces, where they had lived under different and better conditions; of the political frustration amongst educated Africans who saw no prospect of experiencing political power under existing conditions; of the Government's failure to appreciate the importance of the spread of liberal ideas, increasing literacy, and closer contacts with political developments in other parts of the world. To these reasons was added the feeling that Africanisation was a promise, not a policy, which aroused suspicion about government intentions.[45] The Government in reply stressed that it placed its hopes of progress on the African chiefs having a vital part to play in political development,[46] but the Cabinet agreed in October 1949 that there should be some move towards 'a very considerable degree of African participation in the control of policy'.[47]

This did not mean responsible government; and the British were determined to retain the initiative in appointing members to any legislative body. But this determination was shaken by Nkrumah's Convention People's Party's success in the colony's elections in February 1951. The timetable was now adjusted; the process speeded up. The Gold Coast was reasonably prosperous; but more significant in this accelerated process was the existence of an educational system, schools, a small but increasing university-educated class, and a growing political class that had gained experience in city politics and even a few businessmen who supported the Convention People's Party. The Gold Coast also possessed in Nkrumah a political leader of considerable ability who, while he was obliged to spend time in prison, was recognised as a potential figure of some importance. The risk of standing firm was acknowledged by the British Government; and the consolation that the Gold Coast would set no precedent for other parts of Africa helped the Government to respond to this nationalist challenge in a remarkably generous, or at least realistic, way. But, again, there was the comfort of precedent: the tradition of devolving power to whites in South Africa, then to Indians in 1947, could, without too much sense of danger to the empire as a whole, be extended now to an African colony. Whether or not the African élite was quite like the Australians or Canadians who had benefited from this theory of devolution in the nineteenth century was still unclear; but the question might be asked whether the Afrikaaners who gained devolved power in 1910 were quite like Australians or Canadians (though they saw themselves, and were seen, as similar to Irish Nationalists at least). At any rate, the decision to press on with incorporating an African Colony into a system designed for colonies of European settlement was one that seemed consistent with the English way of doing things: of adapting and adjusting, of responding to the need for change, not simply in an expedient way, but in a way consistent with the notion that change and continuity were perfectly compatible. There was, in any event, no white population of any considerable size; trade links, the production of cocoa, were guaranteed. Africans in the civil service had worked well with Europeans. Above all, Nkrumah showed that he had the one great political gift necessary to convince his colonial masters that they must make a move towards granting self-government: staying power. He was not going to go away, and so he must be accommodated. By 1956 he was able to win a victory in general elections; and, driven by these modernising forces, by African political pressure and by the belief that Africans could work their economy better than the colonial government, and work it in their own interests, the Gold Coast was able to win independence as Ghana in 1957.[48] But, in the process, fears expressed by representatives of the north of the country that they would be dominated by the south were over-ridden: this would, said the Under-Secretary of State for Commonwealth Relations on 11 December 1956, 'cripple' the new country.[49]

But the idea persisted that, when it came to dealing with nationalist movements such as that of the Gold Coast, there were nationalisms and nationalisms; some could be accommodated, partly, perhaps mainly out of necessity; but also some were of the order that enabled them to fit into the persisting view that the imperial genius for distinguishing between good and bad nationalisms, and satisfying the former, was undiminished. It was not only that there might be found an élite that could be trusted with self-government; there was also the belief that certain peoples were more innately appropriate to take on the task of governing themselves than were others. Thus East Africans were seen as too far down the social scale, too much of a working class, to enjoy self-government. But in the Gold Coast a British official described his colleagues there as 'in varying degrees, good nationalists'. One former officer described the Negro peoples of West Africa as belonging to a 'quite different stock from the Bantu of Central Africa', seeming to be of a 'higher calibre'.[50] This encouraged the belief that, when the empire met a nationalist challenge, then it was one which must draw an appropriate response and so nationalisms were different in different parts of the empire, and these could be compartmentalised.[51] But this also encouraged the notion that nationalism, if judged 'good', and providing that nationalists were sufficiently trustworthy, and that there was an administrative and political class of the right kind, could be fitted into the general concept that subject peoples, even of different colour, could take their place in the kind of devolved empire that was grounded firmly on precedent. And there was the consoling thought that, as Sir Charles Jeffries, Deputy Under-Secretary of State at the Colonial Office put it in February 1953, 'The problem is not so much what more to concede as how to present the case in such a way that the Gold Coasters are satisfied that they have got the essentials of "self-government", while *we* are satisfied that we have got the essentials of ultimate control.'[52]

The question, then, was to adjust to the new world of nationalism, while not going too far too fast. The example of Cyprus was proof of the drain on resources that a small island, troubled by a sporadic insurgency movement, could exercise on a colonial power, even when it enjoyed broad international support in its perceived role as a bulwark against the communist world. The Greek Cypriot demand for union with Greece – *Enosis* – had important implications for the island, situated as it was in such close proximity to Egypt and Persia. No-one could doubt that Cyprus was vital to British security and her place in the broad alliance against the Soviets. But the problem of ruling a troublesome colony was revealed in the British difficulty in finding a coherent response to nationalism in Cyprus. It was difficult to decide whether or not the priority should be to hold on to the island, and defy Greece; or to seek an accommodation with Greece and thus keep the broader strategic interest in view. There was also the problem of the Turkish Cypriots, whose future in a Cyprus united with Greece would be of concern to Turkey. This made the Cypriot problem especially complex: to grant Greek Cypriot demands would be to sell out on British interests and, less importantly, abandon the Turkish minority to its fate.

The problem of dealing with colonial nationalism was illustrated in another aspect of the Cyprus case: the fact that it would not go away. The *Enosis* movement was durable: history, culture and religion gave the movement its emotional appeal, and helped sustain a terrorist movement that gathered momentum in the 1950s.[53] Oliver Stanley, Secretary of State for the Colonies, had urged in 1944 that Britain make a firm declaration to remain in Cyprus. This would end dangerous speculation. He did not take a short-term view; 'some burdens' must be borne, but because of his feeling

> that in the years to come, without the Commonwealth and Empire, this country will play a small role in world affairs, and that we have an opportunity which may never recur ... of setting the Colonial Empire on lines of development which will keep it in close and loyal contact with us.[54]

Therefore, strategic needs and the British government of the colony would go hand in hand and a declaration of intent would be the means of cementing this connection.

But this underestimated the growing strength of the nationalist movement in Cyprus. In 1947 the *Enosis* movement gathered momentum. Britain still saw this as part of the overall Communist threat, and prepared herself to use military force to maintain order. But her own liberal democratic traditions proved an inhibition, even when used in the face of a violent terrorist campaign. The phrase used by one Colonial Office official – 'a policy of repression in Cyprus in the hope that no one will notice',[55] – turned out to be a policy that everyone noticed. It was made more difficult to apply following a plebiscite in 1950 which returned a clear indication of Greek Cypriot unity on the *Enosis* issue.[56] It was not easy for a colonial power to admit that it was unpopular, and that the people whom it governed for a considerable time might now want to break away from its rule. Then there was the ever-present consideration that concession implied weakness; and that weakness would sooner or later bear a troublesome consequence.

Moreover, in 1950 the British confronted a new and formidable opponent: Archbishop Makarios III (Michael Mouskos). He launched a series of verbal attacks on the British, and was prepared to come to terms with the communist supporters of *Enosis*, who were not natural allies of the Church. Britain sought to counter this with a policy of economic support for Cyprus, building up village economics with welfare grants, supplying piped water and improving agricultural and harbour works. But none of these ameliorative measures blunted the demand for *Enosis*.[57] The level of violence and disorder increased, and from 1954 the terrorist movement developed a momentum which caught the world's attention, and turned out to be a controversial and exasperating war.

Britain reaffirmed her determination that Cyprus could never be given up, owing to its 'particular circumstances'.[58] On 31 March 1955 Colonel George Grivas, a Cypriot-born retired Greek Army officer, began EOKA's terrorist campaign with a series of bomb explosions. Makarios called on Greek Cypriots to 'intensify the struggle'.[59] Over the next five years a series of diplomatic and military policies were tried, talks held, and the counter-terrorist operation mounted against EOKA. The Cabinet was given different and often confusing reports on the Cyprus problem. In March 1957 it was told that the Government of Cyprus was making 'steady progress' against terrorism, and that it would be a sign of weakness to embark on any further discussion with the leader of the Greek community in Cyprus, or with Makarios 'until terrorism had been finally eradicated'.[60] Ten days later it was decided that, despite the 'embarrassment' involved, it would be advantageous, since terrorism was under control, to hold discussions; and that NATO, which earlier must not be allowed to determine policy, must now have its 'frustration' taken into account.[61] Cyprus was not pacified; EOKA was not defeated; and the deportation of Makarios to the Seychelles only made a settlement harder to reach. Faced by this complex problem Britain eventually conceded, on 16 April 1960, a Republic of Cyprus, with Makarios installed as its first President. British strategic needs were secured by her retaining a sovereign base on the island, and undertaking to defend the Turkish Cypriot minority, should the need arise (a p$ \iota \iota $ ise which in the 1970s she reneged upon).

The long-drawn-out Cyprus problem revealed that nationalism, especially if it took a violent form, could push a colonial power to the limit of its endurance; not to the limit of its military power, but to the limit at which that power could be effectively deployed. The Cyprus experience made a mockery of Oliver's desire to see the word 'never' inserted into a declaration of British intent. The attempt to suppress nationalism only succeeded in radicalising the colonial population. Moreover, the United Kingdom was vulnerable to outside pressure over which she had little or no control. In Cyprus the United States was anxious for a settlement, and the Greek and Turkish Governments likewise did not want their clients on Cyprus to decide their foreign policy for them, and certainly not to plunge them into confrontation and possibly war.[62]

The 1950s were a volatile era for the British Empire. But the impact of colonial nationalism was not uniform, any more than its origins were, and it was only one factor pushing the British Government towards re-ordering its imperial priorities. And it is important to stress that what is termed 'colonial nationalism' took a very different form, and was inspired by different economic, social and cultural circumstances. The nationalism that inspired EOKA and the desire for *Enosis* was not the same as that which provoked the Accra riots. It is hard to quote Stalin with any kind of approval, but in his book *Marxism and the National and Colonial Question*, published in 1935, he argued that the struggle for national equality in the colonial empires (from which he excluded the Soviet Union) would become fused with the struggle for social and economic equality. Historical reality had pronounced the doom of the British Empire.[63] This was an over-simplification; but the decade after the Second World War revealed that, for various reasons, British rule was being tested, as discontent became channelled into nationalist ideologies.

It tested the English because it forced them to think in terms of their future imperial role, and not merely to regard the empire as a natural part of their history, and as a natural asset to their policy and economic strength. When the British encountered prolonged, or expensive, or controversial military and police action, they found that concessions must be made. This decade did not mark the end of the empire; but it exposed weaknesses in its condition and, in particular, it revealed that the empire was now exposed to international economic and political pressures.

ar East, that vulnerable part of the empire whose
...d been so cruelly exposed by Japan in 1941–2, that
...the changing context of international politics, and the
...to act as a great imperial power, were most candidly
...gh the transformation of that part of the empire from col-
...overnment was assisted by luck, pragmatic thinking and the
lang.......of transition deployed, again, by the colonial power. But there
was no intention, the Colonial Office reminded the Government in May
1950, to 'abandon responsibility prematurely'; and here the Colonial
Office cited the example of Malaya, a country with a multi-racial people
and a complex social structure which was being moved towards self-
government, but not at the cost of disorder, chaos, or loss of British
interest in the territories.[64]

Between 1942 and 1948 the British had adjusted their government of
Malaya, not least because, as the Public Relations Officer in the Colonial
Office reminded the Government in March 1942, the military disaster
must cause her to revise her assumptions about her colonial territories.[65]
In December 1942 three Colonial Officers of experience pondered on
the 'lessons to be drawn', from the predicament, and noted that the
Government of Malaya was 'alien to the whole of the population save to
the small minority of Europeans'.[66] Some sense of evolution for a post-
war settlement was needed. This would not have prevented the military
collapse, but it was essential nonetheless to work towards the association
of people with government to foster a 'sense of common purpose'.[67]

A new departure was called for. But the Malayan colony increased in
importance as India moved nearer to self-government, and the Colonial
Office gained the Cabinet's endorsement that self-government must be
promoted in the territories. There could be no return to the pre-war
system.[68] However, Malaya – or rather the Malay States, Penang and
Malacca – must have a strong central government.

In 1946 civilian government was restored, but Malayan opposition,
led by her rulers, soon developed. The British acknowledged that if they
wanted to stay in Malaya they needed the support of influential leaders
of Malayan political opinion; non-cooperation could prove troublesome;
Malaya could be infiltrated by communist agitators.[69] The British now
offered a federal solution, but still remained determined to hold Malaya,
establish a strong central government, and work towards common citizenship for the Malayan people, whatever their diversity.[70] The Indian
'Dyarchy' method was chosen, with a division of powers between central
government and the federal states, but the British were faced with a

communist uprising which lasted even beyond the grant of self-government to Malaya.

Self-government must not, however, mean loss of control. In a paper prepared for the Cabinet by the Permanent Under-Secretary of State's Committee in the Foreign Office in October 1949, the view that Britain had a special role to play in post-colonial lands prevailed, and was expressed in the usual language. The British 'cannot dominate the region, but we can and should use our political and economic influence to weld the area into some degree of regional cooperation'. In trying to do so, Britain possessed a special advantage: 'We have been the most successful of the Western Powers in coming to terms with the new Nationalist spirit in Asia. Of our former possessions, India, Pakistan and Ceylon are now independent members of the Commonwealth, and Burma, though outside the Commonwealth, is friendly.' A significant factor was that 'the political systems of all these countries are built upon a British foundation'. By contrast, the Dutch and the French were still in conflict with nationalist movements in Indonesia and Indo-China. Even the United States, for all its power, lacked historical connections with the area.[71]

These high hopes were not realised. American power and penetration in the region were to increase, rather than diminish. But the trend towards self-government for Malaya was hastened by the anti-terrorist war waged against the communists, which involved associating the Malayan people with the armed forces' tactics, and with the police, accompanied by administrative reform and economic development. This process also involved fostering a more democratic political system in the territory. The military commander, Sir Gerald Templar, was doubtful about the readiness of Malaya for political advance,[72] and he set the date for self-government at 1960.[73] But the Malayan Alliance Party (a fusion of the United Malaya National Organisation and the Malayan Chinese Association made in 1951 and formalised in 1953) widened their political ambitions. The British doubted if this alliance would last – the Malays were 'a simple, agricultural people', whereas the Chinese were 'a sophisticated one'[74] – but they were reminded, from various quarters including the Cabinet Defence Committee, that 'the danger lies in too slow rather than too rapid progress'.[75] In 1954 the British, faced with a boycott by the Alliance in response to an over-cautious provision of elected seats for Federal elections, against the background of French colonial defeat in Indo-China, and reminded in January 1955 of the enormous cost of its military operation,[76] stressed the importance of cooperation. The Colonial Secretary, Lennox Boyd, still hoped to keep the progress towards self-government 'reasonably slow',[77] but the hard facts called for a speedy rather than a slow advance. In elections held on 27 July 1955 the Alliance won 51 out of 52 electable seats and the British agreed with the Alliance leader, the Tunku Abdul Rahman, to a federal executive council of ten Alliance Ministers and five British officials. Malaya now possessed a wide measure of internal self-government, and further advance was soon made to local control of defence, security and finance. The British now regarded the Tunku as a safe inheritor of power in a vital area, and they transferred security powers before the grant of full self-government in August 1957.[78]

The accelerated speed towards Malayan self-government was governed by a particular, highly significant conviction, one that was to dominate the last years of the British Empire. It was the recognition that, as Lennox-Boyd's memorandum for the Cabinet on 'Constitutional Advance in the Federation of Malaya', of 7 January 1956 put it, 'the tide is still flowing in our direction, and we can still ride it; but the ebb is close at hand and if we do not make this our moment of decision we shall have lost the power to decide'. He added: 'Not far off, the French have shown us what can happen if such a tide is missed.'[79]

'If such a tide is missed.' The British were aware, by the end of the first post-war decade, that there was indeed a 'tide' and that it could no more be stopped than any tide in the physical world. To 'ride' it required the development of an acute sense of when it was necessary, or essential, to move forward more speedily, should the occasion demand. The post-war context in which the British Empire took stock of itself, redefined itself, was one in which the forces of nationalism, economic decline, American power in the international world and the increasing unfashionability of imperialism required riding the tide; but at least the British Empire was equipped with the discourse that helped it to adjust to this new world, even though Harold Macmillan may have got nearer the heart of the matter when, on 15 August 1957, a decade after Indian independence, he declined to made a radio or television broadcast to mark the independence of Malaya because it would 'celebrate what many people may think as a weakening of the United Kingdom'.[80]

There can be no doubt that the public assumed that the United Kingdom was a great power and should remain so; nor that, within limits, they were prepared to make the sacrifices in men and money to ensure that this status was maintained. England possessed the habit of authority, and believed that the empire was central to her political, strategic and financial leadership. The political élite led public opinion. The empire was the subject of popular interest: films, school textbooks, the Empire Day commemoration, all served to keep it before the public. The Second World War had rekindled the belief that there was 'One King, One Flag, One Fleet, One Empire',[81] an idea propagated by the Empire Day Movement founded as long ago as 1903 to create a bond between the 400 million subjects of the Crown.[82] But the vigour began to drain away from the movement and the imperial idea by the end of the 1950s;[83] soon, to a new generation, such sentiments would seem quaint and irrelevant, only briefly stirred into life by the Falklands War of 1982.[84]

More immediately, as far as politicians, parties and governments were concerned, there was the awareness of the fact that no general elections after 1945 (and very few before then) were fought, let alone won, on imperial issues. In the general election of October 1951 Labour's manifesto devoted 29 per cent of its content to the Commonwealth and Empire; the Conservatives, predictably, scored a much higher percentage, 64 per cent,[85] but in the course of the election the Labour Party managed to brand the Conservatives with the image of 'warmongers' over their demand for a firm British resolve to prevent the Iranian Government from nationalising the Anglo-Iranian Oil Company,[86] an election campaign ploy that was so effective that in the May 1955 General Election Winston Churchill, on the stump for the party he had only recently led, warned against the impact of its repetition.[87] Most people voted for the same party as they voted for in 1951, and the key issues were prices, prosperity and the standard of living.[88]

The essential unimportance of empire when it came to electoral choice was shown in Harold Macmillan's victory in the October 1959 election, only three years after the divisive and publicly important Suez crisis. When preparing for the campaign, Macmillan did mention, not the empire, but one foreign policy question that he thought might strike a chord with young people: 'the fall-out effects from nuclear tests'.[89] But his main concern was to use social and economic policy to buttress Conservative electoral prospects, and the Budget of 1959 seems to have been successful, even if it also harboured future economic troubles.[90] Any mistrust of Conservative leadership occasioned by the Suez crisis evaporated after 1957, and while both manifestos mentioned the Empire/Commonwealth,[91] the central electoral issue was prosperity, and the Conservative appeal to the self-interest of the middle classes won the day.[92] Macmillan's election-winning slogan was a simple and effective appeal to what is now called 'Middle England': 'You have never had it so good.'[93] The message spoke to an electorate that rarely made its choice on any other than domestic and material conditions. Listening to this electorate, and responding to its needs and demands, naturally preoccupied political parties, and the fate of the empire was not central to this democratic process, albeit it sometimes held the headlines – for example over Cyprus, when the Sunday populars vented their spleen, in particular, against Archbishop Makarios, the high-priest of evil. Middle England aspiration was an ever-present part of the context of empire, and one that tended towards a flexible style when the decisions had to be made about its fate.

And in the realm of high policy, flexibility was further reinforced by the Gold Coast experience. Macmillan again showed pessimism about the future of the empire when he replied to his Commonwealth Relations Secretary, Lord Home, in January 1957. Home had written to the Prime Minister that 'I am full of foreboding about the whole Gold Coast experiment.' 'I agree', wrote Macmillan.[94] But in the Colonial Office other voices and opinions were heard. Sir Charles Jeffries, Deputy Under-Secretary of State for the Colonies, noted that:

> there is too much tendency to consider whether the smaller territories are 'ready'. . . . Of course they are not, any more than the Gold Coast is 'ready' for independence, or that one's teen-age daughter is 'ready' for the proverbial latch-key.[95]

'Readiness', then, was not a kind of finite state or condition, and decisions could not be based on any such firm criterion. In this view, 'readiness' was what political necessity, politics itself, recommended. This was not new; it had surfaced in Ireland, India and Burma. But it was soon to push aside other considerations (to the regret of some Ministers at least)[96] and become endowed with the mantle of a manifest destiny.

6

THE CONCEPT OF EMPIRE FROM ATTLEE TO CHURCHILL, 1945–55

The post-war decade was an anxious one for those whose task it was to maintain Britain's pre-eminent position in the world. But this was not new; at the turn of the century British statesmen pondered on what it was that could keep Britain ahead of her competitors. In 1906 L. S. Amery warned Lord Milner that Britain must direct her energies 'into national and imperial channels'.[1] Lord Selborne in October 1901, had expressed concern about the fact that the United States of America, if she wished, could build a navy far superior to that of the United Kingdom.[2] The years after the Great War were also a period of 'unusual self-consciousness' when statesmen, both British and Imperial, 'looked at their Empire with a fresh awareness and wonder', referring to the creation of what Jan Smuts described as 'the only successful experiment in international government that has ever been made'.[3] But in 1931 the Irish Free State Minister for External Affairs announced what he called 'the final demolition of the system which it took centuries to build'.[4] The loss of India might be expected to provoke further gloomy predictions about this work of 'demolition', but the British faced this post-Indian Empire phase of their imperial history with a reasonable degree of confidence.

After 1945 the empire was even more heterogeneous than it had hitherto been. India was a Republic within the Commonwealth; Burma was independent, as was Malaya – though these were not colonies of settlement on which the whole idea of freedom within the empire rested. But the English way of thinking about the empire was firmly based on tradition, on precedent; when Patrick Gordon Walker was invited by Clement Attlee to accept the office of Under-Secretary of State for Commonwealth Relations, he had an interesting exchange with the Prime Minister:

Attlee: I want you to go to Commonwealth Relations.
PGW: I'd be happy to, of course.
Attlee: There won't be much to do in Parliament.
PGW: I've always thought that Britain's greatness lies in the Commonwealth.

Gordon Walker took his task seriously. He identified the problems as:

(1) Change of style in the Commonwealth. We want some name that makes Britain a member of the whole – not Britain and the Commonwealth, but 'nations of the Commonwealth'. Perhaps we should talk of Britain and association nations of the Commonwealth – but I don't like the implications of a lower status. Why not – His Majesty's Commonwealth?

The problem of style was one of political redefinition; the other main problems which he identified were what he called 'economic integration' (he also hoped to 'integrate' India and Pakistan), a forthcoming Commonwealth Conference, and 'the emergence of new Dominions and the coming back of Burma'. [5]

The economic argument for empire was, again, not new; the idea of developing the imperial estate, or mobilising imperial resources to create better social and economic conditions at home, and make the empire into an integrated whole had been put forcefully by Joseph Chamberlain at the turn of the century; L. S. Amery took up the cause after Chamberlain was incapacitated by a stroke, stating his belief in 1906 that in 'our power of increasing the total sum of production' lay 'the total well-being of our people, the total revenue of our State'.[6] Forty years on Amery anticipated Gordon Walker's belief in the urgency of 'integration', noting that 'in spite of Atlantic Charters and all that sort of stuff, it looks as if the world were moving steadily towards more intensive national organisation and if so, our Empire may have to follow suit or fall into the hands of others'.[7] The British Ambassador in Washington warned in 1954 that the United States was extending its influence in Turkey, Saudi Arabia, Persia and perhaps even in Pakistan.[8]

Integration, both political and economic, was the key to British concepts of empire after 1945. Neither was new – imperial federalism in the 1890s was a campaign for political, imperial preference for economic, unity. Now their time seemed to have come – or must come, if the empire was to make sense – and there were some who thought that it did not make sense. Ernest Bevin, in a discussion in the Commonwealth Affairs Committee of the Labour Cabinet on 7 January 1949, observed, in a moment of exasperation, that 'in effect...the Commonwealth ought to be dissolved'. Gordon Walker speculated that his Foreign Office people had 'been at him', for they always thought they could 'run foreign policy better than we can run Commonwealth relations'.[9] But it was significant that when Bevin threatened to break ranks on the Commonwealth, 'most people attacked him and N-B [Philip Noel-Baker] gave a child's lecture on the Commonwealth. Later Bevin warmed up and began to help.'[10]

The idea of guidance – of Britain setting out to direct her colonies towards freedom, freedom that was an essential part of the English political tradition – ran into the danger of a Whig interpretation of the British imperial experience, but it was undeniable that there was material for a Whig theory of the experience: the colony of Barbados claimed what looked like this as long ago as 1649 when its assembly asked 'shall we be bound to the Government and Lordship of a Parliament in which we have no representatives or persons chosen by us?'[11] But the question remained about whether or not this concept of imperial development could be applied to all parts of the empire; India, after all, was different; the British had, in one view, been there a long time, and had established some traditions of parliamentary government, and the Labour Government showed itself anxious to include India in the Commonwealth, even if the central unifying symbol of the Crown was not applicable to India.[12] Writing in 1953, L. S. Amery expressed concern that the British appeared to think that Dominion status would be the goal of all territories. This was not necessarily so: Britain needed something like Malta's system of 'a definite dyarchy', that was, local government and imperial government with clearly defined legislative and financial powers, as in federal systems.[13]

Amery underestimated the British recognition that the empire, though it must be integrated, was not a single, undifferentiated unit. In December 1949 the Colonial Secretary, Arthur Creech Jones, examined the problems of 'Constitutional Development in smaller colonial territories'. He restated what he termed the 'central purpose of British Colonial Policy', which was 'simple':

It is to guide the Colonial territories to responsible self-government within the Commonwealth in conditions that ensure to the people concerned both a fair standard of living and freedom from oppression from any quarter.

This, he pointed out, embodied by implication the 'obvious truth that full independence can be achieved only if a territory is economically viable and capable of defending its own interests'. He divided colonial territories into three classes: those which were potentially capable of achieving full independence; those which could combine with others to form units capable of full independence; and those which fall into 'neither of the above categories'. Creech Jones summarised his argument that 'it is hardly likely that full self-government will be achieved under any foreseeable conditions (apart from association with other territories) by any except Nigeria, the Gold Coast, and the Federation of Malaya with Singapore'. There were also territories where the British aim was to produce closer union or federation in order to build up units capable of independence: South East Asia; the Caribbean colonies, and East and Central African territories.[14]

The term 'closer union' recalled the case of South Africa between 1907 and 1910, and for the same kind of reasons, that territories, if left to pursue their own devices, would never construct a viable economic or political unit; but if harnessed together they could develop into peaceful, harmonious and prosperous states. An example would be the English people in East and Central Africa, who resembled the English of South Africa, in that they were a community rendered secure through the uniting of disparate colonies. Indeed the British attitude towards the white Rhodesians was shaped by their desire to place the English population there in a position to act as a counterweight to the danger of South Africa absorbing the white people of Rhodesia. The federation of the Rhodesias, North and South, with Nyasaland, in 1953 would provide the means of conceding much local autonomy to the white settlers, and thus prevent them from pursuing a policy of apartheid on the South African model.[15]

The idea, therefore, of moving a white population towards self-government as a means of providing political stability, and giving them a sense of security, was not new in the 1950s; the Union of South Africa was a precedent though, as it turned out, it gave the future to the Afrikaaners, whose dominion was accepted by the English as the price of retaining white control of South Africa. But there were smaller territories that could not be conveniently grouped together to form a significant or even viable bloc. In 1948 the Secretary of State for the Colonies enumerated some 25 such territories, placed in five larger geographical groups. Here the procedure was to monitor the character of the smaller territories and the probable trend of their future political development.

Such an inquiry 'could advise whether it is practicable or desirable to define the ultimate objective in the case of particular territories or to lay down any general principle on which policy should be based, to examine any practical steps which might be suggested for promoting healthy political progress, for mitigating the parochialism and other evils to which small and isolated communities are subject, and for giving the peoples of these territories a genuine sense of partnership in the Commonwealth'.[16]

Both the Conservative L. S. Amery and the Labour Party's Arthur Creech Jones, then, believed that not all territories could or should advance towards self-government at the same pace, in the same form or even towards the same goal; some would remain in the category of territories for whom full self-government would be a danger to their own best interests or even their survival. Thus the general idea, central to English assumptions about the empire since the early nineteenth century, that this was an empire the aim of which was to foster free institutions and responsible government, and in the end self-government, was tempered by the acknowledgement that certain conditions had to be met, certain political adjustments made, and a strong guiding hand exercised. The case of the Rhodesias and Nyasaland reinforced the point, and when the question of federating these territories was debated in the House of Commons in the early 1950s the Labour Party was reluctant to divide the House, even though it did insist that the federal idea was contingent upon African acceptance of the proposal.[17] The Prime Minister of the Federation, Roy Welensky, pressed for the granting of Dominion status, which he hoped to use to give what one commentator called 'a stringently restrictive measure of political participation to an African middle class'.[18] But the British had their own standards to judge whether Dominion status should be given or withheld; and these, too, were related, not only to some broad idea of what the Commonwealth stood for, but also to the best way in which British interests might be secured. In the case of the Federation the British were motivated by the fear that, as one Colonial Office man recollected, 'either it was set up, or Southern Rhodesia would go into South Africa'. This was encouraged by Southern Rhodesia's frequent and effective lobbying missions to London in the late 1940s.[19]

Tradition was helpful; and since tradition could be modified in the light of experience it is not hard to see how, even in their most difficult moments, the British were also able to avoid the danger of *hubris*: when ideology was applied more strictly and formally, then it resulted in a weakening of the imperial bond, as the experience of the Anglo-Irish Treaty and its subsequent fate revealed. It was significant that when Britain was faced with Eire's decision to break the last links with the Commonwealth in 1949, Attlee's government considered, but rejected, proposals of making Irish nationals living in Great Britain into foreigners, depriving them of voting rights, and making life difficult for the new Republic (and, in many ways, for Britain as well).

British thinking about the empire was not confined to matters of political and constitutional relations. It was, equally crucially, directed towards putting the empire to work as part of a British post-war recovery strategy. An *Oxford Pamphlet on World Affairs*, published in February 1944, and reprinted in May, claimed that:

> The natural resources of the Empire are comparable to those of the United States and the USSR., but unlike them they are far more widely dispersed, and are not under the control of one political unit, facts which to some extent affect their potential value.

With this reservation the author noted that 'as everyone realises, the resources of the Great Powers are playing a decisive part in the present war, and there is little doubt that they will prove one of the dominating factors in the reshaping of the post-war world'.[20]

But despite Joseph Chamberlain's original design of developing the imperial estate, Britain had done little to assist her colonies, contenting herself with the Colonial Development Act in 1929 which was meant to help service the loans required to develop what were in most cases conditions of extreme backwardness and poverty. The idea of partnership was given a new urgency in the Second World War, and in 1940 a Bill to give colonies grants for 'development and welfare' on the lines of the 1929 Act, but on a more generous scale, was passed. This was followed by the Colonial Development and Welfare Act of 1945. These Acts originated from a mixture of altruistic and selfish motives. They were at the mercy of the time and effort that Colonial Office staff were willing to give to problems of empire. The 1929 Act had suffered from the defect that the poverty of the places to which it was applied was hardly likely to attract private investment. The 1940 Act promised a substantial increase in British Government loans after the war,[21] and substantial sums were made available by the Treasury, possibly as much as £560 million in grants and loans between 1946 and 1964. But the use of this money was left to the discretion of the colonial governments, which concentrated on transport, education, health and the like rather than developing the means of production.[22] In August 1943 a Colonial Office memorandum drew attention to a 'general uneasiness about the slow tempo of action under the Colonial Development and Welfare Acts. We have an alibi, becoming a little worn with use, in war conditions; but I am increasingly dubious whether things will be very much better after the war without radical changes in the present procedure.'[23] 'When the war is over', the memorandum continued, 'we shall be asked where our plans are, and the answer is likely to be somewhat embarrassing.'[24]

The memorandum raised a central point of great importance for imperial thinking in the postwar world. It claimed that private investment was the most effective means of developing colonial economies; but it acknowledged that 'all the signs are that the conditions are not going to be the same. State regulation will be imposed by "priority" requirements, by wide-spreading international economic agreements and by the difficulties of securing private finance even if it is not desired for internal reasons.' The state must therefore find a 'far bigger proportion' of money, for some private investors would not risk their capital in doubtful colonial ventures.[25]

In November 1944 Oliver Stanley, Secretary of State for the Colonies, reviewed the idea of colonial development and concluded that, whatever the cost:

> My feeling is that in the years to come, within the Commonwealth and Empire, we have an opportunity which may never recur, at a cost which is not extravagant, of setting the Colonial Empire on lines of development which will keep it in close and loyal contact with us.[26]

This meant spending government money; but this had to be balanced against the question of how much money Britain could afford to spend; as John Anderson, Chancellor of the Exchequer remarked rather tartly in reply to Stanley's memorandum, 'any increase in assistance under the Colonial Development and Welfare Act is, in fact, an addition to the adverse balance of payments which we have got to correct'. Anderson recognised 'the desirability of making some substantial gesture to justify ourselves before world opinion as a great colonial power and also to reassure the Colonies themselves as to our intentions'. Therefore he offered the concession of extending the period of the Act to give it a ten-year run. But this in itself involved substantial expenditure; and 'after all, £11 million per annum is not a trifling figure for the taxpayers of this country to meet after the war for a purely external payment and I feel that the Colonies should be content with this'.[27]

Anderson's reply made the vital point that Britain had to look after her own interests when the war ended; the colonies could not be her main priority. But the argument could be turned the other way. If Britain wanted to rectify her economic problems, she might then use the empire in partnership as a means of so doing. There was a cost–benefit theory underlying Anderson's memorandum; and cost–benefit, though never absent from British imperial considerations, must loom larger in the economic climate of the post-1945 United Kingdom. The Treasury pressed the Colonial Office hard to devise new ways of eliciting economic advantages from the colonies. The empire might earn dollars for the sterling area and thus ease Britain's own financial hardship. The colonies were to be encouraged to increase primary production. Sir Stafford Cripps warned a conference of African governors, in November 1947, that there was 'a very heavy adverse balance of dollars running at the rare rate of between £600 and £700 millions a year for the sterling area'. In discussing what he called the 'tremendous unbalance', Cripps told the governors that the 'great gravity of the common danger should be realised' and emphasised the need 'for every unit in the sterling area to make the greatest possible contribution to overcoming it'. Cripps' solution was for Britain to sell her goods in the right markets, 'from which we can get an immediate return in the form of essential foodstuffs and raw materials'. Therefore, the 'development of Africa' was 'absolutely vital'. The economies of Western Europe and Tropical Africa were 'so closely interlinked in mutual trade, in the supply of capital and in currency systems that the problems of overseas balance are essentially one'. The 'further development of African resources is of the same crucial importance to the rehabilitating and strengthening of Western Europe as the restoration of European productive power is to the future progress and prosperity of Africa. Each needs, and is needed by, the other.'

But there were, Cripps pointed out, difficulties involved in realising this development policy. The very goods that Britain needed for colonial development – rails, locomotives, port facilities – were what Britain needed for her own rehabilitation as well.[28] This made it hard to plan ahead. The Government was nonetheless determined to use the colonies to promote economic recovery; development was not necessarily the main goal, at least, not when it came to make up leeway in shortages of vital materials at home. The Labour Government's colonial thinking was inseparable from its necessity to revive the home economy, and the scheme for growing groundnuts in Tanganyika was one of the outcomes of this urgent necessity. There was a world shortage of oils and fats, and the Minister of Food, John Strachey, told men working on the project that it depended 'more than any other single factor whether the harassed housewives of Great Britain get more margarine, cooking fats and soap in the reasonable near future'.[29] Sir Stafford Cripps believed that the groundnuts scheme was not the Government's sole answer; indeed, 'we are interested in every method and device that will yield a few thousand tons more of any valuable crop or material'.[30] But Cripps then made a point which revealed the difficulties involved. He wanted 'a quick and extensive development of African resources'. But the key words were 'quick' and 'development'. The groundnuts scheme was slower to work, and much more expensive than had been anticipated; the work of clearing the ground for planting turned out to be much more difficult than had been anticipated. And the question of what 'development' meant was an important one. It did not necessarily mean modern industrial development; if that were pushed 'too far or too quickly', then 'with the present world shortage of capital goods it is not possible to contemplate much in the way of industrial development in the Colonies'. Steel, for example, would be 'better used both from a world point of view as well as from the point of view of the colonies themselves in doing our utmost to increase the supplies of foodstuffs and raw materials'. The colonies, he concluded, 'can make their contribution to the [increasing capital resources] by reducing demands for unnecessary current consumption and directing some of their own earnings to capital purposes'.[31]

The idea of development was one theme of the post-war British Empire; and it was one closely linked with Britain's perceived key role in checking the spread of communism throughout the world. If the poverty, unemployment and deteriorating living conditions of masses of people were an invitation to communism, then for ideological reasons also it was essential to try to improve the lot of Britain's colonial subjects. This was as true in Asia and the Middle East as it was in Africa; the empire of control through influence was as much part of this far-flung battle line as were the directly governed colonial possessions. The idea was floated of an 'economic partnership' in the Middle East through the encouragement of the states to draw up development plans. Early in 1950 the Foreign Secretary, Ernest Bevin, pushed forward what became known as the Colombo Plan. A conference held in Colombo was aimed at strengthening links between Britain and her new Asian members of the Commonwealth, and preventing communist advance in the Far East and South-East Asia. If carefully prepared plans were drawn up, then the United States of America might be persuaded to help with men, money and materials.[32] Ernest Bevin pointed out in December 1950 that 'there was a population of 25 million in Egypt and the Sudan, and with the assistance of water-power in Uganda it should be possible, if the friendly cooperation of these peoples was secured, to develop industries in the Nile Valley which would raise the standard of living in peace and provide a valuable industrial potential for war'.[33]

This was a consideration based upon the supposition that Britain was, and would remain, a great power – the strongest, certainly, of the European powers outside the USSR. But it would be wrong to characterise British Labour attitudes to empire as purely those of world power politics. Labour did set itself the task of modernising the societies that Britain ruled, especially in Africa, where the slowness to develop was attributed to poor educational facilities. The expression 'community development' took hold, fostering ideas of local initiative, local self-help (with official priming), better education, the encouragement of responsible trade unions, and a general raising of enthusiasm for more progressive approaches to economic, social, racial and educational issues. The idea of the empire as one with common citizenship rights was regarded as a real and indeed imperative goal, protecting as it did Britain from criticism of her imperial sway, and protecting also the free world from the propagandist attacks of communism; and also, of course, demonstrating consistency in British imperial thinking, for while individuals and even institutions might operate bars and restrictions on grounds of colour or race, this was never accepted as official policy – certainly not by the Labour Party, which was increasingly hostile to South Africa on grounds of her racial policies and her disruptive potential when Britain came to defend her relations with South Africa in the United Nations.[34]

These developments were the consequence of a Labour Government coping with the consequences of the Second World War and the postwar challenge of remaining a great power, and struggling at the same time to cope with economic shortages at home. In retrospect, the discrepancy between these two goals, or even the pretensions of the first and the realities of the second, seem to make nonsense of both. But it was hard for British politicians to free themselves from the assumptions that Britain had a key role to play in the Cold War, and harder still to abandon the idea that the empire was and would remain an asset. A memorandum on 'The United Kingdom in South East Asia and the Far East', prepared for the Cabinet by the Under-Secretary of State's Committee in the Foreign Office in October 1949, declared enthusiastically that, in the region, 'In all fields, economic and military – the Commonwealth countries of Asia, with the United Kingdom and Australia and New Zealand, present a nucleus on which to build'.[35] It was still a central reference point in British foreign policy; it was what made her friendship and alliance valued in the world. Thus, when the *Round Table* considered the idea of a parliament of Europe, and the whole question of the United Kingdom and European integration, it saw no conflict 'between an obligation to the Commonwealth and Empire and closer unity with Europe'; on the contrary, a united Europe 'which excludes Great Britain would be dominated by Germany'.[36] The Commonwealth and Empire could be mobilised for many different purposes, strategic and economic; and it could, indeed must, be seen as a living, working entity. This was no empire, crumbling because of its immobility, locked in time, vulnerable to the volatile new post-war world. On the contrary, the empire was still seen in long-term perspective. In the longer view the empire had evolved into the Empire/Commonwealth; the coming to independence of the Indian subcontinent, of Malaya, of the Gold Coast, could be easily reconciled with the sense that, historically, this was perfectly compatible with the maintenance of imperial power; or, if not power, then influence. Nicholas Mansergh, in his *The Commonwealth and the Nations*, spoke for official opinion when he commented on the admission of Ceylon to the Commonwealth in February 1948. He quoted Lord Addison, who remarked that:

> this is the first occasion in which a colony, developing the system of self-government of its own accord, has deliberately sought to become a Dominion state in our Commonwealth ... but we hope and expect that it will not be the last.

Mansergh remarked that:

> The impression of orderly progress so notably absent when the Irish Free State, India, and Pakistan acquired Dominion Status is given felicitous expression in the preamble to the Defence and External Affairs Agreements between the United Kingdom and Ceylon: 'Whereas Ceylon has reached the stage in constitutional development at which she is ready to assume the status of a fully responsible member of the

British Commonwealth of Nations, in no way subordinate in any aspect of domestic or external affairs, freely associated and united by common allegiance to the Crown.'[37]

These words echoed the Balfour statement and the Statute of Westminster of 1926 and 1931 respectively; continuity was preserved, and the empire, a long time in evolving, had time and room to evolve still. Or so it might seem.

Whatever the empire lacked in terms of resources, development and the like, British statesmen were not short of ideas. It might be said that the pragmatism provided the secure underpinning of the ideas: thus the Crown, so central to the whole Empire and Commonwealth identity, was challenged by India's declaration of Republican status; and then reconstituted by the idea that India could, indeed must stay in the Commonwealth, for, anyway, its members were all in a sense constitutional monarchies, and thus, in a sense, Republics in all but name.[38] This might be to weaken the Commonwealth definition so much as to render it dangerously close to incoherence. In February 1953 Lord Salisbury minuted that, if small countries 'inhabited by primitive people' were ever to become full members of the Commonwealth club, and were to numerically dominate it by their votes, 'they would, I am sure, rapidly destroy the Commonwealth and the whole influence for good which it exercises in the world'.[39] But this flexibility offered a way forward; the rope of empire had broken, only to have a knot tied in it, and the rope made strong – possibly even stronger – through this exercise in making ideas fit the facts; in using reflections on what was taking place as the basis for concepts of empire. This was indeed to place imperial thinking on a pretty sure footing. And there were other ways of making it even more sure-footed. The British began to think in terms of what they called 'nation building'. Community development was, after all, aimed at breaking down the confines that tribal experience set around Africans; educational policies, the encouragement of local participation in social, economic and, to a limited extent, political life would widen horizons and provide the basis for the making of nations; which, in a very long time scale, might be moved towards greater degrees of self-government. Cyprus, for example, long before it became a major trouble spot, was seen by the British as an example of what must be done by way of making progress towards self-government, and ceasing to regard Cypriots as 'unfit' for such a goal: one official noted that Cyprus was 'both geographically and politically ... in the front line as a test of the sincerity of

H.M.G.'s declared policy of political development in the Colonies'.[40] Africa would take much longer; indeed, Africans generally were regarded as highly unfit for self-government. But here again, the idea that the British were in the business of encouraging political and economic conditions appropriate to constitutional progress was important, though it is possible to treat it with caution, if not cynicism.

Conservative thinking about the empire did not at this time differ markedly from that of the Labour Party. There was the mutual agreement that it must be the object of British policy to encourage 'the greatest possible development of Empire trade'.[41] There was the general commitment to move the empire towards self-government, but at a pace to be decided by the mother country, and on the Conservative as well as Labour side this was qualified by a reluctance to admit that the goal of self-government was suitable for all territories; this struck a chord with L. S. Amery's concern that not all territories were capable of being regarded as advancing towards self-government at the same pace, or to the same end: some, like Malta, would require imperial control of vital interests as was the case in federal systems.[42] This concern about the future of small, non-viable lands was felt by the Conservative Government that replaced Labour in October 1951. The idea of the multi-tiered empire, what one Colonial Office official called the 'special class of Commonwealth country which has complete control over its internal affairs, but which leaves the United Kingdom Government responsible for its external affairs and its defence', seemed feasible. Oliver Lyttelton, Colonial Secretary from October 1951 until July 1954, and Alan Lennox-Boyd, who held the post from July 1954, were far from anxious for change, with Lyttelton referring to the need for what he called a '*mezzanine*' status, with the task of self-government confined to a kind of home rule; these second-class members of the Commonwealth might be placed in a second division, called 'states of the Commonwealth' or 'Colonial Council'.[43]

Yet, though this seemed to differ from the Labour Government's more radical policy, there was still the fact that policy was secreted in the interstices of administration; and that the broad idea of moving colonial territories towards self-rule, however slowly and limited, could not be stopped in its tracks, or even resisted too strongly. When taking up the problem of the Gold Coast, which Attlee's Government had launched on the road to self-government, the Conservatives found themselves pushed along by the expertise of the Colonial officials who were confident that the case of the Gold Coast was one of vital importance for the

whole future of the empire. Once again, the idea of change and continuity was important in making change seem not so much irresistible,
as acceptable, indeed manageable. The idea of inducting local political
élites into power, of giving them steadily advancing experience, was too
deeply embedded in imperial practice to be regarded as novel, dangerous or bad. When the Cabinet discussed this transfer of power, it was
aware of the implications of creating a state in which there were prime
ministers and cabinets. Such words were not merely empty terms; on the
contrary, they foreshadowed the notion of responsible government, and
of conferring great authority on the nationalist leader Nkrumah. Winston Churchill, in particular, was anxious about this; but in 1953 the
issue had already moved beyond the kind of tutelage that the Cabinet
had in mind. It was difficult to see how the movement towards self-
government on a greater scale, once set going, could be checked too
drastically, and the principle of government by consent maintained: the
concept of a divided empire (but not a separating one) remained firmly
placed in Colonial Office thinking. The Cabinet was still anxious about
the style of an African Government, and especially the danger of handing over control of the forces of law and order to an untried, and possibly
authoritarian, administration.[44] But, again, there was the sheer logic of
constitutional change and development; the imperial power might have
limits set in its mind beyond which it would prefer not to advance; but
the process of change was itself unsettling. Ambitious African politicians
could hardly be restrained from seeing each step as simply that – a step
towards the next one, and the next step would then lead on to more
ambitious designs. To use the phrase employed by Robert Lowe when
he opposed the passing of the second Reform Bill in 1866–7, those who
initiated reform were like a man who set a stone rolling down a hill, and
thought he would fix in his mind the point at which it could be brought
to rest.[45] And though it is true that between 1951 and 1957 'not a single
Colonial Office territory attained independence',[46] and that troublesome colonies, such as Malaya, Kenya, Uganda, British Guiana and
Cyprus were dealt with by force, yet the Gold Coast remained central
and, as it turned out, prophetic. In 1956 Nkrumah won his third general
election victory; there could be no doubt that it was safer to decolonise
than to try to delay the process, especially since there was in place a civil
service that had shown it could work well with Europeans, and especially
too as the British believed that they could protect their economic
interests better through granting, rather than withholding, full self-
government.[47]

This experience, as always, ran the risk of provoking a deep debate about what the Commonwealth was, and where it was going, if an African territory was to take its place beside the white-dominated South Africa (itself anxious about the admission of a black country to the Commonwealth). And the Cabinet shared these misgivings, though for different reasons. In December 1954 the Cabinet discussed the implications of living with a non-white Commonwealth, and one in which the new states would not allow Britain to pursue the policy of 'federalism' in the division of powers between the home rule government and the imperial power. It looked as if the Commonwealth would still consist of equal states, equal in their powers if not otherwise. This was a matter of regret to the Cabinet, because

> The admission of three Asiatic countries to Commonwealth member-
> ship had altered the character of the Commonwealth, and there was
> great danger that the Commonwealth relationship would be further
> diluted if full membership had to be conceded to the Gold Coast and
> other countries... it was unfortunate that the policy of assisting depend-
> ent peoples to attain self-government had been carried forward so fast
> and so far.[48]

But there was a counter-argument, and one put in a Colonial Office memorandum in January 1955. The Colonial Office forecast that the Central African Federation, the Federation of Nigeria, the Gold Coast, the Malayan Federation and the West Indian Federation would have achieved 'a fully independent status and become candidates for full Commonwealth membership'. There was much to be gained for the United Kingdom if all these countries were held together in Common-wealth membership – the sterling area, defence potential and the ability of the United Kingdom to prevent new countries from falling under the influence of 'hostile powers'. The Commonwealth was the only effective international organisation which 'links together in an intimate associ-ation both European and non-European peoples', thus providing a 'valuable bridge' between the West and Asia, and it could do the same for Africa. What held them together was not ties of blood, nor their allegiance to the Crown, but their common 'traditions, methods of gov-ernment and political institutions'. This gave them a broad similarity of approach to international affairs. The suggestion that there should be a 'two-tier' Commonwealth was rejected: the tests for membership of the upper tier were not absolute, but matters of judgement. Not all the countries now represented at meetings of the Commonwealth Prime Ministers would qualify for the upper tier (for example, Ceylon). Some new candidates for Commonwealth membership would be reluctant to accept the inferior status of second-tier membership. The lower tier might end up being based on a colour distinction. Colonial territories might be driven into the arms of the USSR; if they became members of the United Nations they would hardly be content with inferior status in the Commonwealth.

But the large argument was that such a division would jeopardise the 'essential purpose' of the Commonwealth – 'to develop a community of outlook among all Commonwealth members on the main international problems of the day'. As countries began to develop their foreign relations they would need help and advice; it was important that they should look to the Commonwealth for these, and they could be prevented from being drawn into other power blocs. The Commonwealth question was raised, in particular, by the admission of the Gold Coast to full Commonwealth membership. South Africa was critical of this, and indeed of Britain granting self-government to the Gold Coast in the first place. But a decision to refuse full admission to the Gold Coast would produce a rift between the old members of the Commonwealth and the Asian members. 'A decision based, or thought to be based, on a denial of racial equality might well lead to a disruption of the Commonwealth as we know it today.'[49]

The Commonwealth Relations Office, for its part, nearly stumbled into an uncharacteristically theoretical distinction between what was termed 'self-government within the Commonwealth' and 'Membership of the Commonwealth'. This distinction was based on the idea that it was the responsibility of the British to advance colonial territories towards self-government; but that admittance to full membership of the Commonwealth of these territories, once self-governing, depended on the consent of the other Commonwealth members.[50] This distinction, however, was less abstract than it first appeared. It was a response to the concerns of South Africa which was uneasy about the admission to the Commonwealth of states which, Dr Malan complained in June 1953, were planning complete African domination. Malan suggested that the old colonial powers, France, Belgium and Portugal, should meet and together work out an 'African charter.'[51] Three years later South Africa pushed the argument further, declaring that full self-government within the Commonwealth meant that membership of such unsuitable territories was a *fait accompli* which South Africa could not but accept. This neat use of the English way of thinking and arguing angered

Anthony Eden, but it served to ease the Empire/Commonwealth into the new era of multi-racial, egalitarian membership, though this was not South Africa's intention. Another milestone had been passed, even though that was not appreciated at the time.

What Britain did appreciate in the early 1950s was that she was a key actor in the Cold War; that her defence arrangements involved the empire; and that she aspired still to fulfil Churchill's doctrine that her foreign policy involved her in three interlocking circles: the Empire, the Anglo-American 'special relationship' and Europe. The concept of Empire, therefore, was deeply influenced by this broad strategy, and in turn influenced it: certain key bases, such as Cyprus, must not be relinquished: there was anxiety and frustration at India's neutrality, and her critical stance on British colonialism; though Sir Norman Brook took comfort in the reflection that the policy of non-alignment was a 'personal fad of Mr. Nehru's rather than a fixed pre-disposition of the Indian people'.[52] The Sudan was granted independence on 1 January 1956, because of considerations of Britain's role in the Middle East; Malaya caused difficulties in that Britain was at one and the same time trying to meet her military commitments in pacifying a guerrilla war and also to prepare, in 1950, for a global conflict with the Soviet Union.[53]

Both Labour and Conservative Governments were, therefore, involved in a phase when Empire was more essential to their concept of the British international role than at any time in her history. The British Empire was, if not a super-power, then a major one. This meant that British notions of the kind of time scale through which colonies would move towards full self-government would be influenced by pressing international claims and considerations. Yet British statesmen brought to these claims and considerations ideas which could be adapted to changing circumstances. They showed a remarkable ability to take decisions that they believed were not entirely selfish, but were compatible with being a great power and also a trustee for nation building in their colonial lands. As Ernest Bevin put it in August 1950:

in our own dependent territories His Majesty's Government are pursuing an enlightened policy of progress towards self-government within the Commonwealth, while seeking to improve the social and economic welfare of the people. That the policy pursued by His Majesty's Government has been the right one, there can be no doubt, and our support of nationalism in South and South-East Asia provides the best possible counter to communist subversion and penetration.[54]

balance of considerations that ushered the Labour and then rvative Governments on towards granting Malaya full self-nt by 1957.

Between 1945 and 1955 the United Kingdom was led by two Prime Ministers, Attlee and Churchill. Of the two, Churchill was of course the more imperialist in this background and belief; in 1941 he told the House of Commons that restoring independence to conquered Europe was 'quite a separate problem from the progressive evolution of self-governing institutions in the regions and peoples which owe allegiance to the British Crown'.[55] His objection to Indian self-government endured until the end. In December 1948 Attlee described him as going 'off the deep end with his usual attitude on Indian matters'.[56] But even Church-ill accepted that the imperial relationship was altering. When General Smuts complained about India's being allowed to remain within the Commonwealth even though she was a Republic, Churchill replied that:

> When I ask myself the question, 'Would I rather have them in, even on these terms, or let them go altogether?' my heart gave the answer, 'I want them in'. And to Lord Salisbury who also rebuked him, Churchill responded prophetically, 'I am glad you realise that the clock cannot now be put back. "The moving finger writes . . . ".'[57]

Churchill believed in the necessity of 'the consolidation of the British Commonwealth and what is left of the former British Empire'[58] rather than a deep and increasing European commitment. The decade after the end of the Second World War was a vital one in British perceptions of her imperial role, because they were years when Britain was at the centre of the bi-polar world created by the confrontation between the USSR and the United States of America. As Nicholas Mansergh (no power-hungry Hobbesian, but rather a Lockean Whig in his political views), put it, 'in the protracted aftermath of the Second Word War it is inevitable that men everywhere should be profoundly concerned, with problems of security and defence'.[59] Mansergh characteristically suggested a partnership between South-East Asia and Britain, and between what he called 'East' and 'West' (by which he meant Asia, and the European and their American allies) as the best means of attaining this security.

Partnership summed up the latest twist in official thinking about the empire after 1945. It was a resonant expression, suggesting as it did a certain kind of equality; yet allowing for the superior power to define the partnership, the terms on which it rested, and the time when – if ever – it might be re-negotiated. It was a word especially appropriate to the English vocabulary of empire: its very imprecision was its greatest strength. It could enable the colonial power to thread its way between the rocks of responding to colonial European populations' demands for imperial protection and security, and the need, perhaps, to set this aside, or at least to modify it, if the occasion demanded.[60] Its chief defects arose from its virtues: was partnership an end in itself, or a means to an end; and if the latter, to what end? Who were the 'partners' to be? Were some African communities likely to prove more easily subsumed into the partnership principle than others? Were there loyal and disloyal African nationalists? Could the disloyal be isolated, even maintained in a kind of political quarantine?

But, for the first decade after the Second World War, it seemed that the empire had indeed discovered a new vitality, through its tradition of devolving power to those ready for it, and the new concept of an empire of partnership which Britain would establish with her African territories in particular. But by the end of that ten-year period a British Government was to undertake a military operation that was to be seen as a defining moment of empire. Lord Milner had spoken grandly of his concept of the British Empire, that great sphere of British influence extending from the centre of East Africa, through to the Sudan, Egypt, Aden and the Persian Gulf to India.[61] India was from 1947 no longer part of that great vision, but Britain's role east of Suez remained; her pillar of empire in the Middle East had to be supported; and the English capacity for adaptation met its severest test yet.

7

PILLARS OF EMPIRE: THE MIDDLE EAST

The British Empire in the Middle East was relatively recent, and differed in important respects from other imperial possessions. Except for Egypt there was little direct imperial government, but rather a series of treaties entered into by Britain to defend her influence in the Persian Gulf; and that interest was stimulated by the need to defend thereby another interest, that of the routes to India, especially after the opening of the Suez Canal in 1869. The Canal was not the only route to India; there were the overland routes via the north Syrian desert, the Euphrates Valley and the Persian Gulf; and another via Alexandria, Suez town and the Red Sea. There was also the sea route by way of the Cape.[1] But the Canal downgraded these alternative routes, despite its disadvantages; for the Canal was highly vulnerable, and might be seized by an enemy such as France. Moreover, the Canal exposed Britain to more dangers; the Russian threat to the Turkish empire was ever-present, and the hopes entertained of sustaining that empire against Russian depredations were slender. Britain's stake in the area was illustrated by Disraeli's purchase, in 1875, of 177,000 out of 400,000 Suez Canal ordinary shares. Then there were commercial considerations; cotton was a particularly valuable crop grown in Egypt and the principle which Lord Cromer, who, as Agent and Consul-General, bore responsibility for Egyptian affairs between 1883 and 1907, laid down – that 'administration and commercial exploitation should not be entrusted to the same hands'[2] – was violated. The Egyptian Treasury's grant of contracts and concessions ended in bankruptcy, and the establishment of dual control by the British and the French in order to restore solvency to Egypt. In 1882, motivated, at least ostensibly, by the need to protect her route to

India, and alarmed by an Egyptian nationalist revolt led by an army officer, Arabi Pasha, Gladstone's Liberal Government sent a small fleet to Alexandria, bombarded the city, and landed a military force which quickly overcame the Egyptian army.

Britain became directly involved in the politics of the Middle East; yet she was anxious not to entangle herself too deeply in the affairs of Egypt. Lord Cromer, who was a student of past empires, looked for lessons from the Roman and Greek experiences. He had no doubt that one of the key purposes, perhaps the key purpose, of imperial rule was to bring order out of chaos. The Roman Emperor Augustus, he wrote in 1910, 'put a stop to those frequent changes of officials which did an infinite amount of harm to the Roman, as they have in our day to the Ottoman, Empire'.[3] Augustus created a 'regular civil service', removed corruption from the courts, appointed governors who 'took a real interest in the well-being of the provincials'.[4] Cromer set his own example by remaining in Egypt for a long time; but he also insisted that the British were essential to keep order. If the British did not keep order then there was, some officials believed, the danger that France would move in. This quest for law and order involved the British in some hard fights, notably the reconquest of the Sudan after the extinction of a British–Egyptian army in 1884, and the death of General Gordon in Khartoum. The Sudan was finally subdued in 1898 by Lord Kitchener and his conquering army.

The British and the French engaged in mutual rivalry in Egypt; but they agreed to administer the country through a condominion in 1899. The British presence remained, yet the British were torn between their acknowledgement of their needs to control Egypt and their desire not to govern it for ever. Lord Milner in 1919 declared that 'Egypt is truly the nodal point of our whole imperial system. But is it, therefore, necessary that we should own it? Is it not sufficient if we have a firm foothold there?'[5] The desire to get the best of both worlds inspired the 1922 constitution which gave Britain control over four main areas of policy vital to her interests: the security of the Canal; defence; the protection of foreign interests; the integrity of the Sudan. Thus did Britain concede her protectorate rule over Egypt, and yet remain in control, it was hoped, of Egypt's destiny.

The First World War considerably augmented the British Empire in the Middle East, adding Transjordan as a mandated territory, which Britain separated from Palestine in 1921, and then established as an Arab kingdom in alliance with Britain in 1923. Palestine was also handed over to Britain as a mandated territory. Iraq was also made a mandated territory in 1920 and Britain sought and obtained an influence over Iran through a treaty arrangement. The importance of the Middle East was enhanced after 1918 by the oil supplies of the region. By 1921, therefore, the Middle East was central to British imperial thinking, which combined the traditional concerns about the route to India with the contemporary need to safeguard oil supplies.

The Middle East presented Britain with the most difficult and intractable of her imperial responsibilities. She found herself in 1917, for good reasons, offering a 'national home' to the Jews in Palestine, despite the fact that there were only some 67,000 Jews there as against some 600,000 other peoples, mostly Muslim. This 'Balfour Declaration' became more difficult to stand over in the 1930s, when persecution of European Jews increased Jewish emigration to Palestine, and Arab fears of the consequences. But the British Government believed that any attempt to set up a Jewish state in Palestine, and thus partition the country, and give the 'non-Palestinian Jews of Central Europe' better opportunities for emigration, would fail. The area of the state alone could not support a high degree of new immigration; the British would still be responsible for the protection of minorities; and the question would arise whether or not British troops would have to be used to 'prevent all the conflicts which seem to lie so close beneath the surface of an enforced partition'.[6]

The outbreak of the Second World War made the problem even more complex, as the British did not wish to alienate non-Jewish opinion in this vital region, and elsewhere in the Middle East, and sought to limit Jewish immigration, only to incur the wrath of Jewish leaders, including influential interests in the United States of America. When the Cabinet met to review its position in Palestine, on 8 July 1946, the Foreign Secretary, Ernest Bevin, noted with a degree of irritation that an Anglo-American Committee of Inquiry, including on the British side Herbert Morrison and Sir Norman Brook, had 'given us no guidance . . . beyond stating that the constitution should be such that mere numerical majority should not give one race the power to dominate the other. They volunteer no suggestion how this result is to be achieved, but admit that their proposal is likely to result in an almost indefinite period of trusteeship.' But, Bevin went on, 'any such arrangement must surely be dismissed as impracticable'. The British were already holding the position, in so far as they were holding it at all, by force of arms, and this would only be made worse if the report was implemented. 'On the one side, we shall have incurred the undying hostility of the Arabs; on the other, we shall still be subjected by the Zionists, in Palestine and in America, to pressure in favour of an ultimate Jewish State and we shall still have to face the problem of illegal immigration, which, at the last, we know ourselves powerless to control.'[7]

Bevin neatly called on the post-war anti-imperial United Nations charter to support his argument. Any draft trusteeship agreement would be 'open to serious challenge' as contravening the United Nations' article laying down one of the bases of trusteeship as that of the 'progressive development towards self-government or independence of the inhabitants of the Trust Territories in accordance with the freely-expressed wishes of the people concerned'. Bevin considered the alternatives, rejecting the idea of rule on the basis of parity as 'one administered by a bureaucratic government under the aegis of the machine-gun', and opting instead for the creation of what he termed a 'semi-autonomous area under a central Trustee Government', giving each community charge of its own area, and ending the present requirement of the British trying to be forever even-handed between the two groups. This would have the advantage that the mandate would remain unaltered, 'our strategic position in Palestine would remain exactly as it is at present, and we should continue to have at our disposal all the facilities which we now enjoy'. The United States could not object, since the British could permit its desired admission of 100,000 Jewish immigrants who would be confined 'to a definite and comparatively small compartment of Palestine', and thus reassure Arab fears about being displaced or submerged. The choice of coming closer together in a kind of federation, or of definite partition, would be left open to the parties concerned.[8]

Bevin's concern, and irritation, about the role of the United States in this problem initiated what was to be a British anxiety for the rest of the century: the proper and most fruitful role for Britain to adopt in her relations with America, and her response to increasing American involvement in world affairs and, therefore, in the affairs of the British Empire, and especially in the British Empire in the Middle East. The Chiefs of Staff reinforced Bevin's concern about the Anglo-American report. On 10 July 1946 they emphasised the danger to stability in the region, and in particular to Britain's interests there, if the report were adopted. They emphasised the importance to Britain of retaining the goodwill of the Arab States, because:

All our defence requirements in the Middle East, including maintenance of our essential oil supplies and communications, demand that

an essential feature of our policy should be to retain the co-operation
of the Arab States, and to ensure that the Arab world does not gravitate towards the Russians. In view of the increasing interest of the United
States in the area it is also of importance to the Americans to retain the
goodwill of the Arabs.

Defence of British interests, now that Britain had no facilities in Egypt,
and without any permanent or assured control of Cyrenaica, necessitated
full control of Palestine. Therefore, the British Army there should be
reinforced; but the Chiefs of Staff acknowledged that this would be difficult, given British commitments in Germany, India and elsewhere. It
might be necessary to recall men to the army; the operation would be
costly; and British troops might find it difficult to act against Arabs when
they, the British, had already suffered attacks from Jewish terrorists.
The Americans could hardly supply troops.[9]

A day later the Cabinet considered the overall position, and decided
that it could not support the idea of a Jewish State, but favoured instead
a compromise which would leave the way open for further advance –
either towards partition into two independent states, or towards partnership in a federal constitution. Again it was emphasised that the
support of the United States for whatever plan was adopted would be
essential; even to the point of requesting military assistance to enforce a
settlement if need be. The essential part of the whole difficulty was that
Britain had, for good reasons, made promises to both sides in the conflict, and had her obligations under the original mandate which, even
though the League of Nations was now extinct, raised what one official
called the 'political and moral obligation to bring our future policy in
Palestine before UNO'.[10]

Ernest Bevin, with characteristic forthrightness, summed up the tangle
in January 1947. The plan for provincial autonomy as drawn up by the
conference of British and American officials in July 1946, was unacceptable to Arab and Jew alike; a unitary independent state was unacceptable to the Jews; partition was unacceptable to the Arabs, and also to
the United Nations. Bevin leaned towards the Arab idea of an independent unitary state. In an Annex to his document, 'The Present Position',
Bevin asked for clear guidance from the Cabinet, a firm decision and its
'resolute enforcement'; or the mandate must be surrendered either to
the United States or to the United Nations. Yet the opinion of the Chiefs
of Staff was that Britain must stay in Palestine; and if this was the case
then one of three plans must be implemented: provincial autonomy,

partition or a unitary Arab state.[11] This was an echo of Sir Henry Wilson's opinion just after the Great War that there were certain places in the world where Britain could either 'knock the gentleman on the head' or come out; and those where she could not knock the gentleman on the head, she consequently must stay in.[12] This assumption, that Britain must stay, determined all future decisions; but these decisions proved more and more difficult to implement. The British delegation at the London Conference on Palestine, due to reopen on 21 January, must enter into serious negotiations with the Arabs, for to do otherwise would be to jeopardise Britain's relations with Iraq, Syria and 'possibly elsewhere', and 'revolutionary nationalism' would sweep the region. To concede a unitary state on democratic principles would be 'in accord with the prevailing trend of world opinion on the treatment of dependent areas'.[13]

The Chiefs of Staff again emphasised the importance of Britain retaining defence facilities in Palestine, not least because they would soon forfeit them in India; and this Palestine presence was irrevocably linked to the defence of the United Kingdom and also to the maintenance of Britain's sea communications. The need to move troops rapidly had been demonstrated by a recent deployment to Basra. They added, rather hopefully, that the military situation would be 'greatly eased if a political solution could be found which was acceptable to both communities'; but if this were not possible, then the best solution was one which appeased the Arabs.[14] Bevin warned that Britain could not impose a solution; there would be widespread disorder in Palestine, and some government or other would bring the matter before the Security Council of the United Nations as endangering 'World Peace'.[15] The Cabinet discussion showed the difficulty of conducting imperial policies in the United Nations context; but there were strong arguments that whatever was to be done must be done soon, otherwise disorder would increase and the British might stand accused of anti-Semitism.[16] Creech Jones, for the Colonial Office, endorsed the view that no policy could be pursued outside the reference of the United Nations; and if they rejected the proposal which he thought the best option – partition – then 'it will be necessary to consider whether we should not announce our intention to withdraw from a situation which will have become impossible'.[17] By 22 January the Cabinet had agreed that, failing an agreed settlement, any solution must come to the United Nations; but it was recognised that the various, conflicting and competing, British promises made in the past posed a potentially embarrassing predicament. Perhaps, then, the

British ought to hand the whole problem over to the United Nations; but, then, British military interests must be secured, and so she could not 'lightly take such a course'.[18] By 6 February, Bevin and Creech Jones stated bluntly that ten days of exploration with the representatives of the Arabs and Jews had failed to find a way forward; partition would not work, since both Jews and Arabs found it could not be reconciled with their views, and the United Nations, which must in any event approve partition, would be unlikely to do so: even the United States could not be relied on. The two ministers recommended a short period of trusteeship with the aim of 'enabling the country to achieve its independence' by building up from the bottom political institutions rooted in the lives of the people.[19] This was familiar language: evolution, trusteeship, the building up of a self-governing state. And this was to be followed by what the Minister of Defence called the reliance on 'a military alliance with an independent State when the period of Trusteeship ended, and there was no reason to suppose that this need be more difficult to obtain in Palestine than it had been in Iraq and Transjordan'.[20]

But on 22 January, Bevin and Creech Jones alerted the Cabinet to the impossibility of having the British plan accepted by the contending parties in Palestine. They considered the option of immediate evacuation of the country, but rejected this because it was a 'humiliating course', saddling the United Kingdom with moral responsibility for any subsequent bloodshed, and incompatible with the obligations that Britain undertook when she first accepted the League of Nations mandate. Britain must continue to shoulder the burden until she could submit the problem to the appropriate organ of the United Nations, 'namely, the General Assembly'. But the volume of illegal Jewish immigration would grow between now and September; the civil administration in Palestine was 'virtually a besieged garrison'; the plight of the military forces was 'little better', with the danger of reaction by British troops if Jewish terrorism continued. If the Cabinet decided to refer the problem to the United Nations, then this must be done without delay. The Government should in this event rehearse the whole history of its mandate in Palestine and explain that it was now unworkable. This proposal was adopted in Cabinet on 14 February 1947.[21] The following September, Bevin warned that the United Nations must not be allowed to propose a settlement for which the British Government could not accept responsibility, and if it did so Britain must withdraw, unconditionally if need be. Bevin consoled himself with the reflection that such a precipitate withdrawal might bring the Arabs and Jews to reach agreement, if the alternative was civil war. But if they did not, then at any rate British lives would be saved by withdrawal, and British resources would not be expended in suppressing one Palestinian community for the advantage of the other; and such a policy, at least compared with other options, would not be 'destructive of our interests in the Middle East'.[22]

The attempt by the United Nations Special Committee on Palestine to oblige Britain to enforce a form of partition fairly favourable to the Zionist cause and therefore damaging to Britain's relationship with the Arab world, caused the British Government to warn that she would withdraw her troops by 1 August 1948, at the latest on 20 September. The Minister of Defence urged the difficulties in Cabinet of trying to maintain law and order over the whole country; other ministers expressed their anxieties about the United Nations' proposal; and the Prime Minister remarked on the close parallel between the position in Palestine and the recent situation in India. He 'did not think it reasonable to ask the British administration in Palestine to continue in present conditions, and he hoped that salutary results would be produced by a clear announcement that His Majesty's Government intended to relinquish the mandate and, failing a peaceful settlement, to withdraw the British administration and British forces'.[23] Winston Churchill, who had for some time doubted the wisdom of British policy in Palestine, was left to muse on the 'element of obstinacy' that had set no time limit for British withdrawal from Palestine, but had done so with serious consequences in India; what had forced this 'particular assertion in the midst of general surrender and scuttle of British will-power in Palestine?'[24]

The British experience in Palestine might be regarded as marginal to the whole British imperial tradition; as the consequences of a mandate undertaken without any conception of how different British promises to the inhabitants of Palestine could be reconciled; and without, of course, the foreknowledge that anti-Semitism in Europe in the 1930s would result in increased Jewish immigration to Palestine, a predicament worsened by the Second World War, as Zionism used the opportunity provided by the desperate experience of Jews in Europe. But in another sense it was a serious blow to the British idea of empire for, as W. K. Hancock remarked in 1937, 'this theory is almost entirely irrelevant to the realities' of Palestine. Hancock referred to his perception of 'something pathetically naive in the reiterated complaint of the Shaw Commission (set up in 1929 to investigate Arab–Jewish disturbances, and reporting the following year) that neither Arabs nor Jews would understand the dual nature of the policy which the Palestine Government have to administer'. Hancock quoted the Commission's conclusion that 'the idea of compromise hardly exists', adding 'how could it exist? ... the will to partnership does not exist ... a hundred Lord Elgins could not under present circumstances achieve a Canadian reconciliation in Palestine, because they could not find the materials on which to work'. He asked what the British had done to create such materials, and made recommendations of his own, while noting that, even as he wrote, another commission, this time a Royal Commission, was 'engaged upon the old task of trying to find a policy in accord with the professed British principles', But he added pessimistically that such principles were not relevant to the realities of Palestine where both Arabs and Jews regarded the issue as one of survival. 'Neither community believes in its heart that it will be safe in its home unless it is master in it.' 'British policy has itself been driven.'[25]

Hancock, characteristically, cut through the rhetoric and revealed the realities of the Palestine predicament; one that turned ideas of imperial progression into mere banalities. He contrasted the Palestine experience with what he perceived as the successful creation of loyal communities that cut across such divisions in Canada and South Africa; he saw comparisons in the conflict between political nationalism in Palestine and the conflict of Unionist and Nationalists in Ireland. The collapse of the Palestine mandate which, if he did not foresee, then at any rate recognised might end badly, was a sign that the British concept of empire was not universally successful; it all depended on local political conditions, local loyalties, local hopes and fears.

And yet the British had a vital interest in the Middle East. The *Round Table*, normally the advocate of agreement and consensus, wrote in March 1947 that 'without security for oil supply in war, the Forces of the Empire will be immobilised, its communications ruptured and its cohesion lost'. Britain must stay; and the journal even linked the need for Britain to maintain the Palestinian mandate with the overall 'respect for the British character in the Middle East' which an 'abdication from the mandate' would destroy.[26] The British decision to relinquish the mandate did not, however, signal a general retreat or 'scuttle'; far from it. The British commitment to the region, for security and oil-supply reasons, remained powerful; but the question of how best to enforce British interests remained an open one. In 1945 Anthony Eden described the Middle East as 'one of the most important strategic areas in the world', the defence of which was 'a matter of life and death to the British Empire'. It was a primary British responsibility to stand there as the paramount power, though this was not incompatible with international cooperation in maintaining security there. But Britain must not 'abdicate'.[27]

The will and power to sustain this role was soon to be tested. Two main trouble spots pointed up its difficulties, and revealed how hard it was for a great power to apply its strength in conditions, political and international, with which it assumed it was familiar, but in the event was not. The first of these was the crisis in Iran between 1947 and 1951. Iran displayed all the complexities of British policy in the Middle East. The British were anxious to secure their oil supplies there, but were in agreement with the USSR that both themselves and the Russians should withdraw their troops simultaneously before 2 March 1946. The British had their eye also on the United States of America, and hoped to prevent any further American commercial penetration into the Middle East. Yet the Minister of Fuel, in October 1945, was aware of the need to get the United States to accept greater political responsibility in this area; and on that account 'we should not resist their seeking further expansion of their oil concessions as contemplated in recent discussions'.[28]

The delicate nature of British and American control of oil was soon revealed when, in April 1951, the Iranian Parliament, under the leadership of Dr Muhammad Musaddiq, approved of the unilateral nationalisation of the Anglo-Iranian Oil Company which had worked in Iran under a concession first granted in 1901. Iran, needing more revenue to finance a seven-year economic plan drawn up for 1949–56, requested a revision of its share of the company. The Foreign Secretary, Ernest Bevin, stated that he was 'not prepared to sacrifice the British Empire', especially since 'if the British Empire fell . . . it would mean the standard of life in our constituencies would fall rapidly'.[29] There was, too, much indignation amongst the British that their enterprise, skill and effort was to be taken advantage of by the Persian Government, which could not have developed the oil industry by themselves; and, above all, a fear of the consequences for British prestige and standing in the region, which must be compromised by concession.[30] Bevin's replacement as Foreign Secretary, Herbert Morrison, prepared for strong measures, and military action was contemplated. But the Government preferred negotiation, even though it supported this by imposing economic sanctions on Iran.[31] But the opinion of the United States of America must be sought, and this too was hostile to military action. The Chiefs of Staff urged intervention to ensure British interests were safeguarded and to prevent communism spreading to Iran. The British Government, faced by these conflicting pressures, opted for the less risky choice. It declared that it was willing to offer the dispute to international arbitration, and the International Court of Justice made an interim ruling, on 5 July 1951, which leaned towards the British position, but warned both sides not to do anything that would worsen the dispute. The Iranian Government rejected the ruling, and the British Government now had to consider what action it might take if the Iranian Government were to put further pressure on the Anglo-Iranian Oil Company and its employees. The first item in their discussions was military action, but this was regarded as 'undesirable' if it were to be implemented to save British property, as distinct from British lives. The United States had offered to send Averell Harriman to Tehran for discussions, and the Cabinet was anxious to impress upon him that his task should not be to mediate between Britain and Iran, but to insist that the Iranian Government comply with the decision of the International Court. The Cabinet also decided to refer the dispute to the United Nations Security Council.[32]

The British Government was anxious not to give the impression that it was about to embark on a bout of Victorian imperialistic enthusiasm. It took account of the fact that it was dealing with a nationalist movement, inspired by the corrupt character of the previous regime; the Cabinet accepted that, if negotiations were resumed, they would be resumed on the basis of its acceptance of the principle of nationalisation, and a willingness to operate the oil industry on behalf of the Iranian Government, 'on a basis of friendly partnership'. There was a sensitivity to the need not to do anything that might humiliate the Iranian Government.[33]

Nevertheless, the Government commissioned a study of the feasibility of using armed force; and the Chiefs of Staff reported on 20 July that what they called Operation Buccaneer was ready. Troops could be flown in at short notice to occupy Abadan 'against any opposition which the Persians unaided would be likely to mount'. The Chiefs of Staff asked the Cabinet to consider under what precise circumstances they would put the plan into effect; the most obvious one being a decision by the Iranians to occupy the oil refinery. Such an operation, they claimed, 'would have obvious advantages': it would enable the refinery to be kept in at least partial production; it would 'demonstrate once and for all to the Persians the British determination not to allow the Anglo-Iranian Oil Company to be evicted from Persia, and might well result in the downfall of the Mussadiq regime and its replacement by more reasonable elements prepared to negotiate a settlement'; it might be expected to 'produce a salutary effect throughout the Middle East and elsewhere, as evidence that United Kingdom interest could not be recklessly molested with impunity. Indeed', they added, 'failure to exhibit firmness in this matter may prejudice our interests throughout the Middle East'; finally, such action 'should be warmly welcomed by those sections of public opinion in this country which have been criticising His Majesty's Government's attitude over Persia as having been unduly weak'.[34]

These last two considerations were vital, and showed again, as did Palestine, that a great power with imperial pretensions found itself almost bound to take action because not to take action would reflect on its standing as a great power; which in turn would weaken its great power ambitions. The Conservatives were certain that Labour had showed less determination than was needed for Britain to secure a satisfactory outcome of this crisis. But there were objections to military operations. The Mussadiq Government, if it did not fall as a result of British military action, might appeal to the Security Council on the grounds that the British had indulged in 'aggression' against Iran; and, 'having regard to the terms of the United Nations Charter, a majority might be found for a resolution enjoining us to remove our troops forthwith'. It was a sign of the new context of an imperial power that the Cabinet acknowledged that, in this event, Britain might have to use her veto, or comply with such a resolution; and so far the British had not exercised their veto. On the other hand, International Law did not prevent a state acting to preserve life and protect its essential interests. But the American dimension was in the Cabinet's mind yet again. America, it was clear, was opposed to the use of force, and 'support of all the old Commonwealth countries cannot be assured'. There was the danger of Russian intervention; the Mussadiq regime might anyway be the author of its own downfall, as its policy had already caused economic hardship in Iran. For Britain to send troops into Iran might only render more remote the chance of a reasonable regime replacing that of Mussadiq. There was the possibility that British action might inflame Arab opinion elsewhere in the Middle East; but on the other hand, 'Arabs have little respect for the Persians', and a display of force might have a salutary effect in deterring any other would-be nationalisation policy in other Middle Eastern states.[35]

The balance of argument was still, therefore, fine; but in September 1951 the Labour Government, in its last Cabinet Meeting, decided not to resort to force in settling the dispute. The first consideration was the American attitude to a British military operation; and this was predicted as the United States' inability 'to support any action' of this kind. The United States was no more favourable to the Mussadiq regime than were the British; but they were anxious to see the dispute settled by some fresh proposal from the British Government. Attlee summed up by saying, clearly and unequivocally, that in view of the attitude of the United States Government, he did not think it would be expedient to use force to maintain the British staff in Abadan. Such action might only unite Iranian opinion behind its government, and result in the defection of Iranian workers in the refinery. The United Nations would be unsupportive.[36]

Ernest Bevin pointed out the difficulties of inaction: it was doubtful if any fresh British proposals could be made with any likelihood of success; if the remaining staff were expelled from Abadan, and the Government's handling of the dispute seemed 'feeble and ineffective', then 'the repercussions throughout the Middle East and elsewhere would be very serious'. Egypt 'might be emboldened to take drastic action to end the military treaty and possibly to bring the Suez Canal under Egyptian control, and British legal rights in many other parts of the world would be placed in jeopardy'. In these circumstances the Government must demonstrate firmness, take whatever action was necessary, and explain to the United Nations Security Council why such action was unavoidable. Such action, the Cabinet was informed, could be mounted within 12 hours; but there was the consideration that an imperial power would find it hard to gain a hearing for military force in the United Nations; the Law Officers warned that action which was not sanctioned by the Security Council would be illegal. This consideration was balanced by the view that states had the right to act in self-defence; but the United States' attitude was the vital aspect of the argument about appropriate action. Given the United States' attitude, force must be ruled out. 'We cannot afford to break with the United States on an issue of this kind.' The United States might see its way to supporting military action if it were to protect lives or stop communism; but such action might endanger British lives, and would not necessarily bring a resolution of the dispute any nearer. The best way forward was for the British to put their case strongly to the United Nations Security Council, which if it were accepted might enlist American support. But negotiations would continue, concessions would be offered to the Shah of Iran, who might dismiss Mussadiq and appoint a more 'reasonable' government. British public opinion expected strong action to be taken; but the Government was aware that this might stop short of the use of force, and it would be advantageous to the Government if it were to point out to the public and Parliament the United States' attitude to the use of military action. The Cabinet agreed to use the mechanism of the Security Council to bring pressure on Iran.[37]

The Conservative Government that succeeded Labour in October 1951 had shown impatience with Labour's handling of the dispute; but it too found itself unable to act in any different way. Sensitivity to the impact of military intervention on Britain's position in the Middle East was reinforced by the consideration that, as Eden put it in August 1952, if the British did not make fresh overtures to Iran, then the United States might make an 'independent offer of financial assistance to Persia with the object of preventing the establishment of a "Communist regime"'.[38] But American policy veered towards the British position, because the United States did fear a communist threat. The deteriorating economic predicament of Iran caused unrest not only for the Shah, who was increasingly anxious about the growing power of his Prime Minister, but the middle classes, politicians, businessmen, landowners and merchants, and the army. The British and Americans now sought material to work on to weaken Dr Musaddiq's hold on power.[39] Ann Lambton, a former press attaché in Teheran, and a person regarded by the British Government as an expert on the country, noted in June 1951 that it might be possible to give 'intelligent Iranians' well-disposed to the British the chance to 'speak out'.[40] But Musaddiq needed a push from the powers to engineer his downfall. Anthony Eden (with some misgivings) acquiesced in the American approach to the dispute; military action was not taken; and he found himself by-passed by the United States Government's expedient of using covert operations to topple Mussadiq from power and replace him by a more 'reasonable' government. Eden, for his part, noted that when this happy event was confirmed, he 'slept better that night'.[41]

The Iranian crisis was of profound importance for Britain's role in the Middle East, as a great power generally, and as a power struggling to come to terms with the changed post-war world, one characterised by the constraints imposed on unilateral action by the United Nations and, in the British case in Iran, by the rising power of the United States in the Middle East: a power exercised not through military action, or even a military presence, but by the unlimited power of America in the world, her economic superiority, her domination of the western European states, and her military potential. There was also a perception, in some quarters of the British Government at least, of the volatile force of nationalism on the region: a nationalism likely to be fuelled, rather than extinguished, by western action, especially the use of force. As one official in the Eastern Department of the Foreign Office put it in November 1943, it was essential for the British to seek to encourage, or to act in partnership with, modern Arab nationalism 'if we are not to produce a Mahdist or pan-Arab revolution, which will spread from wherever it breaks out to the whole Arab world'.[42] This latter policy was not new; British imperial power always rested in some degree on the acquiescence, if not the support, of local power élites, as the case of India revealed. But its importance was sharpened by the emerging force of nationalism after 1945; and the British experience in Palestine and Iran might be expected to confirm the conviction of the Foreign Office man who warned of the dangers of provoking irreconcilable nationalisms. After all, the British had had to leave Palestine with some ignominy, having found themselves sandwiched between Zionism and the Arab reaction to Zionism; and the Iranian dispute revealed that direct action would be more likely to result in the bolstering of a nationalistic regime rather than its demise.

The Iranian crisis and its resolution exercised an influence on British strategic thinking that was to have serious consequences. In July 1956 the Chiefs of Staff reviewed Britain's position in the Middle East from an historical and contemporary perspective. They warned that the balance of change had worked to Britain's disadvantage, producing a 'vicious circle in which a reduction in our ability to influence events leads to loss of prestige', which 'in turn creates both the incentive and the opportunity for countries hostile to us to take action harmful to our interests'. In an appendix they listed some 14 'major factors of an inflammable nature', including nationalism, the United Kingdom dependence on oil supplies from the area, the creation of the state of Israel, the loss of the Indian army through Indian independence, the failure to take a 'strong line' in the Abadan crisis of 1950–1.[43]

This trenchant criticism – Britain's failure to adopt a 'strong line' – was indispensable to the working-out of the British reaction to the next major crisis in the Middle East: Suez, 1956. British Governments were always anxious about their hold over Egypt, and since Lord Cromer's time they had hoped to exercise necessary control without becoming too deeply or directly involved in the administration of Egypt itself. The rise of Egyptian nationalism, and its flourishing after the Great War, always exercised British concern. The nationalist leader of 1920, Saad Zaghlul, provoked deep irritation in British Government circles, and was regarded as the Egyptian version of Sinn Fein; his proposal that Britain transfer her garrison from the Nile Delta to the bank of the Canal, and preferably to its eastern side, was rejected out of hand by Lord Milner as provocative to other great powers, which would be alarmed at the presence of British troops on the Canal Zone.[44] But there was also the belief that Egyptians should be given greater control and responsiblity, and the question of just how Britain could enforce her will on Egypt. Britain moved from military occupation up until 1914, a Protectorate for just over seven years and, from 1932, a period of indirect control which lasted until the signing of the Anglo-Egyptian Treaty of 1936 by which Britain agreed to withdraw its garrison from Cairo to the Canal Zone, sponsor Egypt's membership of the League of Nations, and refer any dispute over a new treaty at the end of the 20-year period to the Council of the League. This, the British Ambassador felt sure, if used with tact and firmness, would enable Britain to retain her influence over Egypt.[45] The importance of Egypt to the British was signalled by the fact that it was the largest British military base in the world, supplying troops and equipment for the Middle East, North Africa and Europe;[46] some 200,000 troops were stationed there at any one time.[47] During the Second World War Britain was active both militarily, in defeating the German and Vichy France forces, and diplomatically, in engineering the presence and security of friendly governments in Egypt and elsewhere in the region.

It is hardly surprising, then, that the Foreign Secretary, Anthony Eden, described the Middle East in 1945 as:

> an area the defence of which is a matter of life and death to the British Empire. . . . Consequently, we are bound to give the Middle East an extremely high priority when allocating our available resources to the areas where we have responsibilities. For this reason alone, we cannot afford to resign our special position in the area (even though in an emergency we may be able to accept the help of others in defending it) and allow our position to become dependent on arrangements of an international character.

Or that the Resident Minister in the Middle East should claim that, given that the Commonwealth was a 'cooperative' body 'of widely separated peoples', whose 'life and strength' depended on freedom of communications, then it could not survive if its communications were likely to be severed by a foreign power. The region was one where the 'British political method must make good if the British way of life is to survive'.[48]

And yet the demands made on Britain by the need to support the American position in western Europe and to participate fully in its defence meant that the Middle East was given a lesser role in British defence policy.[49] But despite the difficulty of maintaining adequate forces everywhere they were needed, and especially in the Middle East, the British were aware of their need to maintain a firm grip in what appeared to them to be as vital a region in the 1950s as it had been in the 1940s. Sir Pierson Dixon of the Foreign Office identified the problem in 1952 as 'the very obvious fact that we lack power'. But Britain must not accept that condition, but must 'build up our lost power'. Power consisted not only of troops and money, but prestige; and so Britain must 'make every conceivable effort to avoid a policy of surrender or near-surrender'.[50] In June 1953 Winston Churchill told the meeting of Commonwealth Prime Ministers that, despite the fact that the whole strategic importance of the Canal had lessened, yet Britain must secure the maintenance of the Canal and the Canal Zone. But he was obliged to use less than enthusiastically imperialist language. Britain had a 'profound imperial and colonial record of which we are not ashamed', but her presence in Egypt was for international, not imperial, reasons 'in the interest of the free world'. But after 'we abandoned Abadan the Egyptians had started to insist upon Britain's withdrawal from Egypt'. Britain had no desire to control Egypt, but she was not going to 'accept any solution of the problem at the expense of British humiliation; there was no question of yielding to an ultimatum'. He referred to the unwillingness of the United States to 'brush aside Egyptian objections to their participation in the discussions' – an ominous sign that the United States, in Britain's eyes, seemed not to recognise its own interests in the area.[51]

Britain, then, had no desire to infringe Egyptian sovereignty. The best way to secure her interests in Egypt, as elsewhere, was to find and support friendly regimes. But the overthrowing of King Farouk by a military coup led by General Neguib, in July 1953, seemed to present no further difficulty for this policy, though Eden, who was its chief advocate, found himself harassed at every turn by Churchill and other Conservatives who warned him against anything that smacked of 'scuttle'.[52] When Neguib was replaced by Colonel Gamel Abdel Nasser, in February 1954, Eden's instinct, and by now Churchill's, was for some kind of settlement by negotiation that would protect British interests. The Americans, for their part, watched this change of leadership with equanimity, and indeed American officials had been in contact with key figures in the original coup, including Nasser.[53] Eden, exasperated by the possibility of American involvement in what had been until now a British preserve, noted that the Americans were 'not more popular in the Middle East than we are' and that it would not be good for Britain's position in the area if she were seen as being unable to settle the matter without help from the United States.[54] The developing influence of America was seen in her determination to secure British acquiescence in withdrawing from the Suez base, which America regarded as 'more a factor of instability than stability', mediating an Anglo-Egyptian settlement, and then creating a defence system of Turkey, Pakistan and Iran on the southern border of the USSR.[55] A new Anglo-Egyptian treaty was concluded in October 1954, which withdrew British troops from the Canal Zone by 1956, with the option of re-entering the base in the event of war or other crises.[56]

The Foreign Secretary, Sir Anthony Eden, was at first favourably impressed with Nasser whom he described as 'most friendly';[57] but the context of British influence in the Middle East was to alter yet again, when Britain signed the Baghdad Pact with Turkey and Iran on 4 April 1955. This seemed to Nasser to threaten any hopes of Arab unity, but also to pose a threat to Egyptian hopes of dominating the whole Middle East area. The Arab masses were invited by Egypt to oppose 'the stooges of imperialism' and remain free from imperialist devices such as the Baghdad Pact. Nasser's hostility to the western powers was increased by their rejection of his requests for military and economic aid, a call made more pressing by the deterioration in Egyptian–Israeli relations in 1955, and especially by an Israeli attack on Egyptian installations on the Gaza Strip.[58]

The British Foreign Office, and its new Foreign Secretary, sought to arouse American hostility to Nasser; but the Americans remained unmoved, and Macmillan noted on 9 November 1955 that 'we should not write off Egypt or drive her into Russia's arms.'[59] Eden sought to manage Nasser rather than oppose him, though his views were coloured by the personal dislike that he had by now conceived for Nasser, which had overtaken his initial favourable impression. Nevertheless, the British, together with the United States, agreed in December 1955 to help finance the construction of a dam at Aswan, a vital project for Egypt which could no longer guarantee to be able to feed her own population. Eden, in Cabinet on 20 October 1955, described this policy as one of 'importance in restoring the prestige of the West . . . in our dealings with Egypt it could be a trump card'.[60]

But Britain's attitude to Nasser was shaped by her general belief that she must dominate the region; and her failed efforts to bring Jordan into

the Baghdad Pact in December 1955 was compounded by Jordan's
dismissal of General Sir John Glubb from command of Jordan's Arab
Legion in March 1956.[61] Eden was under pressure from the Conservative press for not showing sufficient firmness in his Middle East policy.
He felt more assured that the Americans appreciated Britain's point of
view; but he was confronting the difficulty that the Labour Government
had faced in Iran. To talk about firmness was one thing, but to back it
up with an aggressive policy was another. It was possible for Attlee to
talk himself out of the 'firmness' mentality; but Eden, facing criticism
at home and in his party, found himself moving closer towards implementing 'firmness'. When Anthony Nutting, Minister of State in the
Foreign Office, sought to contain Nasser through strengthening the
Baghdad Pact and constructing an Iraqi–Jordanian axis, Eden responded
with a phone call in which he referred to the 'nonsense' of Nutting's
scheme of isolating Nasser, declaring 'I want him destroyed, can't
you understand?'[62] and he believed firmly that if Britain lost out in
the Middle East she was finished. Nevertheless, Eden's weakness in
his whole Middle Eastern policy secured the Cabinet's acceptance of
Nutting's plan.[63]

By now America was more convinced that Nasser must be replaced
with a 'pro-western regime'.[64] The problem for Eden was that America
was not supporting its policy with more vigorous action. But it was pressure from the American Congress that obliged the American Secretary
of State, John Foster Dulles, to withdraw American support for the
Aswan Dam. Nasser responded by nationalising the Suez Canal, much to
the surprise of the Americans, declaring on 26 July 1956 that 'the people
of Egypt alone shall be Sovereign in Egypt'.[65] Eden's instinct was to act,
but he was warned by his Chiefs of State that, while suppressing Mau
Mau insurgents in Kenya was within Britain's capacity (as was nuclear
war) a 'little local episode' in the Middle East was outside her military
planning.[66] As with Iran in 1954, the United States urged caution. But
now the Eden Government moved its plans a stage further, and began to
look for another, and more credible, basis for intervention, with an ally
whose interests in North Africa were perceived to be under threat from
Nasser's support for rebels in Algeria – France.[67] There was also, the
Chancellor of the Exchequer, Harold Macmillan, pointed out, the possibility of cooperation with another power – Israel. Meanwhile, the British developed a powerful propaganda campaign, depicting Nasser as a
second Hitler, and claiming that only Britain could act, in the capacity in
which after all Lord Cromer had always claimed she could act, as that of

the policeman, the guarantor of order, the only barrier to anarchy in this volatile area.[68]

This kind of neo-, or perhaps more accurately bastard-, Cromerism, had much support in Britain, including that of the Labour opposition.[69] The use of force 'as a last resort' was now firmly on the table, as Eden summed the matter up in a Cabinet meeting on 28 August. Operation Musketeer was prepared under the supervision of the Chiefs of Staff, to be succeeded by Musketeer Revise, setting out detailed plans for a military operation.[70] The process of moving from plans to action took place against the background of a divided Cabinet, but the logic of acting was supported by the argument that to stand idly by would destroy British influence, not only in the Middle East but in other colonies, in Aden, Somaliland, Kenya, and Macmillan, for his part, conceived grand plans to re-cast the boundaries of the whole Middle East.[71] Yet there were still doubts; and the advocates of force sought what they had lacked so far – a pretext for intervention that would prevent any use of force being branded as an imperialist adventure; a device made all the more necessary by America's decision to rule out economic sanctions against Nasser and denounce the use of force. Britain had to make up the ground lost when she referred the dispute to the United Nations on 13 September.[72] The move towards a military strike began to take shape, with the plan of using the United Nations as a means of justifying military intervention, instead of acting as a drag on the wheels. America's opaque discussion with Macmillan on 23 September was interpreted by Macmillan as a 'determination ... to bring Nasser down'.[73] Nevertheless, Britain hesitated; force was still a last resort and its possible impact on Britain's position in the United Nations, whose charter outlawed force as a means of tackling international disputes, was an obstacle to direct action.[74] But by October the idea of military collusion between Britain, France and Israel was revived, with Eden referring to the British obligation to intervene, ostensibly to stop the Israelis attacking the Egyptians. Eden's position was by now becoming desperate, for there was the threat that, if he did not participate in the intervention option, then Israel might attack Jordan, and Britain must then support her closest Middle Eastern ally, or join in a war against France and Israel.[75] Still the British hesitated; but by 25 October Eden informed his Cabinet that 'The French Government were strongly of the view that intervention would be justified in order to limit [Egyptian–Israeli] hostilities and that for this purpose it would be right to launch the military operation against Egypt which had already been mounted.'[76]

On 29 October Israel launched an air attack on Egypt, together with a parachute drop into the Mitla Pass. The United States resolved immediately to take the issue to the Security Council of the United Nations, much to Britain's dismay; and Eden proceeded on 30 October to announce in the House of Commons that the British and French were demanding that the Israelis and Egyptians withdraw ten miles from the Suez Canal and allow British and French forces into the Canal Zone 'in order to separate the belligerents and to guarantee freedom of transit through the Canal by the ships of all nations'.[77]

This justification for intervention – as clumsy as it was false, because 'separating belligerents' was a difficult if not impossible military task, and one rarely, if ever, attempted by an army trained not to act as referee but as combatant – was one great flaw in the British plan; the second was the unwillingness of America to support Britain, and a third was the imminent danger of the collapse of Britain's currency reserves.[78] Even at the earliest stage of the crisis these were 'still falling at a dangerously rapid rate'.[79] President Eisenhower pressed in the United Nations for a cease-fire. The British went ahead with their military intervention on 31 October, on the assumption that, as Eden put it to Eisenhower, 'if we had allowed things to drift, everything would have gone from bad to worse. Nasser would have become a kind of Moslem Mussolini, and our friends in Iraq, Jordan, Saudi Arabia, and even Iran would gradually have been brought down.'[80] Twenty-four hours after the military invasion was begun, on 5 November, the Cabinet accepted that it must end. For Britain to continue her operations would be to defy the United Nations' resolution for the despatch of an emergency force, and so to defy Britain's own claim that she would cease operations when the United Nations was ready to take over these responsibilities. There was at least the possibility of Russian intervention; and the value of the pound dropped to crisis proportions. On 3 December the British and French Governments announced that they would withdraw their forces; and within three weeks Britain received nearly 2 billion (US) dollars in loans and aid.[81]

The significance of the Suez crisis for the British Empire, in the Middle East and elsewhere, is still a matter of debate. It was clearly far from the end of British influence in the Middle East. Harold Macmillan, in his first broadcast to the nation two weeks after the Anglo-French invasion of Egypt, spoke of his anxiety to be rid of 'any more defeatist talk about second-class power'.[82] In December 1956 the Chiefs of Staff recommended that Britain must sustain her treaty with Jordan as long as possible, and that she must not withdraw from Libya 'unless the United

States were prepared to take our place'.[83] In May 1958 the Cabinet discussed the possibility of abandoning Cyprus because it was of declining strategic importance, but concluded that 'our prestige throughout the Middle East would be gravely affected if we withdrew from the island at this critical juncture'.[84] Within two years, in July 1958, Britain once again intervened when a revolution in Iraq was met with action by Britain in Jordan; the United States at the same time intervened in the Lebanon, but this was not the joint operation that Macmillan claimed. It was not the end of British ambitions to play a key role in the region. When the Colonial Secretary, Lennox-Boyd, addressed a Conservative Political Centre meeting held in connection with the Conservative Party Conference at Blackpool in October 1958, he listed what he called 'fortress colonies', and included amongst them Aden and Cyprus. He stated that 'our aim is to maintain a balanced all-purpose fleet East of Suez, to discharge our obligation to SEATO and the Baghdad Pact and to carry out our Imperial responsibilities'. [85] He added that:

the hostility of Egypt and Syria has created an air barrier across the Middle East which could affect our oil supplies and our communications with the Far East. This has the effect of greatly increasing the importance of Aden and Libya for Commonwealth defence. The Colony and Protectorate of Aden are in a key strategic position. The Western States of the Protectorate are under constant Yemen pressure, and we have lately assured them of our warm support for a Federation.[86]

British aims could best be secured by diplomacy, and the payment of subsidies, rather than force. But the British Empire in the Middle East, even more than in other areas, was subject to unpredictable local political and social upheavals. The collapse of the British mandate in Palestine, the Iranian oil crisis, Suez, and the Iraqi revolution, not to mention other tensions and instabilities in the Middle Eastern states, revealed how difficult, if not impossible, it was for one power, however apparently great, to act alone in order to protect her interests. British power was susceptible to American ambitions, and when the two coincided, as in Iran, then the British eventually got what they wanted – the removal of Mussadiq. In the wake of the 1958 Iraqi revolution, when Britain sent military support to Jordan, then at least the search for influence was not penalised, even though the United States thought that Britain was 'foolishly exposed'.[87] But there was another problem. Even if intervention were possible – even if Suez had worked militarily (and it might have done) – then Britain would have found herself entangled in the business of reconstructing or, worse still, constructing, an administration favourable to her aims, but also able to govern without depending on British bayonets; for the use of force to topple and then re-create a regime was bound to arouse hostility not only in the conquered country, but throughout the Arab world. The days of one quick volley and then leaving a governor and a handful of civil servants and soldiers to manage the conquered region were long past. As Attlee acknowledged in the Iranian case, 'we could not safely assume that if we succeeded in upsetting the present government, their successors would be less unsatisfactory, and we should risk identifying ourselves with support of an equally undemocratic regime'. Nonetheless, there were in 1951 those like Macmillan, one of the chief advocates of military intervention in Egypt, who held that not to intervene in Iran would mean the 'end of the association of Britain with the development of Persian oil. It means, still more, the collapse of British power in the Middle East.'[88]

After Suez, no-one would have put the issue quite like this. But it could be put another way: that defence needs, and especially the protection of the right flank of NATO, necessitated a British presence in the Middle East, despite the cost – an average 10 per cent of Britain's gross national product – spent on defence. The Government's Command Paper on Defence went on to state that 'in the Arabian Peninsula, Britain must at all times be ready to defend Aden Colony and Protectorates and the territories of the Persian Gulf for whose defences she is responsible. For this task, land, air and sea forces have to be maintained in that area and in East Africa.' Adherence to the Baghdad Pact was essential to prevent the spread of communism in the region, and this required the readiness of British forces to support the alliance.[89]

But all these obligations, and the ambitions they represented, depended upon the support of the United States of America. The Suez crisis involved the Commonwealth only retrospectively. The Commonwealth was neither consulted nor informed of British intervention in Egypt. Australia supported it; New Zealand did, less whole-heartedly; Canada was not in favour of military action; India was totally opposed to the use of force (though critical of Nasser's actions in nationalising the Canal); Pakistan was less opposed, because of her membership of the Baghdad Pact.[90] But these views and differences only revealed that the Commonwealth had, indeed, different views and opinions; they were not vital to the Suez crisis, though they revealed that the Commonwealth was becoming less than coherent. Yet, it is arguable that this was the case as early as 1922, when it was divided over British policy in the Greek–Turkish war. The essential difference between 1922 and 1956 was that in 1922 the Commonwealth's opinions were important; in 1956 they were not. But American reaction was vital. Macmillan worked hard, as Prime Minister, to recover the good offices of the Americans, and especially showed considerable flair in reconstructing and then, in the Kennedy era, of strengthening the Anglo-American relationship. And although the 1957 Command Paper on Defence spoke as if Britain's role was in some sense self-derived, this was to mislead. The central result of Suez was that America and Britain resolved not to come to such a divergence of policies again, if they could avoid it. This was not always easy; there were frictions between the two governments over Britain's decision to help the Sultan of Oman against rebels. Macmillan informed Eisenhower, but he received only a tentative message of support. In August 1957 Macmillan was irritated when America refused to support him at the United Nations when a number of Arab countries tried to call a Security Council meeting to protest against British aggression.[91]

The Iraqi revolution in 1958 against the pro-British King, which deposed the King and his Prime Minister Nuri al Said, and resulted in the murder of both, was hastened by the Suez crisis. It is true that the Iraqi monarchy was struggling to retain its power beyond its borders before Suez; but after Suez it suffered from the accusation that any ally of Britain was a friend of Israel, a lackey of imperialism, a participant in the Anglo-French–Israeli attack upon Egypt. The downfall of the pro-British regime in Iraq was a major blow to the British system of exerting influence where she could not exercise direct power.[92] Britain now accepted that it might be advisable to pursue a *détente* with Colonel Nasser, but Nasser now turned to generating anti-British feeling in south-west Arabia, and especially Aden.

But the assumption that Britain must maintain a presence in the Middle East to enable her to exercise her influence East of Suez, or indeed anywhere that she had to, was hard to shake off. In 1962 Aden was defined as one of the 'three main bases from which to fan out by air and sea . . . Britain, Aden and Singapore'.[93] A year earlier, in July 1961, the British had deployed a substantial military force in Kuwait to support her from Iraqi aggression, even though Kuwait had terminated its 1899 agreement, by which Britain promised her protection, in June. This swift act of deterrence almost seemed to cancel out Suez; a new feeling of confidence infused the decision makers, seen in the statement by the Secretary of State for War in 1962 that 'outside Europe, the Army is prepared to intervene to keep the peace in all parts of the world where our interests or those of our allies are directly involved, and we have proved our ability in Kuwait'.[94] East of Suez was still seen by the Service Chiefs as a more attractive arena for British military involvement than north-west Europe. Britain could count more confidently on the support of the United States of America, which strongly supported her presence in the Aden base, especially as Britain provided a strong presence in the Indian Ocean, whereas the United States had few forces there.[95] Britain also made constitutional changes, incorporating Aden into the federation of Arab Emirates, and seeing the future of the colony as one moving forward to political change in a gradual way. But from December 1963 the base was itself troubled by terrorism, and the military forces there soon found that their chief role was to defend themselves and their families.[96]

And yet Aden must be kept. Again, events as well as tradition seemed to insist on this policy. In 1964 Britain intervened in three former colonies, Kenya, Tanganyika and Uganda, to help restore civilian rule following military coups. There was the fear also that Russian expansionism would mean that she would move into any vacuum left by the diminution of the British presence in the region.[97] Therefore more military resources must be committed.

The Labour Government that came to power in 1964 still harboured ambitions of retaining whatever influence Britain still possessed in the Middle East (which by now meant in effect the Persian Gulf). Wilson stated that Britain could not afford to lose her world role, and America, embroiled in her Vietnam War, was not unwilling to allow Britain to maintain some kind of global role. But the financial cost of maintaining that role was felt, not least in the Middle East, and especially in Aden which, as one critic put it, 'consumed more security than it can ever produce'. [98] In December 1966 the Cabinet considered a joint paper from the Foreign Secretary and the Minister of Defence proposing cuts in British defence spending of up to one-half in Far Eastern Command and one-third in the Middle East and Europe. In the case of the Middle East, Richard Crossman noted, 'there was an instruction in the paper that a special study shall be undertaken on the political assumption of a total withdrawal (but not in the Far East, where the assumption was "that we are there for ever").' [99] In 1966 the British Government resolved to leave Aden, a decision complicated by the approaching conflict between two competing successor movements: the National Liberation Front (NLF)

and the Front for the Liberation of South Yemen (FLOSY). On 16 March
1967 Crossman noted that Denis Healy, the Defence Minister, was 'determined to get us out fast, but with the minimum of dishonour'.[100] On
19 June the Foreign Secretary, George Brown, announced that Aden
would become independent on 9 July 1968, with a new constitution and
military and civilian aid, with British naval and air support to guarantee
its integrity.[101] By September 1967, even as Britain was shifting its support from the NLF to FLOSY, Brown was cutting the Gordian knot: 'we
want to be out of the whole Middle East as far and fast as we possibly
can'.[102] By October the date for departure had been brought forward to
November instead of the following January. 'It now looks as though we
shall get out of Aden without losing a British soldier', Crossman reflected,
'chaos will rule soon after we've gone, and there'll be one major commitment cut – thank God'.[103] This withdrawal was a part of the Wilson
Government's appreciation that it was time to 'wind up our military
commitments in the Middle East as soon as possible',[104] and in July 1968
the Cabinet discussed whether withdrawal from the Middle East should
be made final in 1970–1 or 1971–2, and decided on the earlier date.[105]
The Labour Party had lost the taste for empire; the Conservatives, in
government in 1970, found that the imperial moment had indeed
passed. Political consensus was complete.

When the Chiefs of Staff contemplated Britain's role in the Middle
East after the Second World War, they concluded that:

> if we surrendered that hold and the responsibilities which it entails, we
> would automatically surrender our positions as a world power, with
> the inevitable strategic and economic consequences. We should join
> the ranks of the other European powers and be treated as such by the
> United States.[106]

But the event revealed that it was the United States which made Britain
aware of the weakness of her empire in the Middle East, and it was the
attempt to defy this logic that led to Britain acknowledging that she was
in danger at least of surrendering her position as a world power. The
need to write what *The Economist* called a 'balance sheet' in Palestine[107]
could and indeed must be applied to the whole Middle East; it was not
long before it was applied in other parts of the empire as well.

The Suez crisis, and the other British experiences in the Middle East,
revealed the weaknesses of the British Empire in that vital region. The
network of agreements, pacts, treaties, all carefully constructed and all

providing the framework on which an empire of influence rather than direct control rested, was challenged by the Suez crisis; not even the Israelis regarded their British ally as more than a fair-weather friend. If Palestine, as W. K. Hancock claimed, demonstrated the futility of the British confidence that they knew how to manage conflict, in this case between Zionism and the Arab people of Palestine, then the British experience in Iran and then Egypt revealed the weaknesses of an empire based on influence but unable to be supported by power. The attempt to wield power undermined the influence; yet the influence was not strong enough to protect what Britain at the time regarded as her vital interests, her need to guard her oil supplies, and her desire to play a key role in the world, and not drop to the status of an ordinary European power. Peter Lyon has argued that 'in the Middle East, after 1956, there was to be no post-imperial Commonwealth camouflage to provide some semblance of posthumous vindication for empire or to ease the transition to an era when some local leaders would be able to assume active world roles regardless of whether Britain wished to act as their patron or guardian'.[108] And yet it could be said that the problem of standing down from the imperial role in the Middle East was not so much one of loss of prestige, as the inability to relinquish the prestige with which Britain's once pivotal role endowed her. Even up to the present day, Britain is still regarded as a significant manipulator in the Arab world. Arguably, the withdrawal from the region was one of the least well-managed, least well-considered, least well-defended experiences in the whole of British imperial history. But in an area where the habit of pragmatism seemed to have collapsed so spectacularly in 1956, the British recovery after Suez, for good or ill, revealed yet again that, when it came to scaling down the pillars of empire, the English capacity to reinvent the British Empire in the most unlikely circumstances was – and in the Gulf still is – remarkably resilient, extraordinarily alive.[109]

8

THE CONCEPT OF EMPIRE FROM EDEN TO WILSON, 1955–70

In 1952 Anthony Eden reviewed Britain's overseas commitments and concluded that the defence of Western Europe was 'the first priority'. The imperial dimension and the need to fulfil British international obligations were not, of course, to be scaled down; but the state of the British economy must compel her to make other countries, including Commonwealth countries, bear their share of the burden.[1] Eden summed it up pithily: 'we must now cut our coat according to our cloth. There is not much cloth.'[2] In June 1956 Eden's Policy Review Committee studied a document prepared by the Treasury Officials, the Foreign Office and the Ministry of Defence, warning that Britain had ceased to be a 'first class Power in material terms'[3] though the Commonwealth Relations Office begged to differ: Britain was 'still in its own right a very great power'.[4] Eden, though his name will forever be associated with the Suez débacle (and therefore imperialism) was not much interested in what he rather dismissively called 'these territories' of which he had little 'first hand knowledge'.[5] For Eden the empire, if it had any useful function at all, was that of helping maintain Britain as a first-class power; he did not possess Winston Churchill's instinctive love of empire, nor Attlee's (admittedly partly self-serving) belief in the evolution of the British Empire into the Commonwealth of free nations.

   The Suez adventure, which only in retrospect seems to mark the point at which the British Empire began its final and rapid decline, did invoke some reflections on the place of empire in the post-Suez world. Both the fatally discredited outgoing Prime Minister, Anthony Eden, and the great survivor of the disaster, Harold Macmillan, ruminated on the lessons to be drawn from Suez. In a memorandum, 'Thoughts on Suez', composed on 28 December 1956, Eden drew the conclusion that 'if we are to play an independent part in the world, even on a more modest scale than we have done heretofore, we must ensure our financial and economic independence'. Britain also had to rethink the distribution and use of her strategic bases: 'Do we need', Eden asked, 'so many troops in Malaya?' The need was for a smaller and more mobile and modern force. But Suez, he believed, had 'not so much changed our fortunes as revealed realities'. However, Eden did not anticipate that recognition of such realities necessarily involved the eventual decline of Britain's relationship with the Commonwealth. On the contrary, he thought that Britain should determine to work more closely with Europe, but at the same time 'carrying with us, we hope, our closest friends in the Commonwealth'. But it was, he acknowledged, important that Britain did not live with illusions: Europe would 'not welcome us simply because at the moment it may appear to suit us to look to them'.[6]

When Harold Macmillan settled in as successor to Eden, he too sought a reappraisal of the imperial context in which Britain had always assumed her status as a great power lay. 'I should like', he noted in a memorandum on 28 January 1957, 'to see something like a profit and loss account for each of our Colonial possessions, so that we may be better able to gauge whether, from the financial and economic point of view, we are likely to gain or to lose by its departure.' He went on:

> This would need, of course, to be weighed against the political and strategic considerations involved in each case. And it might perhaps be better to attempt an estimate of the balance of advantage taking all these considerations into account, of losing or keeping each particular territory. There are presumably places where it is of vital interest to us that we should maintain our influence, and others where there is no United Kingdom interest in resisting constitutional change even if it seems likely to lead eventually to cession from the Commonwealth.[7]

This brisk, business-like approach seemed to add up to a turning point in British decolonisation; but the idea of what the British Empire stood for was one not based merely on rationally calculated balance and loss. It was after all a British idea, more specifically an English one, and it was one based (in England's eyes) on more than self-interest; it was based also on self-concept, the notion of what Britain stood for in the world, though the cynic might identify many areas where the two mysteriously coincided.

In any event, the Macmillan Memorandum did not go unchallenged. Lennox-Boyd, the Colonial Secretary, admitted in June 1957 that he was 'suspicious that a reappraisal of the value of the Colonies had been one of the Prime Minister's motives'; and when he and his officials began to draft a full response they believed that their papers struck a 'decent balance between a "defence" and a "factual" presentation' (by which he meant, between the officials' own opinions and a more objective assessment). He added:

> When we in the Colonial Office first began to consider the Prime Minister's directive we felt that what we were being called upon to propose was a real 'profit and loss account' of the Colonial territories. Later, however, when the Official Committee began to consider the draft, we discovered that what the Prime Minister had in mind was a detailed account of the relevant strategic, economic and political factors for each territory, to assist Ministers when they are called upon to consider constitutional changes.[8]

This was perhaps not quite what Macmillan had in mind at all; but the making of opinion was as much a Colonial Office as a Cabinet matter – at least in the Colonial Office's opinion. When the officials began to get to work on what they now interpreted as the Prime Minister's request, they began by listing the territories most likely to obtain independence within the next ten years. These were Malaya, Ghana, the West Indies, the Central African Federation and Singapore. The officials did not list Uganda, but acknowledged that 'there will almost certainly be African pressure for rapid advance', with the possibility of independence by 1967. But Uganda could not be expected to have attained the skills in government by then, or have developed the racial harmony, which would justify the British Government's surrender of authority. In such cases, they urged, the British Government would be obliged to maintain its authority in the face of opposition and criticism.

The emphasis was on what the officials called 'orderly development', and their memorandum listed territories that were most likely to develop towards what the officials called 'internal self-government' in the next decade. This was expected to be 'orderly' but, again, the memorandum revealed the Colonial Office dislike of the 'balance and loss' method of assessing the empire's future. When it came to economic profit and loss, then the officials noted that the net saving when territories got independence was less than imagined, simply because those nearest to independence were in least need of Exchequer assistance. They noted, too, that the colonies as a whole had contributed to the strength of the sterling area in recent years; and they were 'of considerable trade importance to the United Kingdom'. And it followed that, what the officials called a premature transfer of power which resulted in serious political troubles, would badly affect the United Kingdom trading and financial interests in the territory.

The central concept – the word on which the Colonial Office philosophy was based – was 'order'. A premature transfer of power was to be avoided; an orderly transfer would produce benign results. The draft memorandum summed up by claiming that the 'economic considerations tend to be evenly matched', because the economic interests of Great Britain were unlikely in themselves to be decisive in determining whether or not a territory should become independent. If Britain decided on granting independence in her own selfish interests, she would do more damage in delaying independence for a country which was ready for it, than if she gave independence 'negotiated in an atmosphere of goodwill such as has been the case with Ghana and the Federation of Malaya'.

The officials then turned to the political 'balance and loss' account. Here again they fell back on, or re-stated, the language of British decolonisation. They stated that 'Successive Governments in the United Kingdom have for many years pursued, with a broad measure of public support, a Colonial policy of assisting dependent peoples towards the greatest practicable measure of self-government.' They were determined not to accept the logic of Macmillan's request: it was, they wrote, 'presumably not intended to depart from this general policy, nor to weaken it, as regards individual territories, by imposing any delays which could be interpreted as artificial'. But it was important also to follow the 'complementary aspect' of this policy, which was that 'we must retain some measure of jurisdiction or protection when this is patently required in the best interests of peoples whose system of government, or law, or administration, and of political habit, derive from the UK [sic] custom and advice'. The UK stood to win no credit for launching a number of 'immature, unstable and impoverished' territories whose performances as independent countries would be 'an embarrassment, and whose chaotic existence would be a temptation to our enemies'.

The officials therefore stressed British responsibility for integrating peoples of different tribal loyalties. It was a 'slow process' to get them to live in toleration. It was necessary to retain British authority until a transfer of power could be shown to be desired by the inhabitants, and it could be demonstrated that they could live in peace with each other. Creditable standards of government in independent states must be assured. This draft ended with a ringing affirmation of England's mission:

> Any premature withdrawal of authority by the United Kingdom would seem bound to add to the areas of stress and discontent in the world. There are territories over which jurisdiction might be surrendered without prejudice to the essentials of strategy or foreign relations, and at some modest savings to the Exchequer, but would we stand to gain by thus rewarding loyalty to the Crown which is an enduring characteristic of so many Colonial Peoples? The United Kingdom has been too long connected with its Colonial possessions to sever ties abruptly without creating a bewilderment which would be discreditable and dangerous.

This draft was ready by September 1957. It was a refutation of any logic that might lead to a rapid decolonisation on a profit and loss account. A couple of years later officials felt that they had satisfactorily scotched any such ambition. Ian Watt minuted on 9 February 1959 that 'Profit and Loss is no more than a handy title for what is essentially a book of reference.'[9] And on the file lay a letter from a colonial governor, Sir John MacPherson, in Barbados, written in March 1958: 'I am very glad', he wrote, 'to read Para. 15 [the paragraph which underlined the need not to abandon colonial territories prematurely] of the Report by Officials. When I was in England last October I was told by an official of the Conservative Party that Britain should withdraw from useless places like British Honduras in order to save money. Need I say More!'[10]

This was the concept of empire held by the Colonial Office, to be firmly based, as they saw it, on precedent and tradition, on the British way of doing things. Macmillan's Government inherited a set of principles from its Colonial Office that could not easily be set aside. Officials were excited by a series of broadcasts made in 1955 by the constitutional expert, Sir Ivor Jennings, on 'Self-government in the Commonwealth'. Ian Watt minuted on 26 September 1955 that these were 'an interesting and valuable series of talks', and noted on 16 November that the Colonial Office should discuss with the Information Department the best way to 'exploit these lectures overseas'.[11] He stated approvingly that:

> Sir Ivor explains that most of his experience has been in Asia, and does not try to lay down the law too forcibly for those countries, especially

in Africa, which are now going through similar processes of developing self-government as the Asian Countries have accomplished. Nevertheless he does draw many valuable deductions of a general kind. The first of these comes right at the beginning of his series of lectures and it is this – when the United Kingdom Government says that it intends to assist a country to develop self-government, and when it commits itself to any kind of timetable, it keeps that promise.

Watt also approved of Jennings' argument that plural societies, such as Kenya or Central Africa, were bound to proceed at a slower pace towards self-government than homogeneous societies such as the Gold Coast or Nigeria. 'No solution can be tailored to general propositions . . . and no solution which takes account of all the conflicting factors will ever be a perfect one.'

Watt did not believe that Jennings' lectures were suitable for public consumption any more than any other set of lectures; but if they could be directed to politicians in the colonies, and 'such intelligentsias as exist in and around our larger Colonial capitals good and well'.[12]

The lectures were filed by the Colonial Office; key passages were marked in red ink, such as 'the system of government to which all the dependent peoples of the Commonwealth are accustomed is the British system'. Another stressed the value of 'our empirical methods' which did not lay down general propositions but relied on an assessment of local conditions. The need to take time, and not place self-government into inexperienced hands, was likewise marked up. A further passage marked by Watt referred to the need to pay heed to the 'man on the spot'. Paper constitutions were not to be studied; 'there is always a background of knowledge and experience which explains them'.[13]

The Colonial Secretary, Lennox-Boyd, inherited this cargo of ideas and suppositions, and he was in full agreement with the general thrust of Colonial Office thinking. Decolonisation was not, at least not in any stark 'balance and loss' form, on the agenda. 'Nothing is more dangerous', he minuted to the Lord President of the Council on 13 February 1957, 'than to gain a reputation for forsaking one's friends'; and if Britain were to withdraw from any territory 'without being able to hand over a successor government, which could be expected to govern reasonably well in the interests of all its inhabitants, the repercussions might be serious and widespread'.[14] There was also the question of British strategic interests: obligation, he wrote in a memorandum for a first draft of the Colonial Office paper for the use of the Cabinet, was matched by self-interest. A premature withdrawal by the United Kingdom would leave a vacuum which would be filled by a country hostile to the United Kingdom and her allies. This hostility might assume a strategic importance; for example, even though a particular territory might not have great strategic importance for the United Kingdom's system of defence, it could be integrated into the 'defensive system of, say, the USSR'.[15]

J. T. O'Brien of the Colonial Office was certain that the economic arguments for maintaining the Commonwealth link were equally strong: they 'would increase rather than diminish'. He spoke of the factors affecting the cohesion of the Commonwealth and its effective contribution to world peace. There was the 'major revolution' of the admission of the Indian members; the second 'and perhaps the final' revolution would be the admission of the African members. Nevertheless, there was, he believed, no incompatibility between evolving closer ties with Europe, and maintaining the Commonwealth markets; the Commonwealth was not 'an exclusive association'. To take advantage of the expanding markets of Europe did not involve the closure of British markets to the Commonwealth. 'The cohesion of the Commonwealth should not be shaken during the next ten years', he concluded; the strength of the Commonwealth link 'lies in the strength of its combined strands'.[16]

The Cabinet was prepared to follow the advice of its Colonial Office experts, and regard the Commonwealth as an important, indeed indispensable, source of British economic prosperity. In June 1957 it discussed economic aid to the colonies and noted that the 'gradual loosening of the other ties which bound together the members of the Commonwealth made it increasingly important that its economic links shall be strengthened as far as possible'. The Government noted that it was already spending 1 per cent of its gross national product on Commonwealth development resources. Economic support in future would increasingly take the form of technical assistance and services, and 'if these facts were to capture the public imagination, they should be presented in as vivid and constructive a way as possible'.[17] In February 1958 Macmillan, reporting on his Commonwealth tour, said that it was a great success and 'helped to emphasize the strength and unity of the new Commonwealth'. In the Asian countries, especially India, the British people were now held in great respect. Australia and New Zealand were loyal to the United Kingdom, a loyalty based on common origins and common allegiance to the Crown, and the keen desire that the economic development of those countries should be based on British manpower and British capital, which 'reflected the strong emotional urge that these

countries should preserve their British character'. It was natural, therefore, that they shared misgivings about the admission of Asian and
African members to the Commonwealth. 'The United Kingdom', he
went on, 'had a duty to interpret the new members of the Commonwealth to the old, to emphasize the significance of the Commonwealth
association whose members were united by the common belief in the
principles of Parliamentary democracy and individual freedom; and to
indicate the importance of the role which this unique association could
play in the world struggle between the powers of tyranny and of freedom'.[18] In September 1958 Macmillan, briefing the Cabinet on issues
likely to arise in the Commonwealth Conference in Montreal, spoke of
the need to foster a more 'dynamic attitude towards the expansion of
resources and of trade'. But now there was also a more sceptical note.
The underdeveloped Commonwealth countries would continue to press
for Britain to allocate substantial resources from the United Kingdom
for their development at the expense of British prospects of economic
expansion; Britain should counter this tendency by emphasising that
the only genuine remedy for development lay in a just and determined
effort to increase the real wealth of the Commonwealth as a whole.[19] But
when, in December 1959, the Chancellor of the Exchequer explained
the dangers of the European Economic Community to the British economy in the absence of European free trade agreement, and the anxiety
of Commonwealth countries about the EEC and trade discrimination
amongst the European groups, Macmillan warned that a united Europe
was in the best interests of the 'Free World', but that Britain needed to
balance this against her special relationship with the United States of
America and 'the value of our position in the Commonwealth'.[20]

The importance of maintaining good relations, economic and political, with the Commonwealth, and the need to consult it as Britain began
to reconsider her economic relationship with Europe, was emphasised
again and again. On 13 July 1960 Heathcote Amory, the Chancellor
of the Exchequer, stated that, if Britain were to join, she must not
impair her relations with the Commonwealth.[21] And the Commonwealth itself was still regarded by its members as a special organisation.
In a paper prepared for the Cabinet on the 'Constitutional Development
of the Commonwealth', officials from six Commonwealth nations (the
United Kingdom, Canada, Australia, New Zealand, India and Ghana)
reviewed the position, and noted, in language characteristic of the
idea of the imperial relationship since the early twentieth century at
least, that:

member countries of the Commonwealth constitute a free association of independent sovereign states, all of which have, in varying degrees, the following common characteristics: a certain weight of population; political, financial and economic viability; the ability to play a role in world affairs and to carry weight in world councils; and the capacity for self-defence, not least against local acts of aggression. It is, in short, a relatively small group of relatively large countries.

The Commonwealth had exercised a valuable influence in the world; it transcended regionalism. Yet it was growing, and would grow, and perhaps therefore the best way forward was to give full membership to all territories irrespective of size, when they got their independence.[22]

The idea of guiding all the territories of the empire towards Commonwealth status, by way of responsible government, remained unchanged, it seemed, by time. A Colonial Office official wrote to Major J. G. Lockhart, Secretary of the United Kingdom Branch of the Commonwealth Parliamentary Association, in January 1960, describing how this process continued: there would be no timetables laid down in advance; it was to be expected that the Federation of the West Indies, the Federation of Rhodesia and Nyasaland, and certain other territories would one day achieve independence within the Commonwealth 'but we cannot yet say when that day would be'. 'Bold advances' were being made in Tanganyika and 'equally sweeping advances' had been recommended in the recently published report of a Constitutional Committee in Uganda, and these were now under consideration. Other developments were taking place.[23]

But the Foreign Office held a more pessimistic view. In December 1959 the Foreign Office prepared a memorandum on 'Africa – The Next Ten Years', to provide a framework for discussion with 'our Commonwealth partners and our allies', to decide what attitude the West should adopt towards what it called the 'rapid march of events in Africa'. The Foreign Office discussed the influences at work in that continent, examining the development of Pan-Africanism. It noted that there was 'one simple and recognisably common factor in the political ferment at work in all African territories today – namely, the desire on the part of Africans generally to be rid of external European domination and their belief in their right and ability to govern themselves'. Pan-Africanism was an attempt to give practical expression to the concept of 'Africanism' and of an 'African personality' which could play a part in world affairs. Its anti-colonial objectives affected the resolution of some issues, for example Nyasaland, and might encourage Africans to seek solution through violence rather than negotiation.

The Foreign Office memorandum went on to consider the next decade and set out the likely developments in the European colonial territories. It drew pessimistic conclusions. In Uganda the earliest forecast of 'full internal responsible self-government' was 1965 ('probably' 1970). In Kenya the forecast was that a 'viable, non-racial state' was probably not possible before 1970. Tanganyika was 'well on the way' to gaining responsible government by 1965. By 1970 it would probably have gained full self-government but would have to rely on external economic and administrative help. But, 'owing to the backwardness of the majority of Africans in all these territories and the multi-racial nature of Uganda in particular, British authority would remain and would still, in the last resort, prevail'. The Federation of Rhodesia and Nyasaland was bedevilled by African fears of being dominated by local Europeans and of European fears of being submerged by an 'uncivilised' African nationalism. The Foreign Office memorandum envisaged that by 1965 Europeans would be the 'main driving force' of government in Southern Rhodesia, and the Central African Federation. The United Kingdom Government would control the two northern territories. In Northern Rhodesia, Africans would be playing a more substantial part in legislature and participating in the executive. In Nyasaland they were likely to form an unofficial majority in the legislature and playing a 'prominent part' in the executive. The situation would remain stable over the next five years. But the memorandum warned that if the 1960 Conference failed to find a solution, 'the picture grows darker'.

In its general assessment of the future development of Africa the Foreign Office memorandum concluded that Africa would become 'Balkanised': divided into a large number of independent states with blacks in control and with authoritarian governments, but might be nonetheless stable for that. What Britain wanted from Africa was 'peace; political stability; trade; exclusion of subversive influences; safety of whites and other minorities'; and certain defensive requirements. The constitutional advance of Africa, as far as the British parts of it were concerned, was still shaped by British colonial policies, which 'have themselves led the African peoples to believe that independence is the ultimate goal to which they are being directed'. Power must be transferred where there was a 'fairly firm prospect that the territories concerned will remain reasonably stable and viable and will be capable of standing on their own feet'. If power was handed over too soon, then 'internal chaos would develop and the territories would be prey to the hostile external forces which are now seeking to penetrate the continent'. Rising African politicians wanted power in their lifetime; the danger was in going too slow or too fast. And there was the danger also of racial conflict which might even force Southern Rhodesia into the South African orbit. If Britain could not solve the problems of East and Central Africa, then 'our past record of benevolent government will be forgotten'. There was a programme to be pursued: economic links must be sustained; in British territory a currency based on sterling and imperial preferences should be maintained; defence arrangements must be continued; education must be developed. The Foreign Office paper stressed the importance of relations with other colonial powers in Africa. Africa, it concluded, was vital now, but had not been vital until about 1957, 'and the problem is aggravated by the fact that the position and influence of the United Kingdom in the world depend to a large extent on what other countries think of us', and their reactions were brought into focus in the United Nations.[24] On 9 January 1959 the Commonwealth Office added its opinion to the debate, predicting that by 1964 most Africans would live in independent countries, and that Africans would demand 'one man one vote': multiracial states with political arrangements for minority groups would be difficult to justify. If the French failed in what the note called their attempt to create a multi-racial society in Algeria, then this would be used as a force of example against the United Kingdom. Moreover, it was important to see Africa in the context of containing communism, and this necessitated satisfying African demands. It was hardly to be wondered at that Macmillan noted gloomily: 'we have our Algerias coming to us in Kenya and Central Africa'.[25]

But the optimism of the Colonial Office, and the qualified pessimism of the Foreign Office, were soon to be overtaken by events. Vital colonial possessions were to become self-governing entities within less than five years of these deliberations by the departments of state. And, as one official put it in March 1961, 'most of the horses have already bolted, and a number are already so far out of the stable that they cannot be pushed back again'.[26] This throws significant light on the Conservative Party and empire. It was less idealistic than the Labour Party, and indeed lacked the warm glow of satisfaction that Labour felt, rightly or wrongly, about their imperial record. It was not that Labour took their responsibilities to the empire any more or less seriously than the Conservatives. India was not the shining example of preparing a people for statehood that in retrospect it was made out to be. Talk of moving colonies along the familiar road was influential, but often represented *post-hoc* thinking about what Attlee, for example, saw as the danger of 'scuttle' in India.

But there was a sense of greater expediency, even selfishness, in the Conservative approach to the changing empire. Their no-nonsense attitude was not formed immediately after Suez; nor was it quite developed in a deliberate way, as Lennox-Boyd's defence of empire demonstrated. But perhaps it was implicit in Harold Macmillan's analysis as long ago as 1942, when he was for a brief period Colonial Secretary, that 'the Empires of the past have died because they were rigid ... by contrast our Empire has had the great quality of adaptation'. The colonies, he stated, were 'four or five centuries' behind in development. But this would seem to imply a slow, gradualist process of decolonisation. However, Macmillan's next phrase was, at least in the light of later events, important: 'Our job is to move them, to hustle them across this great interval of time as rapidly as we can'.[27]

The use of the word 'hustle' seems appropriate. Ian Macleod, who can be seen as the most enlightened of Conservatives when he came to deal with colonial self-government, can also be regarded as pragmatic to the point of ruthlessness. It was he who, a few months before the general election of October 1959, warned Macmillan of the serious consequences of failing to respond to 'Black Africa' – serious, that is, for the Conservative Party, since the 'Socialists' hoped that this was an issue that could 'turn the tide' for them.[28] In July 1960 he considered in the House of Commons whether or not the Westminster model of government was 'exportable'. He was not overly concerned if it were not. 'It is inevitable that new countries need and will find strong executives, and I do not think we should be perturbed about that.' The idea of a loyal opposition was central to the British system of government; and he hoped that in new states 'opposition in the real sense of the word will come too'. The Conservatives had shown 'a great deal of ingenuity in recent years'; there was 'no fixed mould' into which they could 'pour' all these countries.[29] Later, Macleod defended the policy of 'getting a move on' in Africa. There was a 'deliberate speed-up' and 'in my view any other policy would have led to terrible bloodshed in Africa. This is the start of the argument.'[30] Thus he told the Conservative Party Conference in Scarborough in October 1960 that 'the Socialists can scheme their schemes and the Liberals can dream their dreams, but we, at least, have work do to'.[31]

But there was another side to Conservative ideas: that multi-racialism, that is, the rights of the European peoples in Africa, must be protected.

Duncan Sandys, Secretary of State for the Commonwealth, remarked in November 1961 that the extraordinary feature of the new constitution of Southern Rhodesia was that it 'provides far-reaching advances for the Africans with the full consent of the Europeans'[32] – a claim which African politicians would have denied.

When in July 1960 Ian Macleod discussed the notion of expelling South Africa from the Commonwealth, he advised strongly against; they must not be forced 'into what would then truly be a wilderness',[33] while Macmillan in March 1961 drew attention to the 'links forged by history' between the United Kingdom and South Africa, warning that its expulsion would not help those European people who did not accept apartheid, nor would it help the Africans.[34]

This policy of 'hustle' could, and did, end almost in farce. In November 1959 C. J. M. Alport, Minister of State at the Commonwealth Relations Office, spoke in glowing terms of the year ahead, when 'we in Great Britain have a chance of demonstrating to the world the real significance of British policy in Africa'. In almost every territory something would happen. There followed a substantial list of territories which amounted to a large slice of the continent: 'in Nigeria, Somaliland, Kenya, Uganda, Rhodesia and Nyasaland, Basutoland, Bechuanaland, Swaziland. It is a wonderful story, I submit to the House, of constructive progress and statesmanship.'[35] It was also a somewhat breathless, helter-skelter story. But this list, more than any other statement or document, exemplified the Conservative concept of empire after 1959, and it was one of 'the doctrine of the lesser risk'.[36] Or, in other words, good riddance.

No Conservative Minister with responsibilities for the colonies could be found who would deviate from this line. Reginald Maudling spoke right away, in his first statement to the House of Commons as Colonial Secretary, of his intention to continue to pursue 'a consistent policy designed to bring independence to colonial territories'. One contemporary noted that 'young Tory Ministers strongly felt that the white minorities could not indefinitely stand in the way of African advance and were prepared to put their careers to the test on the issue',[37] and Duncan Sandys, Commonwealth Relations Secretary, went so far as to confess to Sir Roy Welensky, Prime Minister of the Federation of Rhodesia and Nyasaland, that 'we British have lost the will to govern'.[38] R. A. Butler, who was given responsibility for central African affairs in 1962, stated that:

it was not possible in the latter part of the twentieth century even in the cordial atmosphere of the Commonwealth, still less in the far chillier atmosphere of general international relations, to justify or even maintain except by force – except in complete isolation – a policy based on domination over the black.[39]

Not all Conservatives found this easy to accept. The chief opponent of Conservative Government thinking about decolonisation, Lord Salisbury, spoke of his passionate belief in the 'British mission in Africa'. Britain's mission in the 'outer world' was embodied in the preservation by the European communities in Africa of 'what has come to be known as the British way of life'. This relationship was central to the maintenance or the 'shrinkage' of 'British spheres of influence'. But while a minority in the party sided with Salisbury, most accepted what they were told was the inevitable, and went along with the policy of 'hustle'.[40] In any case there was still the hope, indeed expectation, that the kind of 'informal imperialism' that characterised much of British influence abroad, keeping the same rights but fewer responsibilities, could be given a new lease of life.[41]

Conservative thinking on empire was soon to be enmeshed with an issue that had been discussed, off and on, since 1945: the question of the United Kingdom's relationship with the European Economic Community. But now the European issue came into closer focus as the Government began to take the first steps, tentative, then more decisive, towards a closer relationship with the European Economic Community, prompted by the EEC's speedy development of discriminatory tariff arrangements. This was not to be done at the expense of Britain's Commonwealth friends, the Chancellor of the Exchequer, Heathcote Amory, noted on 13 July 1960; Britain must persuade the Commonwealth to relinquish some special advantages in the United Kingdom market to enable her to accept membership in Europe, but Britain must not press the point where it might threaten the Commonwealth relationship. The Commonwealth Secretary, Duncan Sandys, agreed: Britain's wider interests and influences throughout the world depended to a considerable extent on her links with the Commonwealth; and if, by joining the EEC, Britain did fatal damage to those links, she would lose her power to exert her influence on a world scale. Full membership should be considered but special terms must be sought to meet Britain's fundamental interests and those of the Commonwealth.[42] But by 29 June 1961 the President of the Board of Trade stated that:

Commonwealth Governments should be warned that, even if we did not join the Community, it was likely that our existing policies, which gave unlimited access to Commonwealth products, will need to be modified.

In negotiations Britain would try to preserve the Commonwealth markets in the United Kingdom 'to the greatest extent possible'.[43]

Commonwealth concerns were not so easily met. On 21 July the Commonwealth Secretary told the Cabinet of the concerns of Australia, New Zealand and Canada about British application to join the EEC, fearing not only the economic, but also the political, consequences, which 'will lead in one way or another to a political union which must weaken the Commonwealth relationship'. The Commonwealth Secretary assured them that the United Kingdom would favour the larger concept of the Atlantic Union, rather than a purely 'continental system'. But he did not disguise the fact from the Cabinet that 'if we did join the Community this would be an initial shock to the whole Commonwealth system'. But the damage done would not be irreparable, and the Commonwealth would in the end become stronger from 'our increased ability to provide capital for development and to buy more Commonwealth products'.[44] By 22 August 1962 the Cabinet found it necessary to urge the Commonwealth Prime Ministers to 'view their particular problems against the background of the strong economic and political arguments in favour of joining the European Economic Community', and in September R. A. Butler, in the chair, admitted that the attitude of the Commonwealth governments had 'so far, been more critical than had been expected'. It was, he went on natural that they should be concerned about their own economic interests, but 'what was more surprising was their failure to recognise the potential disadvantages which were likely to follow, both for ourselves and for the rest of the Commonwealth, if we remained outside the Community'. In the discussion, the point was made that the Commonwealth governments would 'bear a heavy responsibility if, by their public statements at this stage, they made it impossible for the United Kingdom to join the Community'.[45]

In the event the United Kingdom application fell because of French, not Commonwealth, objections. But it was clear that by then the Macmillan Government had indeed moved towards the kind of 'balance and loss' account of the British relationship with her Commonwealth and imperial lands that Macmillan had asked for in the wake of the Suez crisis. But the idea of the Commonwealth was not yet dead, and indeed was to gain a new lease of life with the victory of the Labour Party in the general election of October 1964. This is not surprising. The brute facts of Britain's much-altered state in the world had been disguised by the evolution of the empire into the Commonwealth, and post-1945 developments in the Commonwealth had only enhanced the idea of the world status that it sustained. Harold Wilson, the first Labour Prime Minister to take office since 1951, had an attachment to the old Dominions that went back to his youth. 'Wilson', a former Foreign Office administrator noted, 'shared the Attlee Government's pride in the notion of transforming the Empire into the Commonwealth.' His personal preference was to place a new emphasis on the Commonwealth, and to work for an expansion of Commonwealth trade.[46] There was also a great Labour tradition of pride in the generally socialist and internationalist appearance of the new third world ex-colonial states, led by India, the great exemplar of a socialist Asian democracy. In 1962 Patrick Gordon Walker (Secretary of State for Commonwealth Relations in 1950–1) published his book *The Commonwealth*, in which he extolled the virtues of the 'cohesion and reality of the Commonwealth' which was 'at root historical'. British imperial rule, he claimed, 'increasingly assumed such a nature that it could fulfil itself only by annulling itself. Otherwise the normal process of imperial disintegration would have taken place: instead of becoming a Commonwealth, the Empire would have extinguished itself in a trail of Americas, followed by a trail of Burmas.'[47]

Gordon Walker did not attribute this happy outcome to Britain alone; on the contrary, it was the result of a 'mutual interaction of all the member countries upon one another'.[48] What he called 'Parliamentary democracy' was common to the member states 'not because the members borrowed their institutions from Britain, but because each country made of its own will a nation of which parliamentary democracy was an integral part'. Thus, 'by creating genuine, autonomous parliaments, adapted to their particular constitutional needs, Britain and all the other members built a specifically Commonwealth type of democracy that moved along the same lines of development and increasingly diverged both from the United States type of democracy . . . and from the democracy practised on the continent of Europe'.[49]

Gordon Walker's panegyric on Commonwealth was almost identical to that of the Prime Minister under whom he had served in the Labour Government that lost office in 1951. In May 1960 Attlee delivered the Chichele Lectures in Oxford on 'Changes in the Conception and Structure of the British Empire during the Last Half Century'. Gordon Walker referred to Britain's decision to 'work closely with the independence movements to achieve a smooth transfer of power';[50] Attlee claimed

that the British Empire was the only one that had 'voluntarily surrendered its hegemony over subject peoples and has given them their
freedom'.[51] Both noted the similarity in constitutional arrangements
within the member states.[52] Cooperation was central to the relationship;
for Attlee this amounted to 'a talk round the table between friends'.[53]
Gordon Walker claimed that one of the essential elements was its multi-
racial character, which meant that it was 'set upon the ending of race-
discrimination of all kinds';[54] Attlee could never recall 'a division of
opinion on racial grounds'.[55]

Gordon Walker, while acknowledging that the members of the Commonwealth would never 'band themselves together by alliances or commitments', claimed that they all assumed 'that they would be bound
together in any great moral cause'.[56] Indeed, it was thus sense of moral-
ity, or high ideas, that particularly appealed to Labour in its celebration
of the Commonwealth. Harold Wilson, then, inherited a powerful
Labour tradition, one that the Conservatives, for all their imperial past
and their role in transforming empire into Commonwealth, could not
share. For Wilson the Commonwealth was not merely a trading area or
a sentimental association, but a 'multi-racial community and potential
force in the world, and one in which there was a post-colonial role for
Britain, guarding the development of poorer regions'.[57] In August 1961
Wilson, referring to the United Kingdom's possible entry into the
EEC, warned that 'we are not entitled to sell our friends and kinsmen
down the river for a problematical marginal advantage in selling wash-
ing machines in Dusseldorf',[58] though he cautiously supported the
policy. For Wilson, Britain's frontiers were not in Europe, but on the
Himalayas.[59]

Between Harold Macmillan's succession to power after Anthony
Eden's resignation, and Harold Wilson's first term in office which ended
in 1970, the shift from Empire/Commonwealth to a new perception of
the United Kingdom's role in the world, and especially in Europe, was
slow and by no means fully predictable. The focus of attention in that
transformation was the last great remaining pillar of empire, the British
colonial territories in Africa. Most of that transformation was carried out
by Conservative administrations; and when Labour won their general
election victory in October 1964 they inherited a continent governed
by independent states that seemed to bear witness to the British genius
for adaptation that Attlee, Gordon Walker and Wilson praised and
hoped to bring to a consummation. It was because the Commonwealth,
and Africa in particular, provided the greatest test of the British way of

decolonisation, and the discourse that accompanied it, that successive governments found themselves engaged in complex and risky negotiations, sometimes in armed conflict and, in Wilson's case, in spending what might otherwise seem a disproportionate amount of time on the last colonial rebellion in British imperial history.

9

PILLARS OF EMPIRE: AFRICA

When in 1953 Winston Churchill, ruminating on his government's decision to withdraw British troops from the Suez Canal Zone, told his Cabinet that 'we are not animated by fear or weakness, but by the need of making a better deployment of our forces, and . . . in my case we are not going to be in any hurry',[1] he expressed what might be regarded as the aspirations of British colonial policy in the post-war era. He also articulated a more general assumption of British policy-makers, that the management of change was well within their capability. Thus the precipitate withdrawal from India in 1947 could be set in the balance by the notion that India had been led, slowly and gradually, towards self-government, though privately the Labour Cabinet on 10 December 1946 admitted that to make a precipitate withdrawal and 'leave India in chaos' might be regarded as 'an inglorious end to our long association with India': 'world opinion would regard it as a policy of "scuttle" unworthy of a great power'.[2]

Worthy or not, that decision was made; but it was not seen as a prelude to further 'scuttle', and certainly not in another set of colonies that were central to the modern British Empire – those in Africa. On 1 November 1946 F. J. Pedler of the Colonial Office described Africa as 'now the core of our Colonial position; the only continental space from which we can still hope to draw reserves of economic and military strength'.[3] The direction of British thinking about Africa fell easily into the general context of ideas of tutelage, development and trusteeship. Official papers spoke a familiar language; phrases that rang down the ages were embedded in government documents: 'legislative councils', 'a chain of representation', 'devolution of responsibility', the general refreshing of the old idea of 'indirect rule': all aimed at managing the growth of nationalism that had been stimulated by the early Japanese victories in the war.[4] And this refreshing of local institutions, the Colonial Office summer conference on African administration was told in August 1951, was 'in the first place the field of activity to which Africans can look for political training'.[5] Responsible government inside the Commonwealth was the 'ultimate goal' in all the African territories, though the different regional and local characteristics, the presence for example of Europeans in East and Central Africa, made the resolution of these colonies' problems, and their march towards the goal of a nation governing itself within the Commonwealth, of no small difficulty.[6]

This broad goal had of course to be reconciled with what Sir P. Mitchell, Governor of Kenya, described in a despatch commenting on the Colonial Secretary Creech Jones' circular of 25 February 1947 as the strategic aspects of colonial policy: that Africa as a whole merited a kind of British version of the American Munro Doctrine, setting out British strategic needs, a 'strategic unity' of Africa 'which is essential to the safety of all the parts'.[7] The advance of the Gold Coast towards self-government was not regarded as heralding any imminent overall change in the British position in Africa; yet, by 1956, Britain's African colonies were on the verge of one of the most remarkable, and swift, decolonisation experiences ever undergone by any colonial power: and all this in what the Colonial Office International Relations Department in 1950 reminded the Government was in a part of the world which, within living memory, was still 'the Dark Continent'.[8]

Between 1957 and 1963 the British Government – and a Conservative Government at that – was responsible for the making of eight new states in Africa, seven of them between 1960 and 1963. The Gold Coast, which became independent on 16 March 1957, was followed by Nigeria in 1960, Sierra Leone in 1961, Uganda in 1962, Kenya in 1963, the Gambia in 1965, and the Federation of Rhodesia and Nyasaland; a federation so painstakingly constructed in 1953 and always regarded by African political leaders as a means of securing white domination in these territories, which was dissolved in December 1963, with Nyasaland (Malawi) becoming independent in July 1964 and Northern Rhodesia (Zambia) in October 1964, leaving Southern Rhodesia to pursue its self-appointed goal of unilateral independence under an all-white government.

The British after 1956 were engaged in recovering, with some apparent degree of success, from the Suez failure; they did not believe that the imperial game was up, and they still believed that change could be managed, and would necessarily take some time. They were aware, as they had been since 1945, of the development of African nationalism; they had encountered it in the Gold Coast, which finally achieved its self-governing status under a Conservative Government. The case of Ghana was seen as a special case. Within a short time it proved to be the harbinger of change in Africa.

I   The View from the Centre

Nonetheless nationalism, as sceptics liked to point out, was more of a theory than a reality in Africa; certainly 'African Nationalism' in the broader sense was hard to locate. There was a series of movements, whose character and progress depended on variables: the emergence of political élites, the growth of political parties, the beginning of political unrest, that were specific to their own regions. But the leader of the newly liberated colony of Ghana, Kwame Nkrumah, saw himself as a sign of a general African awakening, of a pan-African nationalism that would sweep the continent. He analysed the ingredients of African nationalism, which he identified as:

(a)   the emergence of a colonial intelligentsia;
(b)   the awakening of national consciousness among colonial peoples;
(c)   the emergence of a working-class movement; and
(d)   the growth of a national liberation movement.

West Africa, he claimed, 'represents the focus of all these contradictions of imperialism'.[9]

This statement bears closer examination; for it did not place the emphasis only on the 'natural' response of colonial peoples to European rule. Nkrumah stated that imperialism itself contained the seeds of its own decline. The growth of a national liberation movement was preceded by important and necessary political manifestations, arising from intellectual as well as social and economic discontent. This analysis had foundation in fact. The British always needed to create some kind of political structures that enabled them to broaden the base of their rule; and it was the case also that the emergence of political élites, following from this process of (admittedly limited) politicisation, led to their demand for more opportunity to manage their country, and perhaps even seek to move it towards self-government.

But nationalism, wherever it emerges, is a complex phenomenon. The idea that it is simply a modern invention must be qualified in the light of modern research into the traits that contribute to its manifestation. People are not blank sheets on which modern, educated nationalist élites then inscribe their ideologies; there is a dialogue between past and present. 'Primary' resistance to colonial conquest and domination, while not nationalist, at least provides nationalism with the beginnings of a tradition to which it can appeal, though it is true that Africa provided 'no . . . *Risorgimento*, no Gandhi or Sun yat Sen'.[10] Julius Nyerere claimed in 1956, referring to the rebellion of the Maji-Maji against German rule in Tanganyika at the beginning of the twentieth century:

> The people fought because they did not believe in the white man's right to govern and civilize the black. They rose in a great rebellion, not through fear of a terrorist movement or a superstitious oath, but in response to a natural call, a call of the spirit, ringing in the hearts of all men, and of all times, educated and uneducated, to rebel against foreign domination.

It was the purpose of the nationalist not to 'create the spirit of rebellion but to articulate it and show it a new technique'. Another resistance movement in Kenya, in 1906, was invoked in 1963; for on a primary school there was a sign on which was written 'Return our shields and our spears.'[11]

There is, of course, an important difference between the use made by modern nationalists of such historic events, and the connection between these events and modern nationalism.[12] Resistance, once offered and defeated, seemed to leave a long period of quiescence before nationalism re-emerged in the post-Second World War period. Nationalists needed to recall heroic deeds, past resistance; but at least the past deeds were there, in some places, to recall. And even the concept of 'resistance', and its corollary – that resistance, had it been successful, would have given the African peoples a better life – provided some sort of soil in which nationalism could establish itself. Nationalists had to appeal to a new, ambitious modern élite; but few Africans were members of this élite, and the claim, common to most if not all nationalisms, that everyone must benefit from supporting a nationalist movement, was put forward, as Ghana's Nkrumah put it, to 'create' a unified political consciousness. This was helped by the fact that, in most African colonies,[13] especially Kenya and Rhodesia, there was the indisputable reality of white domination. This provided the 'otherness' that nationalism needed to define itself and its community or 'nation' against, though early nationalist leaders often called for their people to work with the European rulers, and even to show themselves 'ambitious, self-interested' men.[14]

The sinews of nationalism were to be found in organised groups and associations: in Northern Rhodesia, for example, there were trade unions; in Nigeria local government officers were organised in trade unions. In Kenya there were the Young Kikuyu Association and other organisations that formed the core of the Kikuyu African Union. The Young Kikuyu Association made its initial impact through drawing attention to the growing problems of the urbanised Kikuyu.[15] In East and Central Africa there were independent churches and schools, and even an early desire to control education.[16] Moreover, there was the incentive for educated Africans to challenge Asians in the colonial territories for influence, better jobs, and even, in the end, political power. In Tanganyika, Asian political ambitions stimulated African political awareness after 1918, as African leaders such as Martin Kayamba called for Africans to demonstrate that 'unity is strength'.[17]

African nationalism did not become a serious challenger to colonial rule until political parties were formed, based on such groups and organisations. But a glance at the style of African nationalist parties, their often religiously expressed rituals, their use of song and chanting, their dependence on the charismatic leader who would take his people into the promised land: all these gave African nationalist movements, however complex their origins, an accessible and attractive political mode of expression. But nationalism was the product of a relationship between governed and governors, and the way in which what might be called this raw material was fashioned into a nationalist movement, ideology and party, varied, emerging at different paces, and with important local idiosyncrasies, but emerging nonetheless as a major problem for British Governments, and especially for the Conservative Government between 1957 and 1963.

Nigeria, which covered nearly 3 per cent of Africa's land surface, contained nearly one-quarter of its population. It was a country of great diversity, social and ethnic; it might have been expected, therefore, to be slow in moving towards any kind of self-government, and indeed the British colonial government was able to play off the two main conflicting groups in order to check any rapid, destabilising political developments. In the south they encouraged the spread of Christian education and created an English-speaking group of Yoruba, in the western region of Southern Nigeria; in the eastern region they did the same for the Ibo people, and both of these groups could be used as intermediaries between local cultures and the British authorities. In the north, which had the larger population balance (more than the rest of the southern regions put together), the British governed through allowing Islam to retain its supremacy, and they guaranteed the Hausa chiefs the right to rule their kingdoms on behalf of the British. Thus the colony was administered by British officials working under the system of indirect rule, introduced by Lord Lugard as High Commissioner of Northern Nigeria after 1900. But this had different impacts in the different areas. In the north it resulted in confirming the conservative character of the region; in the south it only encouraged the activities of rising political élites. The efforts of Sir Hugh Foot, Chief Secretary in the Colonial Office between 1947 and 1951, to defuse political radicalism in the south by sponsoring local committees to examine the sensitive issues of constitutional revision and the Africanisation of the public service, contributed to African political awareness.[18]

The differences between the peoples of Nigeria were further marked by the advance in constitutionalism in the 1950s. In May 1950 the Labour Cabinet agreed on increased Nigerian participation in the executive, at the centre and in the regions, increased regional autonomy and larger and more representative regional legislatures with increased powers.[19] Three political parties emerged: the National Council for Nigeria, strongest in the eastern region; the Action Group in the western region; and the Northern Peoples' Congress in the northern region. These parties were avowedly regional, and represented the different communities that made up the Nigerian people; and when the Conservative Government introduced a federal constitution in 1954, it was significant that the leaders of all the main parties chose to stand for the House of Assembly in their own regions, rather than for the Federal House of Representatives in Lagos.[20] Thus the Ibo, Yoruba and the Conservative Muslim aristocrats were confirmed in their divisions through their political parties. Nkrumah was right: the contradictions of colonial rule were laid bare, in that the need to find some broader basis of political authority necessitated the granting of constitutions and ultimately encouraged the move towards more self-government, which then led to more constitution making, which in turn again stimulated the development of political consciousness. Moreover, the colonial authorities then identified local groups and élites that they felt they could, or must, work with, and this gave these élites a more significant role in the governing of the territory. But Nkrumah's analysis fell short in one important respect: the élites were not nationally minded, but locally minded; and in their localities, minority groups which were not regarded as significant by the colonial power found themselves ignored.

Sierra Leone provided another example of how colonial government shaped the nationalist movements that aimed to overthrow it or, to put it more accurately, to take it over. Here the divisions were between the Creole population (descendants of black slaves brought from eighteenth-century North America after the War of Independence and from Nigeria in the nineteenth century when slaves were freed and settled there under British rule) and the rural population. The Creole National Council dominated Sierra Leone politics from 1951, when the governor, Beresford-Stocke, began the transfer of authority to the elected leaders of the Sierra Leone Peoples' Party. These leaders came from chiefs who lived in the rural areas, and they were useful supporters or collaborators with the British. The British were: colonial rulers; then the appointers of local advisors; then the makers of elected local councils; then the makers of a legislature with limited powers; then the augmentors of those powers, and the granters of a greater degree of responsible government, and then of independence.[21] This process shaped the way in which local participators engaged with the colonial power, which identified certain indispensable local interests in order to balance more securely their colonial government.

Uganda was similar. Here again the pattern emerged, as the British found it necessary to engage with local rulers in order to make their position stronger. They had also to deal firmly with those who seemed to threaten that position. Thus they arrested and exiled the King of Buganda, Uganda's central province, but this elevated him into something of a national figure. The Ugandan education system produced more radical and less traditional political élites, for the Roman Catholic Church's schools taught in an atmosphere hostile to the King of Buganda and to colonial rule alike. In the south of the country these influences helped create a political élite; but the north saw the emergence of another élite, led by teachers and civil servants who formed a 'Peoples' Congress'.[22]

But all these developments had their roots in the earlier colonial history of Uganda. When the British first came there they found in Buganda an impressive, advanced centralised kingdom which, for sound geopolitical reasons, they made the central base of their expansion into what became the Ugandan Protectorate. Colonial rule served to

maintain and even enhance the separation between Buganda and the rest
of the Protectorate. But when the British began to collaborate with the
more professional and radical nationalists in Uganda, Buganda's ruler
and people became alarmed. The British Government rejected Buganda's claim in 1953 to be treated as a separate entity and ruled it directly
from the Foreign Office. Hence the king's exile, which outraged the
Bugandan people, and provoked the crisis of British rule in Uganda;
faced by the consequences of their actions, with their earlier encouragement of Bugandan separation, now reversed with the exile of its ruler,
the British found themselves again in a contradictory position: the selection of Buganda as the core of their authority, and the system of 'indirect
rule', encouraged the sense of difference, and increased the local awareness of 'tradition', and therefore the king's belief in his right to inherit
the post-colonial state. But, as in Nigeria, colonial rule also proved to be
a unifying influence, in that the British saw the nation state as the unit
of political legitimacy (they talked in the Colonial Office about 'nation-
building'), and they felt obliged to deal with new, modern élites, which
they had helped to create, and who saw themselves as the rightful inheritors of power. Colonial rule recognised and intensified diversity in
politics; yet it also denied this when it set itself to create and leave behind
a 'nation state'.

Either way, the experience of colonial rule encouraged politicisation.
This was because the rulers had to search for political leaders and parties
in order to stabilise their rule; but also because, in encouraging diversity
in political terms, they fostered rivalry between competing élites; and
this in turn radicalised these élites and engaged them in political activity,
often of intense mutual rivalry, but political activity nonetheless.[23]

A discussion of black African nationalism is insufficient for an understanding of the political forces that helped shape modern Africa; a political ideology, which can be characterised as a form of loyalism, took root
in Africa amongst the Europeans as well, though necessarily in a different form. The British in the African territories were anxious to defend
their interests against African nationalist movements, though they did
not all speak with one voice. But their belief that they had made Africa,
that European rule was best for Africa, and that Africa's prosperity
depended on maintaining European domination, gave them a kind of
British nationalism, a form of loyalism that chafed against what they
often regarded as the inability of the British Government to apprehend
the true state of affairs in its African colonies. In 1905 Lord Selborne
described the 'main British population' in the Witwatersrand as 'splendid'

men 'whose average is higher, distinctly higher, than you would find in any one British town', but whose resentment against the 'radical press and ... platforms ... excite a bitterness that is politically dangerous'.[24] In July 1942 Sir Arthur Dawe, musing on the possibility of securing white settler domination through a federation embracing all the East African territories, recalled the settlers' defeat of the Wood–Winterton attempt to place Europeans and Indians on the same electoral roll. He described this as the settlers' 'Magna Carta', and compared it to the Ulster crisis of 1914, with ex-soldiers and other settlers mobilising to 'resist by armed rebellion'.[25]

This white nationalism did, in some territories, ask for self-government. Southern Rhodesia lost effective control of its own armed forces and its own High Commissioner in London in 1923; but it had responsible government and its governor-general acted on the advice of Rhodesia's Prime Minister. Southern Rhodesia had a population of 50,000 Europeans out of a total of 2 million people in 1931, of which almost 19,000 were under 21; these would form the white nation of the future, in what they believed was a 'white man's country'.[26] This white population saw itself as the very epitome of loyalty to the British, and stressed their readiness to volunteer to fight for Britain in the Second World War.[27] The purpose of the white Rhodesians was to preserve their paramount position by working towards unity with Northern Rhodesia and Nyasaland, and this aim was shared by the settlers of Kenya, Uganda and Tanganyika, who claimed that they stood for greater economic prosperity, and hoped to work towards unity. The most that they obtained was the establishment in 1949 of an East African High Commission in Nairobi, which had a central legislature but which was confined to purely economic matters and failed to achieve political unity. Tanganyika was, after all, a Trust Territory of the United Nations; there were too few whites in East Africa to make their view prevail, and their economic performance was not impressive.[28] In the 1950s the three territories combined contained only 100,000 whites, two-thirds of them in Kenya. The ratio in British East Africa as a whole was 250:1, and in Kenya 131:1, African to non-African; and the non-Africans included substantial numbers of Asians as well.[29] Nevertheless, these white settlers could make matters difficult for the British Government, or at least for sections of any Conservative Party, with their appeal to kith and kin, and their claim that they had civilised Africa, and were still necessary for its future political and economic stability. And the advance of African nationalist movements in the colonies provoked political awareness among the settlers. Southern Rhodesians were always in advance of their brethren elsewhere, but even in Tanganyika, only acquired from Germany in 1919, there developed the 'time of politics', though here the settlers divided into three groups with the 'red-eyed' small coffee and grain farmers of the north forming the European Union of Tanganyika in 1946, and calling for European mastery of the legislature and an increase in European settlers, and the sisal (a form of fibre) planters showing more concern with economic than political goals, with a third group accepting a multi-racial society.[30]

There was another aspect of white nationalism that must trouble the British Government. The British practice of devolving power to local élites had been tried, and seemed for a time to have succeeded, in South Africa in 1910. But, faced with black nationalism, and argued with by white nationalism, British Governments found themselves in an unenviable position. They sought to discover some kind of brokering role between such rival claims, and African nationalists, for their part, believed that the British Government was inclined towards the white point of view, as the war against the Mau Mau in Kenya seemed to confirm. But in reality the British Government was anxious not to alienate black political élites, and it could not guarantee indefinitely to uphold, let alone support with military force, the claims of the loyal British in the African colonies. Neither the Indian Empire, with its European population confined largely to the civil service and the army, nor the 'white' dominions offered, on the face of it, a precedent for the clash of white and black nationalism in Africa. And this clash was mutually reinforcing: in 1926 the Kenya Native Affairs Department reported that:

> Native agitators take their cue from non-Native bodies, and Native political bodies watch the reported proceedings of non-Native bodies, adopt their tone, and seek to emulate what they gather to be their attitude to those whose views or interests do not coincide with theirs towards constituted authority.

By contrast, Uganda did not have the presence of a large white community, and indeed its colonial governors were, if anything, much more modern in outlook than its tribalist Conservative African leaders.[31]

The British had not been unprepared for this quickening upsurge in African nationalism; on the contrary, they had been alerted to it by a series of far-sighted British colonial experts.[32] And civil servants and politicians warned in 1947 that 'the rate of political progress cannot be regulated according to a pre-arranged plan; the pace over the next generation will be rapid, under the stimulus of our own development programmes, of internal pressure from the people themselves, and a world opinion expressed through the growing international interest in the progress of colonial peoples'.[33] This required a positive approach to African nationalists, who would form the new rulers and administrators. This was a bold vision; but the experience of Uganda and to a lesser extent Sierra Leone showed how difficult it was to put this into practice. The British tended anyway to see nationalism in a functional way only; as a vehicle on which the orderly transfer of power could be smoothly loaded. But nationalism, or at least nationalist politics, had its own dynamic; it could be an engine, not a carriage: for it opened up hopes and fears amongst groups and peoples, and it widened the political aspirations of those who accepted the British concept of the nation state, and sought to get their hands on the levers of power.

Nation states needed educated, modern bureaucrats and political leaders; colonial rule encouraged the emergence of such people. The British recognised this, but thought their emergence, training and preparation for power would take a long time. But time was on no-one's side; and it is hard to envisage such élites waiting decades before they were given what they were now increasingly experiencing: the politics of power. It would be harder to manage political change in African colonies where there were European populations in any proportion. Northern Rhodesia, Nyasaland, Tanganyika and Kenya presented complex problems. Here the first demand for loosening the control of the Colonial Office came from the white colonists.

In Kenya the demand for more self-government developed not in the first instance from African nationalists, but from the Europeans who settled there in numbers from the 1890s and who 'came with the faith and the will to subdue the soil and rule its people'.[34] In 1906 they secured from the Secretary of State for the Colonies a promise (as they saw it) that no settler not of their race could secure land in the Kenyan highlands. They began also to use the language of the English political tradition, speaking of their rights to self-government, and their claims to a share in policy making, which were first met in 1915, when they were allowed elected representatives to a special war council. They were given a new constitution in 1919 with two seats on the executive council and representation by 11 members on the legislative council; the Africans, and the substantial Indian community in Kenya, were excluded from this constitution. But their demand for residential and commercial segregation from Indians raised British official objection; and this in turn provoked the danger of a white rebellion, which, W. K. Hancock observed, 'would shatter the advance "from force to persuasion" which was the only principle by which the British Commonwealth could in the long run endure'.[35]

In 1923 the Colonial Secretary, the Duke of Devonshire, stated that:

> primarily, Kenya is an African territory, and H. M. Government think it necessary definitely to record their considered opinion that the interests of the African natives must be paramount, and that if and when those interests and the interests of the immigrant races should conflict, the former should prevail.

But it qualified this by a surrender to white settler fears:

> Obviously the interests in the other communities, European, Indian and Arab, must generally be safeguarded. Whatever the circumstances in which members of these communities have entered Kenya, there will be no drastic action or reversal of measures already introduced.[36]

And, as for any possibility of self-government, the British Government noted that:

> it cannot but regard the grant of responsible government as out of the question within any period of time which need now be taken into consideration.[37]

The idea of trusteeship must stand in the way of representative or responsible government based on European domination. But the Europeans (and Asians) would also have a future in Africa.

The question for the European community was whether or not the official use of the words 'native paramountcy', was merely a pious declaration, or was to be taken seriously. The Europeans in Kenya in the 1930s sought to subvert any risk that it might be taken seriously by calling for a grand federation linking Kenya with Uganda, Nyasaland, Tanganyika, and the two Rhodesias, in a great 'central African dominion', but the leaders of Northern Rhodesia were unwilling to commit themselves to a venture which exposed them to a risk of African numerical superiority becoming irresistible. In 1929 a report by the Hilton Young Committee declared that the white community of Kenya were not the people of Kenya, politically understood; that public opinion in Kenya was not yet formed.[38] The Kenyan legislative council had only one nominated African member and no directly elected member until 1952. But Kenya too began to experience the impact of the political awakening of Africa. The central group in this transformation were the Kikuyu tribe. They were a farming community whose income was supplemented by those of their community who worked as herdsmen on European-owned dairy farms, as porters for the Asian business community, and in similar employment. By 1952 they were still reasonably well off, but they were becoming alarmed by fears for their economic future, especially by the practice of European farmers employing cheaper, non-Kikuyu labour, and by the impact of labour-saving machinery. This discontent was increased by the experience of Kikuyu who had emigrated to the city, Nairobi, and who found themselves poor and unemployed. In 1948 the Municipal Affairs Officer for Nairobi reported that 'it was disheartening to see legitimately employed Africans sleeping under the verandahs in River Road, in noisome and dangerous shacks in the swamp, in buses parked by the roadside and fourteen-to-the-room in Pumwani, two-to-a-bed and the rest on the floor'. In 1952 in Mombasa 27,000 people were in urgent need of accommodation.[39] Moreover, these conditions existed in a country where, as the East African Royal Commission of 1953–5 noted, 'completely new avenues of life have been opened in the last fifty years in employment, in towns, plantations, forest services, European farms and Government Departments'. Thus, 'The society that was so primitive sixty years ago has been affected by new conceptions of religion, education and economic life.' But these changes, as well as problems, caused frustration: 'An increasing gulf was often made between the educated and the uneducated, and the young and the old; and by tradition the latter were regarded as the wise men of the people'.[40] It was estimated that there were 10,000 unemployed Africans in Kenya out of an African population estimated at 5,251,120 in 1948. Many had sought but failed to get education, or had got it, but not the career choices it was supposed to bring, since Asians held the clerical posts they, the Africans, hoped for. The Kikuyu also suffered directly from discrimination, with restrictions placed on the planting of cash crops, such as coffee, and on the acquisition of land in the white Highlands.[41]

This produced unrest and then rebellion: the Mau Mau troubles of the 1950s and the British military response which was firm and at times severe. The challenge to order in Kenya was inspired by the groups of

Kikuyu speakers who found that their economic and social opportunities were increased, only to be frustrated, by the colonial Government. In 1952 they resolved to abandon cooperation with the authorities, and rebellion spread, resulting in the killing of some white settler farmers and provoking a strong British security response. Considerable casualties were inflicted on the Kikuyu, who suffered from the military action of both the Government and the rebels. 'My guess', declared one Colonial Office official, 'is that, quite unlike the position in Malaya, Mau Mau can be dealt with, or kept under control, fairly readily now that the Government has shown that it is prepared to be tough.'[42] But a military response turned out to be, at best, the means of mounting a holding operation, not a solution.

'Toughness' made a nonsense of any claim by the Europeans to govern themselves as an independent state by giving the British a hold over white security and thus political ambitions. The African political leader who emerged in the 1950s, Jomo Kenyatta, was presumed by some to have Mau Mau connections; but what he did have, which was much more troublesome to the aspirations of the Europeans, was the ability to create and hold together a political party, the Kenyan African National Union, which drew its support from the Kikuyu and also the Luo tribes. He also eventually showed that he could cultivate the European community, win its trust and yet also carry with him the radical nationalist leaders from the western province.[43] This reinforced Nkrumah's point that social and economic distress would fuel African nationalism, and that élites could use this to create a liberation movement. In Tanganyika the desire of the white population to assert its primacy, and the suspicion that the British would put its welfare above that of the Africans, only enhanced the appeal of the Tanganyikan African National Union (TANU). The British sought to introduce racial parity into the Tanganyikan Legislature (which had been established in 1928 with an official majority and without African participation). Three African chiefs had been admitted to the Legislature in 1945, but this institution sat alongside that of indirect rule, and here again officials carefully regulated and supervised the rule of African tribal authorities.

In the 1950s the Colonial Office assumed that it must protect European interests, and it constructed the policy of racial parity in the Legislature, and representation for the minority in committees in the district councils. This provided TANU with an opportunity to gather support throughout the country; Julius Nyerere, the leader of TANU, was dismissed by the British Government as a 'man of straw', and the British sought to revive the power of the chiefs as a makeweight against the new radical élites. But the Government also made the unpopular decision to use coercion in order to implement rural development policies, which only served to undermine the local chiefs, and prepare the ground for TANU. Between 1956 and 1958 TANU grew more, not less, powerful. The chiefs, alienated by British policy in their rural areas, began to cooperate with TANU. In 1958 'parity' in the Legislature was abandoned, and in 1959 abandoned also for the appointment of elected members to the Executive Council. TANU now showed itself willing to cooperate with the Government, and the Government and the European community alike realised that its interests would be best served by cooperation. Once again the impact of colonial rule, this time in response to the effort to protect the European minority, resulted in a radicalising of the main tribe, in this case the Kikuyu, and the recognition that Government could only proceed with their assistance and consent.[44] The Government's education policy of encouraging the use of Swahili in schools itself facilitated the rise of a united nationalist movement;[45] modernisation, the Colonial Officer's favoured option since 1945, contained the seeds of the undermining of the colonial system that it was designed to justify and even to sustain.

The desire to secure European safety, perhaps even maintain European domination, in these African colonies was most significantly present in Rhodesia and Nyasaland. In 1953 the British Government created the Federation of Rhodesia and Nyasaland, with almost complete powers of self-government. This 'Central African Federation' was meant to retain the unity of its component parts and thereby their mutual prosperity (Southern Rhodesia was agriculturally profitable; Northern Rhodesia had great mineral resources; Nyasaland was regarded as too poor to go it alone). But it was based on systems which had, since the 1930s, been less than hospitable to the African population, especially since the 1931 Land Apportionment Act which gave Southern Rhodesia's 148,000 Europeans 1000 acres of land per head of the population.[46] This made it clear to migrant workers from Nyasaland and Northern Rhodesia that they should have nothing to do with any proposed amalgamation of the three territories. The Europeans in Rhodesia were able to take advantage of Britain's concern about South African expansion under the Afrikaaner Nationalists to allow Southern Rhodesia considerable latitude for its ambitions, ambitions which attracted the favourable attention of Northern Rhodesia. Britain was supportive of the federal idea, consoling herself with the reflection that it might better protect African interests, since white fears would be assuaged. Economic improvement was expected to follow and, in the first four years of the Federation's existence, did so.[47]

This initial success encouraged the Federal Prime Minister, Roy Welensky, to press for full Dominion status for the Federation. But the problem of the African majorities could not be set aside. Franchise proposals were put forward in 1957 which were designed not to exclude Africans from power, but to carefully regulate and restrict their power. This action, upheld by the Conservative Government in Britain, only served to inspire African nationalism, especially in Northern Rhodesia and Nyasaland. The African National Congress in both territories began to organise and prepare for systematic opposition. Dr Hastings Banda returned from London to lead the anti-federation movement, landing in Blantyre on 6 July 1958. He was elected President-General of Congress in Nyasaland on 1 August. In Northern Rhodesia there were protests and boycotts against European and Asian shops, and strikes in support of Banda, who believed strongly in pan-African nationalism. A state of emergency was declared in Nyasaland in 1959 and the British Government was forced to intervene, dismissing the Government claims that there was a 'murder plot'.[48] In 1960 the Federation's constitution was revised, as provided for at its inception, and a committee chaired by Walter Monckton reported that each territory should have the right to secede. The aspirations of the European communities of these colonies, with the important exception of Southern Rhodesia, to move towards full self-government in the form of Dominion status, were ended.

The view from the centre, in the sense of the centre as Africa, not London, revealed the quickening pace of change over most of British Africa. Where colonial government encountered African political aspirations, the result was invariably the enhancement of African nationalism. The structure of the colonial state was itself an invitation to emerging political élites to attempt not to overthrow the state in chaos and rebellion (though there were rebellions in some places, and the fear of chaos amongst the European populations), but to supplant the colonial administration, substituting themselves and their followers in place of the present governing élite. Education, the impact of anti-colonialism, the attempts by the British to associate Africans with political change (however slowly anticipated this process was), and in some cases conflict with the European population, served to produce volatile and difficult predicaments for the British rulers of Africa. Within a very few years the measured tones of the British Government yielded to new notes of urgency. The European idea of the nation state was taking root in what were, on the face of it, unlikely and unpromising places. It was significant that Nkrumah prefaced his *Towards Colonial Freedom* with quotations from European thinkers: Mazzini, Wilhelm Liebknecht.

Yet it must be stressed that these African nationalist movements, though they commanded more support from the African masses than their enemies liked to think, left large numbers of Africans untouched. But they affected sufficient of them to arouse political demands: even traditional tribal chiefs were sucked into this expanding political universe. However, much the same process had happened in India since 1918. There the Congress Party had built itself as a mass movement, with its combination of nationalist ideology and its support of local social and economic grievances; there, too, Congress had used new political institutions, in the states, to build a firm political base, from which to dislodge the British and replace them by Congress. Yet the process of leaving India was a protracted one, covering nearly the first half of the twentieth century. Africa turned out differently. Between 1956 and 1963 these nascent nationalist movements sprang into life as successors to the British colonial system. And this rapid transformation was not only presided over, but pushed along, by the British Conservative Party. It is now time to turn to the view from the periphery, the Cabinet, the Colonial Office, the Foreign Office in London, to try to discover why the 'winds of change' blew through Africa with such effect, and in so short a time.

II   The View from the Periphery: British Governments and Africa, 1956–70

The Conservative administrations that governed the United Kingdom from 1951 until 1964 seemed unlikely candidates for presiding over the decolonisation of the British Empire in Africa. The party was traditionally associated with the spirit of imperialism; though when it came to defending British interests, as in Egypt in 1882, Liberals had shown themselves as willing to act imperially as any Conservatives; and Labour after 1945 did not take office with any intention of winding up the empire – certainly not the empire in Africa, which they hoped to develop and turn to good use. But, after all, Winston Churchill had strongly opposed any moves towards self-government for India in the 1930s; he maintained that, after 1945, Britain's interests lay in maintaining what he called the three interlocking circles of her foreign policy: the Anglo-American special relationship; Europe; and the Empire, though for Churchill the European dimension stood short of any fundamental realignment of British policy. Anthony Eden, for his part, was anxious lest British colonial policies were 'moving at a pretty dangerous gallop' [in West Africa];[49] Harold Macmillan, who replaced Eden after the Suez crisis, had been one of the most deeply implicated Ministers in the collusion plan, though he escaped any censure; he, too, hardly seemed a likely candidate for a programme of decolonisation.

Churchill and Eden were Prime Ministers at a time when any fundamental change in the British position in Africa seemed unlikely, with the exception of the Gold Coast. In October 1954 the Colonial Secretary Lennox-Boyd felt confident enough to tell the Europeans in Kenya that they were there to stay, and that they would 'have the full force of Her Majesty's Government behind them'; he even declared that he 'believed in British emigration to Kenya'. The previous Colonial Secretary, Oliver Lyttelton, on a visit to Kenya, told Europeans to 'expect to hold all the political power and to exclude Africans from the legislature and from the government'.[50]

The replacement of Eden by Macmillan after Suez was not at first a significant landmark in the beginning of the end of the British Empire in Africa, despite his 'profit and loss' memorandum of July 1957. Macmillan declared that nothing should be done to 'prejudice' the interests of the Central African Federation, because the Federation 'could make a very important contribution to the maintenance of our position in Central Africa'.[51] In March 1959 the Colonial Secretary warned that if Nyasaland were allowed to secede from the Federation then Northern Rhodesia would claim a similar right. Southern Rhodesia would be 'liable to gravitate into the orbit of the Union of South Africa. The Federation would dissolve and the Government's attempt to create a multiracial partnership in Central Africa would fail.'[52] A week later the Home Secretary, R. A. Butler, argued that public opinion in Britain would not accept the perpetuation of the Federation in the absence of a general review of the continued future of the Federation.[53]

In June 1959 the Prime Minister and the Colonial Secretary interviewed David Stirling, wartime hero and self-appointed expert on African affairs, who had put forward a paper on the future of the Central African Federation. Stirling was concerned that African opinion saw the Labour Party 'as being the quarter to which they would look for support, while Europeans looked to the Conservatives'. This was 'unhealthy', and the

Government should now make a 'Declaration'. Macmillan thought that 'a limited extension of the franchise, coupled with a written constitution' might well bring some form of stability. White people in Africa 'would have to recognise that one day the black majority would have to make itself effective, although not necessarily right away.' Macmillan deployed the language of imperial management: 'If we pressed on too fast with the extension of the franchise, the more reactionary white people might try to join the Union of South Africa. If we did not move fast enough, the Africans would lead the disturbances.' There must be 'some perceptible movement and some declared aim'. But it was 'useful to keep the objectives in front of us rather than at this stage try and say what we were going to do.... The timing depended entirely upon a proper situation having been achieved.'[54] Macmillan admitted the possibility of change, and this was echoed in Nigeria. In 1957 the question of self-government for Nigeria was discussed, and the Government concluded that to consider independence too soon was to risk Nigeria's political disintegration; yet to deny independence would be to provoke animosity and disturbance, and thus disable British chances of influencing Nigerian politics thereafter. This dilemma – which always confronted the colonial power when it tried to work out the best possible programme for political change – was resolved by the Cabinet's decision to state that if by 1959 the Nigerian people wanted early independence within the Commonwealth, it would confer with all the Nigerian regional governments to determine the process by which this wish might be attained, perhaps through a constitutional convention which would make recommendations for self-government. In this discussion the Cabinet was anxious to avoid any commitment to independence by a specific date, especially in view of South Africa's concern about the implications for the Commonwealth of new states such as Nigeria being admitted to its membership, and also because of concern about British strategic interests.[55] But by 1958 the Colonial Secretary told the Cabinet that he was ready to accede to the Northern Region's demand for regional self-government, and stated that if the new Nigerian Parliament asked for independence as a whole, it should be given by the beginning of 1960. At the forthcoming conference on Nigeria's future the governor-general advised the Cabinet that it should set a date in 1960 for full self-government for the Federation 'as a whole'. 'Public opinion in Nigeria was conspicuously loyal to the Crown and the Commonwealth connection, and it would be unwise to alienate this sentiment by reluctance to prescribe a date for the achievement of Federal self-government.'[56]

The appointment of the progressive Ian Macleod to the Colonial Office, in October 1959, hastened the process in Africa generally; even more significant was his deployment of the familiar language of British imperial and colonial arrangement and (if need be) retreat, when at a Lancaster House conference in London to settle the Kenyan problem, MacLeod set out his agenda as that of creating in Kenya 'a nation based on parliamentary institutions on the Westminster model and enjoying responsible government'.[57]

The following year Macmillan himself made a speech which was later seen as the defining moment in his Government's attitude to the British colonial role in Africa: the 'winds of change' speech which he made in Cape Town, South Africa, in February 1960. This declaration, these words, are so central to British colonial reappraisal in Africa that their context merits full consideration.

Macmillan was always good at extricating himself from difficult predicaments, not only with a minimum of damage to himself, but even with honour. By 1960 his Government was increasingly concerned about the future of the Central African Federation because of African unrest at the insensitivity of the federal system to their interests. As African concern and militancy increased, so too did white ambitions, fuelled by the desire to retain power in the Federation. They spoke of moving away from their present status towards full Dominion status and even independence.[58] South Africa was also a source of much anxiety. Despite the long period in office of the Afrikaaner National Party (since 1947), South Africa remained a full, if restless, member of the Commonwealth, though her racial policies occasioned considerable friction with the Labour Government of 1945–51. Yet, for Labour, there was also the consideration that if South Africa were driven out of the Commonwealth, then one of the great building blocks of the Commonwealth system, created in 1910, with the Union of South Africa, would crumble, with serious consequences for the whole Commonwealth tradition. Again, history looked over the shoulders of British statesmen when they came to respond to shifting international and imperial concerns.[59]

At the same time these considerations had to be set against the danger of alienating African opinion, and indeed world opinion, if Britain were seen to be setting her strategic and economic interests in South Africa in the context of the abhorrent apartheid system of the South African state, and thus coming down on its side. And yet there were the ties of the past, which the South African Prime Minister, Dr Malan, played upon in July 1953 when he warned the Secretary of State for Commonwealth

Relations that the 'real strength' and 'real unity' of the Commonwealth lay in the 'common outlook' of the old Dominions. Malan then went on to talk about what he called the 'African problem', warning against the danger of those Africans such as Nkrumah who were planning 'complete African domination'. He suggested that the colonial powers, France, Belgium and Portugal, should meet and, together with Britain, formulate an 'African Charter' to protect their interests. But by 1959 Macmillan was strongly advised by his High Commissioner in South Africa, by his Commonwealth Secretary, Lord Home, and by Kwame Nkrumah, that anything that could be construed as a defence of *apartheid* (or a passive acquiescence in that system) would be damaging to British interests and facilitate the spread of communism. Some statement of principles to which African nationalists could subscribe must be made.[60] These conflicting pressures were felt by Macmillan when he embarked on a tour of Africa in 1960.

When Macmillan addressed the South African Parliament in Cape Town on 3 February he might have found himself in a most unenviable position. To say too much that was critical of South Africa was hardly appropriate; to abstain totally from criticism would have compromised him deeply in the eyes of African nationalists, and of liberal opinion generally. Macmillan's officials served him well with their advice and drafting of his African speeches, and Macmillan responded with a masterly performance: flattering the Afrikaaners, praising their 'beautiful country', their 'great and thriving cities', and recollecting the Union that was forged in 1910 and which was now, as he put it, 'celebrating the Golden Wedding'. He shrewdly reminded his audience that much of South Africa's achievement 'has been financed by British capital'. Then he came to the most enduring part of his address. He analysed the development of African nationalism, and the inevitability of the emergence of new 'nation states' in Africa; he warned that such developments marked (in a phrase that he had used earlier in his African tour) 'the wind of change' that was 'blowing through this continent and, whether we like it or not, the growth of national consciousness is a political fact'. 'We must', he urged, 'all accept it as a fact, and our national policies must take account of it.' He reminded the Afrikaaners of their own growth of national consciousness, and warned South Africa to come to terms with the nationalism now stirring in Africa. To do otherwise would be to 'imperil the precarious balance between the East and West on which the peace of the world depends'. Were the peoples of Africa and Asia to swing to the East or to the West? Would they embrace communism? Or would the great experiments of self-government that were now being made in Africa and Asia, especially within the Commonwealth, prove so successful, and by their example so compelling, that the balance would come down in favour of 'freedom and order and justice?'

Thus emboldened, Macmillan went on to present a context for the working out of Commonwealth future: a global context of communism against freedom. He urged the South Africans to recognise that 'the internal politics of one nation may have effects outside it'. To say 'mind your own business' was all right; but 'in these days I would myself expand the old saying so that it runs: "Mind your own business but mind how it affects my business too".' Now he was able to be, as he put it 'frank'. The British had created new nations – India, Pakistan, Ceylon, Malaya and Ghana; and 'what they will do for Nigeria and other countries now nearing independence ... we do in the belief that it is the only way to establish the future of the Commonwealth and of the Free World on sound foundations'. Macmillan then moved on to stress that Britain's aim was to 'create a society which respects the rights of individuals, a society in which men are given the opportunity to grow to their full stature', which was an indirect indictment of apartheid. But he balanced this with a reference which did not mention the Central African Federation but must call it to mind: Britain was aiming at fostering fellowship in 'countries inhabited by several different races'. He linked the dilemma of South Africa's white population with that of the 'Europeans in Central and East Africa', and stressed that the Commonwealth wanted to give South Africa full support and encouragement; but he warned also that 'there are some aspects of your policies which make it impossible for us to do this without being false to our own deep convictions about the political destinies of free men'. Isolation was impossible in the modern world; all nations were interdependent. But Macmillan also deplored the boycotting of South African goods in the United Kingdom.[61]

This speech, then, operated on several different levels. It gave Macmillan a most favourable press; but it was not an invitation to African nationalists, in South Africa or elsewhere, to push for independence or constitutional change at the expense of Europeans. It was intended to keep South Africa in the Commonwealth by urging her to mitigate the impact of apartheid in the interests of the West in the Cold War. When Macmillan reported to the Cabinet, on 16 February 1960, he noted that in South Africa 'the main political problem arose from the doctrinaire policy of the Nationalist government on race relations. Though we could not endorse that policy, we must remember that it was their responsibility not ours.' It would be a 'tragedy', he claimed, 'if South African links with the Commonwealth were wrecked by reason of differences of opinion on that question. South Africa enjoyed a strong and flourishing economy and had a valuable part to play in the Commonwealth.'[62]

But the 'winds of change' speech seemed to do what it did not set out to do at all: it was interpreted as ushering in a new era in which Britain was firmly set on the course of creating new African-dominated states in her former colonies. But it was meant to keep South Africa in the Commonwealth. The speech's apparent success really marked its failure; but its failure, to keep South Africa in the Commonwealth, turned out to be its success. On 21 March the South African police killed 67 African demonstrators at Sharpeville. In Cabinet on 24 March Macmillan noted that the Opposition had tabled a motion deploring the shootings. He outlined what he called the Government's difficult task. It must observe the convention that one member of the Commonwealth should not interfere in other members' internal affairs; so the Government should avoid lending support to the idea that the shootings were the inevitable result of the racial policies of the Union Government. But, he warned, public opinion in the United Kingdom had been deeply moved; it would expect an expression of sympathy from the Government and so the Government would table an amendment recording the 'deep sympathy with all the people of South Africa at the recent tragic events'. On 29 March the Commonwealth Secretary, Lord Home, warned against offending South Africa, because the 'continued adherence of South Africa to the sterling area was a matter of great importance'.[63] But, despite the Government's carefully modulated response to the Sharpeville shootings (which it maintained in its reaction to a motion in the United Nations put down by Ecuador),[64] South Africa moved towards departure from the Commonwealth. In July South Africa announced its determination to hold a referendum on the issue of whether or not the state should become a Republic. In October the referendum produced a small majority in favour of republican status. Macmillan urged the Commonwealth to delay any decision on South Africa's position in the Commonwealth until a meeting of the Commonwealth Premiers in March 1961, and stressed that it was more likely that South Africa's apartheid policies would be softened by her remaining in the Commonwealth. But Diefenbaker, the Canadian Premier, would have none of this, and his opposition persuaded Macmillan that it was better to hold the Commonwealth together and avoid a split, even at the price of South Africa's withdrawal of its application to stay in the Commonwealth. 'There was a real danger', he told the Cabinet on 16 March 1961, 'that continued controversy on the issue might have led to the disintegration of the whole association in its present form', though Macmillan viewed the severance of South Africa's links with the Commonwealth as a 'matter of deep regret'. The Cabinet agreed to retain friendly links with South Africa and seek to keep her in the sterling area.[65]

So the 'winds of change' speech failed in its key purpose; but it was soon to be seen as the harbinger of change in the British African empire, the change that would be implemented, or accelerated, and would result within a short time in the end of the African colonies and their replacement by new African-dominated states. The reality was less clear-cut. Britain still insisted on her need to maintain her economic and strategic interests, and her prestige in Africa, and to calculate how these could best be secured. In the case of Ghana it was held that they could be met by moving smoothly towards independence. But the idea of 'smooth progress' was quickly transformed elsewhere in Africa to something more like a scramble to get out of Africa.

The 'winds of change' speech was delivered just before Britain conceded independence to Nigeria, Sierra Leone, Tanganyika, Uganda and Kenya, and all between 1960 and 1963. This transformation was not calculated in advance: but it was smoothed by reference to the broad idea that Britain was always in the business of transforming (but not losing) her empire. Lennox-Boyd, Secretary of State for the Colonies, picked his way carefully through this concept in his address to the Conservative Party conference in October 1958. He weighed up the 'too fast' as against the 'too slow' schools of thought. He countered criticism with the argument that seemed, on the face of it, to make little or no distinction between the colonies and any other underdeveloped countries in the world:

> What may well mark the middle of the twentieth century for historians is not the ideological conflict between Russia and the free world but the painful process of adjustment as between the West and the non-European and underdeveloped countries. . . . So the problem of our relations with Colonial peoples is fundamentally no different from that of our relations with independent countries at a similar stage of political, economic and social development.[66]

Lennox-Boyd went on to cast doubt on the possibility that 'independence' could mean anything more than 'inter-dependence' in the modern world. So the process of moving colonies towards independence was, in effect, only moving them towards another type of interdependence. There was also the overwhelming argument of fact. Ian Macleod, Colonial Secretary between October 1959 and October 1961, summed it up: 'we could not possibly have held by force to our territories in Africa. We could not, with an enormous force engaged, even continue to hold Cyprus. General de Gaulle could not contain Algeria.' But Macleod, like Lennox-Boyd, drew upon the well-established vocabulary of the transition from colonial to Commonwealth status. 'The march of men towards their freedom' could be 'guided', though it could not be 'halted'. There were risks in moving quickly, but 'the risks of moving slowly were far greater'.[67]

Kenya, which became independent in 1963, revealed how hard it was to contain or regulate the process of change. The Mau Mau war had required, as Macleod pointed out, the deployment of thousands of troops. The emergency involved Britain in a damaging scandal over a riot in the Hola detention camp in July 1959, when a number of detainees were killed (an episode which Macleod declared was a turning point in his thinking about Africa[68]). In a debate in the House of Commons on 27 July criticism was heard, not only from the Labour Opposition, but from Conservative backbenchers, with Enoch Powell declaring that 'it is argued that this is Africa, that things are different there. Of course they are. The question is whether the difference between things here and there should be upon different principles.' 'We claim', he went on,

> that it is our object . . . to leave representative institutions behind us wherever we give up our rule. I cannot imagine that it is a way to plant representative institutions to be seen to shirk the acceptance of responsibility, which is the very essence of responsible Government.

Powell claimed that, precisely because Africa was different, it was vital for Britain to behave there as she would at home: 'We cannot, we dare not, in Africa of all places, fall below our own highest standards in the acceptance of responsibility.'[69]

The use of force to retain imperial control was not unsuccessful; the British were good at this, as the Malayan emergency revealed; they had experience and professional skills. But they found it impossible to use force in the face of criticism at home, against accusations that the force used was degenerating into mere violence. The Hola incident no more spelt the end of the empire in Kenya than Amritsar had in India. But in both cases it caused some concern that the empire might be perceived as resting on the crude acceptance of violence, not the measured application of statecraft and legal coercive powers.

Between 1946 and 1959 British expenditure in Kenya (excluding the cost of dealing with the emergency) rose from £8.6 million to £4 million. This expenditure included the policies of land consolidation and agricultural reform; and to carry out these policies new staff had to be recruited in the agricultural, veterinary and land departments. The police force doubled to 12,000 between 1951 and 1960. The cost to Whitehall of these projects, allied to the intensification of African involvement in them, meant that the state in Kenya was, for whatever the motive, taking a new and more dynamic shape; and that it was an expensive one for the United Kingdom to sustain.[70]

The question of what was the best 'timetable' for moving the colonies forward to self-government under African majority rule became more acute in the early 1960s. Tutelage could be a long-drawn-out affair, but there seemed to Britain to be less time in which to make this tutelage work: less time and a changing context too. The Berlin crisis of 1961, when the West and the East stood face to face at the Berlin Wall; the growing British concern over entry into the European Common Market; all made decolonisation more of an imperative, less of a free choice for Britain. Yet the timetable did not run as smoothly as these other imperatives might suggest. Macmillan was concerned about the impact of the transition to Kenyan independence on his party. Lord Salisbury and Lord Lambton, he confessed to Lord Kilmuir in 1961, 'could even rally a "settler" lobby here of considerable power', especially since the Kenyan settlement was 'aristocratic and upper middle class (much more than the Rhodesias) and has strong bonds with the City and the Clubs'.[71]

The question that vexed the Colonial Office was what should be done with Jomo Kenyatta. In November 1961 the Colonial Secretary noted that tribal tensions were increasing in Kenya and that the best hope for the future was to work towards a constitutional conference in the early part of 1962 to devise satisfactory safeguards for minority interests. In discussion, Kenyatta was described as an 'evil man who must be held responsible for the brutalities of the Mau Mau movement'. The European minority could not rely on safeguards under a Government controlled by him. Indeed, the 'continuation within the Commonwealth of an independent Kenya would seem to many people to be inconsistent with the moral principles which had hitherto been the basis of the Commonwealth association'. But against this must be weighed the fact that to continue colonial rule 'would involve a heavy financial and political burden'.[72] But by 16 November Reginald Maudling was arguing that there was not much hope for the constitutional conference on Kenya unless Kenyatta was permitted to attend, though there was the possibility of stationing some troops in Kenya after independence to reassure the European minority and give them some degree of confidence.[73] The following February the position became even more stark. Maudling told the Cabinet that the constitutional conference on Kenya would open on 14 February. The transition to full independence would probably take a year to 18 months after the attainment of self-government. He stated bluntly that:

> Refusal to accept an early date for independence would probably lead to further outbreaks of violence, which would further reduce confidence in the country's future and intensify its economic problems. Early grant of independence might leave behind an unstable country – but the first task is to seek agreement on a Constitution with strong safeguards for African minorities and the European settlers.

The Cabinet still thought in terms of independence taking all of five years.[74] But on 20 March the Colonial Secretary confessed to the Cabinet that the 'least palatable feature of these proposals' was that it would be necessary to include Kenya in the coalition government.[75] Within a year Kenyatta was head of an independent government of Kenya within the Commonwealth.

The view from the imperial periphery was as complex as that from the African centre – or centres. Nationalists showed themselves adept as using whatever power structures, however limited, the British idea of partnership provided. These became more important as the partnership idea moved the British to permit direct elections rather than indirect methods of selection as a means of reconciling African political aims with the continuation of imperial rule. Dissent was often fuelled by social and economic deprivation, though this too provided an incentive for political leaders to use discontent to strengthen their demands upon the colonial state, rather than bringing it down in chaos. Mau Mau was a fearful term in the 1950s in Kenya, but nationalists had no desire to destroy a state on whose foundations they were themselves building, and whose institutions and government they sought to inherit. Moreover, constitutional change, which the British found themselves obliged to make in whatever restricted a form, also created a sense of uncertainty

amongst European and African alike. This bred political activity, and led
to the African political élite demanding, and often getting, unswerving
support and loyalty from their followers. Thus armed, nationalist leaders were able to hide the potentially disastrous splits amongst the people
of their territories, tribal and regional; in Kenya the Kikuyu and the Luo
fought hard, if not always comfortably, to establish one monolithic political party, under Kenyatta's leadership.[76] These splits were always likely
to re-emerge, but they were themselves anyway the agents of political
awakenings, and again made government by partnership necessary. The
Kenya African Democratic Union, for example, was able to enjoy the
support of the British administration because of its moderate and multi-
racial character, which stood it in good stead at the Lancaster House
conference in 1962.[77]

Similar patterns emerged elsewhere. In Tanganyika the process of
change was begun by the British, who sought to reform local and central
government, and increasingly associate Africans with the politics of the
colony; local government was reformed, and a new relationship with
central government worked out. Urban and rural discontent helped fuel
African political activity, and pressure from the United Nations (for
Tanganyika was a mandated territory) obliged the British in 1954 to
think, again, of 'timetables' for constitutional advance.[78] By 1958 the
experiment of direct elections was tried; Julius Nyerere's Tanganyikan
African National Union, founded only in 1954, participated in the elections, and became recognised by the Governor, Sir Richard Turnbull, as
an essential partner if disorder was to be averted. In November 1959 Ian
Macleod informed the Cabinet that the Colonial Policy Committee had,
on 23 November, approved the proposal that an acceleration in constitutional advance in Tanganyika should be made in the following month.
There would be an introduction of an unofficial majority in the Council
of Ministers in 1960 (with, if necessary, the introduction of the post of
Chief Minister) and a substantial extension of the franchise. This, he
concluded, was necessary if Britain were to retain the confidence of all
sections of opinion in the country which were united in their desire for
progress towards self-government.[79] TANU was able to present a united
front, with a satisfying absence of tribal rivalries; responsible government was transformed by December 1961 into sovereign nationhood,
and, in this case, the British had no important strategic or defence needs
that called for caution. Once again, African Nationalist centre and British imperial periphery worked not to frustrate a settlement, but to facilitate it.[80] Uganda followed the same pattern. While serving in the Colonial

Office its governor, Sir Andrew Cohen, had been a strong advocate
of decolonisation. Now he moved to implement the process. In 1958
the Executive Council contained two nominated Africans, one elected
African, two nominated Asians and one nominated European, with
seven officials. The Legislative Council comprised, on the official side,
ten Africans, three Europeans, and two Asians, on the unofficial side ten
directly elected Africans, two indirectly elected Africans, one nominated
African, six nominated Asians and six nominated Europeans. In November 1958 the first steps were taken to work towards a direct election
for all members of the Legislative Council on a common roll. A constitutional committee, the Wild Committee, called after its chairman,
noted the absence of modern political parties, but put the electoral cart
before the party horse, in that it declared that the very lack of elections
impeded the growth of parties; the only way to build responsibility amongst
Ugandan educated people was to associate them with responsibility in
government. Ian Macleod ruled out indirect elections on 14 September
1960, in his response to the Wild Report, and agreed to the 'Westminster model' with modifications, so that control of the executive was still
largely in the hands of the governor. But following the objections by the
African members he announced that, in the event of clear-cut results in
the elections, he would reconsider the position at once, and he encouraged the belief that the transition to internal self-government and then
independence would be rapid. In the March 1961 elections major parties emerged: the Democratic Party (founded in 1954) and the Ugandan
Peoples Congress (founded in 1960, by a fusion of part of the Ugandan
National Congress and the Ugandan Peoples Union). Now the pace
quickened further, with Reginald Maudling presiding over a conference
called in September 1961, and promising that the Ugandan people
would be given full responsibility for their own affairs within probably
a year or two. The conference agreed on a Westminster-style system of
government, though Buganda, which had opposed direct elections,
and where the British had originally focused their political organisation
of Uganda, would be united in a federal relationship with the rest of
Uganda. At the close of the conference Maudling announced that
Uganda would achieve internal self-government on 1 March 1962,
and full independence on 9 October of the same year.[81] It was significant that a politically inexperienced territory presented hardly any
difficulty to the British Government, mainly because of its very small
European population. Without white loyalism, decolonisation (given the
appropriate attitude in London) was easy, even if it was at the cost of the

new state acquiring little political experience, and its institutions scant legitimacy.

The 'balance sheet' concept, outlined by Macmillan in July 1957, was, however, a little more complicated than it at first appears. The fear of precipitate retreat, and its impact on British prestige was, after all, part of the balance sheet, as well as trade or strategy. There was the developing European Economic Community dimension to the calculation of British interests; to set against this there was also the fact that Britain enjoyed strong trading links with the Commonwealth. But the danger of going 'too slow' was felt to be real; and this was exemplified in the fate of the Central African Federation.

Lennox-Boyd referred to the special problem in deciding how to respond to the problems posed in territories where, as he put it in his 1958 speech, there were 'people of different races and in different stages of civilisation'. It was not, he confessed, 'an easy task to reconcile the interests of African, European and Asian traditions in the same territory; the capital and skill of Europeans and Asians and the numbers of Africans'. 'Nor', he added 'is it easy to implement the democracy which we have taught the Africans . . . and give security which Europeans, many as much entitled to call themselves Africans as those of darker skin, rightly demand.' Lennox-Boyd outlined the various means by which minorities could be safeguarded: 'Bicameral legislatures, qualitative and quantitative franchises, Councils of State'; but he cut through the argument with a blunt warning that 'we must face the fact that if ultimate control is surrendered it will be surrendered to someone – usually either to an educated and advanced minority or to an uneducated majority'. This could not be done, he argued, 'before genuine confidence and traditions of fair play have been established, so as to ensure that when power is transferred it will be to responsible people of different races who live there'. In this perspective, then, there were 'certain territories' in which 'it is clear that there is no honourable alternative to continuing to maintain our control for quite a long time'.[82]

But maintaining control could mean using stern measures of repression. The increasingly fragile state of social order in Africa was soon to be revealed in a whole wave of unrest which swept the colonial world in the late 1950s, not least in French Algeria and the Belgian Congo. In Nyasaland the British officials identified what they called a 'murder plot', and the suppression of this plot cost 51 African lives. The Devlin Report on these disturbances, published in the middle of 1959, condemned the security response to what it described as African antipathy

to the Federation, denied that the authorities were justified in claiming
that nationalism was confined to a small majority, insisted that the British depiction of Hastings Banda as an extremist was misleading and
unfair, dismissed the claim that there was a 'murder plot', and characterised the authorities' response to the whole situation as that of a 'police
state', albeit one of a temporary duration.[83]

The question of how long was 'quite a long time' remained an open
one. The problem of reconciling European and African in the Central
African Federation was only made more difficult by Macmillan's 1960
tour of Africa. In Lagos he was interpreted as having, in his 'winds of
change' speech, indicated that the African people in the Northern Territory would have some say in any decision about that region staying in
the Federation. In Nyasaland he stated that 'the cause of the Federation
was almost desperate because of the strength of African opinion against
it'.[84] Macmillan hoped that his visit to the Federation would prove reas-
suring; but it turned out more like de Gaulle's visit to Algeria, when de
Gaulle assured the Europeans that he 'understood' them. In February
1960 the Secretary of State for Commonwealth Affairs, Lord Home,
warned that Sir Roy Welensky and Sir Edgar Whitehead felt that 'the
United Kingdom Government were always led by circumstances into
negotiating with the extreme African Nationalists which made it impossible for the position of the settlers to be adequately safeguarded'.[85] On
28 February Macmillan claimed that the 'best hope of regaining normal
conditions in Nyasaland lay in opening discussions with Dr. Banda on
constitutional advance.... Unless some constitutional progress were
made there, the Federation was unlikely to secure the degree of African
confidence necessary for its survival. The Commonwealth Secretary
should put these arguments to Welensky and Whitehead, and should
also assure them that British proposals for constitutional advance in
Nyasaland would be moderate'.[86]

Macmillan understood the Europeans in the Federation; but the Government's Monckton Commission, established in 1959 to review the
future of the Federation, reported in October 1960, and acknowledged
that the 'great majority' of Africans 'expressed opposition to the Federation', and that their opposition was 'widespread, sincere, and of long
standing'; indeed in the two northern territories, 'almost pathological'.
The European demand for dominion status had increased African fears
that the British Government's protection would be withdrawn before
self-government in the northern territories had been secured. The
Monckton Commission did indeed acknowledge that the winds of change

were blowing through Africa; as it pointed out, in 1953, only five countries in the continent enjoyed independent nationhood: South Africa,
Egypt, Ethiopia, Liberia and Libya. 'No single unit of the British, French
or Belgian colonial empires had attained self-government.' But in 1957
'the Gold Coast emerged from its colonial status as the independent state
Ghana, and in so doing started a chain reaction among the still dependent states of Africa'.[87]

These events outside the Federation had an impact within it. It was,
the Commission reported, 'inevitable and natural that the prospect of
independence, seven years ago unthinkably remote, should now appear
to many Africans to be a right from which they should be no longer
debarred'. The Federation appeared as a block on these aspirations, and
their opposition to it was implacable. The Commission concluded that,
despite its economic advantages, and despite too the danger of friction
between the territories, the Federation should be dissolved. Balkanisation was a real threat; but a worse threat was the African dislike of the
Federation, and so the Commission recommended constitutional changes
to improve relations between Europeans and Africans, which would
stabilise the federal states. But it warned that these were not enough
to secure the Federation's future: 'we are convinced that no form of
federal association, however reformed, can succeed so long as many of its
peoples feel that they are being kept in it against their will and can break
out only by force. We therefore recommend that under certain conditions
there should be an opportunity to withdraw from the association.'[88]

This was a balanced conclusion; but it caused difficulties for the
Macmillan Cabinet. Macmillan hoped to adopt the first of the Monckton
Commission's recommendations, constitutional change, and he suggested that African representatives should have something close to parity
with Europeans in the Legislative Assembly for Northern Rhodesia. This
infuriated Roy Welensky, who threatened to boycott the talks which
began in London in December 1960. It also caused concern in the Cabinet. Macleod's impatience for change obliged Macmillan to move him
from the Colonial Office and replace him by Reginald Maudling. In his
farewell speech, at the Conservative Party conference in October 1961,
Macleod again raised the question: was it more dangerous to go too fast
or too slow? The experience of anarchy left behind by Belgium in the
Congo suggested it was more dangerous to go too fast; but there was
'probably greater safety in going fast than in going slow'. There was what
Macleod called a 'tight rope of timing which the Colonial Secretary has
to walk in every territory, every week, sometimes almost every day', in

reconciling majority and minority interests. Macleod warned that social
and economic reform could never be a substitute for political rights:
indeed, reform only sharpened the demand for those rights. Macleod
thus helped dovetail the view from the centre of African Nationalism to
that of the periphery of British colonialism. There was no automatic
right to govern, he added. 'We would never have accepted – we did not
accept this from the Romans. The Irish never accepted it from us.'
Macleod urged partnership. The British Empire would not be 'at one
with Nineveh and Tyre' because 'we are the only empire leaving behind
us a coherent political scheme of development'. The tide of events could
not be turned.[89]

Reginald Maudling pushed ahead with the destruction of the Federation. In February 1962 Northern Rhodesia was given the right to secede,
despite Lord Home's warning that there was a danger that the Europeans 'if driven too far' would take the law into their own hands and form
a European-dominated association of Southern Rhodesia, the Copper
Belt, Angola, Katanga and South Africa, 'fatal to British hopes of multi-
racial cooperation in Africa'. He hoped that the right of secession would
be delayed, with a two-year transitional period.[90] Macmillan hoped
to relieve tension in his government by appointing Butler, in March 1962,
as Secretary of State with special responsibility for Central Africa – a job
likely to keep him out of any potential role as the man who would be
king – of the Cabinet – and Butler put the finishing touch to the break-
up of the Federation. In April 1962 Hastings Banda won a resounding
victory in the general elections in Nyasaland, and demanded immediate
secession. The Government now set its sights on the lesser task of promising as many safeguards as it could for the Europeans, aware that the
end of this complex problem was more of a relief than a disaster for the
empire.

But the end was not quite reached; the relief was only temporary. On
28 March 1963 Butler informed the Cabinet that the Government of
Southern Rhodesia wanted independence at once. He set out the advantages and disadvantages of a British acquiescence in this outcome. If
Britain were to allow Rhodesia to proceed to independence in the normal way, at an appropriate time, then 'we relieve ourselves of a position
whereby, while having no power to compel the Government of Southern
Rhodesia to modify their racial policies, we remained responsible for
defending these policies to world opinion'. But if Britain were to confer
independence on a colony where a European minority sought to impose
its will on an African majority by increasingly repressive measures, then

Britain would be abandoning her consistent policy to defer the grant of final independence to a colony until it had reached the state of constitutional development at which the majority of the population enjoyed the decisive voice in managing public affairs. To depart from this would open the United Kingdom to intense Commonwealth and international criticism. If Rhodesia could not be prevented from seeking to assert formally the independence which they already enjoyed in practice, 'it would be better that they should be seen to do so by a unilateral action which will be unprecedented in the history of the progressive transfer of power to former dependencies'. This essentially hard-headed view – characteristic of the Conservative attitude to the end of empire in Africa – was not formally adopted by the Cabinet; but it informed its attitude, which was summed up by the Prime Minister, who said that the wise course was to defer a decision on the issue for as far as possible.[91] It fell to Harold Wilson to pick up the remaining pieces of this last African pillar of empire.

This apparently minor footnote to British imperial history, occupying what seemed an inordinate amount of the Prime Minister's time, was of deeper significance than at first appeared. The white population of Southern Rhodesia regarded the break-up of the Central African Federation in 1963 as a betrayal, and they had from the 1930s hankered after the status of a Dominion in the Commonwealth, but, though they were in most respects their own masters, this final accolade had been refused. By 1964 Africans were not without some political rights – 15 seats out of 65 in the Legislature were held by Africans, and there was even a 'Bill of Rights' – but the British faced the problem that had confronted them in the 1930s: that of creating an authentic 'public opinion' in Rhodesia which was not yet formed, but which the white Rhodesians seemed determined would not be formed. In April 1964 Ian Smith became Prime Minister of Rhodesia and it soon became clear that he was moving the colony towards independence on his own terms, that of white supremacy. Smith was helped by a split between the black African leaders, with two main groups emerging: the Zimbabwean African Peoples' Union, led by Joseph Nkomo, and the Zimbabwean African National Union, formed by the Reverend Ndabaningi Sithole. This gave Smith the opportunity to claim that this faction-fighting was typical of black African politicians, leading to the kind of anarchy experienced in the former Belgian Congo (now Zaire) since its decolonisation in 1960.[92]

The Rhodesian problem was particularly vexatious for Labour. Labour's concept of the multi-racial, democratic Commonwealth was of course irreconcilable with minority white rule in Salisbury. If Britain did not respond to the Rhodesian challenge, then her standing in the Commonwealth would be weakened. This would deeply affect her position as a world power which Labour, or at least Harold Wilson, believed was inextricably bound up with her leadership of the Commonwealth. This in turn would have serious implications for Wilson's belief that a strong Britain in a United Commonwealth was a great force for influence on world peace.[93] All this was now put at risk. The Tanganyikan Minister for Foreign Affairs said in 1963 that if Britain did not secure majority rule in Southern Rhodesia 'the entire African states' membership of the Commonwealth would have to be considered'. Tanzania, Zambia and Ghana threatened to leave the Commonwealth if Britain, having failed to grant majority rule in Rhodesia, did not end the rebellion by force, and in 1965 Ghana and Tanzania broke off diplomatic relations with the United Kingdom, though they did not withdraw from the Commonwealth.[94]

Wilson later admitted that he had 'no intention' of subjecting what he called the 'Rhodesian people' to the rule of 'an unprepared African majority tomorrow'.[95] But Ian Smith, in threatening to make a unilateral declaration of independence, was attacking the sovereignty of the British Crown and Parliament and these must be defended.[96] Wilson was determined from the first not to succumb to demands by the Commonwealth Conference in June 1965 for military intervention. On 30 October he made a broadcast in which he declared that there could be no 'thunderbolt hurtling through the sky and destroying the enemy, a thunderbolt in the shape of the Royal Air Force'.[97] This expressed the policy agreed on by the Cabinet on 12 September, when it was decided that Britain would exert whatever pressure against Rhodesia that it could, short of military intervention. Wilson even set his face against military intervention from any other quarter; Britain would be 'unwilling' to make a United Kingdom contribution to a United Nations force, and should seek to avert military action being undertaken by such a force.[98] Meetings on 7 and 14 October reinforced this negative stance, though it was noted that it would be difficult for Britain to withdraw her standing offer to provide logistical support for six battalions of a United Nations force, and it might even be desirable to intervene if law and order broke down.[99] Wilson still hoped that the Rhodesians would come to appreciate that the United Kingdom was not insisting on immediate majority rule in Rhodesia.[100] Much of Wilson's diffidence about using force was based on the logistical difficulties; but the Cabinet was also aware that, while public opinion in Britain might be expected to condemn the illegal declaration of independence, nevertheless 'there might be developments, such as action against the white population in other African countries, which could influence sentiment in the United Kingdom once more in favour of the Rhodesian Government'.[101]

The Government's admission that force was ruled out, however understandable, only encouraged Smith and his Cabinet. On 11 November 1965 Smith's Rhodesian Security Council issued its declaration of independence. The result was a long political dispute that was not resolved until 1979; a ruinous war between the Rhodesian armed forces and African nationalist guerrillas; and a weakening of the Labour Party's traditional loyalty to the Commonwealth idea. The Labour Government was pursued by African members of the Commonwealth, and it is hard to resist the conclusion that Wilson was more concerned to find ways of appeasing their impatience with his Rhodesian policy than with bringing down the Smith regime. His decision to apply economic sanctions in place of military force was weakened by the failure to cut off oil supplies right away. At a special Commonwealth Conference, held in Lagos in January 1966, Wilson fended off African criticism by claiming that sanctions would work 'within a matter of weeks rather than months'.[102] Wilson's plight was real; Zambia did not impose an embargo on Rhodesia for fear of its impact on their own economy. But there was suspicion, not without foundation, that Wilson was prepared to go further in negotiations with Smith than seemed appropriate. Certainly, in the negotiations on board HMS *Tiger*, in December 1966, Wilson conceded that the British Government would accept the 1961 constitution, which was based on a gradual transition to black majority rule, with minority rights secured. This would now be constructed on an extended African franchise, but Sir Edgar Whitehead, Prime Minister of Rhodesia in the 1950s, reckoned it might delay majority rule until the next century. For this, Smith must 'return to legality'. Greater concessions were offered in the talks on HMS *Fearless* in October 1968, which would have involved Wilson pressing the 'no sell-out, no slamming the door' argument on the Commonwealth.[103]

The danger to Britain's standing in the world, and to such cohesion as the Commonwealth still possessed, was undeniable; and Wilson was critical of what he called a 'caucus' (Africa, Asia and the West Indies members, except for Malawi and Malaysia) which, he alleged, sought to prevent reasonable compromise. Wilson, summing up the position in Cabinet on 16 September 1966, went so far as to suggest that, after a suitable period of time, 'it might be desirable to review United Kingdom interests in relation to the future of the Commonwealth'.[104] Wilson's dilemma was eased as the white Rhodesians moved further into their pursuit of permanent minority rule. In 1970 he told Barbara Castle that 'we are clearly seen to have been reasonable, while Smith has not. He will have no support from British public opinion now.'[105]

There was, perhaps, a wider context to Wilson's uncertain policy. Since the early nineteenth century, and more so since the South African settlement of 1910, the United Kingdom had preferred to maintain its imperial role through devolving powers to local political élites. When this proved difficult, as it did in Kenya, then the consequences were troublesome. And the Conservative Governments which were responsible for the decolonisation of most of Africa opted to support any military action with a policy that, in some degree at least, reflected Edmund Burke's *dictum* that to act as superintendent of subordinate or, in the twentieth century, equal governments was preferable to the application of sustained force, of which, Burke claimed, the British had 'no experience' in its favour.[106] In reality the British Empire had considerable experience of force by 1964; but they had no desire to get into a long war, like Vietnam; and yet they could not identify and devolve power in Rhodesia to local African élites, because the white Rhodesians stood firmly in their path. Hence Wilson's only option was to play for time, which left the unfinished business to another Government and another day. But it was significant that the other Government, the Conservative Government of Margaret Thatcher, which supervised the transition to black majority rule, was as much a spectator as a participant in the downfall of the Smith regime.

In 1972 Edward Heath's attempt to negotiate a bi-lateral agreement for independence collapsed with ignominy when a commission led by Lord Pearce registered the total unacceptability of the proposed agreement which (it was estimated) would have taken between 30 and 100 years to meet black African aspirations. The outcome of the Heath initiative was that he had shown willingness to fulfil British obligations to build a settlement, satisfied his own Right that he had tried to reconcile a settlement with white Rhodesian security, and done his best to end what Lord Carrington later called 'an irritant – with the Commonwealth, with our European partners and with the United States'.[107] But the Heath initiative also aroused black African opinion and created a greater sense of solidarity amongst those restless under, or opposed to, white rule.

The pressure towards change in Rhodesia came from factors quite outside Westminster or Whitehall – or even Salisbury – control. In

1975 Portugal withdrew from Angola and Mozambique. Now a guerrilla campaign could be launched from these territories. The lesson of
this was not lost on South Africa which, perhaps fearing that it might
have to take on board a crippled Rhodesia, pressed Smith to concede
the principle of majority rule. In 1978 he did so, accepting the government of the country by two African nationalists, Ndabaningi Sithole
and Bishop Muzorewa. But the guerrilla war waged in eastern Rhodesia by Robert Mugabe's armies intensified. It was at this moment that
Mrs Thatcher's Conservative administration took office, and with characteristic energy set out to resolve the long-running and damaging
problem.

The Conservative Government would have found it more congenial
and easier to lift sanctions and recognise the existing regime. But, yet
again, the world could not be set aside, and world opinion, the Commonwealth and the United States would not recognise the Muzorewa
Government. The Conservative Government went for a simpler solution: to treat Rhodesia as a colony whose future would – in the time-
honoured British way – be decided at the conference table. Accordingly,
they summoned all the relevant parties to Lancaster House in London,
cleared the proposed initiative with the Commonwealth in the Lusaka
summit, and in November convened the Lancaster House talks. At these
talks Mrs Thatcher conceded that there would be fresh elections as part
of the settlement to which the Patriotic Front would be admitted; and
that Commonwealth observers would supervise the elections and report
on their fairness. The conference negotiated the difficult issues of the
constitution, the cease-fire arrangements and interim administrative
arrangements. On 11 December 1979 a new governor was installed and
the transfer of power – for such it now appeared to be – proceeded. Elections produced a victory for Mugabe's ZANU (PF) party which won 57 of
the 80 African seats. This was a shock to the British Government, though
it might have reflected on the fact that, as a correspondent put it in the
Round Table 'it is not usual in Africa for any political party to agree to
elections it might lose'.[108] But, although never the master of events, the
British Government could yet again take refuge in the belief that, by
brokering a transfer of power, even one made only after political crises,
humiliations, and violence, it was thereby taming and domesticating the
new masters of a colonial territory. The real master of Zimbabwe was
perhaps the economic facts of life, notably the importance to the economy of white cooperation, Zimbabwe's economic relations with South
Africa, and later, the increasing globalisation of the economy with its

constraints on the policy of all states, even those led by avowedly Marxist leaders such as Mugabe.[109]

Writing to Lord Beaverbrook in March 1976, Wilson described himself as a 'Commonwealth man – and I have even used your house-flag phrase "Empire" on many occasions.'[110] But the Rhodesian crisis, though it played no part in his Government's application to join the EEC in May 1967, was a disillusioning experience for Wilson. His sanctioning of the sale of WASP helicopters, in October 1969, to South Africa on the grounds that they could only at great expense be adapted to riot control, seemed to reveal that his Commonwealth enthusiasm had been shallowly based,[111] though it surfaced again in November 1975, when he requested that Canada be represented at an EEC 'Big Five' meeting proposed by France.[112] His imperialistic tendency was blunted when he was forced to abandon Britain's role East of Suez, a 'psychological' journey which may have begun when he decided to apply for membership of the EEC in 1967.[113]

This left Wilson's claim that Britain's frontiers were on the Himalayas looking threadbare. By now there was a large gap between Harwich and the Himalayas; the frontiers were left with spaces in between. The British influence in Africa soon waned. In the army mutinies in Uganda, Kenya and Tanganyika in 1964, British troops intervened to suppress the mutineers; but a more significant fact was Nigeria's decision in 1962 to annul a defence agreement with Britain.[114] The Conservatives, particularly under the leadership of Edward Health, had fewer illusions about the imperial and Commonwealth role than Harold Wilson, and Mrs Thatcher, though she fought the Falklands War, was mostly concerned to build up and sustain the Anglo-American relationship and, less enthusiastically, maintain the European connection.[115] Deprived of its chief supports, its pillars, the empire began to float off, like some Laputan island, into its contemporary role as a forum for discussion, and sometimes considerable disagreement, but without collective political, military or economic power.

But symbols have their own part to play in politics, as the present state of Anglo-Irish relations testifies. The Irish Taoiseach's musings on the possibility of opening a debate on Ireland rejoining the Commonwealth in order to assuage Unionist fears, and meet their desires for a monarchical political system may come to nothing. But they suggest that the British Commonwealth may yet provide a forum for helping to reconcile a conflict of nationality, even as its great age of power draws to its close.

10

EMPIRE, RACE AND CITIZENSHIP

When J. R. Seeley published his timely book *The Expansion of England*, he compared the British Empire to those of Greece and Rome. He argued that the British Empire was powerful because it was an extension of the state, peopled by Europeans, who were subjects of the Crown. He denied that the British Empire was one of conquest, as the Roman Empire had been, with the exception of India; it was an empire of free peoples who enjoyed a common culture and religion. He was concerned lest the empire, by expanding beyond the limits of this common nationality, would weaken and die. For such was the condition of most empires.

Seeley's description was, even in its day, misleading. From the middle of the eighteenth century Britain incorporated many non-British peoples under her rule, often after conquest. And between the publication of Seeley's book and the end of the Great War the British Empire further developed in the way that Seeley feared; it became even more of an empire of diverse people, cultures and religions. People of European stock governed, policed and administered it; but the diversity underneath even had an impact, at first limited, but later significant, on the peopling of the British Isles, or at least of Great Britain. In the eighteenth century there was a black community in Britain, and the migration of people from the empire inwards to Britain attained considerable proportion by the 1950s.

Britain had no difficulty absorbing this immigration before the 1950s; but the question of what it meant to govern an empire that was (except India) originally European (or to use the contemporary, if highly misleading, expression 'Anglo-Saxon') in composition, and yet contained diverse races and religions, was one that disturbed the idea of the empire as propounded by Seeley. There was a feeling in the developing Commonwealth after 1918 that there was a vital distinction to be made

234

between the Commonwealth (free) and the Empire (subjects) – or, as one Australian put it in 1901, the Australians were 'citizen-subjects', while the Indians were 'subject citizens'.[1] This was not a view held by all the Dominions, but it found expression in their practice of immigration laws and in their treatment of resident Indians. An Australian Shipping Bill of 1907 contained a clause restricting preference to British goods carried on British ships manned by white labour.[2] Their awareness of this attitude provoked the British Government to ask the Dominions to frame their policies so as to 'avoid wanton injury to the self-respect of non-European British subjects', and avoid embarrassing the Government in India, otherwise there could not be any hope of a truly united Empire:

> However close the connection and however perfect the understanding between the Mother Country and the self-governing Dominions, we are not a united Empire unless that understanding spreads to some considerable extent, also to that vast part of the Empire of which, of course, India is the most prominent division, but which also includes all the Crown Colonies which are inhabited by the various native races.[3]

The question of South Africa's place in the empire also raised problems of race. When the Earl of Selborne was presiding over the making of the South African Union between 1908 and 1910, he was fully aware of the danger of depriving those non-whites in South Africa (few in number and confined largely to the Cape Province) who already enjoyed political rights, let alone preventing them from ever attaining rights which they did not yet enjoy. He also exercised about the future of the Protectorates, Bechuanaland, Basutoland and Swaziland, in the new South Africa. His solution to this – which the Liberal Government rejected – was to place them under the Government of South Africa, but have them administered by 'carefully selected officers' and watched over by the imperial parliament.[4] The question of a native franchise also deeply concerned Selborne, who feared that it might wreck closer union. Selborne hoped to save the Cape native franchise by incorporating it into the new constitution; but even if that were secured, there remained the even more vexatious problem of whether or not it might be extended to other native peoples. Selborne advised the drawing up of a 'civilisation test' of native fitness to exercise political rights, and even hoped to establish that by holding out the prospect of an immediate transfer of the Protectorates to the Union government. But he realistically surmised that the only rights likely to be salvaged were those already existing in the Cape, and these rights were entrenched in the constitution, but with no 'open door' for further native advance.[5]

Selborne's attempts to grapple with this issue revealed important aspects of the thinking of a highly religious and fair-minded man to the question of race equality in the British Empire. His search for a 'civilisation test' was based on the notion that Europeans were, simply, at a much more advanced stage in civilisation than non-Europeans. White people, as he put it, were the 'ancestors' of those who 'came into contact with Roman civilisation 2000 years ago'. It was hardly reasonable, then, to apply this standard to Bantus 'whose ancestors first came into contact with civilisation less than 100 years ago'. His civilisation test would be limited to men of 30 years of age and older, who could produce evidence that they had a 'fair education' and had been living an 'industrious life' (a test, it must be said, not unlike that which Victorian liberals sought to apply to the British working man). There must also be checks to ensure that the civilised man's sons had not 'reverted'; a coloured man might be tested at a lower age and might dispense with further proof.[6]

This question, then, raised the wider issue of what these concepts, 'nationality' and 'citizenship', meant in the British Empire. Seeley equated the two: common culture and religion were what underlay common citizenship. The Roman Empire, to which he liked to refer, possessed the idea of common status – a Roman citizen need not be a Roman by birth, but could live in Gaul, Germany or Spain. The common status of citizenship was extended more quickly in the West than the East, but finally it was declared for all the peoples throughout the empire without exception.[7]

The French Empire, as a modern example, professed allegiance to the idea of a common citizenship irrespective of race or doctrine; it also offered its colonial peoples the full benefits of the French civilisation. The idea of the natural equality of all men, however diluted in practice, could not be set aside or abandoned. But the British Empire was as diverse in its attitude to nationality and citizenship as in the character of its empire. The empire was multi-cultural; but it also contained its senior white division, and it permitted the white division to erect barriers against the non-white peoples of the empire. In the 1850s the Australian colonies initiated policies to restrict the entry of Asiatics, which were applied not only to the Chinese, but also the Queen's Indian subjects. Natal in the 1890s framed laws against British Indians, though she was obliged to substitute an education test to attain the same ends. Joseph

Chamberlain, at the 1897 Imperial Conference, requested the Australian colonies to 'arrange a form of words which will avoid hurting the feelings of any of Her Majesty's subjects', but he sympathised with the white colonies' desire to protect themselves against the influx of people 'alien in civilisation, alien in religion, alien in customs, whose influx, moreover, would seriously interfere with the legitimate rights of the existing labour population'.[8]

The British Government fully accepted the principle – which all the white colonies found ways of implementing – of these restrictive discriminations. In 1911 Lord Crewe dismissed the idea that every subject of the King could travel or settle in any part of the empire; the British Government, he declared, 'fully accept the principle that each of the Dominions must be allowed to decide for itself what elements it desires to accept in its population'.[9] This at least had the effect of causing New Zealand to withdraw a resolution asserting that, in order to preserve imperial harmony, 'every race should be relegated to its own zone'. Oddly enough, the Indian delegation in 1918 accepted this principle of restriction on immigration,[10] and Basil Williams was justified in his claim that, if Britain had failed to make real the concept of 'common citizenship' for her Indian subjects, the fault lay not with her, but in the 'entire liberty granted to all British communities to decide on their own composition and destinies'.[11]

There was another barrier which race or colour raised in the empire – that of the importation of cheap indentured labour, such as Lord Milner introduced in South Africa to work the Transvaal gold mines and enable South Africa to recover from the ravages of war. 'Chinese Labour' was a label that liberals fastened around Milner's neck; yet the idea of free movement of labour might be linked to the making of a melting pot, or at least the granting of citizenship rights to the immigrants. This would hardly work in South Africa, where the idea of race equality, denied to natives and applied to Cape coloured peoples, only under strict controls, was unlikely to be extended to incoming Asians.[12]

The British Empire, then, was evolving into a series of separate nationalities, but these diverse communities might yet be granted equal rights; and the United Kingdom itself consisted, after all, of different nationalities (Welsh, English, Irish, Scottish) but enjoyed a common citizenship, that of a British subject. But, despite this possible model, it was clear by the 1930s that the Dominions which received non-European immigrants were by no means uniform in their treatment of these races. Some like the Australian states (except Western Australia) admitted

Indians to the franchise: but in Canada British Columbia was nervous of so doing, fearing that, if the Indians were given these rights, the more numerous Chinese and Japanese would claim them too.[13] The growth of Dominion authority, the development of Dominion status, was not bringing with it the equal treatment of non-European members.

Nowhere was the nationality/citizenship question more complex than in the British attitude to India – that part of the imperial realm that Seeley identified as the most difficult to reconcile to the empire of common culture and religion. There was no one simple response to the government of a large subcontinent containing many different religions, linguistic groups and marked by regional diversity, and no simple attitude to its role in an evolving British Empire. India was indeed different; but that difference need not exclude her from being taken in hand and advanced, slowly but gradually, along the road to self-government. But the problem for British administrators and soldiers in India was that the very people who were likely to play a part in that process, and indeed benefit from its outcome – civil servants, professional people, lawyers, teachers – were the kind of people who were likely to be found in the forefront of the nationalist movement that seemed to feel no gratitude to the British for what the Raj thought was its stern, but just, rule. Moreover, the idea of trusteeship could easily be translated into a special kind of superiority: not only of crude racialism (though that was present) but one of regarding the people of India as necessarily backward. The governor of the Punjab, Sir Michael O'Dwyer, wrote in his memoirs that the Sikhs (whom he greatly admired as fighting men) were 'slow witted'.[14] It was a sense of duty, General Dyer claimed when he confronted the Hunter Committee on the Amritsar massacre in 1920, that obliged him to teach the 'rebels' of the Punjab a lesson, to do them 'a jolly lot of good', to show them that they must not be wicked, and thus make the moral point that the Raj was not to be disobeyed. O'Dwyer, for his part, vehemently denied that he was opposed to Indian self-government; rather, he feared that it was being driven by ignorant politicians in Britain, and demanded by dishonest agitators, such as Gandhi, in India.[15] Britain must not abandon her loyal friends in India, the vast bulk of the India people; this would be a betrayal and 'unworthy of our great past'.[16]

The *Round Table* group, as always, was quick to offer answers to these vexing questions, claiming that India was not unlike England, in that both possessed 'highly educated, thoughtful and competent people.... It has numberless country gentlemen exactly like the country gentlemen of England', and a professional middle class which was making increasing demands to have a say in the making of public policy. India was not like Africa, and was clearly the centre of the whole future development of the empire. If the Indian problem could be solved, if a responsible, self-governing Dominion could be created, and if that Dominion elected to stay in the empire, then 'we shall have solved the greatest difficulty which presents itself in the world today'.[17] This was to move British imperialist thinking from the authoritarian Roman model, which was most popular at the turn of the century, to the Greek concept of an empire based on a large-scale civilised community which transcended local and national differences, which was part of the development of the 'higher life of the human race'.[18]

The problem of race in the empire, then, was one that worked on several levels. There was the British attitude to her non-European nationalities; the Dominions' attitude to their non-European peoples (both 'native' and immigrant); and the attitude of one member of the empire to another, especially the running battle between South Africa and India over the Union's treatment of Indians in South Africa, which Gandhi drew attention to, and which the Viceroy of India criticised in 1913, claiming that the Government of India had a 'deep and burning sympathy' with Indians in South Africa.[19] At times, for example in 1924, this threatened to damage the Commonwealth and deprive it of any sense of moral unity, that moral unity that seemed central to the whole concept of the uniqueness of the British expansion in a world of European empires.[20] The Government of India also intervened on behalf of Indians in Kenya and Uganda in 1920, demanding adequate political representation.[21] The potentially disruptive impact of race was seen when some European settlers threatened to rebel against their governor and set up their own government.[22] In the course of the crisis the British Government, in a white paper issued in 1923, stumbled on the presence of another set of people in Kenya: the Africans. It committed itself to act as the guardians of trusteeship on their behalf, and the ultimate goal of Kenya as an 'African territory'.[23] The Indian community, for its part, outdid the whites in their opposition to the statement that there should be reciprocal rights for all separate communities, a proposal which would place them in a permanent political minority: Natives first, Europeans second, and Indians third.[24]

These controversies revealed the difficulty in establishing the British Empire on any kind of firm citizenship footing. The disruptive potential of race was felt far and wide; emotional language was spoken. For colonies to be moved towards self-government required the formation of a public opinion. But in most African countries (except South Africa) there was as yet no 'public opinion' that embraced the majority of the peoples; in India there was a tendency for the Government to deny that the main Indian political party, Congress, represented the 'real' people of India, but was the voice of an élite, and a devious and untrustworthy élite at that. And in South Africa there was clearly the making of a white man's country, which would not in the foreseeable future acknowledge the political presence of the African population.

Despite this troublesome background the Labour Government between 1946 and 1948 clarified the question of where the Commonwealth stood on citizenship and nationality. It had to respond to the Canadian intention to enact a citizenship bill 'inconsistent with the prevailing practice of a single common code of British nationality applicable throughout the Commonwealth',[25] whereby Canadian citizenship would be local and separate, and there would be a general recognition that all persons possessing such citizenship would be recognised as British subjects throughout the Commonwealth. Canadians would have citizenship as Canadians, and would only secondarily be British subjects. This was to challenge one of the fundamental links of the Commonwealth; but the British Government acknowledged that there would be certain advantages in the new law. It set up a committee to review nationality law in the Commonwealth generally, and this 'Committee of Experts', chaired by a Home Office official, reported favourably on the Canadian idea, calling for a further conference of experts from the self-governing nations. A conference in Canada in February 1947, attended by representatives from the United Kingdom, Canada, Australia, New Zealand, South Africa, Ireland, Rhodesia, Burma and Ceylon, with the Indian High Commissioner in attendance as an observer, concluded that the Commonwealth should reconcile citizenship with nationality, with each country determining by legislation who were its citizens. The combined total of the citizens of the various Commonwealth countries would form the general body of 'British subjects'.[26] This was to adopt in essence the Canadian model, with local citizenship combined with a recognition of all persons possessing this citizenship as British subjects throughout the Commonwealth. The British Government passed a nationality bill enacting that all persons who were citizens of any Commonwealth country (except Eire) should, by virtue of their respective citizenships, be British subjects, and this was done 'in a spirit which would not create such bitterness between the two countries as might diminish the chances of Eire's ultimate return to the Commonwealth',[27] though it was acknow-

ledged that Eire was retaining the advantage of Commonwealth membership while renouncing her obligations.[28] The bill recognised the reality
that each local independent Commonwealth country was an individual
entity, but that all were (it was hoped) united in a common association
as British subjects (changed to 'Commonwealth citizen' after Indian
objections).

In the event some Commonwealth countries allowed dual nationality;
others, such as South Africa, India and Ceylon, did not. The free entry of
British subjects was, by the end of the 1940s, only allowed by Great Britain, India and Pakistan. Typically, the British handled the delicate issue
of Irish citizens' status in Great Britain by treating them to all intents and
purposes as British subjects, on the grounds that the inconvenience to
both countries made this essential: they even continued to operate the
Dublin Liaison Office to match job vacancies in Britain with prospective
emigrants in Ireland.[29] *The Round Table*, surveying the 1948 Nationality
Act, grumbled that Irish citizens, 'apparently to satisfy Mr. de Valera',
should be singled out for treatment as 'international hermaphrodites',
and went on to ask whether 'a Commonwealth of Nations which, at least
for the moment includes India, Ceylon and Pakistan, not to mention
South Africa, Canada and Ireland' could be described as 'British', and
doubted if the term 'subject' any longer indicated 'the true relation of its
peoples'. Would it not be 'wiser and more realistic to recognise publicly
that the Commonwealth is now an alliance of independent states, which
can no longer be described as Dominions, and which are bound together
in a common citizenship and purpose under one King by consent rather
than allegiance?'[30]

In an article entitled 'Personal Loyalties in a Changing Empire', the
Round Table accepted that the British Commonwealth was 'a creature of
growth. Its nature and justification are pragmatic; it works because it
lives . . .'. But it described the British Nationality Bill as a 'disintegrating'
one. The key to nationality was the concept of British 'subjecthood',
which was the common status of all subjects of the Crown whichever of
its dominions they were born in. This system gave reality to the proud
boast *civis Britannicus sum*, enabling citizens of different parts of the
Commonwealth to intermarry without the risk of losing their nationality
or complicating the nationality of their children. Now the idea that to be
a British subject was the guarantee of their 'basic nationality' had gone,
and local citizenship in each Commonwealth country would replace it.
There would be British subjects without citizenship, and 'it would be
hard to find any phrase more obnoxious to the ancient system with its

proud boast of the rights of British subjects everywhere'.[31] This, more-over, was a 'sudden invention', and quite at odds with the British way of proceeding.[32] Had the *Round Table* known the details of inner dis-cussions, it would have been even more alarmed: for civil servants assumed that the idea of full British nationality for colonial peoples would be a 'violation of geography and common sense'. Fortunately the Labour Government did not take to the principle of discriminating against any British subjects and the government retained open entry to Britain.[33]

The South African question, though it was far from posing the only problem of race and citizenship in the British Empire, was nonetheless the very epitome of the problem – or at least was soon to become that. After 1945 the Union Government began its policy of apartheid on a systematic and determined scale. The Colonial Secretary, Creech Jones, described it in 1949 as a 'wicked racial policy'.[34] In Britain there were various liberal-minded groups and individuals who showed concern about apartheid, and accepted Britain's special responsibility in acting to expose and if possible destroy it. An organisation called the National Peace Council's African Committee convened a conference in June 1950, composed of 'representatives of political, social and religious societies' to discuss 'The Humane Crisis in Africa'. It acclaimed the 'moral awaken-ing' of Africa and approved 'its support for the . . . welfare of Africa'. This concern embraced all the African peoples, and in the early 1950s the problem of race began to be regularly debated, with concern expressed at the dominance of European minorities at the expense of black Africa. The Fabian Colonial Bureau told the Commonwealth Relations Society in March 1950 that its members 'noted with some alarm an attitude of appeasement towards white opinion in South, East and Central Africa'. And in February 1951, in the House of Commons, a motion sponsored jointly by Fabian and left-wing MPs reaffirmed

> its confidence in the course of British Commonwealth and colonial policy in the last five years and, whilst recognising the difficulties encountered today in countries where different races have reached different stages of development, calls upon white people everywhere to free themselves from the conception of racial superiority and follow courses directed towards the brotherhood of man.

This was signed by 106 Labour MPs, nearly half the Party's back-benchers.[35]

This was impressive as far as it went. But the politics of race in the British Empire were more complex than these ringing declarations made it out to be. There were good reasons why a Labour Government (or for that matter any government) should want to move carefully on the apartheid issue. There were strong economic links between Britain and South Africa; there were the historic ties, with South African involvement in the two world wars; there was the need to cooperate with the Union on defence policies, with the importance of the naval base at Simonstown a major consideration; the Nationalist Party in South Africa was strongly anti-communist and its Prime Minister, Dr Malan, had publicly pledged support for Britain in any war with Russia arising from 'Russian Aggression'; it was important not to strain the ties of Commonwealth, which rested upon 'the principle of tolerance'.[36] At the same time it was acknowledged that the South African race policy was at odds with everything the British believed they stood for in their policy towards African problems: South African policy towards African development was 'fundamentally different to ours' aiming as it did at 'a stratified society in order to safeguard the economic and political domination of the European and, above all, the Dutch community'. It was these misgivings, and the doubts about reaction in other Commonwealth states such as India, that caused the Government to question the wisdom of handing over South-West Africa to the Union.[37]

The Secretary of State for Dominion Affairs and the Colonial Secretary found themselves at odds, with the former adhering to the idea that the Dominions constituted the 'first division' in the Commonwealth, and expressing opposition to the interference of the United States and the United Nations, and the latter expressing concern about the 'maintenance of the trusteeship principle'.[38] The High Commission territories, which Lord Selborne had hoped to incorporate into the Union on its formation in 1910, raised another issue over which South Africa and Britain disagreed. The Commonwealth Relations Office, when drafting a letter in reply to the Union's request for their transfer, wrote sympathetically of South Africa's desire to 'maintain the present standard of living and way of life' for South Africans of European stock; but it hoped that the Union would appreciate the difficulties for the United Kingdom in any transfer:

The United Kingdom controls many African territories inhabited by various *indigenous* peoples at many different stages of development. It is the experience of the United Kingdom Government that *these peoples* in any one part of the Continent attach great importance to promises – or indeed to anything which may be interpreted as a promise – made to *other peoples of their race* elsewhere.

Transfer therefore could take place only with the consent of the inhabitants of those territories.[39] The fear was that, as one Colonial Office member put it in September 1950, the United Kingdom would be 'tarred with the apartheid brush'.[40]

The balance was always one between fulfilling obligations to the African races on the one hand, and maintaining good relations with South Africa in order to retain her as part of the struggle against communism, and her value to the British military position in the Middle East; and it is fair to say that the Labour Government tried hard not to abandon the African Commitment, yet could not downgrade the strategic consideration. In February 1951 the South African Prime Minister, Malan, warned the British that the Commonwealth had changed its character since the days when it had a 'sufficient similarity of culture and political outlook'; 'Link of common kinship was not strong enough in the case of Ireland, India and Burma and in any case was too remote and vague to exercise any real effective force in the long run.'[41] Patrick Gordon Walker, in April 1951, urged that the best way forward was, as he put it, to 'contain' South Africa and prevent spread of its influence in the other British African Colonies, yet remain 'friendly' towards the Union.[42] But, in a memorandum written by Sir E. Baring to Gordon Walker in June 1951, a more pessimistic picture was painted, one in which Baring foresaw the likely breaking of the 'strong tie of sentiment', the declaration of a Republic, and the decay of 'interest in and love for all things British'.[43]

The 'strong tie of sentiment' was one that worked both ways; it was also one that provoked liberal and left-wing opinion in Britain to demand that British Governments use their links with, and influence over, South Africa to change her apartheid policy. The Fabian Colonial Bureau continued its propaganda work following the defeat of the Labour Government in the General Election of 1951. Its 'Future Policy' declared that it would help colonial peoples advance themselves, and that it would work for the clarification of 'the concept of partnership' in East and Central Africa. In June 1952 it stated that it sought to '*help* peoples in Africa in opposing unfair discrimination and inequality of opportunity and to foster cooperation between races'.[44] It organised meetings, distributed literature and published a monthly *African Report*.[45]

The Labour left organised a committee to monitor African affairs, and in March 1954 a new organisation, the 'Council for Colonial Freedom', was founded, with support from Labour MPs and leading churchmen to defend the right of colonial peoples and to uphold the Declaration of Human Rights against the Colour Bar.[46] This organisation gained widespread publicity, and by the mid-1950s the debate on race equality, centring on South Africa, was fairly in the centre of at least the British political élite. The Labour Party had by now emerged as a main promoter of the rights of colonial peoples, and the issue of race in the British Commonwealth and Empire was given greater political significance than ever before.

This marked a major shift from the idea of an empire falling into two divisions – the white old dominions and the new non-white countries – to one of a multi-racial Commonwealth; and this in turn made the point that no nation state which aspired to join, or remain within, the Commonwealth, could also pursue policies based on the concept of racial inequalities. But the British Government, for their part, were conscious of the need to weigh up this undeniably moral code – one that seemed to provide moreover a coherent identity for a widespread and heterogeneous Empire/Commonwealth – and its desire not to drive South Africa out of the Commonwealth, thus forfeiting important strategic and economic interests. The control of the Simonstown naval base revealed the British concern to balance its strategic needs as against the rising tide of Afrikaaner nationalism. Britain was anxious to retain the facilities of this base after its transfer to South African control in 1955; and this transfer was not made without misgivings, not least about the signals that transfer would make about British imperial weakness in the post-war world. But it also involved the British Government in successful negotiations ensuring the protection of the rights of 'coloured' workers on the base. The South African Government's belief that it had a role to play in the defence of British world power enabled the agreement to be made on conditions that satisfied the British Government that its use of the base was guaranteed (unlike that of the Irish 'treaty ports').[47]

This successful negotiation, highly satisfactory to both sides, was to prove a liability in political terms, even if it were successful in the strategic context. The hostility to South Africa's apartheid policies intensified in the 1950 and 1960s, threatening to disrupt the Commonwealth, let alone embarrass the British Government. The decision of South Africa in 1961 to become a republic and also to let her membership of the Commonwealth cease was something of a relief to the British, though the Simonstown question continued to harass the Government, anxious not to concede this vital naval base, and referring in moral terms to Britain's 'obligation' to supply arms to South Africa because of her agreement on the Simonstown base.[48] The Conservative Government's compromise – to sell arms only for external defence and not for internal security operations[49] – proved unconvincing to critics. Edward Heath's Conservative Government promised to resume arms sales in 1970, but opposition from the Commonwealth, with none of the 47 members (except Malawi) supporting the British position, discouraged Heath, and in the event only a handful of helicopters and spare parts were supplied; efforts by the South Africans to entice further sales by the bait of lucrative contracts for frigates to be built by British shipyards were ignored.[50] Finally, in 1975 the Labour Government ended the Simonstown agreement. Pressure on South Africa because of apartheid spread into other areas, not least international sporting contacts which, while they might seem trivial compared to wider military contacts, were nonetheless deeply damaging to South Africa's international standing, increasing her sense of isolation. The issue of race, then, had profound implications for South Africa's status as well as her security in the modern world. And the Commonwealth had negotiated itself through one of its most troublesome and disruptive issues; though the resolution of the race question in South Africa itself was not yet in sight.

The Empire/Commonwealth was declaring itself, and through its criticism of South Africa putting into practice its character as a multi-racial institution. But there was another, equally important, dimension to the question of race, nationality and citizenship in the empire: that of the right of nationals from members of the Commonwealth to settle permanently in the United Kingdom, be accorded full citizenship rights, and demonstrate that indeed the British Empire was a Roman Empire in that it recognised that common citizenship (which Lloyd George fought strenuously for in the Anglo-Irish Treaty negotiations of 1921) was a reality; and a reality firmly located in the heart of the empire itself. In his *The Third British Empire*, Professor A. E. Zimmern argued that the term used by Dilke, 'Greater Britain', applied not only to the 'overseas British' who had migrated to the white dominions, but to any subject of the King. 'When Lord Palmerston nearly went to war with Greece because he claimed that a British subject had not been paid adequate compensation by the Greek Government, it made no difference that that British subject was a Maltese Jew.'[51] But the question of Britishness in the homeland became a significant issue in the post-1945 world, as the United

Kingdom began to experience for the first time a sustained and considerable degree of immigration from the Commonwealth (at first mainly from the West Indies). Some 35,000 immigrants were estimated to have come in 1955; in 1961 the number was 115,000. This immigration was largely for economic reasons: jobs were sought and were available in the United Kingdom. But the notion of Britain as a natural place for immigrants to settle in was undoubtedly influenced by the sense of common culture, and reality of common language, fostered by the imperial connection. It was not an idea shared by the Colonial Office which, in June 1948, described a passenger load of 492 Jamaicans as an 'incursion'.[52] British Governments moved uncertainly in dealing with this new development. In 1948 the British Nationality Act offered free access to the United Kingdom for all Commonwealth citizens – indeed, the term 'Commonwealth citizen' was, on Patrick Gordon Walker's advice, included in that Act.[53] In February 1954 Winston Churchill warned about the consequences of the policy of allowing unrestricted entry of British subjects into the United Kingdom, warning that the 'rapid improvement of communications' was 'likely to lead to a continuing increase in the number of coloured people coming to this country, and by their presence here would sooner or later come to be resented by large sections of the British people'.[54] In March Lord Salisbury wrote to Lord Swinton that immigration faced Britain 'with a problem which, though at present it may be only a cloud the size of a man's hand, may easily come to fill the whole political horizon'. He blamed this on the coming of the Welfare State, which meant that so long as 'the antiquated rule obtains that any British subject can come into this country without any limitation at all, these people will pour in to take advantage of our social services'. He suggested that a Commonwealth Conference might be held to try to establish some uniformity of legislation on immigration: 'this coloured problem is potentially of a fundamental nature for the future of our country'.[55] The Cabinet considered the issue in July 1956, but noted that 'in spite of the strong arguments in favour of assuming power to control the flow of coloured immigrants', the majority of the Cabinet's Committee on Immigration's conclusion, that controls would be disadvantageous, was accepted. Immigrants were, after all, prepared to take jobs that British workers would not accept and, in any case, unemployment was rising and this would by itself check the number of immigrants.[56] Two years later the then Colonial Secretary, Lennox-Boyd, addressed the Conservative Party Conference in Blackpool on the immigration issue. He welcomed the fact that many of the peoples of the British overseas

possessions in the Caribbean – Jamaica, Trinidad, Barbados, the Wind-
ward and Leeward Islands – had come over to Britain as immigrants,
and acknowledged their contribution to the British economy. They
'naturally' looked on Britain as the mother country. He welcomed the
strong action taken to quell the race riots that had recently occurred in
London and elsewhere. But he also warned that there were difficulties
involved in accepting the immigrants, 'social, housing and lately economic'. There was considerable West Indian unemployment and the
chances of absorbing them into employment were not good. Yet he
urged that 'it would be a tragedy to bring to end the traditional right of
unrestricted entry into the Mother Country of Her Majesty's subjects,
and quite unthinkable to do so on the grounds of colour'. The deportation of a few undesirables was not inconsistent with this 'historic
policy'.[57] This speech reflected Cabinet concern about the volume of
immigration into Britain. On 1 July 1958 the Lord President of the
Council, Lord Hailsham, noted that legislation was not yet required to
control coloured immigration, but administrative action should be taken
to restrict it from India, Pakistan and the West Indies. Immigration
must be kept under review, and in discussion the Cabinet agreed that
the 'unrestricted coloured immigration might have serious social consequences in the long term'.[58] In September 1958 the Home Secretary
said that it was desirable to seek to establish some form of control over
coloured immigration at their countries of origin, similar to those that
Britain had recently persuaded India and Pakistan to introduce. This
might be discussed with the government of the West Indies. However, it
was stressed that there must be no major pronouncement on this policy,
no discussion of principle. The Government would 'continue to deal
with this problem empirically' and should base its action on the 'practical
considerations of the availability of housing and the capacity of the
labour market'.[59]

In November 1960 the Home Secretary turned again to the immigration question. There had been a 'startling increase' in the rate of immigration from the West Indies. The Cabinet agreed that this was 'disquieting'
and should be kept under review; and although it would be a breach
with tradition, 'it might be necessary to introduce legislation to control
immigration from the Commonwealth and to empower the Secretary
of State to deport Commonwealth citizens', though this must not be
done in a 'discriminatory way', otherwise it would have a 'damaging
effect on the Commonwealth'.[60] In May 1961 the Lord Chancellor
informed the Cabinet that the early part of the new year saw yet another

'startling increase' in Commonwealth immigration. If this continued, the figures might rise to 2 million within the next 15 years. The Commonwealth Migrants Committee noted that the time was coming when legislation would be needed to control immigration, and favoured a form of management based on employment and the issuing of work permits to the unskilled. This was flexible and avoided the accusation of race distinction.[61] In October the Home Secretary indicated that it was now time to introduce legislation to control immigration.[62] In November the new bill was debated in the House of Commons, and Labour, still defending the Commonwealth idea, attacked it on the grounds that it was an 'affront to all Commonwealth countries ... the whole lot', and alleged that the Conservatives, who prided themselves on being the party of the Commonwealth, 'do not know the first thing' about it.[63] 'They are still our Colonies', said Hugh Gaitskell, 'they think of themselves ... as British people. Oh, yes, they do. It is rather moving.'[64]

In 1962 the Commonwealth Immigration Act was passed to control immigration, by requiring immigrants to obtain employment vouchers, the first of a series of measures which Governments of both shades of political opinion felt essential to prevent racial disharmony, overcrowding and social unrest. Despite these prudent measures, a speech made in 1968 by the Conservative MP for Wolverhampton, Enoch Powell, prophesied that the volume of Commonwealth immigration into the United Kingdom must end in disaster: 'Like the Roman, "I seem to see the River Tiber foaming with much blood."'[65] This provoked expressions of support and opposition and made immigration a major and divisive issue in the Conservative Party.

But it was not only the Conservatives who moved to abolish the right of unrestricted entry; the 1964 general election saw race become an issue in Birmingham, where in the Smethwick constituency Patrick Gordon Walker lost his seat. Harold Wilson may have been a genuine enthusiast for the Commonwealth relationship, but his Home Secretary Frank Soskice was forced to abandon what Richard Crossman called 'his purely liberalistic attitude' for a 'recognition that we have to combine tight immigration controls, even if it means changing the law, with a constructive policy for integrating into the community the immigrants who are there already'. Crossman, a Midland MP, noted that 'here I really do represent my constituents. Ever since the Smethwick election it has been quite clear that immigration can be the greatest potential vote-loser for the Labour Party if we are seen to be permitting a flood of immigrants to come in and blight the central areas in all our cities.'

By July 1965 the only Cabinet Ministers who resisted tighter controls were Barbara Castle, Tony Greenwood and Arthur Bottomley, who were departmentally responsible for the Commonwealth; but Crossman observed that even these three 'didn't adopt the 100 per cent pro-immigration line and arguments with which Hugh Gaitskell and George Brown opposed the Tory Immigration Act, lock, stock and barrel, only three years ago. The atmosphere has changed since then.'[66] In August 1965 a White Paper announced a reduction in the provision of entry vouchers for Commonwealth immigrants from 208,000 per annum to 8500, a decision which Crossman believed had 'taken the poison out of politics' in the Midlands, though he regretted that the Government had not had 'even more preliminary negotiations with Commonwealth countries than we did'.[67] In March 1968 the Labour Government passed a new Immigration Act, imposing a quota on the number of Kenyan Asians allowed to enter Britain each year. It was clear that any idea of a Commonwealth based on Lloyd George's assertion of a common citizenship – one made in the high tide of the white Commonwealth and its 'first division' status – was only another Commonwealth dream. The enlargement of the Commonwealth, and the blurring of the 'divisions', meant that citizenship now raised a question of race. That the Southern Irish were still permitted unrestricted entry into the United Kingdom only reinforced the point, though Wilson for his part was anxious about the implications of this anomaly for the Commonwealth relationship.

The Government led by Edward Heath which won a general election victory in June 1970 had now to grapple with this problem. The Conservative Party, in opposition between 1964 and 1970, was divided on immigration, and found itself coping also with the Rhodesian crisis, with its resonances of 'kith and kin' white people rightly struggling to be free from black majority rule. Enoch Powell's speech on the grave consequences of immigration further divided the party, and forced Heath to dismiss him, but brought Powell a huge volume of popular support. Heath now announced his party's intention of introducing much tougher controls over immigration, ensuring that Commonwealth immigrants, like aliens, would enjoy no right of permanent residence; they must have a job, a specific time to work and a specific place to work.[68] In 1971 Heath, now in government, oversaw the Immigration Bill which replaced the 1962 temporary measure with permanent legislation which placed Commonwealth immigrants on the same footing as aliens, with the need to apply for work permits instead of employment vouchers. It also created a new class of person, 'patrials', who were defied as citizens of the United Kingdom and colonies whose parents and grandparents were born in the United Kingdom; a citizen of the United Kingdom and colonies who had settled in the United Kingdom for five years; and a Commonwealth citizen who had a parent or grandparent born in the United Kingdom.[69] In its passage the Bill was amended to tighten these restrictions further, but allowed Commonwealth immigrants to have the statutory right to bring in their wives and children.[70] The British Government still did not abandon the more pragmatic response to citizenship that was exemplified in its response to Eire's leaving the Commonwealth in 1949. When Pakistan seceded from the Common-wealth in January 1972 the Heath Government continued to treat Paki-stani citizens in the United Kingdom as having rights as British citizens. But the expulsion of Asians from Uganda provoked another immigra-tion crisis, and here again the Heath Government acted honourably, allowing the expelled Asians to settle in Britain, though at the cost of a considerable rise in support for the right wing National Front.[71] In November 1972 the Government suffered a defeat on the immigration rules introduced to implement the Immigration Act of 1971, a setback inspired partly by the Government's giving effect to the Treaty of Rome which laid down rules for the free movement of workers between Euro-pean Community members. Some Conservatives struck a last blow for the idea of retaining the closest ties with the white Commonwealth coun-tries, in particular Canada, Australia and New Zealand.[72] When this was seen in the context of the instinctive sympathy of many Conservatives for white Rhodesians, and the resentment against the Government's accept-ance of Ugandan Asians, then it was clear that the Conservative Party and its supporters were in full and final flight from the concept of *civis Britannicus sum*, except insofar as it referred to their kith and kin in the old Commonwealth.

The 1981 Nationality Act further restricted the definition of the Brit-ish subject by stipulating that from 1986 only the British-born children of British-born or naturalised British people would inherit British cit-izenship. The 1988 Immigration Act removed the right of certain British citizens to be joined in the United Kingdom by their spouse, which must most directly affect those immigrants of recent origin whose customary social tradition or economic circumstance would make them likely to seek a marriage partner from their countries of origin.[73]

This suspicion that Britain responded more readily to the appeal of 'kith and kin' was reinforced by the British response to the Argentine invasion of the Falkland Islands in 1982. The strong Conservative reaction to the invasion was fully supported by the front bench and most of the back bench of the Labour opposition. If it was a long way to Rhodesia, and if military action was a hazardous enterprise, then the same could be said of the Falklands. Of course, the cases were different. Any army dispatched to Rhodesia must be sent by air; and the task of evicting an Argentine Army from the Falkland Islands was simple compared to the complex and almost certainly protracted role that Britain must play in destroying a white Rhodesian government and then reconstructing a mixed race, or a black one in its place.

But there were other suspicions in the 1960s and 1970s that Britain was indeed turning back on the idea of common treatment of all Commonwealth nationalities. Common citizenship, with all that that implied, was clearly a rapidly disappearing concept; the various Acts restricting Commonwealth immigration, the subsequent narrowing of definitions of British nationality and citizenship, bore witness to that. But the claim was made that Britain was showing less concern about punishing South Africa for her apartheid policy: that she was placing economic considerations above moral precepts; that she was even regressing in her attitude to apartheid, with the Conservative Government's decision in 1970 to resume arms sales to South Africa.[74]

South Africa continued to act as a kind of moral critique on the British Government in the 1980s. The previous decade saw the emergence of a younger generation of blacks who began to assert themselves in a deteriorating economic climate that rendered their employment prospects even bleaker than before. Political activists now found fertile ground for their work, inspired by the fear that a new handicap would be fixed on them by an obligation to learn Afrikaans as the medium of education. The South African Government's response was to use force; and the world was treated to the spectacle of school children being chased and beaten by the police. The South African Government appeared to be able to hold its own, even destabilising the so-called 'front-line' African states, and using military force to penetrate their borders and destroy guerrilla bases. But South Africa lost ground again when the end of the Cold War in 1989 meant that South Africa was no longer perceived as a link in the containment of world communism.[75] These developments, and the sudden acceptance by the Nationalist Party that it could not hope to stand against majority rule and also maintain order and economic prosperity in South Africa, saw the 'wind of change' finally blow through white government of non-white peoples.

This was an extraordinary and for many an emotional decade, cul-
minating in the inauguration of Nelson Mandela as President of the
Republic of South Africa on 10 May 1994, with world leaders attending
the formal transfer of power.[76] But throughout these momentous
changes there remained the suspicion that the Thatcher Government
had behaved sluggishly, even meanly. The chief ground of criticism was
the Thatcher Government's refusal to implement full economic sanctions
against the Republic in the 1980s. The Government did urge the need for
change; and its case against economic sanctions was based on the premise that they would only result in the injury of all South Africans, black
and white, and destroy any hopes of a peaceful transition to majority
rule. There was some justification for this: it was the white business class
that was most confident that it could work with black capitalists as easily
as white ones. The desire to save the economy and, through a political
settlement, encourage foreign investment in South Africa was a significant one; and the arguments were more finely balanced than Mrs
Thatcher's detractors would like to admit. Nevertheless, the last decade
of white rule in South Africa, and the reluctance of Britain to engage
actively in engineering its downfall, seemed to indicate that not only
had old notions of common citizenship, common culture, even moral
obligation been set aside or had withered, but that the sense of British
moral obligation to subjects of her former Empire/Commonwealth had
diminished.

All this took place against the background of British involvement in
the European Union – an experience itself dogged with anxiety as the
British Government in the 1980s adjusted itself to the consequences
of what, in 1973, it had decided to do. Whatever Britain's difficulties in
finding a constructive role in Europe, and yet one that would not compromise 'a thousand years of history', the very fact that British Euro-
Sceptics spoke in terms of a thousand years of history (referring to the
perceived essential free and independent role of Britain and especially
of her Parliament) spoke much about her present relationship with her
former empire and present Commonwealth. The slowing down of free
Commonwealth immigration; the dissolving of links with the former
empire in economic and political terms; the defining of British interest
as either resting in Europe, half in Europe, or virtually outside Europe
brought no renewed interest in the Commonwealth, even though the
'simple fact of a shared history' still had resonances – and sometimes
ironies, when one former colony, Bermuda, voted in a referendum to
remain under British rule rather than endorse independence.[77]

The twentieth century witnessed the underlying weakness of Lloyd George's demand that the Irish delegates in the Treaty negotiations of 1921 accept what he called the 'common citizenship' of Ireland and Great Britain and the Irish 'adherence to and membership of the group of nations forming the British Commonwealth of Nations'. The term 'group of nations' itself implied, and indeed recognised, the developing autonomy of the white Dominions; they could hardly then, by 1921, be described as Seeley characterised them in 1883 as an 'extension' of the British state. It also witnessed the failure of the idea of common citizenship for all subjects of the empire, which the Labour Government accepted in the concept of the 'Commonwealth citizen', but found itself, like the Conservatives, obliged to introduce immigration controls, the logical outcome of which was the definition of British nationality in terms which restricted even the rights of British Commonwealth people of European stock to claim full British nationality.

It might be said, then, that both the Roman imperial idea of citizenship and the Greek idea of a cultural civilisation transcending local differences had failed equally to give the British Empire a coherence, and therefore strength, to turn it into the kind of world organisation that Britain had hoped and believed it would become in the late nineteenth and most of the twentieth century. But it could be argued that this failure, an inevitable one, since the British never attempted to make their territories an integral part of the metropolitan core as the French sought to do, in the end facilitated the relatively easy decline of the British Empire. British politicians and at times the public, when they were interested, might assert the claim that India must remain in the empire; but while they insisted that India should stay under British rule, they never claimed that India was British in the sense that the French claimed 'Algérie Française'. No British paratroops threatened to descend on London to overthrow a government in the interests of white Rhodesians; conversely, no British Government, including the Labour Governments of the 1960s and 1970s, was prepared to push matters too far in the interests of black South Africans. This fundamental insularity of the English when it came to questions of nationality and race, in one sense, served the empire well. Had it indeed been an 'extension of the state' then the fate of white Rhodesians would have been a matter of grave political consequence; had it been one based on common culture, or common citizenship, then the question of immigration might have indeed fulfilled Enoch Powell's dire predictions. As it was, the incoherence of the British Empire and Commonwealth facilitated its end, and helped prevent the traumas that afflicted French imperial decline. But the price was one of a diminishing of the idea of what it meant to be a British subject or citizen. In August 1941 Mr O. G. R. Williams, Head of the West Africa Department of the Colonial Office, referring to the need to educate 'the Great British Public' in order to enlighten them about race and prejudice, minuted that

> As for educating public opinion (including my own prejudices) into a more tolerant attitude, I am all for it, but how is it to be done? We must have some kind of snobbery to keep us going and the more levelling there is of class distinctions the more racial distinctions are likely to acquire snobbery value.[78]

This was a disappointing and unworthy gloss on the imperial experience, which, with its idea of Britishness, British nationality and British citizenship, whether applied in the United Kingdom or the empire, enabled a broad, multi-national British state and empire, symbolised by the Crown, to encompass a variety of multiple identities. Catholic as well as Protestant Irish, Scots and Welsh, and a host of peoples outside the British Isles, found in the empire a comfortable and flexible arena to pursue their interests and realise their abilities. As R. B. McDowell remarks, 'almost all Irishmen are in a sense Anglo-Irish. That is to say they have an English or British component of varying proportions in their cultural make-up.'[79] This applies to many nations and races beyond Ireland; which perhaps makes the point that the English themselves, paradoxically, were the people who willingly, it seems, gave up the search for some idea of nationality or citizenship that would have given real and lasting meaning to the expression which used to be on Englishmen's lips: *civis Britannicus sum*. One Colonial Office man noted in 1902 (drawing upon classical allusion): 'If and when the doctrine of "*civis Romanus sum*" is finally interred . . . there will be very little left of the British Empire'.[80] But the gradual dismantling of the project means, once again, that the retreat from empire, while it diminished British citizenship, left England herself relatively untroubled.

EPILOGUE: THE CONTRACTION OF ENGLAND

It is not easy today to think of the English as Seeley defined them over a century ago as an imperial people, as an 'Anglo-Saxon' nation that spread its peoples and its power over the globe. And the last half of this century has witnessed the demise of an empire whose apparent permanency was summed up by the historian D. W. Brogan in 1947:

> Nevertheless, as a rule, when Divine Providence has put a part of the world under English rule, it has usually stayed, often quite willingly, in the state unto which it pleased God to call it. And contemplating this fact we are inclined to agree with Mark Twain: the English *are* mentioned in the Bible.

Today only some 16 'Imperial relics' remain, comprising a total population of less than 200,000.[1] Most contributors to the imperial debate point to certain legacies of empire: sport, architecture, the English language, even the presence of something called 'Commonwealth literature', which takes its place ambiguously on library shelves beside Scottish and Irish literature – themselves ambiguous enough categories. And there can be no question that the history of British expansion transcends the merely political, and encompasses religious, social and cultural experiences of a most profound kind. Ironically, the least significant impact for many post-colonial territories is the institutional; most of Africa, for example, has rejected western political ways, in substance if not always in form. The Prime Minister of Singapore, Lee Quan Yew, for example, declared that his country could not afford the luxury of the British game of government and opposition. Other countries would make the same claim, and on the whole Britain has quietly accepted this notion: even the 'Emergency' decreed by Mrs Indira Gandhi in India in 1975, met with approval in some circles in Britain: at least now the Indian trains would run on time, and anyway, India was best suited to a new form of enlightened despotism.

256

It is hard, too, to assess the impact of empire on the English people them-selves. In 1937 the South African journalist and politician K. B. Long complained of the 'preoccupation of the British public with sport; its entire ignorance about the Empire'.[2] But the same cannot be said about the English state, nor the British state that it constructed. The Anglo-Saxons liked to speak of their *imperium* over all the 'English' peoples north of the Humber. Post-Norman Conquest writers described with satisfaction how King Edgar was rowed on the river Dee by eight subject-kings visiting his court.[3] A near-contemporary authority wrote that 'all the kings who were in this island, of the Cumbrians and the Scots, once came to Edgar, eight kings on one day, and they all submitted to Edgar's direction'.[4] As the English state expanded, King Edward I, conqueror of the Welsh, 'Hammer of the Scots', showed great interest in the myth of King Arthur as King of Britain, with all the rights that the British kings supposedly held in the British Isles.[5] Dominion over part of France was sought until the early modern age. Dominion swung west-wards into the new world, and east into Asia. Dominion, it seemed, came naturally to the English, and their British compatriots, and the idea was again taken up and refurbished by Seeley in his *Expansion of England*. At the élite level, in a state that was an oligarchy tempered by democracy until at least 1918, the Empire and Commonwealth came to be associ-ated, and rightly so, with Britain's rise to world power status, with the making of 'The British Empire as a Super Power'. The determined efforts made by British politicians of all persuasions to retain the imper-ial link for this purpose bears witness to this perception: India must be kept in the Commonwealth, even if she became a republic; South Africa must be retained as a vital defence component, even if her apartheid policy raised objections on the humanitarian plane. A role East of Suez was vital, even after the empire lost India, and some would even place the Falklands War of 1982 in the context of a desperate attempt by a disappointed nation to reassert its great past – though it is possible to exaggerate the popularity of this episode, as against a sense of unease as the crisis developed into war, and the war produced casualties.

The loss of empire was bound up with the emergence of Britain as a great power. But the way in which it declined – the evolution of the Commonwealth principle, the idea that the empire was not declining but was merely being transformed – enabled England to escape serious self-doubt, though it also stood in the way of the kind of fundamental reassessment of her position in the world. Whatever the centrality of empire to the French sense of where they stood as a nation, they never doubted that they were first and foremost a European power, with a tradition of dominating Europe, and contesting, or latterly sharing, that domination with Germany. The British Government assumed that Britain was a great world power. As Macmillan put it as early as 1952:

> with the commonwealth behind us and holding, as we should, a balance between France and Germany, Britain would be the unchallenged leader of the European Confederation. This, in itself, would further strengthen our position in the Commonwealth. As the leader, moreover, of both the Commonwealth and Europe we should be able to establish a more equal partnership with the United States both in the immediate task of containing Russia and in the long run.[6]

This predominance must be maintained – if not through empire, then by membership of the European Common Market. The campaign for membership of the EEC always placed as much, if not more, emphasis on the need to maintain Britain as a major power as on the purely economic benefits of access to more markets.

But in what sense were the English an imperial nation in their way of thinking about their own nationality? It has been claimed that imperialism was an essential ingredient of the making of 'British' nationality; shared religion (Protestantism) united with shared participation in the imperial enterprise. And since the Scots and Irish, in particular, gained from this shared enterprise, then this further enhanced the sense of British identity, giving the British a sense of destiny and superiority. This became embedded in the popular perception: the victories of British arms in late eighteenth-century India were celebrated in the streets of London; and from there to the celebrations that accompanied the news of the relief of Mafeking in the Boer War in 1900 was but a short, and continuous, journey. The empire was one of dominion over different, and inferior, peoples. Thus the British nation's empire was like that of Rome and was epitomised in the Government of India: a Government defined by ideals of law and order and united by 'roads and rulers'.[7]

But there are problems with this analysis. There never was a British nation: national identities in the British Isles remained, though compatible with, even complementary to, Britishness. But Britishness itself was hard to define, though the sense of 'otherness' as Britons soldiered, administered or worked in the imperial territories must have had some impact on it: though, again, a limited one, for the confusion of the terms 'British' and 'English' meant that the empire that 'Britons' helped build was claimed by the English as essentially theirs. Even if Joseph Chamberlain's hope of making the Westminster Parliament into the governing institution of the empire had come to be, it would have confronted the same difficulties that it did in absorbing the Scots, Welsh and Irish representatives: that it would have been essentially an English Parliament with bits added on – late-comers who would not fundamentally alter the English origin and character of the institution. There would be no real 'Imperial' parliament, at least, not unless the whole British constitution was to be fundamentally revised and altered: which most Englishmen would not wish to allow.

Recently a lively and scholarly attempt has been made to inject a significant non-English (that is, Irish) dimension into the history of British imperialism.[8] A convincing case can be made out for the claim that Ireland and the Irish have established their place in the imperial story, with the Scots, and perhaps to a lesser extent the Welsh, also playing their parts. But, while the players who took the field wore jerseys of varying national colours, the rules of the game, the refereeing, and the moving of not only the goal posts, but even the touch lines, were all under English control. It is significant that the great unifying occasion of 'Empire Day' was inspired by the Earl of Meath; even more significant was the fact that its originator belonged to the Southern Irish Unionists, a people abandoned by the British Government in the Anglo-Irish Treaty of 1921.[9] Britishness, and the imperial culture that underpinned it, had more meaning for the multi-national peoples of the empire than it had for the English, for whom it was axiomatic that to be English was to be British, and that, therefore, to be British was to be English. As Keith Jeffrey observes, the traces which Ireland has left in the British Empire, and vice-versa, 'may most abundantly be found in social and cultural resonances, rather than in any concrete constitutional, political or even economic structures'.[10]

Seeley's seminal work, after all, was entitled *The Expansion of **England***, though he thanked the Celtic nations for their contribution. And only 100 years separate his great work (or timely essay) from a recognition that England moved in that relatively brief period from expansion to contraction. Attempts were made in this century to write a book, or books, that would capture the changing nature of the empire, and match Seeley's book with a more appropriate exposition. Several stand out: A. E. Zimmern's *The Third British Empire* (1926); Reginald Coupland's *The Empire in These Days* (1935); and the irrepressible Lionel Curtis's *Civitatis Dei*, published between 1933 and 1937.

Sir Alfred Zimmern (1879–1957) was Professor of International Relations in University College Aberystwyth from 1919 to 1921, and Montague Burton Professor of International Relations in Oxford from 1930 to 1944. He sought to breathe new life into the concept of empire; but he did not embrace the notion of racial solidarity upon which Seeley based his analysis. Zimmern began by thinking upon the fall of the great, prewar empires, the German, Russian, Austro-Hungarian and Ottoman. 'But there still remains a British Empire'.[11] Why had it survived? Because it possessed a 'principle of vitality which the other empires lacked. And that principle, that seed of continuing life, is the spirit of liberty.' The British Empire became the British Commonwealth of Nations.[12] Zimmern looked to the British political tradition to explain how this had happened; and he identified 'practical genius' to account for the means by which the 'largest single political community in the world' survived. Freedom was the principle that saved the British Empire, despite its geographical, racial, religious, cultural and governmental diversity.[13] The Great War showed that liberty was the basis of power; this generated a spirit of loyalty. When John Morley reviewed Seeley's book in February 1884 he doubted that Australians would ever interest themselves in the neutrality of Belgium, but they did so, not because of Seeley's desire for a tightly organised Empire, but precisely because the empire was not tightly organised and controlled.[14] Zimmern did not, therefore, believe that this loyalty, shown in the late war, should or could lead to imperial federation on the old lines: the war served to enhance Dominion nationality,[15] and in any case the Durham Report had scotched any such possibility, for it 'recommended the cutting off of King Charles's head'.[16] But the broad *principle* of federation was ideally suited to the present day, for the world was now, by way of the League of Nations, being organised on just such principles: internationalism, liberty and an organised world political system. If we lived in 1827, not 1927, Zimmern wrote, we would have to 'bow the head and accept the verdict of destiny', for then the world was 'anarchic, individualistic ... restless for change' and devoid of organisation. Now, in 1927, the age was one of integration and international cooperation, and the British Empire's experiment in those values was of 'vital concern to the whole world'.[17] Democracy was now the orthodoxy in this new order.[18] The League of Nations was the *deus ex machina* of the British Commonwealth,[19] and the Commonwealth would best serve as a league within this larger League.

Lionel Curtis, by now a Fellow of All Souls College, Oxford, wrote on similar lines, but in even more idealistic language. The British Empire was the manifestation of the Kingdom of God on earth. It stood for responsible government, internationalism, the hatred of war, and the Dominions should federate 'to form the first international community'.[20] Reginald Coupland, Beit Professor of Colonial History at Oxford, another disciple of the *Round Table* group, wrote in his essays and lectures, collected together under the title *The Empire in These Days*, that it would be a 'paradoxical blunder to dissolve the international unity of our lesser league within the League of Nations'. For the empire served the interests of the world as a whole. He hoped for 'genuine comradeship, yoking Europe and Asia in free service for the common weal', which was part of the 'long, hard march towards the brotherhood of man'.[21]

None of these Oxford men's books enjoyed the popularity enjoyed by Seeley the Cambridge man's *Expansion of England*, which was reprinted eight times between 1883 and 1894, and the second edition of which was reprinted twice between 1897 and 1899. It could be said of them, as Curtis's biographer, Deborah Lavin, remarked of his *Civitatis Dei*, 'few books could have defined a vision of the future so out of touch with the real world of the 1930s'.[22] But they provided a moral justification for empire. Seeley's *Expansion of England* was, as Andrea Bosco noted, a mechanical view of empire, which stressed the significance of industrialisation and predicted that the United States of America and Russia would have overtaken Europe in economic and military power, just as the great nations of the sixteenth century had overtaken Florence.[23] This view, far from being irrelevant by the 1930s, was depressingly appropriate for the Hobbesian world of international politics in the inter-war years. But their moral, as distinct from Seeley's mechanical, view eased the British Empire into the new age, and comforted British statesmen as they sought not so much to contain change as to arrest it, and retain British great power status. What one historian has called 'soft' federalism would be based on ever-increasing cooperation by way of inter-governmental coordination and 'functional integration'.[24] This was expressed at the official level: in 1926 a report by a committee on inter-imperial relations was adopted by the Imperial Conference, and it included a definition of what the empire meant. Federation was impossible because of geographical and other conditions; autonomy was the way forward, but

> no account, however accurate, of the negative relations in which Great Britain and the Dominions stand to each other can do more than express a portion of the truth. The British Empire is not founded upon negations. It depends essentially, if not formally, on positive ideals.

Free institutions are its life-blood. Free co-operation is its instrument
... and, though every Dominion is now, and must always remain, the
sole judge of the nature and extent of its co-operation, no common
cause will, in our opinion, be thereby imperilled.

Function was important too; but function, though vital to deal with questions of diplomacy and imperial defence, also required 'flexible machinery – machinery which can, from time to time, be adapted to the
changing circumstances of the world'.[25] But its updated, morally based
idea of an empire of power was abandoned by the *Round Table* after
1940. The notion of the empire as an institution of power gave way to
the idea of an empire founded on the cultivation of relationships between
different peoples.[26]

This concept worked tolerably; at times, remarkably well, until the
1960s. But from the late 1960s onwards a series of books, by historians
and others, marked a sharp change in the perception of Empire and
Commonwealth alike. These works emphasised 'decline', 'eclipse', 'delu-
sions of grandeur', 'Britannia's burden', 'Britannia Overruled'. The terms
most often used were 'winding down', 'national decline' and the like.
Perhaps the culmination of this kind of writing and analysis was Paul
Kennedy's *The Rise and Fall of the Great Powers*, first published in 1988,
which spoke in Rankean terms of the changes in the world economic
system which 'posed considerable, and ultimately insuperable, problems
for a British Empire which now found it much more difficult to defend
its global interests than it had done half a century earlier'.[27] This book
was a best-seller throughout the world and, in particular, it singled out
Britain as vulnerable to this massive shift in world politics.

Some thought that the contraction of England was not confined to the
world scene, but was detectable in domestic United Kingdom politics as
well. In the 1970s, as British politics became more volatile, with violence
in Northern Ireland, damaging industrial disputes, governments brought
down by trade unions, and 'ungovernability' becoming a word on everyone's lips, the possibility of the 'break-up of Britain' seemed to some to
be imminent. This was the title chosen by Tom Nairn for his analysis of
the British condition in 1977. Nairn's book, though quickly dated, nonetheless struck what seemed to be a significant note. The British Empire
was a 'myth'; a 'new generation' had emerged which found its 'sacred
traditions' 'meaningless or comic'.[28] Nairn called for a 'federative' solution, using the (as it turned out) rather unhappy analogy of the need to
create a 'Yugoslav' resolution of Britain's territorial problems rather

than the 'Habsburg' one he originally thought inevitable. Nairn acknowledged the difficulties of federating the 'British Isles', and singled out
'England's indurate metropolitanism – that hegemonic arrogance which
such long experience has turned into daily bread'.[29] Were devolution to
fail, then the break-up of Britain 'will be more imminent, and its form
more predictable'.[30]

Devolution, let alone federation, failed in 1979, but the United Kingdom did not break up. On the contrary, under the Conservative leadership of Margaret Thatcher it became more centralised, more uniformly
governed, with the exception of Northern Ireland which, after the 1985
Anglo-Irish Agreement, was seen anyway as ever more exceptional, and
irrelevant to the integrity of the United Kingdom. The imperial experience was now, of course, a thing of the past.

Harold Wilson was the last Prime Minister to whom it meant anything.
James Callaghan held a sensible, if unadventurous, watching brief, in
Rhodesia and the Falkland Islands, where his decision to overrule his
Defence officials and retain the vessel *Endurance* in Falkland waters
deterred Argentine adventurers.[31] Edward Heath and Margaret Thatcher, the Conservative leaders between 1970 and 1989, had no feeling
for empire whatsoever. This was not a generational matter; Heath was
born in 1916, the same year as Wilson, and Thatcher was born only some
nine years later. What shaped their attitude to empire was their willing
inheritance of what R. F. Holland has neatly dubbed the 'grammar
school aspirants', 'new people' whose dislike of colonialism and empire
reflected their repulsion at the sentimental and sinecure-ridden Conser-
vatism which they despised. Mrs Thatcher's view of the world had no
brief for giving financial support to the former colonies, and her silence
'in the face of Third World debts was deafening'.[32] But Heath and Thatcher were the disciples, in this respect, of the Conservative decolonisation of Africa in the late 1950s and early 1960s, sharing Ian Macleod's
unrelentingly realistic assessment of the relationship between the United
Kingdom and the Empire, and emptying their minds, as he emptied his,
of any sentimental attachment to England's mission.

The Falklands War was an echo of the great power status that the
empire, admittedly, helped to create. But it was not an attempt to resus-
citate England's imperial mission, though it had resonances of earlier
popular imperialism.[33] Mrs Thatcher saw the war as a means of exorcis-
ing the ghost of Suez, of arresting the feeling of decline that had haunted
Britain since 1956, and of reasserting Britain's position in the world. 'We
have ceased to be a nation in retreat', she claimed. Britain's name meant

more than it had.[34] But this, in a way, influenced her role in, or willingness to wind up, outstanding post-imperial problems. The settlement at
last of the Rhodesian tangle in 1980 took place in London, but owed
little or nothing to British policy; and it was clear that the United Kingdom was not going to square up to China over the future of Hong Kong.
Indeed, the Foreign Office was anxious not to work too hard even to
secure democratic institutions in the colony before its transfer to communist rule, or to offer citizenship to more than a few of its people.

The contraction of England in the British Isles was at least checked by
Mrs Thatcher, but the question of national identity that it raised would
not go away; nor would the Scottish, Welsh and Northern Irish questions vanish. On the contrary they returned in the 1990s, a decade which
saw the Conservative successor to Mrs Thatcher, John Major, defending
the Union (with reservation over Northern Ireland). Tony Blair, the
Labour leader elected in May 1997, accepted the need for devolution in
Scotland and Wales; and William Hague, Major's replacement in 1997,
admitted in February 1998 that his party had been wrong to reject the
re-ordering of the United Kingdom on the basis of devolved government. These ideas of re-ordering the constitution were expressed in
piecemeal, even fragmented, fashion; there was no great scheme of British federation, as the *Round Table* group had advocated between 1910
and 1919.

The loss of empire, the contraction of England, were forecast by John
Morley in his review of Seeley's *Expansion of England* in 1884. Morley
argued strongly against the idea of imperial federation and customs
union. The question was 'simply whether the good of the members of
our great English union all over the world will be best promoted by
aiming at artificial centralisation, or by leaving as much room as possible
for the expansion of individual communities along lines and in channels
which they spontaneously cut out for themselves'.[35] But it was all less
traumatic than it might have been, partly because there existed a tradition to which Morley's ideas belonged, which acted as a facilitator of
British withdrawal from empire. As Norman Stone (a Scottish observer
of English *mores*) put it, 'Europe modernized through the state and
much time and not a little blood was expended in fighting about institutions. The English just took institutions and made them do something
else.'[36]

The lions of Trafalgar Square, it would seem, offer a more impressive
architectural–political legacy than the Blue Channel at Heathrow or
Gatwick airports. The imperial theme has run its course. Enoch Powell

dismissed it altogether in an address to the Royal Society of St George in 1964:

> There was this deep, this providential difference between our empire and those others, that the nationhood of the mother country remained unaltered through it all, almost unconscious of the strange fantastic structure built around her – in modern parlance, 'uninvolved'. The citizenship of Rome dissolved into the citizenship of the whole ancient world; Spain learnt to live on the treasure of the Americas; the Hapsburgs and the Hohenzollerns extended their policy with their power. But England, which took as an axiom that the American Colonies could not be represented in Parliament and had to confess that even Ireland was not to be assimilated, underwent no organic change as the mistress of a World Empire. So the continuity of her existence was unbroken when the looser connections which had linked her with distant continents and strange races fell away.[37]

But this eloquent and persuasive argument, though shrewd and, up to a point, accurate, is wrong, and profoundly so, on two counts. The idea of Britishness, as distinct from Englishness, was enhanced by the immigration from the new Commonwealth, for the epithet 'British' was most easily adopted by immigrants; and in an age when the United Kingdom bears at least some marks of disintegrating, the new Britons offer a counterweight to the continuing dilution of British identity. Secondly, the United Kingdom experience as both an imperial and yet a European power has had repercussions. In November 1925 Austen Chamberlain, defending the Government's decision to define, without reference to the Dominions, its policies on the Locarno Agreements which sought to facilitate the stability of post-war Europe, told the House:

> I could not go, as the representative of His Majesty's Government, to meeting after meeting of the League of Nations, to conference after conference with the representatives of foreign countries, and say, 'Great Britain is without a policy. We have not been able to meet all the Governments of the Empire, and we can do nothing.' That might be possible for an Empire wholly removed from Europe, which existed in a different hemisphere. It was not possible for an Empire the heart of which lies in Europe and next door to the continent of Europe, and

where every peril to the peace of Europe jeopardised the peace of this country.[38]

An empire whose heart also lay in Europe: this contradiction was a legacy that, Enoch Powell's claim notwithstanding, helps explain, in part at least, the political history of post-imperial England.

CONCLUSION: COLONISATION AND DECOLONISATION – A PERSPECTIVE

The history of decolonisation is a fascinating one, and one that has attracted some of the best academic analysis. It benefits, too, from the quickened pace of the release of British official documents, which has produced a flood of papers, memoranda, Cabinet discussions, correspondence, secret, as well as merely confidential, that throws new light on the process of decolonisation, and will continue to do so. Many of these documents have found their way into print, with the series *British Documents of the End of Empire* providing an invaluable source for historians of Empire, and a corrective to facile views such as that the empire was doomed by the granting of Indian self-government in 1947, or by the Suez crisis. Indeed, so complex is the picture now emerging that the expression 'end of empire' might be better replaced by something like 'old empires never die, they just fade away'.

This book has emphasised the long view of imperial growth and decline. And it has done so because, in some ways at least, it is as important to understand not only the 'why' of imperial decline, but also the 'how'; indeed, the how is arguably as significant, if not more significant, than the why. It is so because it helps explain the relative ease with which England got rid of her empire. This is not to deny that there were hard and difficult decisions to make: lives were lost, military and police repression was used from time to time, there was a suspicion of racial partiality (in Central Africa for example). But the thing was done with remarkably few scars, or so it was perceived; even the human catastrophe that accompanied the partition of India was seen as taking second place to the success of finally moving India to her ultimate goal, that of nationhood, and of nationhood equipped and supported by English-style institutions.

Understanding this requires the longer view, as well as the contingencies revealed in the official papers which no historian can ignore. There is, of course, always the risk that, in taking the long view, the historian

sinks to a teleological level, with the outcome of the process determining
the way in which it is interpreted. Contingency and the unexpected are
an essential part of the story; but the guiding notions of empire are a
part of it as well.

The pressures moving Britain, and other colonial powers, towards
relinquishing hold on their empires came from many quarters: economic decline, post-war nationalisms, after 1918 and 1945, the inability
to match military and economic commitments, the declining asset of
empire in military and financial terms, the rise of super-powers, all these
are significant factors undermining the European empires. But, in the
case of the British Empire, these pressures were exerted in the context of
English ways of thinking about politics and government.

When, in the late nineteenth and early twentieth century, England
tried to rationalise her empire, it proved not only unsuccessful but
divisive. Incorporating the colonies into a grand theory, whether it was
federalism or economic unity, was self-defeating, frightening the Dominions into a greater awareness of the benefits of upholding informal
links with the mother country. Plans for common imperial defence
foundered on the rock of colonial reluctance to pay for ships of the Royal
Navy that might then sail off into other waters, such as the somewhat distant North Sea. Plans for common economic policies, such as the Ottawa
Agreement of 1932, proved divisive, and instead of goodwill they 'bred
questionings and consciousness of divergent interests'.[1] As Sir Keith
Hancock put it in his Marshall lectures in Cambridge in 1950, the British
response to the world economic crisis was to take to her lifeboat, but the
'lifeboat of imperial design', called Ottawa was unserviceable, because
Britain was at the centre of a discriminating trade system. Foreigners
resented this; some Dominions benefited from it; but, except for the
sugar and tobacco colonies, the colonial peoples believed that dearer
imports were too high a price to pay for shelter in the imperial market.[2]

This did not prevent the Dominions, and not only the Dominions, ral-
lying to the British war effort in 1914 and 1939; but the Second World
War was the last sustained common enterprise, even though the Commonwealth enabled Britain to retain her image as a great power after
1945. And any idea of a great imperial nationality, either in the cultural
or political meaning of the term, was soon compromised by British and
Dominion nationality and citizenship laws. Even the Indian politician,
Sir J. P. Sinha, recognised as early as in 1918 the right of the 'several
communities of the British Commonwealth, including India, that
each should enjoy complete control of the composition of its own

population by means of restriction on immigration from any of the other communities'.[3]

England did not relinquish her imperial and great power status easily. If she was obliged to change, then she did so in order to stay the same: she aspired to remain a great power, or at least influence, in, for example, the Middle East, even after the Suez crisis. But when she was obliged to change, to accept Edmund Burke's *dictum* that the time for change was when it could no longer be resisted, then at least she was possessed of a whole vocabulary that implied adjustment, accommodation, gradualism. Words like free association, partnership, responsibility, self-government (which she was able to distinguish from 'independence'), trusteeship could be drawn upon, not merely as expedients, but rather as in some degree informing, even influencing, what officials and politicians did. Ian Watt, an influential figure in the Colonial Office in the 1950s, minuted on 4 June 1960 that, in drafting a response to a Foreign Office document referring to the political future of 'backward' countries, the Colonial Office should emphasise 'that in Colonial Office experience political leaders demanding self-government pay us the compliment of insisting on systems which come as close as written constitutions can to the Westminster pattern . . . we should add the point that the UK is ill-equipped by tradition or experience to attempt to teach any regime how to conduct itself in an authoritarian way.'[4]

In fact the imperial power was perfectly capable of behaving in an authoritarian way, with (in Cyprus and Suez, to mention just two examples) troublesome consequences. As P. J. Marshall put it, 'Although their bellicosity was more and more to be mitigated by prudent calculations of cost and consequences, the British were at intervals to make war on their imperial subjects until the 1950s.'[5] But it was also able to recognise that, if there were risks in decolonisation of 'going too fast' there were equally dangerous risks in 'going too slow'.[6] How 'fast' or 'slow' were to be determined in each event, in any given case. But this mode of behaviour made imperial policy-making like the Duke of Wellington's description of his Peninsular army: it was like a length of rope and, when it broke, he simply tied a knot and carried on. When Clement Attlee remarked complacently to Pandit Nehru in March 1948 that the 'course of Irish history resulted in the establishment within the Commonwealth of a republic which was, however, linked to the other states by the Crown', he ignored the fact that in the 1930s Neville Chamberlain's Government was not in a position to stop the Irish achieving this end. He concluded that 'it is, as so many things British are, illogical, but it works'.[7] It was certainly illogical to retain India in the Commonwealth as a republic in 1949 while, only a year earlier, excluding Burma because she desired republican status, and accepting the secession of Ireland as a fully declared republic. But the government had good, practical reasons for its inconsistency, based on political calculation; so had India. But Attlee was right in the sense that this policy decision, taken in the context of British colonial discourse since the nineteenth century, did result in a more liberal definition of the Commonwealth.

For nearly 200 years empire was deemed indispensable to England's greatness; but, despite the belief held by some that she suffered from a post-imperial depression, England underwent remarkably few traumas as a result of the end of empire. This is because grand ideas of imperial federation, a new moral order and the like made little headway against the English tradition of resolving political issues in a way that enabled the old order to give way to the new, and that combined the benefits of practical thinking with the language of constitutional development. Underpinning these was the fact that England's empire was based on various systems of government, which could be altered and rearranged and yet which (it was believed) sat firmly in the tradition created by the North American experience, the lessons taught by the loss of the 13 colonies and the (apparently) satisfactory example set by the Durham Report, which was to the empire what the Great Reform Bill of 1832 was to English domestic politics: a precedent, though arguably a much-misunderstood one, but one which could be accommodated to practical politics, and used by politicians to justify, explain, or sometimes even motivate, their responses to particular problems. By contrast, the French proclaimed at a conference in Brazzaville in 1944, which debated the future of their colonies, that the objectives of the 'task of civilisation undertaken by France in the colonies exclude all idea of autonomy, all possibility of evolution outside the French block of the Empire'. Therefore, the eventual, 'even remote, creation of self-governments in the colonies is excluded.'[8] Ireland, and the Anglo-Irish Treaty of 1921, offers one of the few parallels with France; here definition and the desire for a core commonwealth link showed, once more, the exceptionalism of Ireland. But this was unusual. English history and political practice helped create a discourse that wrote the epitaph of her empire, but also explains its not-infrequent resurrections and, above all (and fortunately for England at least), its thankfully anticlimactic demise.

NOTES

Abbreviations used in the notes:

BDEE   *British Documents of the End of Empire*
Cab.   *Cabinet Office papers*
C.O.   *Commonwealth Office*
JICH   *Journal of Imperial and Commonwealth History*

Notes to the Introduction

1. J. C. D. Clark, '"The Strange Death of British History?" Reflections on Anglo-American Scholarship', *Historical Journal*, 40: 3 (1997), pp. 787–809 at pp. 803, 809.
2. S. R. Ashton and S. E. Stockwell (eds), *British Documents of the End of Empire*, series A, vol. I: *Imperial Policy and Colonial Practice, 1925–1945*, part I: *Metropolitan Reorganisation, Defence and International Relations, Political Change and Constitutional Reform* (London: HMSO, 1996), p. xxxix. Some general statements were collected, with statements on individual colonies, and submitted to Harold Macmillan, who dismissed them as 'scrappy, obscure and jejune, and totally unsuitable for publication' (ibid., pp. 169–70).
3. Clark, ' "The Strange Death of British History" ', p. 803.
4. Alfred Cobban, *The Nation State and National Self-Determination* (London: Fontana, 1969; first issued 1945), pp. 305–6.
5. Ibid., p. 306.
6. For a penetrating analysis of English constitutional thinking see William M. Johnston, *Commemorations: The Cult of Anniversaries in Europe and the United States Today* (New Brunswick and London: Transaction Publishers, 1991).
7. Elizabeth Mancke, 'Another British America: a Canadian Model for the Early Modern British Empire', *JICH*, 25: 1 (January 1997), pp. 1–36, at p. 3.

1   The Expansion of England

1. R. A. Griffiths, '*This Royal Throne of Kings, this Scept'red Isle': The English Realm and Nation in the later Middle Ages* (Swansea, 1983), pp. 14–15.
2. Ibid., p. 30.
3. J. R. Seeley, *The Expansion of England: Two Courses of Lectures* (London: Macmillan, 1885).

4.   Ibid., p. 46.
5.   Ibid., p. 50.
6.   Ibid., pp. 42–3.
7.   Ibid., pp. 17–36.
8.   Ibid., p. 43–5.
9.   Ibid., p. 46.
10. Ibid., p. 46.
11. Ibid., p. 46.
12. Ibid., pp. 29–30.
13. Frederick Madden and David Fieldhouse, 'The Empire of the Bretaignes', *1175–1688: The Foundations of a Colonial System of Government* (Westport, Conn., and London: Greenwood Press, 1985), pp. 215–17.
14. T. O. Lloyd, *The British Empire, 1558–1983* (Oxford: Oxford University Press, 1984), pp. 22–4.
15. Madden and Fieldhouse, 'Empire of the Bretaignes', pp. 307–9.
16. Anthony Pagden, *Lords of all the World: Ideologies of Empire in Spain, Britain and France, c. 1500–1800* (Yale, Conn.: Yale University Press, 1995), p. 127.
17. Kenneth R. Andrews, *Trade, Plunder and Settlement: Maritime Enterprise and the Genesis of the British Empire, 1480–1630* (Cambridge: Cambridge University Press, 1984), pp. 9–10.
18. Ibid., pp. 3–4
19. David Fieldhouse, *The Colonial Empires: A Comparative Survey from the Eighteenth Century* (London: Macmillan, 1986), p. 66.
20. Andrews, *Trade, Plunder and Settlement*, p. 35.
21. P. J. Marshall, 'The British Empire in the Age of the American Revolution', in William M. Fowler and Wallace Coyle (eds), *The American Revolution: Changing Perspectives* (Boston, Mass.: Northeastern University Press, 1979), pp. 193–212, at p. 194.
22. Fieldhouse, *Colonial Empires*, p. 76.
23. Lloyd, *British Empire*, p. 258.
24. Brigadier General Sir C. E. Callwell, *Field Marshal Sir Henry Wilson: His Life and Diaries* (2 vols, London: Cassell, 1927), vol. ii, pp. 240–1.
25. Newfoundland was created a Dominion in 1917, but its financial predicament cost it that status in 1934.
26. See, e.g., J. A. Cramb's panegyric, *Reflections on the Origins and Destiny of Imperial Britain* (London: Macmillan, 1900), pp. 139–40.
27. W. D. Hussey, *The British Empire and Commonwealth, 1500 to 1961* (Cambridge: Cambridge University Press, 1963), p. 35.
28. P. J. Marshall (ed.), *The Cambridge History of the British Empire* (Cambridge: Cambridge University Press, 1996), p. 8.

2   North America, 1775–1850: Lessons from History?

1.   J. C. D. Clark, *The Language of Liberty, 1660–1832: Political Discourse and Social Dynamics in the Anglo-American World* (Cambridge University Press, 1994), pp. 240–1.
2.   Richard Koebner, *Empire* (Cambridge University Press, 1961), p. 223.

3. 'A Much Maligned Monarch', in W. M. Fowler and W. Coyle (eds), *The American Revolution Changing Perspectives* (Boston, Mass.: Northeastern University Press, 1979), pp. 213–31.
4. W. D. Hussey, *The British Empire and Commonwealth, 1500 to 1961* (Cambridge, 1963), pp. 343–4. Durham was the author of the celebrated report on the Canadian problem in 1839; Grey was Parliamentary Under-Secretary for the Colonies; Elgin was governor-general of Canada in the late 1840s.
5. Robert W. Tucker and David C. Hendrickson, *The Fall of the First British Empire* (Baltimore and London: Johns Hopkins University Press, 1982), p. 41.
6. Gareth Jones, *The Sovereignty of the Law: Selections from Blackstone's Lectures on the Laws of England* (London: Macmillan, 1973), pp. 71–2.
7. J. C. Beckett, *The Making of Modern Ireland, 1603–1923* (London: Faber, 1966), p. 164.
8. Clark, *Language of Liberty*, p. 93.
9. For a discussion of these points see Koebner, *Empire*, pp. 132–9.
10. Peter J. Stanlis, *Edmund Burke: The Enlightenment and Revolution* (New Brunswick: Transactions Publishers, 1991), pp. 20–1.
11. Tucker and Hendrickson, *Fall of the First British Empire*, p. 69.
12. Koebner, *Empire*, p. 191.
13. Clark, *Language of Liberty*, p. 121.
14. J. G. A. Pocock, 'Political Thought in the English-speaking Atlantic, 1760–1790: part I: The Imperial Crisis', in J. G. A. Pocock (ed.), *The Varieties of British Political Thought, 1500–1800* (Cambridge: Cambridge University Press, 1993), pp. 246–82.
15. Tucker and Hendrickson, *Fall of the First British Empire*, pp. 182, 193.
16. Koebner, *Empire*, pp. 193, 203
17. Ibid., p. 215.
18. Tucker and Hendrickson, *Fall of the First British Empire*, p. 400.
19. Richard Koebner and Helmut Dan Schmidt, *Imperialism: The Story and Significance of a Political Word, 1840–1960* (Cambridge: Cambridge University Press, 1964), p. 52.
20. John Manning Ward, *Colonial Self-Government: The British Experience, 1759–1856* (London: Macmillan, 1976), pp. 4–20.
21. Chester W. New, *Lord Durham* (Oxford: Clarenden Press, 1929), pp. 333–4; Basil Williams, *The British Empire* (London, 1937), pp. 135–7.
22. Peter Burroughs, *The Canadian Crisis and British Colonial Policy, 1828–1841* (London: Edward Arnold, 1972), p. 4.
23. Ibid., p. 9.
24. Ibid., pp. 13–14.
25. Helen T. Manning, *The Revolt of French Canada, 1800–1835: A Chapter in the History of the British Commonwealth* (London: Macmillan, 1962), ch. VIII.
26. Ged Martin, *The Durham Report and British Policy: A Critical Essay* (Cambridge: Cambridge University Press, 1972), p. 6.
27. New, *Lord Durham*, pp. 326–7.
28. Burroughs, *Canadian Crisis*, p. 91.
29. D. K. Fieldhouse, *The Colonial Empires* (2nd edn, London, 1982), pp. 254–5.
30. Burroughs, *Canadian Crisis*, pp. 97–8.

31. New, *Lord Durham*, p. 322.
32. Martin, *The Durham Report*, p. 18.
33. Ibid., p. 28.
34. Burroughs, *Canadian Crisis*, p. 100.
35. New, *Lord Durham*, p. 322.
36. Ibid., p. 329.
37. Ibid., pp. 333–4.
38. Burroughs, *Canadian Crisis*, p. 101.
39. Martin, *The Durham Report* (London, 1902 edn), p. xiii.
40. Ibid., pp. 44–5, 227.
41. Ibid., pp. 244–5.
42. Burroughs, *Canadian Crisis*, p. 105.
43. New, *Lord Durham*, pp. 503–4, 509.
44. Manning Ward, *Colonial Self-Government*, pp. 195–208.
45. Ibid., p. 247.
46. Ibid., pp. 248–9.
47. Ibid., pp. 249–50.
48. New, *Lord Durham*, p. 505.
49. Martin, *The Durham Report*, pp. 54–5.
50. Burroughs, *Canadian Crisis*, pp. 113–14.
51. Clark, *Language of Liberty*, p. 384.
52. Stuart J. Reid, *Life and Letters of the First Earl of Durham, 1792–1840* (2 vols, London: Longman, 1906), vol. II, pp. 313–14.
53. Ibid., pp. 137–8.
54. Eric Stokes, *The Utilitarians and India* (Oxford: Oxford University Press, 1959), p. 44.
55. *Hansard, Commons Debates*, 3rd series, vol. IX, col. 389 (New York Reprint, 1971).
56. D. George Boyce (ed.), *The Crisis of British Power: The Imperial and Naval Papers of the Second Earl of Selborne, 1895–1910* (London: Historians' Press, 1990), pp. 203, 258.
57. S. R. Ashton and S. E. Stockwell (eds), *BDEE, Imperial Policy and Colonial Practice*, Part 1: *Metropolitan Reorganisation, Defence and International Relations, Political Change, and Constitutional Reform* (London: HMSO, 1996), pp. 105–6.
58. Gowher Rizvi, 'Transfer of Power in India: a Restatement of an Alternative Approach', *JICH*, XII: 3 (1983–4), p. 141.
59. Ashton and Stockwell, *BDEE, Imperial Policy and Colonial Practice*, p. 331.
60. D. W. Brogan, *The English People: Impressions and Observations* (London: Hamish Hamilton, 1947).

3   Rationalism and Empire, 1850–1914

1. P. J. Marshall, *Cambridge History of the British Empire* (Cambridge: Cambridge University Press, 1994), pp. 29–30.
2. Bernard Porter, *Britannia's Burden: The Political Evolution of Modern Britain, 1851–1990* (London: Edward Arnold, 1994), p. 89.

3. Peter Burroughs, 'Liberal, Paternalist or Cassandra? Earl Grey as Critic of Colonial Self-Government', *JICH*, 18:1 (1990), pp. 33–60, at pp. 35–6.
4. Ibid., p. 41.
5. J. L. Morison, 'Emigration and Land Policy, 1815–1873', in J. Holland Rose *et al.* (eds), *The Cambridge History of the British Empire*, vol. II: *The Growth of the New Empire, 1783–1870* (Cambridge: Cambridge University Press, 1940), pp. 449–50; T. O. Lloyd, *The British Empire, 1558–1983* (Oxford: Oxford University Press, 1984), p. 145.
6. Ged Martin, *The Durham Report and British Policy: A Critical Essay* (Cambridge: Cambridge University Press, 1972), p. 57.
7. Ibid., pp. 57–8.
8. Ged Martin, *Britain and the Origins of the Canadian Confederation, 1837–1867* (Vancouver: University of British Columbia Press, 1995), pp. 246–51.
9. Bruce A. Knox 'The Rise of Colonial Federation as an Object of British Policy, 1850–1870', *Journal of British Studies*, 11 (1971–2), pp. 92–112.
10. Burroughs, 'Liberal, Paternalist or Cassandra', p. 53.
11. A. B. Keith, *Selected Speeches and Documents on British Colonial Policy, 1763–1917* (London: Oxford University Press, 1953 edn), pp. 193–6.
12. Knox, 'The Rise of Colonial Federation', p. 112.
13. Douglas Cole, 'The Problem of "Nationalism" and "Imperialism" in British Settlement Colonies', *Journal of British Studies*, 10 (1970–1), pp. 160–82, at pp. 174–5, 177.
14. David Fitzpatrick, *Oceans of Consolation: Personal Accounts of Irish Migration to Australia* (Cork: Cork University Press, 1994), ch. 21.
15. *Whitaker's Almanac* (1906), pp. 511, 523.
16. Ibid., pp. 584, 590.
17. George Bennett, *The Concept of Empire from Burke to Attlee, 1774–1947* (London: Black, 1953), p. 234.
18. Ibid., p. 237.
19. Ibid., pp. 238–9.
20. Sir Charles Wentworth Dilke, *Problems of Greater Britain* (London: Macmillan, 1990), pp. 685–9.
21. Ibid., p. 689.
22. Ibid., p. 691.
23. Ibid., p. 692.
24. W. E. Gladstone, 'Aggression in Egypt and Freedom in the East', *Nineteenth Century*, 2 (August–December 1877), pp. 149–66.
25. Edward Dicey, 'Mr. Gladstone and our Empire', op. cit., pp. 292–308.
26. Earl Blatchford, 'The Integrity of the British Empire', op. cit., pp. 355–65.
27. W. F. Forster, 'Imperial Federation', *Nineteenth Century*, 17 (January–June 1885), pp. 201–18; see also his 'A Few More Words on Imperial Federation', op. cit., pp. 552–6.
28. Michael Burgess, 'The Federal Plan of the Imperial Federation League, 1892: Milestone or Tombstone?', in A. Boscoe (ed.), *The Federal Idea*, vol. I (London: Lothian Foundation, 1991), pp. 139–53.
29. Henry Thring, 'The Fallacy of Imperial Federation', *Nineteenth Century*, vol. 19 (January–June 1886), pp. 22–34. For a further discussion of their anti-federal view see John Kendle, *Federal Britain* (London: Routledge, 1997), pp. 46–51.

30. Robert Stout, 'A Colonial View of Imperial Federation', *Nineteenth Century*, 21 (January–June 1887), pp. 351–61.

31. John Merriman, 'The Closer Union of the Empire', op. cit., pp. 507–16.

32. Sidney Low, 'The Problem of an Imperial Executive', *Nineteenth Century*, 74 (July–December 1913), pp. 419–37.

33. Major Desmond Chapman Huston, *The Lost Historian: A Memory of Sir Sidney Low* (London: John Murray, 1936), pp. 192–6.

34. D. C. M. Platt, 'The National Economy and British Imperial Expansion before 1914', *JICH*, II: 1 (1973–4), pp. 3–14.

35. P. J. Marshall, *Cambridge Illustrated History of the British Empire*, p. 57.

36. Henry Birchenough, 'Mr. Chamberlain as an Empire Builder', *Nineteenth Century*, 51 (January–June 1902), pp. 360–8.

37. Robert Giffen, 'The Dream of a British Zollverein', *Nineteenth Century*, 51 (January–June 1902), pp. 693–705.

38. Henry Birchenough, 'Preferential Tariffs within the Empire: a Reply to Sir Robert Giffen', op. cit., pp. 891–9.

39. L. S. Amery, *My Political Life*, vol. I: *England before the Storm, 1896–1914* (London: Hutchinson, 1953), pp. 231–2.

40. Ibid., pp. 232–3.

41. D. George Boyce (ed.), *The Crisis of British Power: The Naval and South African Papers of the Second Earl of Selborne, 1895–1910* (London: Historians' Press, 1990), p. 25.

42. Iain Smith, *The Origins of the South African War* (London: Longman, 1996), p. 148.

43. Boyce, *Crisis of British Power*, p. 99.

44. Ibid., pp. 222–62.

45. Ibid., p. 206.

46. Ibid., p. 203.

47. J. A. Hobson, *The War in South Africa: Its Causes and Effects* (London: Nisbet, 1900), p. 310.

48. Boyce, *Crisis of British Power*, p. 255.

49. Ibid., p. 9.

50. Ibid., p. 18.

51. Ibid., p. 252.

52. Ibid., p. 216.

53. D. George Boyce and J. O. Stubbs, 'F. S. Oliver, Lord Selborne and Federalism', *JICH*, V: 1 (October 1976), pp. 53–81, at p. 56.

54. Philip G. Wigley, *Canada and the Transition to Commonwealth: British–Canadian Relations, 1917–1926* (Cambridge: Cambridge University Press, 1977), pp. 10–11.

55. *Round Table*, vol. 1 (1910–11), pp. 1–6, and Special Commemorative Volume, vol. 60 (1970), p. 382.

56. Boyce and Stubbs, 'F. S. Oliver', p. 64; Deborah Lavin, *From Empire to International Commonwealth: A Biography of Lionel Curtis* (Oxford, 1995), pp. 105–20.

57. Bernard Porter, *The Lion's Share: A Short History of British Imperialism*, 2nd edn (London: Longman, 1989), p. 112.

58. Boyce, *Crisis of British Power*, p. 107.

59. Ibid., p. 115.
60. Ibid., p. 124.
61. Ibid., p. 124.
62. Ibid., p. 143.
63. Ibid., p. 142.
64. Ibid., p. 171.
65. Ibid., pp. 184–90.
66. Ibid., p. 160.
67. Ibid., pp. 194–5.
68. K. M. Wilson, *The Policy of the Entente: Essays on the Determinants of British Foreign Policy, 1904–1914* (Cambridge: Cambridge University Press, 1985), pp. 80, 81–4.
69. Ibid., p. 80.
70. Lord Curzon, 'The True Imperialism', *Nineteenth Century*, 63 (January–June 1908), pp. 151–65.
71. B. K. Long, 'The Empire in 1914', in E. Thomas Cook (ed.), *The Empire in the World: A Study in Leadership and Reconstruction* (Oxford: Clarendon Press, 1937), p. 71. Long was for nearly 15 years editor of the *Cape Times*, and a Member of the Cape House of Assembly, later of the South African Union Parliament. He took part in the negotiations and discussions leading to the making of the Union.
72. Smith, *The Origins of the South African War*, pp. 422–3.

4   Pillars of Empire: Ireland and India, 1914–49

1. J. J. Bumstead, *Interpreting Canada's Past* (2 vols, Oxford: Oxford University Press, 1993), vol. II, ch. 17.
2. Sheila Lawlor, *Britain and Ireland, 1914–1923* (Dublin: Gill and Macmillan, 1983), pp. 87, 94.
3. Susan Marion Trofimlakoff, 'Quebec in the Great War', in Bumstead, *Canada's Past*, ch. 18.
4. Deborah Lavin, *From Empire to International Commonwealth: A Biography of Lionel Curtis* (Oxford: Oxford University Press, 1995), pp. 128–30.
5. Bernard Porter, *The Lion's Share: A Short History of British Imperialism* (London: Longman, 1984 edn), pp. 235–6.
6. S. R. Ashton and S. E. Stockwell (eds), *BDEE, Imperial Policy and Colonial Practice, 1925–1945*, part 1: *Metropolitan Reorganisation, Defence International Relations, Political Change and Constitutional Reform* (London: HMSO, 1996), pp. xxxi–xxxii.
7. Ibid., p. xxxii.
8. Ibid., p. xxxiii.
9. D. George Boyce, *Englishmen and Irish Troubles: British Public Opinion and the Making of Irish Policy, 1918–1922* (Aldershot: Gregg, 1994), pp. 135–41.
10. Ibid., p. 170.
11. Lavin, *From Empire to International Commonwealth*, p. 186.

12. Ibid., p. 212.
13. John Campbell, *F. E. Smith, First Earl of Birkenhead* (London: Jonathan Cape, 1983), p. 576.
14. Cyril Falls, 'Ireland: Some Truths', *Nineteenth Century and After*, I (January–April 1922), pp. 222–8, at pp. 225, 228.
15. Keith Middlemas, *Tom Jones: Whitehall Diary*, vol. III: *Ireland, 1918–1925* (London: Oxford University Press, 1971), p. 109.
16. Ibid., p. 145.
17. Lavin, *From Empire to International Commonwealth*, pp. 189–90.
18. Ibid., pp. 192–3.
19. Middlemas, *Tom Jones*, p. 177.
20. R. Curtis and R. B. MacDowell, *Irish Historical Documents, 1172–1922* (London, Methuen 1977 edn), p. 322.
21. Ibid., pp. 326–7.
22. Boyce, *Englishmen and Irish Troubles*, p. 173.
23. Ibid., pp. 176–8.
24. Ibid., p. 179.
25. Ibid., p. 174.
26. Ibid., p. 174.
27. Lloyd George to Sir James Craig, 14 November 1921, quoted in St John Ervine, *Craigavon: Ulsterman* (London: Allen & Unwin, 1949), pp. 452–3.
28. Ibid., p. 453.
29. Basil Williams, *The British Empire* (London, 1928), pp. 238–9.
30. R. F. Holland, *Britain and the Commonwealth Alliance, 1918–1939* (London: Macmillan, 1981), pp. 59–60.
31. Ibid., pp. 58–9.
32. Porter, *The Lion's Share*, p. 261; for a detailed breakdown of trade figures see Thomas Cook (ed.), *The Empire in the World* (London: Oxford University Press, 1937), pp. 172–3.
33. Martin Kitchen, *The British Empire and Commonwealth: A Short History* (London: Macmillan, 1996), p. 78.
34. L. S. Amery, *My Political Life* (3 vols, London, 1953–5), vol. 1: *England before the Storm* (London: Hutchinson, 1953), pp. 228–9.
35. Holland, *Britain and the Commonwealth Alliance*, pp. 135–6.
36. Ibid., p. 141.
37. Cook (ed.), *The Empire in the World*, p. 313.
38. W. K. Hancock, *Survey of British Commonwealth Affairs*, vol. 1: *Problems of Nationality, 1918–1936* (London: Oxford University Press, 1937), p. 251.
39. Ibid., 252.
40. Ibid., p. 61.
41. Deirdre McMahon, *Republicans and Imperialists: Anglo-Irish Relations in the 1930s* (New York and London: Yale University Press, 1984), p. 1.
42. Porter, *The Lion's Share*, p. 296.
43. Hancock, *Survey of British Commonwealth Affairs*, pp. 275–6,
44. Ibid., pp. 280–1.
45. Ibid., p. 283.
46. Ibid., p. 321.

47. Deirdre McMahon, '"A Transient Apparition": British Policy towards the de Valera Government, 1932–1935', *Irish Historical Studies*, XXII (September 1981), pp. 331–61, at p. 331.
48. Ibid., p. 331.
49. Ibid., p. 339.
50. Hancock, *Survey of British Commonwealth Affairs*, p. 344.
51. Ibid., p. 348.
52. McMahon, '"A Transient Apparition"', p. 343.
53. Ibid., p. 344.
54. Ibid., p. 352.
55. Angus J. Nolan, 'Joseph Walshe and the Management of Irish Foreign Policy, 1922–1946: A Study in Diplomatic and Administrative History' (PhD, University College Cork, 1997), p. 84.
56. Donal Lowry, 'The Alliance that Dare Not Speak its Name': Afrikaaner and Irish Nationalists and the British Empire/Commonwealth c. 1902–1961'. Paper delivered at the Institute of Commonwealth Studies, 14 November 1996, p. 22.
57. McMahon, *Republicans and Imperialists*, p. 391.
58. Hancock, *Survey of British Commonwealth Affairs*, p. 391.
59. For a discussion of this relationship see Tom Fraser, 'Ireland and India', in Keith Jeffrey (ed.), *An Irish Empire? Aspects of Ireland and the British Empire* (Manchester: Manchester University Press, 1996), ch. 3, and H. V. Brasted, 'Irish Models and the Indian National Congress, 1870–1922', *South Asia*, 8: 1/2 (June, December 1985), pp. 24–45. For some contemporary observations see Sir Michael O'Dwyer, *India as I Knew it, 1885–1925* (London: Constable, 1925), pp. 12–15, and Mahadev Desai's analysis of the Irish struggle for independence, and his belief that India might improve on the Irish example by using less violence (Francis G. Hutchins, *India's Revolution: Gandhi and the 'Quit India' Movement* (Cambridge, Mass., 1973), pp. 291–2.
60. Boyce, *Englishmen and Irish Troubles*, p. 51.
61. Reginald Coupland, *The Constitutional Problem in India*, part I: *The Indian Problem, 1833–1935* (Oxford, 1945), p. 52.
62. Ibid., p. 59.
63. Coupland, *Constitutional Problem*, p. 61.
64. Lavin, *From Empire to International Commonwealth*, p. 136.
65. *Hansard*, HC debates, 5th series, vol. 116, cols 635–40 (22 May 1919). See also Michael Woods, 'The Montagu–Chelmsford Reforms (1919): A Reassessment', *South Asia*, 1: XVII: 1 (1994), pp. 25–42.
66. Hancock, *Survey of British Commonwealth Affairs*, p. 172.
67. Judith Brown, *Gandhi: Prisoner of Hope* (New Haven and London: Yale University Press, 1989), p. 167.
68. P. N. Pandey, *The Indian Nationalist Movement, 1885–1947: Select Documents* (London: Macmillan, 1979), p. 60.
69. Judith Brown, *Modern India: The Making of an Asian Democracy* (Oxford: Oxford University Press, 1985), p. 238.
70. Coupland, *Constitutional Problem*, p. 88.
71. Ibid., p. 93.

72. Ibid., p. 106.
73. Ibid., p. 16.
74. Ibid., pp. 132–46.
75. Ashton and Stockwell (eds), *BDEE, Imperial Policy and Colonial Practice, 1925–1945*, part I, pp. 263–8.
76. Williams, *The British Empire*, p. 216.
77. Coupland, *Constitutional Problem*, p. 184.
78. Brown, *Modern India*, p. 322.
79. Tom Fraser, 'Ireland and India', in Jeffrey (ed.), *An Irish Empire?*, p. 91.
80. Nicholas Mansergh (ed.), *Constitutional Relations between Britain and India: The Transfer of Power, 1942–1947*, vol. I: *The Cripps Mission, January–April 1942* (London: HMSO, 1970), p. 14.
81. Ibid., pp. 45–50, 81–90.
82. Ibid., pp. 110–12.
83. Mansergh (ed.), *Constitutional Relations*, vol. III: *The Reassertion of Authority: Gandhi's Fast and the Succession to the Viceroyalty, 21 September 1941–12 June 1953* (London, 1971), pp. 250–2.
84. Anita Inder Singh, *The Origins of the Partition of India, 1936–1947* (Delhi: Oxford University Press, 1987), p. 73.
85. Coupland, *Constitutional Problem*, pp. 273–8.
86. Nicholas Mansergh, *The Commonwealth and the Nations* (London: Royal Institute of International Affairs, 1948), p. 17.
87. Francis G. Hutchins, *Spontaneous Revolution: The 'Quit India' Movement* (Delhi: Oxford University Press, 1971), p. 191.
88. Ibid., pp. 216–17.
89. Mansergh (ed.), *Constitutional Relations*, vol. IV: *The Bengal Famine and the New Viceroyalty, 15 June, 1943–31 August, 1944* (London, 1973), p. 259.
90. Ibid., pp. 378–80, 387–8.
91. Mansergh (ed.), *Constitutional Relations*, vol. V: *The Simla Conference, 1 September, 1944–28 July, 1945* (London, 1974), pp. 1–6.
92. Mansergh (ed.), *Constitutional Relations*, vol. VI: *The Post-War Phase: New Moves by the Labour Government, 1 August, 1945–22 March, 1946* (London, 1976), pp. 765–6.
93. Mansergh (ed.), *Constitutional Relations*, vol. VII: *The Cabinet Mission, 23 March–29 June, 1946* (London, 1977), pp. 1084–9.
94. Mansergh (ed.), *Constitutional Relations*, vol. VIII: *The Interim Government, 3 July–1 November, 1946* (London, 1979), pp. 348–9.
95. Mansergh (ed.), *Constitutional Relations*, vol. IX: *The Fixing of a Time Limit, 4 November, 1946–22 March, 1947* (London, 1980), pp. 602–9.
96. T. O. Lloyd, *The British Empire, 1558–1983* (Oxford: Oxford University Press, 1984) p. 324.
97. Nicholas Owen, '"More than a Transfer of Power": Independence Day Ceremonies in India, 15 August, 1947', *Contemporary Record*, 6: 3 (Winter, 1992), pp. 415–51, at pp. 421–3.
98. Ibid., pp. 442–3.
99. Robert Pearce (ed.), *Patrick Gordon Walker: Political Diaries, 1932–1971* (London: Historians' Press, 1991), pp. 182–3.

100. Ronald Hyam (ed.), *BDEE*, series A, vol. 2: *Labour Government and the End of Empire, Part IV* (London: HMSO, 1992), pp. 205–7.
101. Mansergh, *The Commonwealth and the Nations*, p. 178.
102. *House of Commons Debates*, 5th Series, vol. 464, col. 373 (28 April 1949).
103. Hugh Tinker (ed.), *Constitutional Relations between Britain and Burma: The Struggle for Independence*, vol. 1: *From Military Occupation to Civil Government, 1 January, 1944 to 31 August, 1946* (London: HMSO, 1983), pp. 131, 186.
104. Ibid., vol. II: *From General Strike to Independence, 31 August, 1946 to 4 January, 1948* (London: HMSO, 1984), p. 202.
105. Ibid., pp. 209–10.
106. Ibid., p. 525.
107. Ibid., pp. 574–5.
108. Ibid., pp. 615–18.
109. Lorna Lloyd, 'Britain and the Transformation from Empire to Commonwealth: The Significance of the Immediate Post-war Years', *Round Table*, no. 343 (1997), pp. 333–60, at pp. 337–8.
110. F. J. McEvoy, 'Canada, Ireland and the Commonwealth: the Declaration of the Irish Republic, 1948–1949', *Irish Historical Studies*, XXIV (November 1985), pp. 506–27.
111. Ronald Hyam (ed.), *BDEE*, series A, vol. 2: *Labour Government and the End of Empire*, part 1: *High Policy and Administration* (London: HMSO, 1992), p. lx–ix.
112. Ibid., p. lxix; and *BDEE*, part IV: *Race Relations and the Commonwealth*, pp. 162–3 (Cabinet Conclusions, 28 October 1948), pp. 166–7 (Cabinet Conclusions, 12 November 1948), pp. 174, 176 (18 November 1948).
113. Hyam (ed.), *BDEE*, part IV, p. 161 (Cabinet Conclusions, 28 October 1948).
114. Ibid., p. 175 (Cabinet Conclusions, 18 November 1948).
115. McEvoy, 'Canada, Ireland and the Commonwealth', op. cit., p. 511.
116. *BDEE*, part IV, p. 162 (Cabinet Conclusions, 28 October 1948).
117. Ibid., p. 184 (Cabinet Conclusions, 12 January 1949).
118. Ibid., pp. 203–4 (Cabinet Conclusions, 8 March 1949). For the Ireland Act and the Irish propaganda campaign see D. George Boyce, *The Irish Question in British Politics, 1868–1996* (London: Macmillan, 1996), pp. 100–3. For a survey of the policy of the various parties to the dispute see D. W. Dean, 'Final Exit? Britain, Eire, the Commonwealth and the Repeal of the External Relations Act, 1945–1949', *JICH*, 20: 3 (September 1992), pp. 391–418.
119. *House of Commons Debates*, 5th Series, vol. 464, col. 1953 (11 May 1949). See also ibid., col. 375 (28 April 1949).
120. *Round Table*, no. 157 (December 1949), p. 27.
121. Ashton and Stockwell (eds), *BDEE, Imperial Policy and Colonial Practice, 1925–1945*, part I, pp. 291–6.
122. *Round Table*, no. 154 (March 1949), p. 155.
123. Hyam (ed.), *BDEE, Labour Government and the End of Empire*, part IV, p. 207.
124. Sir Charles Jeffries, *Ceylon: The Path to Independence* (London: Pall Mall Press, 1962), p.135.

125.   Hyam (ed.), *The Labour Government and the End of Empire*, part 1, pp. 71–2.
126.   Ibid., p. xxvi.
127.   Jeffries, *Ceylon*, p. 134.

5   The Changing World of Empire, 1939–59

  1.   S. R. Ashton and S. E. Stockwell (eds), *BDEE*, *Imperial Policy and Colonial Practice 1925–1945*, part I, p. 299.
  2.   Ibid., p. 303.
  3.   Ibid., p. lix.
  4.   Ibid., p. 310.
  5.   A. J. Stockwell (ed.), *BDEE*, series B, vol. 3: *Malaya*, part I: *The Malayan Union Experiment, 1942–1948* (London: HMSO, 1995), pp. 1–7.
  6.   Ibid., p. 19.
  7.   Ibid., p. 21.
  8.   Ibid., pp. 22–3.
  9.   Ibid., pp. 25–7.
 10.   Ibid., pp. 27–9.
 11.   Ibid., pp. 44–5.
 12.   Ibid., p. 51.
 13.   Ibid., p. 70.
 14.   Ibid., p. 71–3.
 15.   Ibid., p. 87.
 16.   For an excellent analysis of the impact of war see John Darwin, *Britain and Decolonisation: The Retreat from Empire in the Post-War World* (London: Macmillan, 1988), ch. 2. For the Middle East see Elizabeth Monroe, *The British Moment in the Middle East, 1914–1956* (London: Chatto and Windus, 1963), pp. 124–9.
 17.   Trevor Reese, *Australia in the Twentieth Century – A Short Political Guide* (London: Chatto and Windus, 1964), p. 110.
 18.   Ibid., pp. 122–3.
 19.   Duncan Anderson, 'Slim', in John Keegan (ed.), *Churchill's Generals* (London: Weidenfeld, 1991), p. 314.
 20.   Reese, *Australia*, pp. 115–16.
 21.   Ashton and Stockwell, (eds), *BDEE*, *Imperial Policy and Colonial Practice*, pp. xxxix, 167–70.
 22.   N. Mansergh (ed.), *Constitutional Relations between Britain and India*, vol. III (London: HMSO, 1971), pp. 656–7.
 23.   W. R. Louis, 'American Anti-Colonialism and the Dissolution of the British Empire', *International Affairs*, 61: 3 (Summer 1985), p. 395.
 24.   L. S. Amery, quoted in Louis, 'American Anti-Colonialism', p. 401.
 25.   Louis, 'American Anti-Colonialism', pp. 403–5.
 26.   Ibid., p. 408.
 27.   D. A. Low and A. Smith (eds), *History of East Africa*, vol. 3 (Oxford: Clarendon Press, 1976), p. 175.
 28.   Ibid., pp. 175–6.
 29.   'Internal Security in the Colonies', 29 December 1954, Cab. 129/72.

30. Cabinet Conclusions, 28 March 1957, Cab. 128/31.
31. D. Reynolds, *Britannia Overruled: British Policy and World Power in the Twentieth Century* (London: Longmans, 1991), p. 178.
32. Ibid., p. 179.
33. David Goldsworthy (ed.), *BDEE*, series A, vol. 3: *The Conservative Government and the End of Empire*, part I: *International Relations* (London: HMSO, 1994), pp. liv-lv.
34. R. F. Holland, *The Pursuit of Greatness: Britain and the World Role, 1900–1970* (London: Fontana, 1991), pp. 132–3; Lorna Lloyd, 'Britain and the Transformation from Empire to Commonwealth', *Round Table*, no. 343 (1997), pp. 346–7.
35. Reynolds, *Britannia Overruled*, p. 208.
36. John Gallagher, *The Decline, Revival and Fall of the British Empire*, ed. Anil Seal (Cambridge: Cambridge University Press, 1982), p. 73.
37. R. Hyam (ed.), *BDEE, Labour Government and the End of Empire, 1945–1951*, series A, vol. II, part 1: *High Policy and Administration* (London: HMSO, 1992), p. 141.
38. Kwame Nkrumah, *Towards Colonial Freedom: Africa in the Struggle against World Imperialism* (London: Heinemann, 1963).
39. J. A. Hobson, *Imperialism: A Study* (London, 1902).
40. David Boucher, 'British Idealism, the State and International Relations', *Journal of the History of Ideas*, 55 (1994), pp. 682–3.
41. David Goldsworthy, 'Keeping Change within Bounds', *JICH*, 18: 1 (1996), pp. 81–108.
42. Thomas R. Mockaitis, *British Counterinsurgency, 1919–1960* (Manchester: Manchester University Press, 1990), pp. 111–24.
43. Goldsworthy, 'Keeping Change within Bounds', p. 85.
44. 'The Future of Commonwealth Membership', January 1955, C.O. 1032/50.
45. G. E. Metcalfe, *Great Britain and Ghana: Documents of Ghanaian History, 1807–1957* (London: Nelson, 1964), pp. 682–3.
46. Ibid., p. 687.
47. Prosser Gifford and W. R. Louis, *The Transfer of Power in Africa: Decolonisation, 1940–1960* (London: Yale University Press, 1982), p. 137.
48. D. Birmingham, *The Decolonisation of Africa*, (London: University College Press, 1995), pp. 26–9.
49. Metcalfe, *Great Britain and Ghana*, p. 726.
50. Low and Smith (eds), *History of East Africa*, p. 9.
51. Ibid., p. 10.
52. D. Goldsworthy (ed.), *BDEE, Conservative Government and the End of Empire*, Part II: *Politics and Administration*, pp. 188–9.
53. G. H. Kelling, *Centralism and Rebellion: British Policy in Cyprus, 1939–1955* (New York: Greenwood Press, 1990), pp. 1–16.
54. Ibid., p. 50.
55. Ibid., pp. 102–3.
56. Ibid., pp. 103–4.
57. Ibid., pp. 125–6.
58. Ibid., p. 141.
59. Ibid., p. 151.

60. Cabinet Conclusions, 18 March 1957, Cab. 128/31.

61. Cabinet Conclusions, 28 March 1957, Cab. 128/31.

62. R. F. Holland, *European Decolonisation, 1918–1981: An Introductory Survey* (London: Macmillan, 1985), pp. 258–9.

63. W. K. Hancock, *Survey of British Commonwealth Affairs*, vol. I: *Problems of Nationality*, pp. 497–9.

64. Hyam (ed.), *BDEE, Labour Government and the End of Empire*, part I, pp. 334–5.

65. Stockwell (ed.), *BDEE*, series B, vol. 3: *The Malayan Union Experiment, 1942–1948*, pp. 1–7.

66. Ibid., p. 38.

67. Ibid., p. 39.

68. Ibid., p. iv.

69. Ibid., p. 231.

70. Ibid., p. lxiii.

71. Stockwell (ed.), *BDEE, Malaya*, part II: *The Communist Insurrection, 1948–1953* (London: HMSO, 1995), pp. 158–60.

72. Ibid., pp. 393–6.

73. Stockwell (ed.), *BDEE*, part I: *The Malayan Union Experiment*, p. lxxii.

74. *BDEE, Malaya*, part II, p. 330.

75. Ibid., pp. 264–5.

76. Ibid., part III: *The Alliance Route to Independence, 1953–1957*, p. 87.

77. Ibid., pp. 95–7.

78. Ibid., part I, pp. lxxvi–lxxvii.

79. Ibid., part II, p. 236.

80. Ibid., part III, pp. 412–13.

81. John M. MacKenzie, *Propaganda and Empire: The Manipulation of British Public Opinion, 1880–1960* (Manchester University Press, 1996) p. 235.

82. Ibid., pp. 231–3. See also Thomas G. August, *The Selling of Empire British and French Imperial Propaganda, 1890–1940* (Westport, Conn.: Greenwood Press, 1985), *passim*.

83. MacKenzie, *Propaganda and Empire*, p. 257.

84. Ibid., p. 11.

85. David Butler, *The British General Election of 1951* (London: Macmillan, 1952), pp. 35–6.

86. Ibid., pp. 112–18, 247.

87. David Butler, *The British General Election of 1955* (London: Macmillan, 1955), p. 91.

88. Ibid., p. 164.

89. John Turner, *Profiles in Power: Macmillan* (London: Macmillan, 1994), pp. 146–7.

90. Ibid., p. 241.

91. David Butler, *The British General Election of 1959* (London: Macmillan, 1959), pp. 264, 278.

92. Ibid., pp. 195, 197.

93. Turner, *Macmillan*, p. 253.

94. D. Goldsworthy (ed.), *BDEE, Conservative Government and the End of Empire, 1951–1957*, part I: *International Relations*, p. liv.

95. Ibid., p. liv.
96. Turner, *Macmillan*, p. 258. Lord Home was particularly regretful.

6 The Concept of Empire from Attlee to Churchill, 1945–55

1. L. S. Amery, *My Political Life*, vol. I: *England before the Storm, 1896–1914* (London: Hutchinson, 1953), p. 255.
2. D. G. Boyce (ed.), *The Crisis of British Power* (London: Historians' Press, 1990), p. 133.
3. W. K. Hancock, *Survey of British Commonwealth Affairs*, vol. I: *Problems of Nationality* (London: Oxford University Press, 1937), p. 1.
4. Ibid., p. 1.
5. Robert Pearce (ed.), *Patrick Gordon Walker: Political Diaries, 1932–1971* (London: Historians' Press, 1991), p. 168.
6. Amery, *My Political Life*, vol. I, p. 255.
7. Ibid., p. 401.
8. W. R. Louis, 'American Anti-Colonialism and the Dissolution of the British Empire', *International Affairs*, 61: 3 (Summer 1988), p. 395.
9. Pearce, *Patrick Gordon Walker: Political Diaries*, p. 182.
10. Ibid., p. 182.
11. Hancock, *Survey of British Commonwealth Affairs*, p. 9
12. Pearce (ed.), *Gordon Walker*, p. 183.
13. Amery, *My Political Life*, vol. II: *War and Peace, 1914–1939* (London: Hutchinson, 1953), p. 364.
14. A. N. Porter and A. J. Stockwell, *British Imperial Policy and Decolonisation, 1938–1964*, vol. 1: *1938–1951* (London: HMSO, 1987), pp. 302–6.
15. Prosser Gifford, 'Misconceived Dominion', in Prosser Gifford and W. R. Louis (eds), *The Transfer of Power in Africa; Decolonization, 1940–1960* (London: Yale University Press, 1982), pp. 387–416 at pp. 392–5.
16. Porter and Stockwell, *British Imperial Policy*, pp. 302–6.
17. Gifford and Louis, *Transfer of Power*, pp. 398–9; for Labour's timidity in framing a policy of moving African colonies towards self-government see P. S. Gupta, *Imperialism and the British Labour Movement, 1914–1964* (London: Macmillan, 1975), pp. 276–8.
18. Gifford and Louis, *Transfer of Power*, p. 403.
19. Andrew Porter makes this point in Nicholas Owen (ed.), 'Decolonisation and the Colonial Office', *Contemporary Record*, 6: 3 (Winter 1992), p. 529.
20. Jasper H. Stembridge, *An Atlas of the British Empire* (Oxford: Clarendon Press, 1944), p. 5.
21. David Fieldhouse, 'Decolonisation, Development and Dependence: A Survey of Changing Attitudes', in Gifford and Louis (eds), *Transfer of Power*, pp. 483–514, at p. 486.
22. Ibid., p. 487.
23. Porter and Stockwell, *British Imperial Policy*, p. 183.
24. Ibid., p. 185.
25. Ibid., p. 185.
26. Ibid., p. 211.

27. Ibid., pp. 206–7.
28. Ibid., pp. 278–83.
29. Gifford and Fieldhouse, 'Decolonisation, Development and Dependence', in Gifford and Louis (eds), *Transfer of Power*, pp. 487–8.
30. Porter and Stockwell, *British Imperial Policy*, p. 282.
31. Ibid., pp. 278–83.
32. Hyam (ed.), *BDEE, Labour Government and the End of Empire*, part I, pp. xlviii–xlix.
33. W. R. Louis, *The British Empire in the Middle East, 1945–1951: Arab Nationalism, the United States, and Post War Imperialism* (Oxford: Clarendon Press, 1984), p. 16.
34. Hyam (ed.), *BDEE, Labour Government and the End of Empire*, part I, pp. lx–lxviii.
35. Porter and Stockwell, *British Imperial Policy*, p. 170.
36. *Round Table*, no. 157 (December 1949), p. 20.
37. N. Mansergh, *The Commonwealth and the Nations* (London, 1948), p. 22.
38. Hyam (ed.), *BDEE, Labour Government and the End of Empire*, part I, p. lxx.
39. Goldsworthy (ed.), *BDEE, Conservative Government and the End of Empire*, part II, pp. 5–6.
40. Hyam (ed.), *BDEE, Labour Government and the End of Empire*, part I, p. xxxix.
41. Lorna Lloyd, 'Britain and the Transformation from Empire', *Round Table*, no. 343 (July 1997), p. 347.
42. Amery, *My Political Life*, vol. 2, p. 364.
43. David Goldsworthy, 'Keeping Change within Bounds: Aspects of Colonial Policy during the Churchill and Eden Governments, 1951–1957', *JICH*, 18: 1 (1990), pp. 81–108, at pp. 96–8.
44. Ibid., pp. 88–92.
45. For an analysis of Lowe's thought see James Winter, *Robert Lowe* (Toronto: University of Toronto Press, 1976), pp. 199–202, 212–14.
46. Goldsworthy, 'Keeping Change within Bounds', p. 81.
47. David Birmingham, *The Decolonisation of Africa* (London, 1995), pp. 26–9.
48. Goldsworthy, 'Keeping Change within Bounds', p. 98.
49. C.O. 1032, January 1955.
50. Goldsworthy, 'Keeping Change within Bounds', p. 95.
51. Porter and Stockwell, *British Imperial Policy*, vol. II, pp. 234–7.
52. Sir Norman Brooke, Minute, 26 January 1955, C.O. 1032/50.
53. A. J. Stockwell, 'British Imperial Policy and Decolonisation in Malaya, 1942–1952', *JICH*, XIII: 1 (October 1984), pp. 68–87 at p. 79.
54. Ibid., p. 73.
55. John D. Hargreaves, *The End of Colonial Rule in West Africa* (London: Macmillan, 1979), p. 16.
56. Hyam (ed.), *BDEE, Labour Government and the End of Empire*, part IV, p. 177.
57. Martin Gilbert, *Winston S. Churchill*, vol. VIII: *'Never Despair', 1945–1965* (London: Heinemann, 1988), pp. 472–3.
58. Goldsworthy (ed.), *BDEE, Conservative Government and the End of Empire*, part I, p. xxx.
59. Mansergh, *The Commonwealth and the Nations*, p. 162.
60. Low and Smith, *History of East Africa*, p. 51.
61. Louis, *British Empire in the Middle East*, p. 46.

7   Pillars of Empire: The Middle East

1. Ronald Hyam, *Britain's Imperial Century, 1815–1914: A Study of Empire and Expansion* (Cambridge: Cambridge University Press, 1993), pp. 174–5, 176–7.
2. Lord Cromer, *Ancient and Modern Imperialism* (London: John Murray, 1910), p. 69.
3. Ibid., p. 53.
4. Ibid., pp. 53–4.
5. J. Gallagher, *Decline, Revival and Fall of the British Empire*, ed. Anil Seal (Cambridge: Cambridge University, 1982), p. 110.
6. S. R. Ashton and S. E. Stockwell (eds), *BDEE, Imperial Policy and Colonial Practice 1925–1945*, part I, pp. 120–9.
7. Ronald Hyam (ed.), *BDEE, Labour Government and the End of Empire*, part I, pp. 17–18.
8. Ibid., pp. 19–20.
9. Ibid., pp. 21–2.
10. Ibid., pp. 23–4, 27.
11. Ibid., pp. 39–41.
12. Major General Sir C. E. Callwell, *Field Marshal Sir Henry Wilson: His Life and Diaries* (2 vols, London: Cassell, 1927), vol. II, p. 294.
13. Hyam (ed.), *BDEE, Labour Government and the End of Empire*, part I, pp. 39–45.
14. Ibid., pp. 45–6.
15. Ibid., p. 47.
16. Ibid., pp. 49–50.
17. Ibid., pp. 51–5.
18. Ibid., pp. 56–7.
19. Ibid., pp. 57–9.
20. Ibid., p. 62.
21. Ibid., pp. 63–9.
22. Ibid., p. 75.
23. Ibid., p. 78.
24. Martin Gilbert, *Winston S. Churchill*, vol. VIII: *'Never Despair'* (London: Heinemann, 1988), pp. 299–300.
25. W. K. Hancock, *Survey of British Commonwealth Affairs*, vol. 1: *Problems of Nationality* (London: Oxford University Press, 1937), pp. 484–5.
26. *Round Table*, no. 146 (March 1947), pp. 105, 107.
27. Ashton and Stockwell (eds), *BDEE, Imperial Policy and Colonial Practice, 1925–1945*, part I, pp. 228–31.
28. Hyam (ed.), *BDEE, Labour Government and the End of Empire*, part I, pp. 2–3.
29. Ali Reza Moussavizadeh, 'British Foreign Policy towards Iran, with Special Reference to the Nationalisation of the Anglo-Iranian Oil Company, 1948–1954' (PhD, University of Wales, Swansea, 1993), p. 34.
30. Ibid., pp. 44–5.
31. Ibid., p. 60.
32. Hyam (ed.), *BDEE, Labour Government and the End of Empire*, part I, pp. 87–8.
33. Ibid., pp. 89–90.

34. Ibid., p. 91; James Cable, *Intervention at Abadan: Plan Buccaneer* (London: Macmillan, 1991), pp. 51–63, 80–1.
35. *BDEE*, op. cit., p. 91–3.
36. Ibid., p. 93; Cable, *Intervention at Abadan*, pp. 98–9.
37. *BDEE*, op. cit., pp. 93–6.
38. Moussavizadeh, 'British Foreign Policy', p. 110.
39. Ibid., pp. 130–1.
40. Ibid., p. 145.
41. Ibid., p. 145.
42. W. R. Louis, *The British Empire in the Middle East, 1945–1951* (Oxford: Clarendon Press, 1984), p. 47.
43. Goldsworthy (ed.), *BDEE, Conservative Government and the End of Empire*, part I, pp. 149–58.
44. W. R. Louis and R. Owen, *Suez, 1956* (Oxford, 1989); *The Crisis and its Consequences* (Oxford, 1989), p. 19.
45. Ashton and Stockwell (eds), *BDEE, Imperial Policy and Colonial Practice*, part I, pp. 75–6.
46. S. Lucas, *Britain and Suez: The Lion's Last Roar* (Manchester: Manchester University Press, 1996), p. 7.
47. Louis, *British Empire in the Middle East*, p. 9.
48. John Kent, *British Imperial Strategy and the Origins of the Cold War, 1944–1949* (Leicester: Leicester University Press, 1993), p. 50; Phillip Darby, *British Defence Policy East of Suez, 1947–1968* (London Oxford University Press, 1973), pp. 153–6.
49. Ibid., p. 205.
50. John Kent, 'The Egyptian Base and the Defence of the Middle East, 1945–1954', *JICH*, 21: 3 (Sept. 1993), pp. 45–65, at p. 51.
51. Martin Gilbert, *Winston S. Churchill*, vol. VIII, pp. 840–1.
52. David Dutton, *Anthony Eden: A Life and Reputation* (London: Edward Arnold, 1997), pp. 357–8.
53. Lucas, *Britain and Suez*, p. 9.
54. Dutton, *Anthony Eden*, p. 362.
55. Lucas, *Britain and Suez*, pp. 9–10.
56. Ibid., p. 10.
57. Dutton, *Anthony Eden*, p. 366.
58. W. R. Louis and Roger Owen (eds), *Suez, 1956*, pp. 36–7; Lucas, *Britain and Suez*, p. 12.
59. Lucas, *Britain and Suez*, p. 17.
60. Tony Shaw, *Eden, Suez and the Mass Media: Propaganda and Persuasion during the Suez Crisis* (London: I. B. Taurus, 1996), p. 7.
61. N. J. Ashton, *Eisenhower, Macmillan and the problem of Nasser* (London: Macmillan, 1996), pp. 61–3.
62. Lucas, *Britain and Suez*, p. 27.
63. Ibid., pp. 27–8.
64. Ibid., pp. 28–30.
65. Ibid., p. 46.
66. Ibid., p. 47.
67. Dutton, *Anthony Eden*, pp. 402–3.

68. Shaw, *Eden, Suez and the Mass Media*, p. 12.
69. Lucas, *Britain and Suez*, p. 53.
70. Louis and Owen, *Suez, 1956*, pp. 115–16.
71. Ibid., p. 118; N. Ashton, 'Macmillan and the Middle East', in R. Aldous and S. Lee (eds), *Harold Macmillan and Britain's World Role* (London: Macmillan, 1996), pp. 37–65, at p. 44.
72. Lucas, *Britain and Suez*, pp. 63–4; Dutton, *Eden*, pp. 405–8.
73. Lucas, *Britain and Suez*, pp. 67–8.
74. Ibid., p. 71.
75. Dutton, *Eden*, pp. 417–19.
76. Lucas, *Britain and Suez*, p. 86; Dutton, *Eden*, pp. 119–20.
77. Lucas, *Britain and Suez*, pp. 89–91.
78. Louis and Owen, *Suez, 1956*, pp. 128–9.
79. Dutton, *Eden*, p. 429.
80. Lucas, *Britain and Suez*, p. 101.
81. Ibid., pp. 110–11.
82. Anthony Seldon, *Churchill's Indian Summer: The Conservative Government, 1951–1955* (London: Hodder and Stoughton, 1981), p. 433.
83. Goldsworthy (ed.), *BDEE, Conservative Government and the End of Empire*, part I, p. 173.
84. Cabinet Conclusions, 1 May 1958, Cab., 128/32.
85. A. N. Porter and A. J. Stockwell (eds), *British Imperial Policy and Decolonisation, 1938–1964* (2 vols, London: Weidenfeld & Nicolson, 1987, 1989), vol. II: *1951–1964*, p. 495.
86. Ibid., pp. 495–6.
87. Ashton, 'Macmillan and the Middle East', in Aldous and Lee (eds), *Harold Macmillan*, p. 53.
88. Louis, *British Empire in the Middle East*, pp. 669, 671.
89. Porter and Stockwell, *British Imperial Policy*, pp. 452–64.
90. Louis and Owen, *Suez, 1956*, pp. 404–5.
91. John Turner, *Profiles in Power: Harold Macmillan* (London: Longman, 1994), p. 203.
92. Louis and Owen, *Suez, 1956*, pp. 383–4.
93. Karl Pieragostini, *Britain, Aden and South Arabia* (London: Macmillan, 1991), p. 3.
94. Ibid., pp. 28–30.
95. Ibid., pp. 30–1.
96. Ibid., p. 60; G. Balfour-Paul, *The End of Empire in the Middle East* (Cambridge: Cambridge University Press, 1991), pp. 78–9.
97. Ibid., pp. 76–8; Darby, *British Defence Policy*, p. 66.
98. M. Dockrill, 'The Defence of the Realm: Britain in the Nuclear Age', in Alan O'Day and A. Gourvish (eds), *Britain Since 1945* (London: Macmillan 1984), pp. 147–8; Darby, *British Defence Policy*, pp. 215, 284; G. Balfour-Paul, *The End of Empire in the Middle East*, p. 85.
99. Richard Crossman, *The Diaries of a Cabinet Minister*, vol. II: *Lord President of the Council and Leader of the House of Commons, 1966–1968* (London: Hamish Hamilton, 1977 edn), pp. 155–6.
100. Ibid., p. 279.

101. Ibid., p. 388.
102. Ibid., p. 402.
103. Ibid., p. 541. In fact, 135 soldiers were killed between 1 December 1963 and shortly before withdrawal (Balfour-Paul, *The End of Empire*, p. 95).
104. Ibid., p. 454; Darby, *British Defence Policy*, pp. 324–5.
105. Ibid., p. 635.
106. Louis, *British Empire in the Middle East*, p. 405.
107. Ibid., p. 476.
108. Louis and Owen, *Suez, 1956*, p. 273.
109. For a discussion of British policy after Suez see Ashton, *Eisenhower, Macmillan and the Problem of Nasser*, chs 6–15, esp. ch. 15: 'Postscript'.

8   The Concept of Empire from Eden to Wilson, 1955–70

1.   D. Goldsworthy (ed.), *BDEE*, series A, vol. 3, *Conservative Government and the End of Empire, 1951–7*, part 1: *International Relations* (London: HMSO, 1994), p. xxvi.
2.   Ibid., p. xxix.
3.   Ibid., p. xxviii.
4.   Ibid., p. 95.
5.   Goldsworthy, 'Keeping Change within Bounds', *JICH*, 18: 1 (1996), p. 84.
6.   PREM 11/1138, 28 December 1956.
7.   C.O. 1032/146, 28 January 1957.
8.   C.O. 1032/146.
9.   C.O. 1032/147.
10. Ibid.
11. C.O. 1032/93.
12. Ibid.
13. Ibid.
14. C.O. 1032/146. See also Dan Horowitz, 'Attitudes of British Conservatives towards Decolonisation in Africa', *African Affairs*, 69 (1970), pp. 9–26.
15. C.O. 1032/144.
16. J. T. O'Brien to E. R. Hammond, 13 July 1959, C.O. 1032/174.
17. Cabinet Conclusions, 4 June 1957, Cab. 128/31.
18. Cabinet Conclusions, 10 February 1958, Cab. 128/32.
19. Cabinet Conclusions, 8 September 1958, Cab. 128/32.
20. Cabinet Conclusions, 15 December 1959, Cab. 128/33.
21. Cabinet Conclusions, 13 July 1960, Cab. 128/34.
22. Cabinet Papers, 11 August 1960, Cab. 12 (3102).
23. A. N. Poynton to Major J. G. Lockhart, 11 January 1960, C.O. 1032/236.
24. 'Africa: The Next Ten Years', December 1959, F.O. 371/137972.
25. R. Ovendale, 'Macmillan and the Wind of Change in Africa, 1957–1960', *Historical Journal*, 28: 2 (1995), pp. 455–77, and pp. 465–71.
26. C.O. 1032/241.
27. George Woodcock, *Who Killed the British Empire?* (Toronto: Fitz Henry & Whiteside, 1974), p. 320.
28. PREM 11/2583, Macleod to Macmillan, 25 May 1959.

29. *House of Commons Debates*, vol. 626, cols 158–9, 4 July 1960.
30. Nigel Fisher, *Ian Macleod* (London: André Deutsch, 1973), p 142.
31. Ibid., p. 165.
32. *House of Commons Debates*, vol. 648, col. 1110 (8 November 1961).
33. *House of Commons Debates*, vol. 626, col. 162 (4 July 1960).
34. *House of Commons Debates*, vol. 637, cols 444–5 (22 March 1961).
35. *House of Commons Debates*, vol. 685, cols 804–6 (2 November 1959).
36. Fisher, *Ian Macleod*, p. 143.
37. Horowitz, 'Attitudes of British Conservatives towards Decolonisation in Africa', *African Affairs*, 69, p. 20.
38. Ibid., pp. 20–1.
39. Ibid., p. 21.
40. Ibid., pp. 21–2.
41. Paul B. Rich, *Race and Empire in British Politics*, 2nd edn (Cambridge: Cambridge University Press, 1990), p. 210.
42. Cabinet Conclusions, 13 July 1960, Cab. 128/34.
43. Cabinet Conclusions, 29 June 1961, Cab. 128/35.
44. Cabinet Conclusions, 21 July 1961, Cab. 128/35.
45. Cabinet Conclusions, 13 September 1962, Cab. 128/36.
46. Ben Pimlott, *Harold Wilson* (London: Harpercollins, 1992), pp. 433–4.
47. Patrick Gordon Walker, *The Commonwealth* (London: Secker and Warburg, 1962), pp. 9, 15.
48. Ibid., p. 21.
49. Ibid., p. 23.
50. Ibid., p. 22.
51. Clement Attlee, *Empire into Commonwealth* (London: Oxford University Press, 1961), p. 1.
52. Gordon Walker, *The Commonwealth*, p. 217; Attlee, *Empire into Commonwealth*, p. 51.
53. Attlee, *Empire into Commonwealth*, p. 25.
54. Gordon Walker, *The Commonwealth*, p. 381.
55. Attlee, *Empire into Commonwealth*, p. 27.
56. Gordon Walker, *The Commonwealth*, p. 380.
57. Pimlott, *Wilson*, p. 434.
58. Philip Ziegler, *Wilson: The Authorised Life* (London: Weidenfeld and Nicolson, 1993), p. 131.
59. John Darwin, 'British Decolonisation since 1945: A Pattern and a Puzzle', *JICH*, 12: 3 (1983–4), p. 191.

9   Pillars of Empire: Africa

1. D. Goldsworthy, 'Keeping Change within Bounds: Aspects of Colonial Policy during the Churchill and Eden Governments, 1951–1957', *JICH*, 18: 1 (1996), p. 102.
2. Ronald Hyam (ed.), *BDEE*, series A, vol. 2: *Labour Government and the End of Empire, 1945–1951*, part I: *Higher Policy and Administration* (London: HMSO, 1992), p. 32.

3. Ibid., p. 117.
4. Ibid., pp. 111–18, 121, 143–5, 149, 182–3.
5. Ibid., p. 185.
6. Ibid., pp. 338–9.
7. Ibid., pp. 139–40.
8. Ibid., p. 336.
9. Kwame Nkrumah, *Towards Colonial Freedom: Africa in the Struggle Against World Imperialism* (London: Heinemann, 1962), p. 39.
10. Thomas Hodgkin, *Nationalism in Colonial Africa* (London: Muller, 1956), p. 179.
11. Ali A. Mazrui, *Africa's International Relations: The Diplomacy of Dependency and Change* (Boulder, Col.: Westview Press, 1984), p. 28.
12. For which see the two articles by T. O. Ranger, 'Connexions between "Primary Resistance" Movements and Modern Mass Nationalism in East and Central Africa', part 1, *Journal of African History*, IX: 3 (1968), pp. 437–53; part II, op. cit., IX: 4 (1968), pp. 631–41.
13. G. E. Metcalfe, *Great Britain and Ghana: Documents of Ghanaian History, 1809–1957* (London, 1964), pp. 688–9.
14. John Iliffe, *A Modern History of Tanganyika* (Cambridge: Cambridge University Press, 1979), pp. 263–5.
15. Thomas Hodgkin, *Nationalism in Colonial Africa*, pp. 131, 140–2; Robert I. Rotberg, 'The Rise of African Nationalism', *World Politics*, XV (October 1962–July 1963), pp. 75–90, at pp. 79–82; A. J. Hughes, *East Africa: Kenya, Tanzania, Uganda* (London: Penguin, 1969 edn), pp. 100–1.
16. John Lonsdale, 'The Emergence of African Nations: A Historiographical Analysis', *African Affairs*, 67 (1968), pp. 11–28, at pp. 16–17.
17. Iliffe, *A Modern History of Tanganyika*, pp. 263–7.
18. John D. Hargreaves, 'Towards the Transfer of Power in British West Africa', in Prosser Gifford and W. R. Louis (eds), *The Transfer of Power in Africa: Decolonisation, 1940–1960* (London, 1982), p. 138.
19. Hyam (ed.), *BDEE, Labour Government and the End of Empire*, part I, p. xxxvii.
20. Muriel Chamberlain, *Decolonisation: The Fall of the European Empires* (Oxford: Blackwell, 1985), p. 36.
21. W. P. Kirkham, *Unscrambling an Empire* (London: Chatto & Windus, 1960), pp. 32–3.
22. D. Birmingham, *The Decolonisation of Africa* (London: University College of London Press, 1995), pp. 46–7.
23. Grace S. Ibingira, 'The Impact of Ethnic Demands on British De-colonisation in Africa: The Example of Uganda', in Gifford and Louis (eds), *Transfer of Power*, pp. 283–314.
24. D. George Boyce (ed.), *The Crisis of British Power; The Imperial and Naval Papers of the Second Earl of Selborne, 1895–1910* (London: The Historians' Press, 1990), p. 222.
25. For an admirably clear discussion of this phenomenon see Donal Lowry, '"Shame upon "Little England" while "Greater England" stands! Southern Rhodesia and the Imperial Idea', in Alex C. May (ed.), *The Round Table and British Foreign Policy* (London, 1998), pp. 305–41.

26. Alan Megahey, *Humphrey Gibbs Beleaguered Governor: Southern Rhodesia, 1929–1969* (London: Macmillan, 1998), pp. 21–2.
27. Lowry, op. cit., pp. 326–8.
28. J. D. Fage, *A History of Africa* (London: Hutchinson, 1978), pp. 450–1.
29. Ibid., p. 451.
30. Iliffe, *A Modern History of Tanganyika*, pp. 477–8.
31. A. J. Hughes, *East Africa*, pp. 21–2, 166.
32. But for an exception see Sir P. Mitchell, Governor of Kenya, in Hyam (ed.), *BDEE*, *Labour Government and the End of Empire*, part 1, pp. 136–41.
33. C. Pratt, 'Colonial Governors and the Transfer of Power in East Africa', in Griffith and Louis (eds), *Transfer of Power*, p. 253.
34. W. K. Hancock, *Survey of British Commonwealth Affairs*, vol. 1: *Problems of Nationality* (London: Oxford University Press, 1937), p. 214.
35. Ibid., pp. 215–22.
36. Zoe Marsh and G. W. Kingsnorth, *An Introduction to the History of East Africa* (Cambridge: Cambridge University Press, 1963), pp. 182–3.
37. Hancock, *Survey of British Commonwealth Affairs*, p. 224.
38. Ibid., pp. 230–2.
39. Marsh and Kingsnorth, *History of East Africa*, p. 242.
40. Ibid., p. 243.
41. Ibid., pp. 243–4.
42. Frank Furedi, *Colonial Wars and the Politics of Third World Nationalism* (London: I. B. Taurus, 1994), p. 163.
43. Birmingham, *Decolonisation of Africa*, p. 46.
44. Pratt, in Gifford and Louis (eds), *Transfer of Power*, pp. 272–81.
45. Birmingham, *Decolonisation of Africa*, p. 50.
46. P. Griffith, 'Misconceived Dominion', in Gifford and Louis (eds), *Transfer of Power*, p. 391.
47. Ibid., pp. 400–2.
48. Ibid., p. 408.
49. D. Goldsworthy, 'Keeping Change within Bounds', *JICH*, 18: 1 (1996), p. 84.
50. George Bennet and Alison Smith, 'Kenya: from White Man's Country to Kenyatta's State, 1945–1963', in D. A. Low and Alison Smith (eds), *History of East Africa* (Oxford: Oxford University Press, 1976), p. 136.
51. Cabinet Conclusions, 18 November 1958, Cab. 128/32.
52. Cabinet Conclusions, 13 March 1959, Cab., 128/33.
53. Cabinet Conclusions, 23 March 1959, Cab. 128/33.
54. 'Note for the Record', 11 June 1959, PRO, PREM 11/2583/0414.
55. Cabinet Conclusions, 22 May 1957, Cab. 128/31.
56. Cabinet Conclusions, 11 September 1958, Cab. 128/32.
57. Low and Smith, *History of East Africa*, p. 147.
58. A. N. Porter and A. J. Stockwell (eds), *British Imperial Policy and Decolonisation 1938–1964*, vol. II: *1951–1964* (London, 1987), p. 61.
59. Hyam (ed.), *BDEE*, *Labour Government and the End of Empire*, part I, pp. lxiv–lxv.
60. Porter and Stockwell (eds), *British Imperial Policy*, pp. 234–7; R. Ovendale, 'Macmillan and the Wind of Change Speech in Africa, 1957–1960', *Historical Journal*, 38: 2 (1995), pp. 455–77; Cab. 21/3156, 3157.

61. Porter and Stockwell, op. cit., pp. 522–31.
62. Cabinet Conclusions, 16 February 1960, Cab. 128/34.
63. Cabinet Conclusions, 24 and 28 March 1960, Cab. 128/34.
64. Cabinet Conclusions, 1 April 1960, Cab. 128/34.
65. Cabinet Conclusions, 16 March 1961, Cab. 128/35.
66. Porter and Stockwell (eds), *British Imperial Policy*, pp. 491–2.
67. Ibid., p. 332.
68. Low and Smith (eds), *History of East Africa*, pp. 144–5.
69. Porter and Stockwell (eds), *British Imperial Policy*, pp. 498–513.
70. Bennet and Smith, 'Kenya: From White Man's Country', in Low and Smith (eds), *History of East Africa*, pp. 137–8.
71. John Turner, *Harold Macmillan* (London: Longman, 1994), p. 200.
72. Cabinet Conclusions, 9 November 1962, Cab. 128/35.
73. Cabinet Conclusions, 16 November 1962, Cab. 128/35.
74. Cabinet Conclusions, 8 February 1962, Cab. 128/36.
75. Cabinet Conclusions, 20 March 1962, Cab. 128/36.
76. Low and Smith (eds), *History of East Africa*, pp. 148–9.
77. Ibid., pp. 249–50.
78. Ibid., pp. 163–77.
79. Cabinet Conclusions, 26 November 1959, Cab. 128/33.
80. Low and Smith (eds), *History of East Africa*, pp. 185–95.
81. Hughes, *East Africa*, pp. 166–87; Grace S. Ibingira, 'Ethnic Demands on British Decolonisation in Africa', in Gifford and Louis (eds), *Transfer of Power*, pp. 283–304.
82. Ibid., p. 494.
83. John Darwin, *Britain and Decolonisation*, pp. 248–51.
84. Turner, *Macmillan*, p. 183.
85. Cabinet Conclusions, 2 February 1960, Cab. 128/34.
86. Cabinet Conclusions, 18 February 1960, Cab. 128/34.
87. Porter and Stockwell (eds), *British Imperial Policy*, p. 542.
88. Ibid., pp. 543–57.
89. Ibid., pp. 556–61.
90. Cabinet Conclusions, 26 February 1962, Cab. 128/36.
91. Cabinet Conclusions, 28 March 1963, Cab. 128/37.
92. Muriel Chamberlain, *Decolonisation*, pp. 44–5.
93. Ziegler, *Wilson*, p. 219.
94. Peter B. Harris, *The Commonwealth* (London, 1957), p. 107.
95. Austin Morgan, *Harold Wilson* (London: Pluto Press, 1992), p. 274.
96. Pimlott, *Harold Wilson*, pp. 366–7.
97. Ibid., p. 371.
98. Cabinet Conclusions, 12 September 1965, Cab. 128/39.
99. Cabinet Conclusions, 7 October 1965, Cab. 128/39.
100. Cabinet Conclusions, 14 October 1965, Cab. 128/39.
101. Cabinet Conclusions, 9 November 1965, Cab. 128/39.
102. Pimlott, *Wilson*, pp. 376–7.
103. Megahey, *Humphrey Gibbs*, pp. 128–31, 157–8.
104. Cabinet Conclusions, 16 September 1966, Cab. 128/41, Part II.
105. Pimlott, *Wilson*, p. 455.

106. D. Boucher and A. Vincent, *A Radical Hegelian: The Political and Social Philosophy of Henry Jones* (Cardiff: University of Wales Press, 1993), p. 151.

107. Christopher Hill and Christopher Lord, 'The Foreign Policy of the Heath Government, 1970–74', in Stuart Ball and Anthony Seldon (eds), *The Heath Government, 1970–1974* (London: Longman, 1996), pp. 285–314, at p. 295.

108. R. Lewis, 'From Zimbabwe–Rhodesia to Zimbabwe', *Round Table*, 70 (1980), pp. 6–9.

109. John Darwin, *Britain and Decolonisation*, pp. 319–23; Sir Anthony Parsons, 'Britain and the World', in Dennis Kavanagh and Anthony Seldon (eds), *The Thatcher Effect: A Decade of Change* (Oxford: Oxford University Press, 1989), pp. 154–65, at pp. 156–7

110. Ziegler, *Wilson*, p. 434.

111. Morgan, *Harold Wilson*, p. 322.

112. Ziegler, *Wilson*, pp. 464–5.

113. Pimlott, *Wilson*, pp. 466–7.

114. John W. Harbeson and Donald Rothschild (eds), *Africa in World Politics: Post Cold War Challenges* (Boulder, Col.: Westview Press, 1995), p. 30.

115. Parsons, 'Britain and the World', in Kavanagh and Seldon (eds), *The Thatcher Effect*, pp. 161–5.

10 Empire, Race and Citizenship

1. W. K. Hancock, *Survey of British Commonwealth Affairs*, vol. 1: *Problems of Nationalism, 1918–1935* (London: 1937), p. 166.

2. Ibid., p. 167.

3. Ibid., pp. 167–8.

4. D. G. Boyce, *The Crisis of British Power* (London: The Historians' Press, 1990), p. 11.

5. Ibid., p. 12.

6. Ibid., pp. 388–9.

7. Hancock, *Survey*, p. 175.

8. Ibid., p. 173.

9. Ibid., p. 174.

10. Ibid., pp. 174–5.

11. Basil Williams, *The British Empire* (London: Thornton Butterworth, 1937), pp. 217–18.

12. Hancock, *Survey*, pp. 180–1.

13. Ibid., pp. 184–5.

14. Sir Michael O'Dwyer, *India as I Knew It* (London: Constable, 1925), p. 414.

15. Ibid., pp. 424–32.

16. Ibid., p. 453.

17. Paul B. Rich, *Race and Empire in British Politics* (Cambridge: Cambridge University Press, 2nd edn, 1990), pp. 58–9.

18. Ibid., pp. 60–1.

19. Hancock, *Survey*, p. 201.

20. Ibid., pp. 205–6.

21. Ibid., pp. 209–19.
22. Ibid., p. 221.
23. Ibid., p. 224.
24. Ibid., pp. 226–7.
25. R. Hyam (ed.), *BDEE*, *Labour Government and the End of Empire*, part IV, p. 143.
26. Ibid., p. 143.
27. Cabinet Conclusions, 28 October 1948, in Hyam, op. cit., p. 161.
28. Cabinet Conclusions, 18 November 1948, ibid., p. 176.
29. Kathleen Paul, 'The Politics of Citizenship in Post-War Britain', *Contemporary Record*, 6: 3 (Winter 1992), pp. 452–73, at p. 456.
30. *Round Table*, no. 151 (June 1948), p. 705.
31. Ibid., pp. 655–63.
32. Lorna Lloyd, 'Britain and the Transformation from Empire into Commonwealth', *Round Table*, no. 4343 (1997), p. 340.
33. Ibid., p. 663.
34. Hyam (ed.), *BDEE*, *Labour Government at the End of Empire*, part I, p. lxiv.
35. D. Goldsworthy, *Colonial Issues in British Politics, 1945–1951* (Oxford: Clarendon Press, 1971), pp. 153–7.
36. 'Relations with the Union of South Africa', by Patrick Gordon Walker, 25 September 1950, in Hyam (ed.), *BDEE*, part IV, pp. 285–6; see also the Colonial Office memorandum, 'Cooperation with the Union of South Africa', 5 July 1949, ibid., pp. 255–6.
37. Cabinet Conclusions, 13 May 1946, ibid., p. 239.
38. Ibid., pp. 240–1.
39. Ibid., pp. 272–5.
40. Ibid., p. 279.
41. Ibid., pp. 296–8.
42. Ibid., pp. 305–15.
43. 'South Africa: Review of Affairs, 1944–1951', 25 July 1951, ibid., pp. 347–57.
44. Goldsworthy, *Colonial Issues in British Politics*, p. 267.
45. Ibid., pp. 268–9.
46. Ibid., pp. 275–7.
47. Peter James Henshaw, 'The Transfer of Simonstown: Afrikaner Nationalism, South African Strategic Dependence and British Global Power', *JICH*, XX: 3 (1992), pp. 419–44.
48. Cabinet Conclusions, 1 August 1963, Cab. 128/37.
49. Cabinet Conclusions, 11 July 1963, Cab. 128/37.
50. Christopher Hill and Christopher Lloyd, 'The Foreign Policy of the Heath Government', in Stuart Bell and Anthony Seldon (eds), *The Heath Government, 1970–74* (London: Longman, 1996), pp. 285–314, at pp. 292–4.
51. A. E. Zimmern, *The Third British Empire* (2nd edn, London, 1927), pp. 150–1.
52. Kathleen Paul, 'Politics of Citizenship', *Contemporary Record*, 6: 3, p. 457.
53. Robert Pearce (ed.), *Patrick Gordon Walker: Political Diaries, 1932–1971*, pp. 178–9.
54. Martin Gilbert, *Winston S. Churchill*, vol. 8: '*Never Despair*' (London: Heinemann, 1988), p. 949.

55. Goldsworthy (ed.), *BDEE, Conservative Government and the End of Empire*, part III, p. 394.
56. Ibid., pp. 401–2.
57. A. M. Porter and A. J. Stockwell (eds), *British Imperial Policy and Decolonization*, vol. 2: *1951–1964* (London: Macmillan, 1989), pp. 496–7.
58. Cabinet Conclusions, 1 July 1957, Cab. 128/32.
59. Cabinet Conclusions, 8 September 1958, Cab. 128/32.
60. Cabinet Conclusions, 25 November 1960, Cab. 128/34.
61. Cabinet Conclusions, 30 May 1961, Cab. 128/35.
62. Cabinet Conclusions, 10 October 1961, Cab. 128/35.
63. House of Commons Debates, 5th series, vol. 649 (16 November 1961), cols 709, 712.
64. Ibid., col. 800.
65. Powell's speech is printed in John Wood (ed.), *J. Enoch Powell: Freedom and Reality* (London: Batsford, 1969), pp. 213–19. The quotation here is on p. 219.
66. Richard Crossman, *The Diaries of a Cabinet Minister*, vol. 1: *Minister of Housing, 1964–66* (London: Hamish Hamilton and Cape, 1977), pp. 148–9, 270.
67. Crossman, *Diaries* vol. 2: *Lord President of the Council and Leader of the House of Commons, 1966–68* (London: Hamish Hamilton and Cape, 1977 edn), p. 689.
68. Zig Layton-Henry, 'Immigration and the Heath Government, 1970–74', in Ball and Seldon (eds), *The Heath Government, 1970–1974*, pp. 221–3.
69. Ibid., p. 225.
70. Ibid., p. 226.
71. Ibid., pp. 228–9.
72. Ibid., pp. 231–3.
73. David Cesarini, 'Citizenship and Nationality in Britain', in David Cesarini and Mary Fulbrook (eds), *Citizenship, Nationality and Migration in Europe* (London and New York: Routledge, 1996), pp. 66–7.
74. Dennis Judd, *Empire: The British Imperial Experience, from 1765 to the Present* (London: Harpercollins, 1996), p. 382.
75. David Birmingham, *Decolonization of Africa*, pp. 81–3.
76. For a vivid description of this, see Judd, *Empire*, pp. 410–11.
77. Ibid., p. 431; but Judd states that 'the decision seemed to owe a great deal to expediency and the instinct for self-protection'.
78. Ashton and Stockwell (eds), *BDEE, Imperial Policy and Colonial Practice, 1925–45*, part I, p. xcii.
79. R. B. McDowell, *Crisis and Decline: The Fate of Southern Unionism* (Dublin: Lilliput Press, 1997), p. 195.
80. P. G. Wigley, *Canada and the Transition to Commonwealth: British–Canadian Relations, 1917–1926* (Cambridge: Cambridge University Press, 1977), p. 2.

Epilogue

1. On 16 April 1997 *The Times* calculated that some 14 colonies remained, before the departure of Hong Kong; the *Independent* offered 17 before

Hong Kong's relinquishment (17 April 1997). The difference lies simply in the grouping of some of the smaller territories.

2.   E. T. Cook (ed.), *The Empire in the World* (London: Oxford University Press, 1937), p. 153; see also Bernard Porter, *Britannia's Burden, The Political Evolution of Modern Britain, 1851–1990*, (London: Edward Arnold, 1994), p. 125.

3.   Patrick Wormald, 'The Making of England', *History Today*, 45 (1995), pp. 26–32.

4.   Dorothy Whitelock, *The Beginnings of English Society* (London: Penguin, 1962), pp. 60–1.

5.   Ralph A. Griffiths, *'This Royal Throne of Kings, this Scept'red Isle': The English Realm and Nation in the Later Middle Ages* (Swansea, 1983), pp. 29–30.

6.   John Turner, *Macmillan* (London: Longman, 1994), p. 89.

7.   Thomas R. Metcalf, *Ideologies of the Raj* (Cambridge: Cambridge University Press, 1994), p. 4.

8.   Keith Jeffrey (ed.), *An Irish Empire?* (Manchester: Manchester University Press, 1996).

9.   R. B. MacDowell, *Crisis and Decline: The Fate of Southern Unionists* (Dublin: Lilliput Press, 1997), p. 21.

10. Jeffrey, *An Irish Empire?*, p. 18.

11. A. E. Zimmern, *The Third British Empire* (London: Oxford University Press, 1926), p. 1.

12. Ibid., pp. 2–3.

13. Ibid., pp. 6–7.

14. Ibid., p. 11.

15. Ibid., p. 12.

16. Ibid., p. 26.

17. Ibid., pp. 56–7.

18. Ibid., pp. 61–2.

19. Ibid., p. 70.

20. Deborah Lavin, *From Empire to International Commonwealth: A Biography of Lionel Curtis* (Oxford: Clarendon Press, 1995), pp. 268–9, 273.

21. Ibid., pp. 5, 18. Even the hard-headed L. S. Amery believed by 1949 in the idea of the Commonwealth as the 'one great world nation group' which 'transcends the boundaries of race and creed' (P. S. Gupta, *Imperialism and the British Labour Movement, 1914–1964* (London: Macmillan, 1975), p. 299).

22. Ibid., p. 273.

23. Andrea Bosco, 'National Sovereignty and Peace: Lord Lothian's Federalist thought', in John Turner (ed.), *The Larger View: Lord Lothian and the Problem of National Sovereignty* (London: Lothian Foundation, 1988), pp. 116–17.

24. Alex May, 'The *Round Table* and the Post-War Commonwealth, 1945–1966', in *Round Table*, no. 341 (1997), pp. 95–107, at p. 96.

25. Cook (ed.), *The Empire in the World*, pp. 81–2.

26. May, *Round Table*, no. 341, p. 102.

27. Paul Kennedy, *The Rise and Fall of the Great Powers: Economic Change and Military Conflict from 1500 to 2000* (London: Fontana, 1989 edn), p. xx.

28. Tom Nairn, *The Break-up of Britain* (2nd edn, London: Verso, 1981), pp. 266, 274.
29. Ibid., p. 404.
30. Ibid., p. 305.
31. K. O. Morgan, *The Peoples' Peace: British History, 1945–1990* (Oxford: Oxford University Press, 1990), pp. 407–8.
32. R. F. Holland, *European Decolonisation, 1918–1981: An Introductory Survey* (London Macmillan, 1985), pp. 273, 191–2.
33. John A. MacKenzie, *Propaganda and Empire: The Manipulation of British Public Opinion, 1880–1960* (Manchester: Manchester University Press, 1986), p. 11.
34. Bernard Porter, *Britannia's Burden: The Political Evolution of Modern Britain, 1851–1990*, p. 375.
35. F. W. Hirst, *Early Life and Letters of John Morley* (2 vols, London: Macmillan, 1927), vol. II, p. 181.
36. J. P. Kenyon (ed.), *The Wordsworth Dictionary of British History* (Hertfordshire, 1994), preface.
37. John Wood (ed.), *A Nation not Afraid: The Thinking of Enoch Powell* (London: Hodder and Stoughton, 1965), p. 144.
38. *House of Commons Debates*, 5th series, vol. 188, col. 521, 18 November 1925.

Conclusion

1. A. Cobban, *The Nation State and National Self-Determination* (London: Fontana, 1969), p. 165.
2. Sir W. K. Hancock, *Wealth of Colonies* (Cambridge: Cambridge University Press, 1950), pp. 46–7.
3. Cobban, *The Nation State*, p. 159.
4. C.O. 1032/241.
5. P. J. Marshall, 'Empire and Authority in the Late Eighteenth Century', *JICH*, XV: 2 (January 1987), pp. 105–22, at p. 119.
6. See, e.g., Attlee's statement at the Cabinet in December 1946 on India, that 'there is an obvious risk in moving so fast, but an equal risk of disturbances if the return to civil government is delayed' (Hyam (ed.), *BDEE, Labour Government and the End of Empire, 1945–51*, part I, p. xxv). See also the statement by Sir John Johnson, who held various distinguished positions in the colonial service between 1947 and 1968, in the oral witness symposium conducted at the Institute of Contemporary British History on 25 November 1988, in *Contemporary Record*, 6: 3 (Winter 1992), pp. 508–9, and that of Aaron Emanual, in the service between 1943 and 1961 (ibid., p. 514).
7. Hyam (ed.), *BDEE, Labour Government at the End of Empire*, part IV, p. 153.
8. John Keay, *Last Post: The End of Empire in the Far East* (London: John Murray, 1997), p. 144.

SELECT BIBLIOGRAPHY

NB: All works are published in London unless stated otherwise.

1 Standard Works

The history of British decolonisation is well served by its practitioners. John Darwin, *Britain and Decolonisation: The Retreat from Empire in the Post-war world* (1988); T. O. Lloyd, *The British Empire, 1558–1983* (Oxford, 1984); Bernard Porter, *The Lion's Share: A Short History of British Imperialism 1850–1995* (1996); Dennis Judd, *Empire: The British Imperial Experience, from 1775 to the Present* (1996); Brian Lapping, *End of Empire* (1985); D. A. Low, *Eclipse of Empire* (1991) and L. James, *The Rise and Fall of the British Empire* (1994) all offer insightful and well-written analyses. John Darwin's *The End of the British Empire: The Historical Debate* (Oxford, 1991) is an excellent summary of the main points at issue. The comparative dimension is well served in M. Chamberlain, *Decolonisation: The Fall of the European Empires* (Oxford, 1985), R. F. Holland, *European Decolonisation, 1918–1981: An Introductory Survey* (1985), and David Fieldhouse, *The Colonial Empires: A Comparative Study from the Eighteenth Century* (1986). The economic explanation is given modern treatment in P. J. Cain and A. G. Hopkins, *British Imperialism: Innovation and Expansion, 1688–1914* (1993) and the second volume, *Crisis and Decolonisation, 1914–1990* (1993).

The ideas of imperialism and decolonisation are traced in R. Owen and B. Sutcliffe (eds), *Studies in the Theory of Imperialism* (1972); A. P. Thornton's classic study *The Imperial Idea and its Enemies* (1959), C. C. Eldridge, *England's Mission: The Imperial Idea in the Age of Gladstone and Disraeli, 1868–1880* (1973); two books by Richard Koebner, *Empire* (Cambridge, 1961), and (with Helmut Dan Schmidt) *Imperialism: The Story and Significance of a Political Word, 1840–1960* (Cambridge, 1964), while George Bennett (ed.), *The Concept of Empire from Burke to Attlee, 1774–1947* (1962) offers documentary extracts which treat imperialism in a conceptual way. Still helpful are W. P. Kirkham, *Unscrambling an Empire: A Critique of British Colonial Policy, 1956–1966* (1966) and C. Barnett, *The Collapse of British Power* (1972). John Gallagher, *The Decline, Revival and Fall of the British Empire* (Cambridge, 1982) is, as always, provocative and incisive in equal amounts. The by now somewhat aged J. Holland Rose *et al.* (eds), *Cambridge History of the British Empire* (8 vols, 1929–59) still should be read, both for its important detail and its views, from a period when the Empire/Commonwealth was a reality. P. J. Marshall's one-volume *Cambridge History of the British Empire* (Cambridge, 1996) is no

300

mere general survey, but contains much new research and thinking. The first two volumes in the new *Oxford History of the British Empire*, vol. I (ed. Nicholas Canny): *The Origins of Empire: British Overseas Enterprise to the Close of the Seventeenth Century* (1998) and P. J. Marshall, vol. II: *The Eighteenth Century*, promise as well as deliver much. Decline is traced in Paul Kennedy, *The Rise and Fall of the Great Powers: Economic Change and Military Conflict from 1500 to 2000* (1989) and A. L. Friedberg, *The Weary Titan: Britain and the Experience of Relative Decline, 1895–1905* (Princeton, N. J., 1988). Tom Nairn, *The Break-up of Britain* (2nd edn, 1981) predicted disaster, but John Kendle, *Federal Britain* (1997) takes a more positive view.

2   Classic Explanations of Imperialism

The starting point in the exercise of seeing oneself as one sees oneself is of course J. R. Seeley, *The Expansion of England: Two Lectures* (1885); that of seeing oneself as others see one is J. A. Hobson, *Imperialism: A Study* (1902). Sir Charles Wentworth Dilke, *Problems of Greater Britain* (1890) was another influential work. Lord Cromer, *Ancient and Modern Imperialism* reminds us how much classical thinking went into British imperial practice. A. E. Zimmern, *The Third British Empire*, was a brave attempt to impose coherence on the incoherent (2nd edn, 1927). Bernard Holland, *Imperium and Libertas* (1902) assesses the contradictions of imperialism implied in his title.

3   Monographs

Anthony Pagden, *Lords of all the World: Ideologies of Empire in Spain, Britain and France, c. 1500–1800* (Yale, 1995) is a superb introduction to the origins, not only of empire, but of ideas of how empire should be organised. The twentieth century is well served by D. Reynolds, *Britannia Overruled: British Policy and World Power in the Twentieth Century* (1991), R. F. Holland, *The Pursuit of Greatness: Britain and the World Role, 1900–1970* (1991) and John Kent, *British Imperial Strategy and the Origins of the Cold War, 1944–49* (Leicester, 1993). Imperial wars are traced in Thomas R. Mockaitis, *British Counterinsurgency, 1919–1960* (Manchester, 1990) and, less sympathetically, in Frank Furedi, *Colonial Wars and the Politics of Third World Nationalism* (1994). For the interaction between imperial and home politics see P. S. Gupta, *Imperialism and the British Labour Movement, 1914–1964* (1975), and D. Goldsworthy, *Colonial Issues in British Politics, 1945–1951* (Oxford, 1971). Paul B. Rich, *Race and Empire in British Politics* (2nd edn, 1990) is indispensable for the study of a dimension of the imperial experience often oddly neglected. John MacKenzie, *Propaganda and Empire: The Manipulation of British Public Opinion, 1880–1960* (Manchester, 1996) likewise explores a strangely neglected subject. The older study by W. K. Hancock, *Survey of British Commonwealth Affairs*, vol. 1: *Problems of Nationality, 1918–1936* (1937), is full of ideas, insights and information that make it still, after more than 60 years, indispensable.

4   Diaries and Other Published Collections of Documents

Here the field is held by *The British Documents of the End of Empire (BDEE)* series. Full details are given in the Notes. So far 12 volumes have been published (HMSO, 1992–6). The historian can only stand amazed at the scope and vitality of the enterprise, which has combed out documents which it would take many hours, perhaps years, of the lone scholar's life to unearth. More are promised in this major venture. Another excellent series is that launched by Frederick Madden and David Fieldhouse in 1985, *Select Documents on the Constitutional History of the British Empire and Commonwealth* (1985–95), which offers speeches, extracts from official documents and the like, and covers imperial expansion from the earliest times (*The Empire of the Bretaignes, 1175–1888: The Foundations of a Colonial System of Government*, 1985) to the present time. Theirs is not a dry-as-dust example of constitutional history, but a fine illustration of its relevance to social, economic and political affairs, which is the right way to do it. Nicholas Mansergh has left his mark in many books on empire, and his *Documents and Speeches on Commonwealth Affairs, 1952–1962* (1963) must be consulted, as must his magisterial compendium, *Constitutional Relations between Britain and India: The Transfer of Power, 1942–1947* (12 vols, 1970–83). The same treatment is given to Burma in Hugh Tinker and Andrew Griffen (eds), *Constitutional Relations between Britain and Burma: The Struggle for Independence, 1944–1948* (two vols, vol. I: 1983; vol. II: 1984), whose title, compared with that of the Mansergh series, tells much about contrasting notions on the end of empire. A. N. Porter and A. J. Stockwell's *British Imperial Policy and Decolonisation, 1938–64*, vol. I: *1938–51* (1987) and vol. II: *1951–64* (1989), pale only beside the *BDEE* series, as does everything. Some diaries and letters are useful. J. Barnes and D. Nicholson, *The Leo Amery Diaries*, vol. I (1981) and vol. II (1988), contain commentary and analysis as well as the thoughts of a leading imperialist. The second volume of D. G. Boyce's edition of the papers of the Second Earl of Selborne, *The Crisis of British Power* (1990) likewise deals with a deeply committed imperialist who in this case sensed the advent of Kipling's recessional before it became generally acknowledged. Important diaries include Robert Pearce (ed.), *Patrick Gordon Walker: Political Diaries, 1937–71* (1991) and Richard Crossman, *The Diaries of a Cabinet Minister*, vol. I: *Minister of Housing, 1964–66* (1977 edn) and these reflect the quick reorientation of the Wilson Government from Commonwealth aspiration to European reality.

5   Biographies and Autobiographies

These are of variable quality, but the researcher can find good material in Harold Macmillan's volumes, especially vol. V: *Pointing the Way* (1972) and vol. VI: *At the End of the Day* (1973), and in Denis Healey's *The Time of my Life* (1989). Historians' assessment of their subjects is more astringent and in most respects more valuable. Notable biographies are K. Harris, *Attlee* (1982), John Turner, *Profiles in Power: Harold Macmillan* (1994), David Dutton, *Anthony Eden: A Life and Reputation* (1997), three studies of Harold Wilson by Austen Morgan (1991), Ben Pimlott (1992) and P. Ziegler (1993). The most important volume (for this subject) of Martin Gilbert's mammoth *Churchill* (8 vols, 1966–88) is vol. 8, but Clive Ponting takes a more critical view in his *Churchill* (1994). Nigel Fisher's *Ian Macleod* deals with the rapid decoloniser of Africa in a far-from-bleak light (1973), but it is back to scepticism for Richard Lamb in his *The Macmillan Years, 1959–63: The Emerging Truth* (1995). Debora Lavin's thoroughly researched study of Lionel Curtis, *From Empire to International Statesman* (Oxford, 1995) deals with one of the great enthusiasts.

6 Histories of Particular Countries or Regions

North America

William M. Fowler and Wallace Coyle (eds), *The American Revolution: Changing Perspectives* (Boston, Mass., 1979), J. C. D. Clark's *The Language of Liberty, 1660–1832: Political Discourse and Social Dynamics in the Anglo-American World* (Cambridge, 1994), and Robert Tucker and David Hendrickson, *The Fall of the First British Empire* (Baltimore and London, 1982) all cover the vital American experience; also important is J. G. A. Pocock, *The Varieties of British Political Thought, 1500–1800* (Cambridge, 1993). For Canada see John Manning Ward, *Colonial Self-government: The British Experience, 1759–1956* (1976); Chester W. New, *Lord Durham* (Oxford, 1929); Peter Burroughs, *The Canadian Crisis and British Colonial Policy, 1828–1841* (1972); Helen T. Manning, *The Revolt of French Canada, 1800–1835: A Chapter in the History of the British Commonwealth* (1962), and Ged Martin's lively revisionist works, *The Durham Report and British Policy: A Critical Essay* (Cambridge, 1972), and *Britain and the Origins of the Canadian Confederation, 1837–1867* (Vancouver, 1995).

India

The standard work is Judith Brown, *Modern India: The Making of an Asian Democracy* (Oxford, 1987). Thomas Metcalf's volume in the New Cambridge History of India, *Ideologies of the Raj* (1994), is especially useful. Indian nationalism has two fine studies, P. N. Pandey, *The Indian Nationalist Movement, 1885–47: Select Documents* (1979) and Anil Seal, *The Emergence of Indian Nationalism* (Cambridge, 1971). Sumit Sarkar, *Modern India, 1885–1947* (Cambridge, 1989) gets down to the basics of nationalism and imperialism. The climactic years of 1937–47 have attracted much attention: see C. Campbell-Johnson, *Mission with Mountbatten* (1951); D. A. Low, *Congress and the Raj* (1977); R. J. Moore, *The Crisis of Indian Unity, 1917–1940* (Oxford, 1974) and also his *Churchill, Cripps and India* (Oxford, 1979) and *Escape from Empire: The Attlee Government and the Indian Problem* (Oxford, 1983). For a view highly critical of the British role in partitioning India see Anita Inder Singh, *The Origins of the Partition of India, 1936–47* (Delhi, 1991). G. Rizvi's *Linlithgow and India* (1976) is more nuanced, but Francis G. Hutchin, *Spontaneous Revolution: The Quit India Movement* (Delhi, 1971) is not. Judith Brown's books on Gandhi (*Gandhi: Prisoner of Hope* (1989) is particularly good, but her *Gandhi's Rise to Power* (1972) and *Gandhi and Civil Disobedience* (1977) complete the picture) are central as is S. Gopal's *Jarwarlal Nehru*, vol. 1:

1889–1947 (1975). Reginald Coupland's *The Constitutional Problem in India* (Oxford, 1945) remains important, not least for its detailed extracts from documents.

Ireland

Ireland is certainly not a typical imperial possession, and there is still some degree of resistance to treating Ireland in the Imperial context, despite David Harkness' pioneering work, *The Restless Dominion* (1969). Deirdre McMahon, *Republicans and Imperialists: Anglo-Irish Relations in the 1930s* (1984) is an excellent modern study, and Keith Jeffrey (ed.), *An Irish Empire? Aspects of Ireland and the British Empire* (Manchester, 1996) is lively and challenging. Keith Middlemas (ed.), *Tom Jones: Whitehall Diary*, vol. III: *Ireland, 1918–1925* (1971) offers superb insights into British Government thinking. Two books at the opposite ends of the chronological spectrum by R. B. MacDowell, *Ireland in the Age of Reform and Revolution, 1760–1801* (Oxford, 1979) and *Crisis and Decline: The Fate of Southern Unionism* (Dublin, 1997) not only make the connections, but do so in an elegant, humane and lively way. J. E. Kendle, *The Round Table Movement and Imperial Union* (Toronto, 1975) unites Irish, British and imperial themes.

The Middle East

This area is very well served, notably by John Darwin, *Britain, Egypt and the Middle East: Imperial Policy in the Aftermath of War, 1918–1922* (1981); W. R. Louis, *The British Empire in the Middle East, 1945–1951: Arab Nationalism, the United States, and Post-war Imperialism* (Oxford, 1984); P. Darby, *British Defence Policy East of Suez* (1973) and E. Monroe, *Britain's Moment in the Middle East* (1963). For Palestine see M. J. Cohen, *Palestine: Retreat from the Mandate* (1978). For Iran see J. A. Bill and W. R. Louis, *Musaddiq: Iranian Nationalism and Oil* (1988) and J. Cable, *Intervention at Abadan* (1992). The Suez crisis, not surprisingly, has attracted much attention. The best studies are Tony Shaw, *Eden, Suez, and the Mass Media: Propaganda and Persuasion during the Suez Crisis* (1996); N. J. Ashton, *Eisenhower, Macmillan and the Problem of Nasser* (1996); W. R. Louis and R. Owen, *Suez, 1956: The Crisis and it Consequences* (Oxford, 1989) and S. Lucas, *Britain and Suez: The Lion's Last Roar* (Manchester, 1996). Karl Pieragostini, *Britain, Aden and South Arabia* (1991) and G. Balfour-Paul, *The End of Empire in the Middle East* (Cambridge, 1991) widen the scope.

Africa

Thomas Hodgkin, *Nationalism in Colonial Africa* (1956) is still essential reading, and David Birmingham, *The Decolonisation of Africa* (1995) is an excellent short survey. M. Crowder (ed.), *The Cambridge History of Africa*, vol. 8: *1940–75* (Cambridge, 1984) and H. S. Wilson, *African Decolonisation* (1994) are further modern studies. Prosser Gifford and W. R. Louis, *The Transfer of Power in Africa: Decolonisation, 1940–1960* (1982) and *Decolonisation and African Independence* (New Haven, 1988) are indispensable. A good collection of documents is G. E. Metcalf, *Great Britain and Ghana: Documents of Ghanaian History, 1807–1957* (1964). John Iliffe,

A Modern History of Tanganyika (1979), A. J. Hughes, *East Africa: Kenya, Tanzania and Uganda* (1969), Zoe Marsh and G. W. Kingnorth, *An Introduction to the History of East Africa* (Cambridge, 1963), A. G. Hopkins, *An Economic History of West Africa* (1973), D. A. Low and A. Smith (eds), *History of East Africa* (1976), and D. Austin, *Politics in Ghana* (1970), cover the regions. For Rhodesia/Zimbabwe see Lord Blake, *A History of Rhodesia* (1977), and for the last years of white rule see Alan Megahey, *Humphrey Gibbs: Beleaguered Governor, Southern Rhodesia, 1929–64* (1998). D. Thorp, *The Economic and Social Origins of Mau Mau, 1945–53* (1987) covers one of the most explosive and significant aspects of African resistance.

The Dominions and Commonwealth Studies

R. F. Holland, *Britain and the Commonwealth Alliance, 1918–1939* (1981), D. Judd and P. Slinn, *The Evolution of the Modern Commonwealth, 1902–80* (1982), J. D. B. Miller, *Survey of British Commonwealth Affairs: Problems of Expansion and Attrition, 1953–1969* (1974), and W. D. McIntyre, *Commonwealth of Nations: Origins and Impact* (Oxford, 1977) are standard works. H. Duncan Hall, *Commonwealth: A History of the British Commonwealth of Nations* (1971) is rather uncritical, but has useful details. M. Beloff's two volumes, *Imperial Sunset: Britain's Liberal Empire, 1897–1921* (1987 edn) and *Dream of Commonwealth, 1921–42* (1989 edn) trace the failure of the Commonwealth to live up to its protagonists' hopes. W. J. Hudson and M. P. Sharp, *Australian Independence* (Carlton, Victoria, 1988) helps explain why. For a general treatment see Martin Kitchen, *The British Empire and Commonwealth: A Short History* (1996). Nicholas Mansergh's older but evocative *The Commonwealth Experience* (1969) must be read, again not least for the author's own predilections.

7 Selected Articles and Chapters in books

The best source for articles is the *Journal of Imperial and Commonwealth History* (*JICH*), but other journals and books offer excellent research. A *select list only* follows. These are listed in alphabetical order by author.

Ashton, Nigel, 'Macmillan and the Middle East', in Richard Aldous and Sabine Lee (eds), *Harold Macmillan and Britain's World Role* (1996), pp. 37–65.

Boyce, D. George and Stubbs, J. O., 'F. S. Oliver, Lord Selborne and Federalism', *JICH*, 5 (1976), pp. 53–81.

Burgess, Michael, 'The Federal Plan of the Imperial Federation League, 1892: Milestone or Tombstone?', in A. Boscoe (ed.), *The Federal Idea*, vol. I (1991), pp. 139–53.

Caterall, Peter (ed.), 'The East of Suez Debate', *Contemporary Record*, 7 (Winter 1993), pp. 612–57.

Cesarini, David, 'The Changing Character of Citizenship and Nationality in Britain', in David Cesarini and Mary Fulbrook (eds), *Citizenship, Nationality and Migration in Europe* (London and New York, 1996), pp. 57–73.

Cole, Douglas, 'The Problem of "Nationalism" and "Imperialism" in British Settlement Colonies', *Journal of British Studies*, 10 (1970–71), pp. 160–82.

Darwin, J. G., 'The Fear of Falling: British Politics and Imperial Decline Since 1900', *Transactions of the Royal Historical Society*, 5th series, 36 (1986), pp. 27–43.

Darwin, J. G., 'British Decolonisation since 1945: a Pattern and a Puzzle', *JICH*, 12 (1983), pp. 187–209.

Dean, D. W., 'Final Exit? Britain, Eire, the Commonwealth, and the Repeal of the External Relations Act, 1945–49', *JICH*, 20 (1992), pp. 391–418.

Dockrill, M., 'The Defences of the Realm: Britain in the Nuclear Age', in Alan O'Day and A. Gourvish (eds), *Britain Since 1945* (1991), pp. 135–57.

Goldsworthy, D., 'Keeping Change within Bounds: Aspects of Colonial Policy during the Churchill and Eden Governments, 1951–1957', *JICH*, 18 (1976), pp. 81–108.

Hemming, Philip E., 'Macmillan and the End of the British Empire in Africa', in Richard Aldous and Sabine Lee (eds), *Harold Macmillan and Britain's World Role* (1996), pp. 97–121.

Henshaw, Peter James, 'The Transfer of Simonstown: Afrikaaner Nationalism, South African Strategic Dependence and British Global Power', *JICH*, 20 (1992), pp. 419–44.

Hill, Christopher and Lord, Christopher, 'The Foreign Policy of the Heath Government, 1970–1974', in Stuart Ball and Anthony Seldon (eds), *The Heath Government, 1970–74* (1996), pp. 285–314.

Horowitz, Dan, 'Attitudes of British Conservatives towards Decolonisation in Africa', *African Affairs*, 69 (1970), pp. 9–26.

Kent, John, 'The Egyptian Base and the Defence of the Middle East, 1945–54', *JICH*, 21 (1993), pp. 45–65.

Kyle, Keith, 'The Politics of the Independence of Kenya', *Contemporary British History*, 11 (1997), 42–65.

Layton-Henry, Zig, 'Immigration and the Heath Government, 1970–74', in Stuart Ball and Anthony Seldon (eds), *The Heath Government, 1970–74* (1996), pp. 215–34.

Lloyd, Lorna, 'Britain and the Transformation from Empire to Commonwealth: the Significance of the Immediate Post-war Years', *Round Table*, 343 (1997), pp. 333–60.

Lonsdale, John, 'The Emergence of African Nations: an Historiographical Analysis', *African Affairs*, 67 (1968), pp. 11–28.

Louis, W. R., 'American Anti-colonialism and the Dissolution of the British Empire', *International Affairs*, 61 (1985), pp. 395–420.

Lowry, Donal, '"Shame upon 'Little England' while 'Greater England' stands!" Southern Rhodesia and the Imperial Idea', in Alex C. May (ed.), *The Round Table and British Foreign Policy* (1998), pp. 305–41.

McEvoy, F. J., 'Canada, Ireland and the Commonwealth: the Declaration of the Irish Republic, 1948–49', *Irish Historical Studies*, 24 (1985), pp. 506–17.

McMahon, D., '"A Transient Apparition": British Policy towards the de Valera Government, 1932–5', *Irish Historical Studies*, 22 (1981), pp. 331–61.

Mancke, Elizabeth, 'Another British America: A Canadian Model for the Early Modern British Empire', *JICH*, 25 (1997), pp. 1–36.

Marshall, P. J., 'Empire and Authority in the Late Eighteenth Century', *JICH*, 15 (1987), pp. 105–22.

May, Alex, 'The Round Table and the Post-war Commonwealth', *Round Table*, 341 (1997), pp. 95–107.

Ovendale, R., 'Macmillan and the Wind of Change in Africa, 1957–1960', *Historical Journal*, 28 (1995), pp. 455–77.

Owen, Nicholas, (ed.), 'Decolonisation and the Colonial Office', *Contemporary Record*, 6 (1992), pp. 497–535.

Owen, Nicholas, (ed.), '"More than a transfer of power": Independence Day Ceremonies in India, 15 August, 1947', *Contemporary Record*, 6 (1992), pp. 415–51.

Paul, Kathleen, 'The Politics of Citizenship in Post-war Britain', *Contemporary Record*, 6 (1992), pp. 452–73.

Ranger, T. O., 'Connections between "Primary Resistance" Movements and Modern Mass Nationalism in East and Central Africa, part I', *Journal of African History*, 9: 3 (1968), pp. 437–53; part II, 9: 4 (1968), pp. 631–41.

Rotberg, Robert J., 'The Rise of African Nationalism', *World Politics*, 15 (1962–3), pp. 75–90.

Stockwell, A. J., 'British Imperial Policy and Decolonisation in Malaya', *JICH*, 13 (1984), pp. 68–87.

Woods, Michael, 'The Montagu–Chelmsford Reforms (1919): a Reassessment', *South Asia*, 17 (1997), pp. 25–42.

INDEX

308